Political Economy of Resource, Human Security and Environmental Conflicts in Africa

Kelechi Johnmary Ani · Victor Ojakorotu ·
Kelvin Bribena
Editors

Political Economy of Resource, Human Security and Environmental Conflicts in Africa

palgrave
macmillan

Editors
Kelechi Johnmary Ani
Department of History
& Strategic Studies
Alex Ekwueme Federal University
Ndufu-Alike, Nigeria

Victor Ojakorotu
Department of Politics
& International Relations
North-West University
Mafikeng, South Africa

Kelvin Bribena
Faculty of Law
Niger Delta University
Yenagoa, Nigeria

ISBN 978-981-16-2035-5 ISBN 978-981-16-2036-2 (eBook)
https://doi.org/10.1007/978-981-16-2036-2

This Palgrave Macmillan imprint is published by the registered company Springer Nature Singapore Pte Ltd.
The registered company address is: 152 Beach Road, #21-01/04 Gateway East, Singapore 189721, Singapore

Foreword by P. C. Enwereji

Global peace and security are universal concern. The history of international organizations and international non-governmental organizations is the history of concerted efforts towards achieving world peace and security. The world is faced with multiples initiatives towards diverse global, regional and sub-regional efforts to moderate or influence the activities of man in relation to moderation of human activities in managing resources competition, human security and conflicts in different parts of the world. From the United Nations Organization (UNO), to the World Trade Orgnization (WTO), the World Bank (WB), the World Wildlife Fund (WWF), the International Labour Orgnization (ILO), the African Union (AU), the European Union (EU), the Economic Community of West African States (ECOWAS), the Southern African Development Community (SADC), etc., there are multi-dimensional efforts in ensuring that the life of man is safe.

As the world continues to evolve, the tactics and strategies for attaining global peace and security are constantly being revised and refined to meet and reflect the current realities of time. The greatest forces that have influenced this dynamism are globalization and information communications technologies (ICTs). These two phenomena have brought countries in different continents of the world hitherto perceived to be far apart, very close now. With the advent of these two forces, a challenge in the remotest country of the world is being regarded now as universal and thus elicits global reactions. This is evident in the global attention devoted to poverty, terrorism, conflicts, governance, etc. Ironically, the place of resource exploitation in global relations has been neglected by men. The countries in the North continuously penetrate the states in the South or periphery to explore their human and natural resources. Ironically, Africa has been on the receiving side of resource exploitation by the West and Asian giants.

The African continent is the second-largest continent in the world with fifty-four countries and most of the countries are richly blessed with natural resources. This resource endowed countries include Algeria, Angola, Botswana, Burkina Faso, Burundi, Cameroon, Central African Republic, Chad, Cote d'ivoire, Democratic Republic of Congo, Egypt, Equatorial Guinea, Eritrea, Ethiopia, Gabon, Ghana, Guinea, Kenya, Liberia, Libya, Mali, Madagascar, Mauritania, Morocco, Mozambique, Namibia, Niger, Nigeria, Republic of Congo, Sierra Leone, Somalia, South Africa, South Sudan, Sudan, Tanzania, Tunisia, Uganda, Zambia and Zimbabwe. And the resources are mainly oil (petroleum), gas, gold, diamond, aluminium, copper, uranium, iron ore, nickel, cobalt, platinum, graphite, coal, titanium, pozzolana, phosphates, timber, tobacco, coffee, tea and fish, which are found in large quantities within the African environment. The competition between local and international resource exploiters on the one hand and the host community on the other hand, in many cases remains violent, thereby threatening human security. This implies that there is a symmetrical relationship between natural resources and environment. In other words, contentions over natural resource can lead to environmental conflicts and resource-related conflicts could manifest as environmental conflicts, which in any case threatens the security of lives and properties. This scenario is often the case in many African countries leading to resource curse.

In the annals of the continent's chequered history, most of these countries endowed with natural resources have either experienced or experiencing environmental conflicts. Some of the causes of these conflicts include but are not limited to competition over resources, environmental degradation, climate change, population explosion and politics of resource management. At the centre of these conflicts is resource management politics over access, control, ownership, distribution of resources and management of resource revenues by both community, national and international actors. It should be noted that environmental conflicts can manifest in one or combination of two or more of the following types of conflicts: border conflict, ethnic conflict, religious conflict and resource conflicts. While these conflicts have devastating effects like communal clashes, insecurity, human rights abuses, environmental pollution, food shortage, hunger, development challenges, internal displacement, forced migration, etc., on host countries, they equally have global consequences like refugees and irregular migration.

Harnessing resource and mitigating environmental conflicts where they exist, respectively, are equally global concern. The book is a robust discourse in this direction focusing primarily on the push and pull effects between resources, human security and conflicts in Africa. It recognizes the need for resources in Africa to be processed into finished goods in order to influence global market and redefine the pattern of trade relations with powerful countries of Asia, America and Europe in shaping the destiny and future of African countries. The achievement of this laudable objective is plagued by the security challenges which are directly or indirectly linked to resource-related conflicts rocking most of the resource endowed countries in the continent, thereby, threatening global peace and security. To deal with this menace in the continent, it requires global co-operation and support of foreign governments, international organizations, international non-government organizations, governments of host countries and its citizens.

In view of the above, the consciousness that most of these natural resources are non-renewable is a fact that must be laid bare before governments of host countries and its citizens. What are the implications when these resources are depleted in the mono-economy of many African states? The interrogation of this question is very crucial and seems to not had been taken into due cognizance by host governments of resource endowed African countries in the governance and use of natural resources respectively. This accounts largely why the politics of resource management is characterized by corruption, waste of resources, loss of resource revenues, exploitation, environmental degradation, absence of infrastructure and neglect of the people, which often elicit violent reactions resulting in conflicts with its attendant consequences.

The raging conflicts in most resource endowed countries in Africa may have beclouded the governments and parties in the conflicts from perceiving the stark reality noted above. This is because conflicts play diverse roles in places where they exist. For instance, its provides cover for wanton looting of resources and resource revenues, as those who benefit immensely from it will always devise means of engineering and sustaining conflicts. However, these challenges are not intractable and insurmountable. Nevertheless, what is required is initiating the appropriate mechanisms to arrest the situation, build peace among the governments, its citizens and other stakeholders (like multinational corporations) and providing both human and physical infrastructure that will sustain lasting peace.

The book is organized systematically in thirteen chapters. The structure and pattern of presentation reflect a chronological order of the issues discussed above. The chapters relied on the cases and experiences of countries that are endowed with resource, as well as have experienced different forms of human insecurity and have witnessed environmental conflicts in its analysis, which make the discourse interesting and quite educating.

P. C. Enwereji, Ph.D.
School of Public Management
Governance and Public Policy
University of Johannesburg
Johannesburg, South Africa

Acknowledgements

Special appreciation goes to all the scholars whose works have been cited in the process of the development of this book. May God bless the contributors and those who assisted in the review and editorial phase of the book.

Contents

Notes on Contributors

Victor Achem holds a Bachelor's Degree in Sociology from Ahmadu Bello University Zaria and obtained a Master's Degree in Sociology from the University of Ibadan. He is presently a Researcher and Doctoral candidate at the University of Ibadan. He specializes in social research and data deconstruction towards informed policy baiting and justified intervention. His areas of interest include Victimology, Armed Conflict, Forced Migration and Restorative Justice. He is particularly interested in social problems born out of human interaction most specifically as it relates to collective identity, shared values and goals. Substantively, Victor is interested in analysing sustained conflict, renewed violence, victimization and forced migration which are relative to "*identity politics*" and resource manipulation that has led to several sectarian games in the African geopolitical space. Victor has worked to investigate the victimhood experiences of displaced farming communities in Nigeria as it focuses on support systems available to victims and strategies for reintegrating displaced communities affected by herders-farmers conflict which is ubiquitous in Nigeria and other parts of West-Africa. Victor has written and won several travel grants. He is also one of the eight young scholars and winners of the 2020 New-Med Research Network Youth call 3rd edition (Exploring New Approaches to Economic Cooperation, Security and Migration) by Istituto Affari Internazionali in Rome, Italy.

Omolola Oluwakemi Ajayi is a Doctoral Student and Teaching/ Research Assistant in the Department of Wildlife and Ecotourism

Management, University of Ibadan, Nigeria. She obtained her Masters and first degree in the fields of Wildlife and Ecotourism Management in the same institution. Her research interests include the linkage of tourism with community development, environmental management, human security, protected areas sustainability, hospitality and climate change. To this effect, she has 16 publications. Her current research focuses on travel behavioural constructs specifically environmental attitude, motivation and place attachment as it influences conservation, destination management and competitiveness. Her favourite places to carry out research works are eco-themed tourism destinations in Africa such as National Parks, Waterfalls, Zoological Gardens and Beaches.

Kabiru Babatunde Amusa is of the Department of History, University of Ibadan, Nigeria.

Kelechi Johnmary Ani holds a Bachelor of Arts degree in History and International Relations from Ebonyi State University, Abakaliki (Second-Class Upper). He bagged a Post-Graduate Diploma in Education from Kashim Ibrahim College of Education—University of Maiduguri affiliated and a Masters' degree in International History and Diplomacy from the University of Maiduguri, all in Nigeria. He proceeded to North-West University, South Africa where he graduated with a Ph.D. in Peace Studies. He has peace, conflict and African political history as his areas of research interest. Dr. Ani is also a Lecturer in the Department of History and Strategic Studies, Alex Ekwueme Federal University Ndufu-Alike, Ikwo, Ebonyi State, Nigeria. He was a Post-Doctoral Research Fellow in the Department of Politics and International Relations, North-West University, Mafikeng Campus, South Africa before his appointment as research fellow in the School of Public Management, Governance and Public Policy, University of Johannesburg, South Africa. Dr Ani was also appointed an International Doctoral Thesis Examiner in the Graduate School of Business and Leadership, University of KwaZulu-Natal, South Africa.

Ani is Regular Member of International Peace Research Association (IPRA); Member, South African Association of Political Studies (SAAPS); Member, Historical Society of Nigeria and Member, Africa Peace Research and Education Association (AFPREA). Ani, K. J. is the Editor of *Environmental Conflicts and Peacebuilding in Africa: A Festschrift for Victor Ojakorotu*, Academica Press: Washington-London (2019); Co-editor with Victor Ojakorotu, & Kelvin Bribena in *Conflicts and Human Security Threats in Africa,* Academica: Washington (2019); and Co-editor with Kayode Eesuola in the book, ***International Relations and Security Politics in Africa: Essays in Honour of Professor Victor Ojakorotu,*** St James Studies in World Affairs, Academica: Washington, DC (2019). Dr. Ani was Member, Editorial Board, *Africana Studies Review,* Centre for African and African American Studies, Southern University at New Orleans, United States and Guest Editor; *Journal of Nation Building and Policy Studies,* UK.

Kelvin Bribena, Ph.D. was educated in the well-known University of Ado-Ekiti in South-Western Nigeria and at the Nigerian Law School, Abuja, where he obtained his Bachelor of Law and Barrister-at-Law degrees in 2001 and 2003, respectively. He subsequently proceeded to the famous Premier University of Ibadan, Nigeria, where he bagged the Master of Laws degree in 2006. In 2011, Dr. Kelvin Bribena obtained the Doctor of Laws degree from the prestigious North-West University, Mafikeng, South Africa. Again, he recently bagged a Master of Science (M.Sc.) degree on Intelligence and Security Studies from Novena University in Delta State of Nigeria. Besides the stated degrees, Dr. Kelvin Bribena is also a Chartered Arbitrator, and he holds a Certificate in Legal Advisory and Prosecutorial/Trial Advocacy skills. He is Member of the Nigerian Bar Association; an Associate Member of the Chartered Institute of Arbitrators (Nigeria); Life Member of the Society of International Law (Nigeria); Member of the Nigerian Institute of Management (NIM); Member and Country co-ordinator of Hope for the Niger Delta Campaign (Netherlands); Member of the International Research and Development Institute (Nigeria); Member of the National Institute of Marketers of Nigeria (NIMN); and President of the Conflict Resolution Scholars Association (CRSA) of Nigeria.

As an academic, he has taught and mentored law students at the Niger Delta University, Bayelsa State, Nigeria, from 2008 till date. His area of research interest includes International Economic Law, Arbitration and Conflict Resolution in Africa. Besides teaching and direct mentoring, Dr. Kelvin Bribena has made very significant contributions to knowledge through copious well-researched works. He has written several scholarly articles published in accredited journals of international acclaim. He is the Editor of *Conflict Resolution & Societal Reviews* published by the Conflict Resolution Scholars Association of Nigeria. He has also written chapters in books and has well-researched essays yet to be published. Dr.

Kelvin Bribena worked with the famous law firm—Falana and Falana. He was also a Senior State Counsel in the Ministry of Justice, Bayelsa State, Nigeria between 2006 and 2008, before joining the Niger Delta University, Bayelsa State as a lecturer in the Faculty of Law in 2008 till date. Clearly, it was in recognition of Dr. Kelvin Bribena's sterling contributions toscholarship and society, that made the present Governor of Bayelsa State, hisExcellency, Rt. Honourable Henry Seriake Dickson, appointed him to the Office of the Executive Personal Assistant to the Governor at the inception of hisadministration in February 14, 2012, till date. Presently, he is the MD/CEO. Bayelsa State Hotels and Tourism Development Company LTD., Nigeria and the GM/CEO, Bayelsa State Housing and Property Development Corporation, Nigeria.

Ijeoma Genevieve Anikelechi holds a degree in Civil and Water Resources Engineering from the University of Maiduguri. She has a Post-Graduate Diploma in Education and Master's degree in Science Education from the National Open University of Nigeria, Abuja and currently a Doctoral Candidate in the Department of Integrated Science, Nnamdi Azikiwe University Awka, Nigeria. She is a part-time Teacher in the Department of Physics, Enugu State College of Education Technical Enugu and she has a number of published journal and edited book chapter articles.

Kazeem Oyedele Lamidi, Ph.D. is a Lecturer in the Department of Local Government Studies of the Obafemi Awolowo University, Nigeria. He holds a Bachelor of Science Degree in Local Government Studies, Master of Science and Doctorate Degrees in Public Administration of the same University. The author has keen research interests on local governance, peacebuilding, community and policy studies as well as electoral analysis.

Nelson Goldpin Obah-Akpowoghaha, Ph.D. is Political Theorist, Peace and Conflict Studies Expert. He obtained all his degrees in Political Science from the prestigious Obafemi Awolowo University formally called the University of Ife (i.e. B.Sc. Ed.; M.Sc.; and Ph.D. in Political Science). Currently, he is Postdoctoral Fellow at North-West University, Mafikeng, South Africa and a Senior Lecturer in the Department of Political Science, University of The Gambia. He is a Member of Nigerian Political Science Association (NPSA); Social Studies Association of Nigeria (SOSAN); and a Reviewer to British Journal of Education, Society and Behavioural Science.

Uche Nwali has a Master's degree in Political Science and is currently a Ph.D. candidate in the Department of Political Science, University of Lagos, Nigeria. He has co-authored scholarly publications in national and international journals. His areas of research interest include but are not limited to money politics, state fragility, human security and political economy in Africa.

Professor Victor Ojakorotu, Ph.D. obtained a First-Class Bachelor of Science degree in 1994 from the Department of International Relations, Obafemi Awolowo University, Ile-Ife, Nigeria. Based on his impressive performance at the undergraduate level, he was employed as a Graduate Assistant in the Department of International Relations, Obafemi Awolowo University, Ile-Ife, Nigeria. He quickly engaged in the Master's degree programme in International Relations, while teaching some undergraduate courses and offering tutorial classes to students of the Department. He bagged his Master's degree and left for South Africa. In 2007, he earned his Ph.D. in International Relations from the University of the Witwatersrand, South Africa. He earned the University of the Witwatersrand, Post-Graduate Merit Award, 2002, 2003 and 2004; and Laureates, Governance Institute, CODESRIA, Dakar (2002). He taught at the School of Politics, University of KwaZulu-Natal, Pietermaritzburg Campus, South Africa between 2004 and 2007 and proceeded to Monash University, South Africa between 2007 and 2011 before joining the North-West University, Mafikeng Campus where he became a full Professor in 2014 and a C2 rated South African professor by NRF in 2019. He has served as Editor and Reviewer to the following journals: *Gender and Behaviour, Journal of Gender Information and Development in Africa, Journal of Reviews on Global Economies, African Renaissance,* and *Ubuntu: Journal of Conflict and Social Transformation* (all Scopus and IBSS Accredited). He has been an External Examiner for Masters and Doctoral degrees from 2007 to present at the University of Cape Town, University of KwaZulu-Natal, University of Zululand and University of Witwatersrand, all in South Africa.

Enoch Ndem Okon, Ph.D. holds B.Sc. and M.Sc. in International Relations and Political Science from the Obafemi Awolowo University and

University of Lagos, respectively. He has just concluded a Ph.D. in International Relations with the University of Calabar, Nigeria. He has interest in African Regional Governance, Security, Peace and Conflict Resolutions.

Samuel Nwite Okoro graduated from the Department of History and Strategic Studies, Alex Ekwueme Federal University Ndufu-Alike, Ikwo Nigeria. He was a staff of the Department of Social Studies, Ebenezer College of Education, Edda, Nigeria. His area of research interest includes social and political history of pre-colonial African societies, where he has a number of articles.

Bamidele Olajide is currently a Doctoral Student at the department of Political Studies and International Relations, North-West University, Mafikeng, South Africa. He is a lecturer in the Department of Political Science, University of Lagos, Nigeria.

Chijioke Francis Onyebukwa, Ph.D. graduated with a Bachelor of Science degree in International Studies from the Ahmadu Bello University, Zaria, Kaduna State, Nigeria in 2000. He proceeded to South Africa, where he bagged his Masters of Arts degree in 2013 and Doctor of Philosophy in International Relations in 2017 from the Department of Politics and International Relations, Faculty of Human and Social Science, North-West University Mafikeng Campus, South Africa. His areas of research interest include peace, security, conflict and conflict management, diplomacy as well as politics and electoral violence in Africa. Dr Onyebukwa Co-authored *The Struggle for Leadership Relevance between Nigeria and South Africa,* Berlin: Lambert Academic Publishers in 2013 with Ojakorotu Victor and Maseng Jonathan Oshupeng. He has also presented many papers at academic fora including seminars, workshops and conferences locally and internationally. Dr Onyebukwa was a senior Researcher in Governance, Politics and Conflict with African Heritage Institution Enugu State Nigeria before joining the Department of International Relations, Madonna University, Okija, Nigeria and lately Department of International Relations, Eastern Palm University, Nigeria. He has also worked as an Academic Writing Consultant at the Academic Development Center, North-West University Mafikeng from 2014–2016.

Lawson Onyema Chukwu was the Best Graduating Student of the Department of History and Strategic Studies, Alex Ekwueme Federal University Ndufu-Alike, Ikwo Nigeria in 2018 and a Post-Graduate

Student at the Department of History and International Studies, University of Nigeria. He is a Commentator on Nigerian national issues and Post-Graduate Student in the Department of History and International Studies, University of Nigeria Nsukka. His areas of research interest include peace, conflict and African social and political history.

Olufunke Joy Oyebade is a Ph.D. Student in the Department of Wildlife and Ecotourism Management, University of Ibadan, Nigeria. She obtained her first and Master's degrees from the same institution with First-Class Honours and Distinction, respectively. In this regard, she earned the title of a University Scholar and served as a Teaching Assistant during her Master's programme. Her research interest lies in the area of Hospitality and Tourism Management, specifically on Food and Beverage management. Her past works have focused on the acceptability of local snacks among tourists in Oyo State, Nigeria.

Godwin Ezurike Uchegbu holds a B.Sc. degree in sociology from University of Calabar and MSc in Political Science from University of Lagos all in Nigeria. He is currently a doctoral candidate in political science in political science, University of Lagos. His research interest is in political theory and research methods.

List of Figures

List of Tables

CHAPTER 1

Mineral Resources in Africa and Politics of Exploration: An Introductory Synopsis

Victor Achem and Ijeoma Genevieve Anikelechi

Introduction

There is approximately one-third of the world's mineral resources in Africa, but most people in the continent remain so terribly poor and do not benefit from the abundance of natural resources. The African continent has got a productive and resource-rich environment characterized by a huge quantity of minerals also comprising of renewable resources like, fisheries and forestry, as well as energy resources like raw materials, biomass, oil and natural gas. According to the Ghana Chamber of Mines and International Council on Mining & Metals 2015 Report, Ghana is the second-largest gold producer in Africa. South Africa has large reserves

V. Achem (✉)
University of Ibadan, Ibadan, Nigeria

I. G. Anikelechi
Department of Integrated Science, Nnamdi Azikiwe University Awka, Awka, Nigeria

K. J. Ani et al. (eds.), *Political Economy of Resource, Human Security and Environmental Conflicts in Africa*,
https://doi.org/10.1007/978-981-16-2036-2_1

of Platinum Group Metals (PGM) (Statistics South Africa, 2017). Statistically, the Republic of South Africa holds 33% of global chromium, 77% of global manganese and 88% of platinum group metals reserves, while Zambia and Congo Democratic Republic account for 52% of global cobalt reserves (USGS, 2008). All the regions of Africa are rich in one form of mineral resource or another. Many developing African economies manage mineral resources to improve the living standard of their various communities. These nature's assets are the source of income and livelihood for a great per cent of the African people and serves as a significant source of financing and economic strength.

In the right conditions, the production and transformation of these resources from the cottage sector to the manufacturing industry can be a significant driver for economic growth and cognitive development. In essence, natural resources could be efficiently utilized in transforming the weak economies of Africa from just a resource export economy to an industrialized economy.

This is because resource export is one means of lifting most of the poorest African countries from low revenue status thereby raising the scale of national economies. The natural resource endowment in every African country can produce significant social, economic and political advantages for Africa but that can only be achievable when it is used transparently and responsibly in compliance with the basic human rights of the people.

Sadly, natural resource valuations have only in some ways caused a complex development mechanism in many African countries. This is primarily due to the lack of right policies in relation to enhancing resource development and also establishing institutional reforms. This however implies that the main drive to diversify and expand industrial production in the resource-rich African countries is still very difficult to create. The risk is that most of Africa will not be industrialized and stagnate in a simple trap that is reliant mostly on outputs from a few minerals that are hardly refined by domestic African companies. Rather, the foreign multinational corporations ensure their dominance in the area, while other foreign countries dominate the formal and informal trade on these African resources, which they often process in their country and resale to Africans at a geometric high cost. The situation is worsened by the presence of local actors in the mineral resource sector of almost all African states that are directly armed or militarized by the foreign actors who ensure that the local economy is undermined and charactered by heavy resource violence in their bid to ensure continuous grip on the African natural resources.

Regional and Foreign Actors' Interest Group

There are a number of actors in the natural resource industries in Africa. It should be noted that the exploration of natural minerals is not only limited to African nations, but often include foreign nations or clamouring groups within borders of most fragile state. Foreign powers engage in the mining of the natural resources of a wide variety of countries in Africa through various means. They sometimes create and disseminate mechanisms of "war enterprises" and ethnic conflict among groups as well as through strong military action to either assist the existing government or the armed rebels. In a bid to attain that goal, they ensure that the policies of many African states are weak and dependent on the position of the West and their emerging foreign allies.

Unfortunately, state weakness caused by violent resource conflicts has a variety of ripple economic implications that several surrounding nations are confronted with as direct effects of conflicts or "proxy" economic relations. For example, the related conflicts in Liberia and Sierra Leone has enabled vast amounts of wood and diamonds to be trafficked off by proxy businessmen and extraction firms to Western states (Humphreys, 2005). The position of proxy foreign governments trying to benefit from resource-rich nations in Africa is a significant feature of resource exploration and a driver of the crisis. Unfortunately, most of the African diplomatic agreements with these non-African actors are sustained by the rich mineral resource exchanges from Africa. On the other hand, most civil wars in African states and the renewed violence especially in the Democratic Republic of Congo, Angola and Libya represent little other than the political war that is strongly rooted in the dynamics or push and pull effects of the relationship surrounding natural resources, power and violent conflict.

Another problem is the business culture of major multinational companies that are exploring oil in Africa. The presence of international actors in Africa, particularly private security companies, multinationals and NGOs has increased in the past decade. International participation has been more discreet. This international presence is categorized into two major groups. Global mercenaries, imprecisely identified as private security agencies (PSOs) of the multinational corporations (MNCs), who are among the first and by far the most problematic to the African hosts or landlords in every natural resource environment where there is the presence of MNCs. Financial liberalization especially in unstable African countries in which there are significant benefits has resulted in higher income from natural resource mining activity. It has however motivated local uncertified miners to go into the natural resource industry and compete with the multinational companies, who often invest more and lobby government officials to ban the activities of local miners.

While politics and business elite interest influence resource mining in Africa, the foreign influence in African environmental conflicts is often through the international multinational resource extraction firms, many of whom have used internal conflicts to increase their company gains. Unfortunately, the mining sector does not dislodge and evacuate as problems occur. While some multinational exploration companies are known to reallocate themselves in circumstances of uncertainty and aggression, their usual trend is to contribute to and continue to bear the burden of potential losses in a bid to maintain their grip on the monopolistic or widespread imperial resource exploitation in Africa. Undoubtedly, in Africa, there are many vulnerable and failing states, and the market activities of multinational exploring companies have helped to foster violence in different ways thereby weakening the competitiveness of African states in the endowed natural resource politics and diplomacy (Ballentine, 2004).

International Influence and Control of African Natural Resources

The fluid existence of international power relationships and competitiveness can be deeply aided by natural resources with several facets of conventional foreign policy dynamics. Mineral resources continue to draw large and wide concerns from international corporations to world powers. Also, the risk of armed confrontation is considerably higher in Africa due to widespread poverty. In the African continent, natural resources must be mined, refined and sold in order to sustain the huge international industrial economy. Since they are primarily found in far and wide parts of the globe, the geographical borders of statehood just slow down connectivity and delivery facts. According to Bradshaw (2009), the allocation of production and consumption institutions for natural resources may theoretically have major effects on government and non-government conduct. For instance, the manner in which nations view their alternatives and initiate their preferences over environmental resources is, in effect, affecting world energy security policy. The "new" position played by regions, such as Asia pacific, especially Brazil as well as the stance taken by democratic, corporate and intergovernmental organizations in defining standards, backed by the growing credit derivatives of resource development exploitation, and the sweeping pressures of the population to expand ownership of mineral wealth, are some of the key signs to international relations in the mineral resource production politics.

Despite of all these arising issues, the increasing presence of developing economies such as China, India or Brazil in the exploration industry of several African countries have made global political shifts dramatic in the last decade (Runge, 2008). A debate of global power ties and natural resources with no need for a disruptive transfer of influence into developing markets are now impossible. These countries already play a major role as the origin of new investments in the mining sector of Africa, which will be crucial for the leadership systems to develop within the next 10–15 years. The Chinese administration ties its—African bilateral infrastructure assistance policy to mineral rights needed to guarantee its ongoing access to raw materials. However, China's Export-Import Bank has financed development projects in Angola to the tune of $4.5 billion in 2004 for the sole purpose of oil (Bermúdez-Lugo, 2011). In 2008, China's Export-Import Bank also spent $6 billion on the Democratic Republic of Congo's infrastructural development for cotton and copper from the Kolwezi Copper Mine (Villoria, 2009). These developments underline how Chinese-African policy has combined its two geopolitical priorities in the rising, resource-hungry market with both the oil security issues to explore the resource-rich continent.

The mining industry continues to be a major revenue stream in Zambia and draws strong investment thresholds from China, Switzerland, the UK, Canada, Australia and several other nations. Copper is the principal foreign exchange earner of the country for a long time, and the survival of the entire financial market primarily relies on the status of the economic copper sector in the international market (Larmer, 2010). However, Zambian growth and the increase in copper prices as observed in the late 2000s and the swift rebound following the 2008 global financial crisis have so far not generally agreed with the worsening level of poverty. Zambia has been one of the main beneficiaries of Chinese projects in Africa, as China has been spending trillions of dollars in Zambia's mining reconstruction, but has also created new crises and raised unrest among the local people. There are strong worries throughout the region that Zambia doesn't really profit from the nation's mineral resources and a general perception that the nation is not reasonably coping with friendly mining and tax policies that are in favour of exploring firms and companies.

Social analysts in Zambia also raise concerns about privatization as well as the recent rise in dividends from 3 to 6% to shifting corporate tax systems, accountability problems, labour regulations and ensuring inexpensive and efficient energy with electricity, which primarily comprises 15% of mining companies' operating costs. Ironically, Zambia remains obviously a big case study on the alignment between its production of capital, investment flows, various investor compliance frameworks and dis-satisfaction in citizens' aspirations (Palale & Ravat, 2012).

Mineral Resources Access and Armed Militarization in Africa

The militarization of several of the mineral extraction locations is among the consequences of this current foreign resource exploration crisis in Africa and its implications on foreign policy remain progressive. The militarization of mineral resource-rich states aims at maintaining energy supplies, establishing competitive advantages, but as the increasing insecurity of several resource development locations indicates, it already seems to be having the opposite impact. This has left resource stability uncertain for developed and newly industrialized countries. Thus, global forces in African countries are gradually deploying foreign military mercenaries to protect their resource interest. Much of these operations have been related to oil mining sites and are frequently justified or communicated as the assistance of the United States in the fight against terrorism. Interestingly, nearly all African states have wealth of global strategic importance from Nigeria's oil to Niger's uranium. Although the installation of troops is often affected by other factors, insecurity is certainly critical in a world with global vital resources (Akcinaroglu & Radziszewski, 2013).

The involvement of private military contractors or private security firms in mineral-rich locations is even more disturbing than the installation of military forces by foreign nations. Private military contractors face a very particular kind of risk, as they are known to have a lower transparency standard and are embroiled in several of the most egregious human rights violations that humanity have been seeing over the past 10 years (Halakhe, 2014).

However, the whole description of private military forces or businesses participating in resource conflicts has not empirically been observed to exist in strong terms within Africa. Rather, it is the state in many African countries that supply the multinational companies with armed security forces and often gives them cover for their excessive human rights abuses on individuals, groups and mineral resource host communities. These security organizations are, for example, also hired with the aim of providing support for company buildings and personnel in locations in which there are no ongoing civil conflicts, but low-level armed conflicts, such as the Niger Delta in Nigeria. In Nigeria's oil delta in the mid-1990s, the Anglo-Dutch national petroleum, Shell, was associated with a greater likelihood of gross violations of human rights by private security forces authorized by the Federal Government of Nigeria (Okonta & Douglas, 2003).

What we have above indicates that mineral resources mining is indeed so risky and impoverishing that several nations find that perhaps these areas need to be protected. Militarization does not inherently promote security and prosperity but it often incites parties to commit human rights abuses and eventually produce new streams of violence.

There are some fundamental questions that must be examined within the context of mineral deposition and exploration in Africa. Could it be perhaps the effect on dispute more important as it is easier to exploit and disperse the land resources than those participating in the natural resource competition? Are resources like diamonds, for example, quickly exported and marketed with comparatively simple procedures, likely to create conflict rather than oil and gas reserves that need more advanced production methods? Are they more feasible? These concerns indicate that the mineral class and associated complexity of a particular mineral or resources will have an impact on how social ties can be established and the possibility that tension will either be created or escalated.

In Africa, where countries use oil sales to support weapons procurement and oil wealth leads to domestic conflict, oil and weapons are intrinsically connected (Le Billon, 2003) and evidence of that has been established through civil wars in Chad, Angola, the Republic of Congo, Sudan and Nigeria (Ross, 2004). In 2000, the World Bank issued a loan of $3.7 million to the Central African nation of Chad to fund the development of a natural gas pipeline for the export of Chad's oil to the Atlantic Port via two US energy firms, Exxon Mobil and Chevron (Services, 2003). The World Bank put stringent restrictions on using oil royalties and received assurances from the Chadian authorities underneath the influence of the state, national and foreign NGOs that perhaps the funds would be spent on inclusive growth benefits. Ironically, President Idriss Deby has since spent $4 million on weapons to fight against the forces of rebellion with a first transaction of $25 million. This guarantee oil revenues to expand the civil war in Chad and minimize the odds that a permanent dispute settlement can be sought (Volman, 2002).

However, oil has been driving mass genocide, competition and other abuses of human rights in Sudan (Jemera, 2002). Oil income in 2001 was estimated at $580 million, representing over 40% of total national income. Sudan invested 60% of this oil income on military expenditures and the development of a local military industrial complex. The authorities could attack and evacuate communities with military jet, weapons and military armoured assault vehicles as well as protect the next oil reservation zone military armed units. This policy can be replicated before any petroleum field and transport route has been cleared and put under strong military control to secure the oil payable for by the watchman (Fearon & Laitin, 2003).

Interestingly, the government earns about 55% profit from Shell Oil Corporation, so consider that the government is earning about 95% of its overall income from all US petroleum firms (i.e. Texaco, Exxon and so on) and that Government spending in the American oil market is about 95%. As a strategic alliance with Nigeria's energy firms, the Nigerian National Oil Company runs the Nigerian state oil production and development under this initiative. The government is making large-scale petroleum exploration projects, but it does not display the political will to help its people. Most Nigerians' hostile response to the petroleum industry stems from the government's greed.

Several factions in the Niger Delta region demand damages from Shell for oil from which the Government of Nigeria, along with petroleum firms, has obtained trillions of dollars of oil and gas since 1956 from Nembe and others in the Niger Delta, without providing anything to the citizens in exchange (Oronto & Okonta, 2003). Some of these groups are using attacks and aggressive acts as a way of payment, operating projects or even financing developing school programmes, as a reaction to the policies of the government of Nigeria and oil businesses. The disfigurement of Niger Delta environment has led to violent attacks on the people and their cultures. Unfortunately, the Nigerian political representatives and petroleum corporations are also not responding to all quest for environmental governance and their action remain unexplained. For 40 years, Shell has been exploiting and abusing Nigeria's climate without providing sustainable financial and environmental support. The Nigerian oil communities seem fed up with the government and petroleum corporation, hence they tend to focus exclusively on compensation.

Mineral Resources and Corruption

Corruption is indeed a significant hurdle in some countries in their quest for fair allocation of mining resources and income generated thereof. Many businesses in the mining industry are involved in a number of illegal practices, they feel obligated and are willing to bribe the authorities as to the means of securing authorizations. They are often committed to gaining state monopoly control to circumvent rivals. Such corrupt lobbying is sometimes made by businesses in the pursuit of corporate productivity, but inevitably such a scheme does significant harm not only to the social structure of a society, but also to the national development plan and impair overall performance. Consequently, it delays economic development and potentially leads to chaos violent resource conflicts and war. Essentially, corruption also strips away financial resources for countries to spend in economic growth. Indeed, the link between high corruption rate and poor human growth tends to be very significant (Schloss, 2002).

Each nation is to some degree impacted by corruption. The established democracies are under close supervision. Many influential lawmakers in the UK, France and Germany were heavily criticized for allowing bribes from businesses seeking to obtain special privileges. Although as resources and demands are broader and regulatory mechanisms also become weakened, the African countries are by far the most susceptible to corrupt practices. Many politicians in the African states receive quite low pay and also pursue other skill sets to contribute to their earnings. Therefore, they can be severely inclined to take up bribery as their profits. Simultaneously, institutional and administrative processes can indeed be awful. Numerous administrators have the extensive capacity to work under little or no oversight and take actions that have tremendous consequences on mining firms. Dishonest politicians often recognize that they are unlikely to be discovered or much less disciplined, since monetary auditing processes are either feeble or dishonest too. In brief, poor governance raises the incidence of corruption.

Conclusion and Recommendations

Conflicting problems in the mineral resources sector in Africa include, in general terms, the collapse of the government, the democratic process and the unequal sharing of national wealth, and the lack of accountability in the industry. The unequal allocation of the profits of natural resources causes most resource-related disputes and violence. The government and elite reap the advantages of exploiting capital in combination with multinational businesses, but host populations face a worsening effect on the environment. Furthermore, host communities' contributions have been insufficient with the amount of restitution received for their houses, polluted land and water, e.g. economic standards which are below those causing distress and violent responses.

The problem is compounded by the lack of a rule of law that enables the distressed stakeholders to take actions within that natural resources field with no judicial or regulatory redress and undemocratic control actions. However, land resource is sometimes allocated for mineral extraction operations without engaging community members concerned and hence, host societies really aren't properly informed with respect to developments in their spheres of mineral resource influence and deposition. Considering mineral resource connection to peoples' land, peoples' primary revenue source; history has shown that such people's attitudes overtime becomes hostile and aggressive out of the perception of continuous subjugation, resource manipulation, exploitation and violent environmental degradation that undermines the standard of living of the masses. However, the absence of integrity and openness are therefore part of the dispute process in resource conflicts, as coercion, gross resource mismanagement and thus the diversion of the money to be provided for construction and development programmes reinforces environmental crises.

However, if energy-related political problems are to be resolved, these complex governance concerns shall be fully integrated into the natural resources' governance structure. It is expected that core values such as collaborative decision-making will be followed and promoted within the structure of sovereignty throughout the administration of natural resources. Policy choices on the utilization of mineral resources could perhaps take note of the opposing opinions of the multiple parties intended to profit or influenced by continuous usage of natural resource by extending collaborative decision-making to the regulation of mineral wealth. Yet another law that often reinforces the concept of democratic representation is the Environmental Impact Assessment, the laws regulating natural resources production and exploitation, though the law is just one part of effective and successful management of natural resources.

Finally, the successful use of mineral wealth, including the current architectural governance system, seems to be at the core of almost every effort to encourage effective resource exploration and societal development of host communities. While they conform with the various concepts set out initially, they are defined to illustrate the value of quality and fairness in the usage of natural resources as having distinct value for the immediate host communities. The concept of inequalities in wealth allocation is another aspect that fuels resentment and leads to the rise of wars and conflicts in mineral-rich nations in Africa. The heterogeneity of desires and players in mineral-rich nations can also be expressed in such a democratic system. Such a system will understand the interests of rural populations who obtain mineral resources from the nation's population at large. It further addresses environmental issues and the effect of development of natural resources on the livelihoods of host population wherein processing or exploration of mineral resources occurs.

References

Akcinaroglu, S., & Radziszewski, E. (2013). Private Military Companies, Opportunities, and Termination of Civil Wars in Africa. *Journal of Conflict Resolution, 57*(5), 795–821.

Ballentine, K. (2004). *Natural Resources, Governance, Development and Conflict.* Fafo Institute.

Bermúdez-Lugo, O. (2011). *The Minerals Industry of Angola.* Retrieved from Minerals Yearbook Online: http://minerals.usgs.gov/minerals/pubs/country/2011/myb3–2011-ao.pdf.

Bradshaw, M. (2009). The Geopolitics of Energy Security. *Geography Compass, 3*(5), 1920–1937.

Fearon, J., & Laitin, D. (2003). Ethnicity, Insurgency, and Civil War. *American Political Science Review, 97*(1), 75–90.

Halakhe, A. (2014, June 6). *The West Renews Appetite for African Military Adventure.* Retrieved from mgafrica.com: http://mgafrica.com/article/2014-06-06-the-west-renews-appetite-for-african-military-adventure.

Humphreys, M. (2005, August). Natural Resources, Conflict, and Conflict Resolution. *Journal of Conflict Resolution, 49,* 508–537.
Jemera, R. (2002). *Sudan: Oil and War.* ACAS Bulletin 64.
Larmer, M. (2010). Historical Perspectives on Zambia's Mining Booms and Busts. In A. Fraser, & M. Larmer (Eds.), *Zambia, Mining and Neoliberalism: Boom and Bust on the Globalized Copperbelt* (pp. 31–58). Basingstoke: Palgrave Macmillan.
Le Billon, P. (2003). *Fuelling War: Natural Resources and Armed Conflicts.* Oxford: Oxford University Press for the International Institute of Strategic Studies.
Okonta, I., & Douglas, O. (2003). *Where Vultures Feast: Shell, Human Rights, and Oil in the Niger Delta.* Verso: London.
Oronto, D., & Okonta, I. (2003). *Where Vultures Feast: Shell, Human Rights, and Oil in the Niger Delta.* San Francisco: Sierra Club Books.
Palale, P., & Ravat, A. (2012). Resource-rich But People Poor. *Shaping our Future Conference* (pp. 29–30). Lusaka: British Council.
Ross, M. (2004). What Do We Know About Natural Resources and Civil War? *Journal of Peace Research, 41*(3), 337–356.
Runge, P. (2008, November). *Potholes and Profits: Business & other Conversations & Experiences from Africa.* Africa Project Access Publication.
Schloss, M. (2002). *Transparency and Governance in the Management of Mineral Wealth* (Working paper, World Mines Ministries Forum and Transparency International) Retrieved from Transparency International: http://www.transparency.org/working_papers/mining_mineral/trans_govmineralwealth.html.
Services, C. R. (2003, October 9). *CATHOLIC RELIEF SERVICES STATEMENT ON THE LAUNCH OF CHAD-CAMEROON OIL PIPELINE PROJECT*. Retrieved from pwypdev.gn.apc.org: http://pwypdev.gn.apc.org/sites/pwypdev.gn.apc.org/files/crs_chad_091003.pdf.
Statistics South Africa—Stats SA. (2017). Environmental Economic Accounts Compendium Report, No. 04–05–20.
USGS. (2008). *Mineral Commodity Summaries.* Washington, DC: US Geological Survey.
Villoria, N. B. (2009, March 25). China and the Manufacturing Terms-of-Trade of African Exporters. *Journal of African Economies, 18*(5), 781–823.s
Volman, D. (2002). *Oil, Arms, and Violence in Africa.* ACAS Bulletin 64.

CHAPTER 2

Chinese Resource Policy and Human Security in Africa: A Discourse

Enoch Ndem Okon and Victor Ojakorotu

Introduction

Sino-African relation is on the increase especially since the dawn of the new millennium. This has been institutionalized with the founding of the Forum on China-Africa Cooperation (FOCAC) framework in October 2000. This development is seen as part of the "Go abroad" policy of the Chinese government which is expected to open vistas of opportunity for the Asian giant to make impression on Africa and other parts of the world in order to strengthen and expand its economy through trade and investment. Specific to Africa is the abundance of natural resources and market for Chinese products which are cheaper in comparative terms to similar products imported from Europe and other Asian

E. N. Okon
Department of Political Science, University of Calabar, Calabar, Nigeria

V. Ojakorotu (✉)
Department of Politics and International Relations, North West University, Mafikeng, South Africa

K. J. Ani et al. (eds.), *Political Economy of Resource, Human Security and Environmental Conflicts in Africa*,
https://doi.org/10.1007/978-981-16-2036-2_2

countries. Principally, the resurgence of Chinese trade and investment in Africa has heavily tilted to the natural resource sector where the 'Angolan model' or 'resource-backed loan' has facilitated exploitation and exports of resources to China. The impacts of these activities include: the rising wave of economic growth, increase in the Africans share of international trade and investment, as well as improvement on infrastructural facilities of benefitting countries. Some scholars have seen Chinese activities on the continent as a good omen capable of turning the 'resource curse' and engendering win-win outcome as emphasized by the Asians (Ayodele & Shotola, 2014; Brautigam, 2011; Kelly, 2012). Howbeit, others are pessimistic over the long-term impact of these engagements which may lead to imperialism, environmental degradation, concretization of totalitarian democracy, human right abuses de-industrialization of the continent and possible outbreak of war between China and the West (Chang, 2007). Nevertheless, scholars have not discussed the impact of the Chinese resource policy on human security on the continent, and this is the objective of this study. It is divided into six sections including the introduction. Section two reviews some relevant literature. Section three highlights the methodology of the study. Section four presents the findings, section five discusses the findings, and section six concludes the study with some recommendations.

China's relation with Africa has a rich historical tradition. While some scholars trace the interaction to pre-colonial era, others dwell on the contemporary historical milieu after China emerged as a nation state, from the rubble of Communist Revolution on October 1, 1947, and its leadership's identification with the Global South on critical issues in the international system. In the 1970s, late Premier Zhou Enlai embarked on state visits to many African countries to drum up support for 'one China' policy and the recognition of the People Republic China as the authentic representative of the Chinese people in the comity of nations and a permanent member of the UN Security Council. The Asians relation with Africa was also prompted by ideological expansion of the Cold War when the bipolar belligerents were recruiting allies to defend and expand their ideological preferences with aid and technical assistance. Consequently, Chinese were instrumental to the construction Tanzanian railway in East Africa, as well as other structures in Egypt and other parts of the continent as signposts of friendship and persuasion on the continent (Alden & Alves, 2009; Helstrom, 2009).

Howbeit, the phenomenal ascendency of Chinese presence in Africa is adduced to the new policy of 'Go global' which was enunciated in 2000 by the Chinese government. Its objective among others is to expand the Chinese influence and engagement with other parts of the world, given the consistent growth of the domestic economy which required outward flow of goods and services and the inward flow of raw materials which is the reminiscent of the European scramble for Africa in the eighteenth and nineteenth centuries (Ayodele & Sotola, 2014) In spite of the similarities in motive of the Europeans and Asians engagements, the Chinese model is remarkably different in that it seeks the consents of Africans, besides, the terms of engagement are spelt out in agreements and contracts. Hence, the Asian model supports the provision of infrastructure in exchange for African resources. This is a replica of Japanese deal with Chinese in their developmental years when Deng Xiaoping suggested that in order to hasten the exploration of our coal and petroleum, it is possible that on the condition of equality and mutual benefit, and in accordance with accepted practices of international trade such as deferred payments, we may sign long-term contracts with foreign countries and fix several production sites where they will supply complete sets of modern equipment required by us, and we will pay for them with the coal and oil we produce (Morrison, 1978: 692).

The beauty of this model lies in giving the home country the rights and powers to choose the nature and sector of engagement. Here, the Chinese needed industrialization in exchange for its resource export with the Japanese which contrasts the West prescriptive solution to Third World economic woes, as provided by IMF/World Bank. Thus, China benefited from this model as the Japanese supplied high tech equipment, extractive technology and finance to the Chinese coal and oil for efficient production and exports. The recovery of initial investment encouraged the Japanese to further invest in Turnkeys projects worth 10 Billion dollars in 1978 (Takamaine, 2006: 97). According to Brautigam (2011: 5), this model of project financed by line of credit with deferred repayment in resources was instrumental to Chinese implementation of its modernization program. Its replication in Africa is expected to generate similar ripples in the economy and provide the grounding of Chinese resource policy in Africa.

Africa has become a theatre for worldwide quest for natural resources due to its holding of about 30% of global mineral reserves and production of about 60 known minerals, ores and metals. He further observes that the emerging economies are very active in the scramble for African resources. Top on the list is China, whose import from the continent in 2009 shows the dominance of extractive resources, with mineral fuel and lubricant accounting for 60.8% and crude materials composing 17.9% (African Economic Outlook, 2011). Again, exports from five African oil producers—Angola, Nigeria, Algeria, Equatorial Guinea and Sudan—have about 67.5% continental net exports to China and these are in line with other scholars' assertion that Chinese interest and activities in Africa are dictated by the need for energy resource and other natural resources, such as timber copper, aluminium and iron ore (Ayodele & Shotola, 2014; Edinger & Pistorius, 2011; Konings, 2007). Besides, the need to diversify the sources of these resources is of strategic importance to the Chinese given the lesson learnt from the Arab oil embargo in 1974 against western countries and it intimidating impact on the targeted countries, hence Chinese interest in African resources, may as well serves guide against over-dependence on the Middle East for its oil supply. According to International Energy Agency (2007), Middle-East oil giants—Saudi Arabia, Iran and Oman supply, 44% of Chinese crude oil imports, this was followed by Africa—Angola, Sudan and Nigeria which accounts for 32% and Russia, 11%. Therefore, increasing Chinese share in African oil guards against the uncertainty inherent in the politically fragile Middle East (Cherp & Jewell, 2014; Yergin, 2006). Besides, China has a strategic view of energy security which prefers the ownership of oil fields in Africa rather than depending on the forces of demands and supply inherent in global oil market (Cheung & Xinwang, 2009; Shalmon & Lee, 2008).

On the other hand, Butts and Bangus assert that Africa is endowed with strategically important metals/minerals, such as bauxite, copper, coltan, iron ore, phosphate rock, coal and uranium. They further explained that strategic minerals like cobalt, chromium, platinum group of metals and manganese applications in weapon systems and the dearth of substitute make their concentrated reserves in Africa attractive to China as they are to other industrialized nations in South Africa, Zimbabwe, Democratic Republic of Congo (DRC) and Zambia. Statistically, the Republic of South Africa holds 33% of global chromium, 77% of global manganese and 88% of platinum group metals reserves, while Zambia and Congo DR account for 52% of global cobalt reserves, (USGS, 2008). The centrality of these strategic minerals in Sino-African relations accounts for the dominance of South Africa as the most outstanding trading partners with the Chinese with 33% of the Asian trade and destination of Foreign Direct Invest (FDI), on the continent in 2012, Angola followed with 21%, Nigeria was third with 6% and Egypt and Libya were joint fourth with 5% apiece. In terms of Sino imports from Africa, South Africa still had the largest volume of 42.3%, Angola followed with 31.7%, Libya was third with 6.0%, Congo Brazzaville followed with 4.3%, Congo DR was fifth with 3–3% and Zambia, 2.6%, while the rest of the continent accounted for 9.7% (Thrall, 2015: 27–29). These trade, FDI and Chinese imports indexes further confirm the thesis of resources' security, as the bedrock of China engagement with Africa (Kobylinski, 2012).

Chinese resource policy is underpinned by basic principles such as the 'noninterference' in the internal affairs of the host states, and 'non-prescription' of solution to socio-economic and political challenges in the domestic environment of other states. The imperative of these principles ensures that the Asian giant engages in resource scrambling in both democratic and non-democratic states. Consequently, China has several mining agreements with regimes considered pariah by the West such as Zimbabwe, Sudan and Democratic Republic of Congo. These states also are regarded as high-risk nations by the West because of incessant conflicts and inherent insecurity (Edinger & Pistorius, 2011: 38; Helstrom, 2009; Kobylinski, 2012). Another aspect of the policy is the provision of credit line for infrastructure development secured by resources supply (Alden & Alves, 2009). Several countries have benefitted from this model of infrastructure financing tagged 'Angola mode' as it was first introduced by the Chinese in Angola. For instance, DR Congo secured a deal worth 9bn USD in 2007 for copper and cobalt to build about 3900 kilometres of road, 3200 kilometres of railway, 32 hospitals, 145 health centres and two universities (Whewell, 2008). Earlier on, 2004 Chinese had provided a credit line of 4.5 bn USD to Angola to finance energy water supply and education projects in exchange for the supply of 10,000 bpd of oil. In Gabon, the Chinese invested about 3bn USD in infrastructural development which includes the building of 560- kilometre railway that links Belinga to the coast, a deep-water mining harbour, a hydro-power dam on the Ivindo River and the iron mining factory as part of Belinga iron ore deal (Alves, 2008: 4–5). Apart from the 'Angola mode', Chinese also struck traditional contract, which give them access to gold mine in Eritrea, manganese in Cote d'ivoire, Ghana and Gabon, bauxite in Guinea, titanium in Kenya, uranium in Niger, chromium in South Africa, copper in

Zambia and coal in Zimbabwe (Helstrom, 2009: 14). The place of human security in all these Chinese deals cannot be neglected.

Human security is a concept popularized by the paradigm shift of security studies from the traditional state-centric and politico-military model of the Cold War years to the safety and overall well-being of individuals and groups in their habitation. It places premium on the availability of condition and environment which guarantees dignifying human existence and opportunity for self-realization and actualization. It is therefore an outcome of the widening scope of security studies and securitization of non-military and political issues. Therefore, it was modelled to protect the vital core of all human lives in a way that enhances human freedoms and human fulfilment. Human security means protecting fundamentals freedoms—freedoms that are essence of life. It means protecting people from fear critical (severe) and pervasive (widespread) threats and situations on it means using process that build on people strength and aspirations. It means creating political, social, environmental, economics military and cultural systems that together give people the building block of survival, livelihood and dignity (CHS, 2003: 4).

Given the widening of security scope by the model, the following factors are considered as threats to security: economics security—persistent poverty and unemployment; food security—hunger and famine; health security—deadly infectious diseases, unsafe food, malnutrition and lack of access to basic health care among other; environmental security—environmental degradation, resource depletion, natural disaster and pollution; personal security—physical violent, crime, terrorism, domestic violent and child's labour; community security—inter-ethnic, religious and other identity-based tension; and political security—political repression and humans right abuses (UNDP, 2004). According to Alkire (2003: 2), human security as a framework provides protective values for individuals and communities as they are threatened by occurrences beyond their border and control. Such occurrences include: financial crisis, AIDS, violent conflict, terrorist attack, budgetary cut in public health care, drought, chronic destitution or pollution which are more destructive since they are spontaneous could be managed if there are early warning signals to individuals, communities and government to initiate preventive or palliative measures. The strength of this framework lies on its understanding of the mutual inter-connectedness and reinforcement nature of threat in two ways first they are interlinked in a domino effect in the sense that each threat feeds on the other. For example, a violent can lead to deprivation and poverty which in turn leads to resource depletion, infections disease and education deficit among others. Secondly, threats within a given country or area can spread into a wider region and have negative externalities for regional and international security (United Nations, 2009: 7–8).

Human security emphasizes on the security and well-being of individuals and communities globally and this distinguishes it from earlier security studies framework, especially realism; in addition, it focuses on persons, irrespective of gender, religion, race, citizenship, ethnicity or other categorical difference More so, it multi-sectoral approach, comprehensiveness and context-specific compensate for inadequacies of the previous framework of analysis in the field (Alkire, 2003; CHS, 2003; Morgenthau, 1978).

Historically, resource policies of Great powers had and still have a remarkable impact on human security in Africa. The non-consensual scramble and partition of the continent by European powers in the nineteenth century and consequently colonialism in the twentieth century remain foundational threats and inventors of other threats to human security in Africa (Okon & Ojakorotu, 2018). Earlier on the iniquitous slave trade by Europeans quest for human resources had led to the destruction of communities and dislocation of the social system as well as the alteration of the economic well-being of Africans. In addition, the slave raids facilitated the introduction of small arms and light weapons to the continent. This threatened individual, community and environmental security, given the environmental pollution inherent in violent conflict (Rodney, 1972; Collins & Burns, 2007). During this era, many Africans with knowledge of traditional medicine were killed, displaced or sold as slaves to the Europeans. The net impact was the dearth in traditional medical personnel on the continent and resulted in the death of many Africans who would have been treated by these traditional physicians. More so, continuous slave raid resulted in the collapse of food production since the atmosphere was no longer conducive for farming, but also ensured that the productive age brackets on the continent were carted away. Furthermore, European weapons in the hands of their stooges destroyed power structure within African communities and the social stability anchored on power-parity, this raised the stake and promoted zero-sum conflicts or wars of annihilation which were hitherto rarely achievable. Given these scenarios, social bond and cohesion between communities were destroyed and cynicism, intrigues, betrayal and other vices endemic in the state of nature prevailed. Again, many Africans who lost their home were exposed to extreme weather conditions and diseases which eventually killed them. Thus the resources policy of the Europeans during the slave trade era was antithetical to human security in Africa, as economic socio-political, cultural, environmental, community and health security of Africans were disastrously threatened during and after the era (Dike, 1956; Hodges, 1932; Mentan, 2002; Rodney, 1972).

As mentioned earlier on the age of European imperialism and subsequent colonialism were characterized by negative human security on the continent. The introduction of plantation agriculture and the so-called legitimate trade did not only lead to forceful dislocation of communities on the continent and land grabbing, but it also emphasized on production to meet the needs of the Europeans at the detriment of food production in Africa (Collins & Burns, 2007). In addition, forced labour was used by the colonialists and every form of resistance was crushed by the force of arms. Also worthy of note was the political exclusion of Africans in the decision-making process, as well as the destruction of African political and social structures. Many African leaders were captured and exiled, as experienced by Oba Ovaromwem, and King Jaja of Opobo of Benin and Opobo in Southern Nigeria irrespectively. Besides, African culture was desecrated and replaced by European/Judeo-Christian culture which remained till date; therefore, ancestral worship and different rites of passages both for the living and the death were seen and condemned as 'barbaric'. Furthermore, African communities that were hitherto built on egalitarianism as exemplified by the Igbo pre-colonial system were stratified with the appointment of "Warrant Chiefs" and subsequent allegiance to the Europeans. This led to different forms of human right abuses. Indeed, Africans did not have political right or any form of human rights during the colonial era (Okon & Esin, 2018; Reid, 2014). More worrisome was the discriminatory labour practices by Europeans on the continent in goldmines and other mining locations on the continent where many Africans lost their lives due to the collapse of the mines. Besides, African miners and other workers lived in overcrowded shanties with the very poor sanitary condition, thus so many Africans died of illnesses due to poor hygiene and epidemic outbreak. Also relevant here was the poor remuneration and the prohibition of the labour union by the Europeans, this led to the sustenance of exploitative wages and working condition on the continent. All said, this era was absolutely detrimental to human security on the continent, as the resource policies of Europeans were meant to serve the interest of their home countries at the detriment of the Africans in order to establish core/periphery relations in the world economic system (Wallerstein, 1967).

The post-colonial era starting from the 1960s had elements of change and continuity in the resource policy of Great Powers in Africa and its impact on human security. For instance, the desire to control the mineral resources of DR Congo was responsible for the political intrigue which led to the murder of Prime Minister Patrice Lumumba by Western-backed Mobutu Sese Seko and the reign of tyranny in the resource-rich country for over thirty years. Similarly, decades of civil war in Angola cannot be divorced from resource policies of external actors. More importantly, the dominance of western Multinational Corporations in the resource sector of the African economy ensures the continuity of threats to human security on the continent. In Niger Delta region as in elsewhere in, Africa, the environmental pollution arising from the oil exploration by MNC is phenomenal and has led to violent conflicts which further reinforce threat to other component of human security such as health, economy, personal, political, food and community (Akpabio & Akpan, 2010; Ajala, 2016). Indeed, the institutionalization and sustenance of Apartheid in South Africa was a direct outcome of some Great Power desire to dominate and exploit the resources of the country. A similar motive was responsible for settler colonialism in Zimbabwe and Namibia among others. The threat of Apartheid and settlers' colonialism to human security on the continent is legendary as Southern Africa has been struggling with effective policies to contain the enduring dynamics of these threats in the region (Hull & Derblom, 2010; van Nieuwkerk, 2012, Muntschik, 2011).

Methodology

This study adopts exploratory research design which entails the discovery of ideas and insights into the relationship between variables in a flexible manner, in order to consider different aspects of the problem under study through the analysis of insight stimulating examples (Kothari, 2004: 36). This research design is preferred because of its capacity to unveil diverse impacts of Chinese resource policy on human security in Africa. The study relies principally on secondary data which were sourced from textbooks, magazines, scholarly journals and internet. The data was presented qualitatively and analysed with content analysis technique (Table 2.1).

Table 2.1 Summary of the finding on the Chinese resource policy and human security in Africa

Nature of human security	*Contribution to human security*	*Threats to human security*
Economic security	Investment on infrastructure such as roads, rails and ports provides employment and stimulate economic activities on the continent and reduce poverty. China provides an alternative to Western market for African resources and a fairer deal in terms of economic partnership. It has also helped resource-rich countries like Angola to pay up their debt and increase budgetary expenditure. Chinese scramble for African resource has raise the price of these resources in global market	Chinese concessional loan to poor African states has increase the debt of these states. It may also lead to 'debt trap' due to the accumulation of the loan overtime. Recently, there was a rumour of possible Chinese takeover of Zambia Electricity Company because of debt default. This raises the fear of tacit colonialism. Again, Chinese engagement in betty trading as well as the dumping of cheap goods on the continent lead to de-industrialization of the continent and closure of factories across Africa
Political security	Chinese contribution to political security on the continent is low. The Asian giant is an authoritarian state and the crushing of Tiananmen square protest in 1989 is instructive on its position on human rights and political repression. Thus it took the pressure of Western countries on China to support, intervention in Darfour despite widespread human right abuse by the Sudanese government	The 'non-interference' and 'no conditionalities' of the Chinese investment in authoritarian states like Sudan, Zimbabwe and Gabon work against democratization of these countries. It promotes political repression of incumbent regime, since there is alternative source of investment from the west. More so, Chinese was alleged to be in arms deal with both Gaddafi government and the rebel National Transitional council in Libya during the 'Arab. Spring' in 2011. Arms supply is a threat to political security on the continent

Nature of human security	*Contribution to human security*	*Threats to human security*
Community security	Chinese armed forces have participated in un peacekeeping operations in Africa. It has also supplied military assets to the UN missions in Darfur, Cote d 'Ivoire, Congo and Western Sahara. A Chinese, Major General Zhao Jingmin, was the force commander in Western Sahara in 2007. Chinese has about 4500 troop in Sudan to protect oil. Installation. It participates in naval patrol of East African water to contain piracy in the region	China has become a major supplier of military hardwares to resource-rich countries which are used by these states against communities within the states. It weaponry was instrumental to Sudanese genocide in Darfur region. The Asian also supplied Zimbabwe with military equipment which was used against opposition. China is a major supplier of cheap small arms and light weapons (SALW) which is the major driver of threat to community on the continent
Environmental security	Chinese construction of roads, rails, drainage and hydro-power facilities has added value to environment in the benefitting countries and improves the hygiene of these communities. Drainages have supported flood and erosion management on the continent	Chinese hardly pay attention to environmental issues in their investment in Africa. The controversy on the hydro-power dam project in Gabon and Sudan is instructive. Fundamentally Chinese are engage in expropriation of non-renewable resources on the continent which is depleting. Besides, the environmental degradation associated with the extraction of these resources is enormous
Health security	Chinese have built hospitals on the continent, such as Orotta Hospital in Asmara, Eritrea, 32 hospitals and 145 health centres in DR Congo. They have organized conferences, seminars and provide tools for the prevention of malaria and HIV/AIDS. These and other similar projects have promoted health security in Africa	Flooding of Africa with substandard equipments, goods, foods and drugs are dangerous to human health. Besides, environmental pollution from the extraction of oil and other minerals is hazardous to human health. They cause various diseases including cancer, lung inflammation and increase in infant mortality rate

(continued)

Table 2.1 (continued)

Nature of human security	*Contribution to human security*	*Threats to human security*
Food security	Chinese are investing in the agricultural sector in Africa, where they produce food crop. This has contributed to food production and promotes food security. Besides, the technologies and infrastructure provided by the Chinese also assist small-scale farmers to improve in their operations and easily evacuate their produce to market, thereby strengthening food distribution chain on the continent	The accusation of land grabbing and dislocation of communities which hitherto depended on the allocated land to the Chinese leads to food shortage and poverty. Chinese population of about a million people on the continent puts pressure on food and other consumables; this further threatens food security
Personal security	Chinese supply of arms and equipments to African states has enhance personal security, since the arms bearing security operators are equipped to contain violence crime, terrorism, ethnic and religious crises. More so, in enhancing the logistics capacity of UN peace-keepers on the continent and participating in some of the operation, Chinese have made tangible contributions to personal security in Africa	Africans work in Chinese companies under terrible inhuman condition. For instance, many Nigerian factory workers died in an inferno overnight in Ikorodu, Lagos in September 2012, because they were locked up in the building by a Chinese foreman. Similar instances are abounds elsewhere on the continent. Casualization of labour is also common in Chinese companies. This does not guarantee job security, but leads to discontentment and crime

Source Compiled by the author

Presentation of Findings

Discussion of Findings

Chinese resource policy is a double edge sword to human security in Africa. It strengthens at one end and threatens at the other as captured by table. Detailed discussion of the findings is done below:

Economic Security

Chinese investments, loans and aids which are components of its resource policy have enhanced economic security on the continent. The provision of infrastructures such as roads and rails has opened up and linked communities and regions which facilitates the transaction between individuals and regions. These generate income and reduce poverty among the populace. Besides, Chinese hydro-power projects on the continent have increased power generation. This stimulates the efficiency of small- and medium-scale enterprises on the content. Indeed, the infrastructures built by the Chinese in resource-rich countries have made significant contributions to poverty alleviation and employment generation in many countries (De Lorenzo, 2007; Helstrom, 2009). Similarly, China's demand for African resources has improved the global prices of these resources and consequently the revenue earnings of these countries. For instance, Ayodele and Sotola (2014) have observed the reverses in the dwindling global prices of aluminium, copper and other minerals on the continent since the incursion of Chinese into its extractive sector. More so, the Asians are investing in high-risk countries where others would not, such as Angola, DR Congo, Zimbabwe and Sudan. This reduces the economic volatility of these countries to Western dependency. Consequently, even the so-called pariah states have received economic succour from the Chinese which has multiplier effects on poverty alleviation and employment (Kobylinski, 2012, Thrall, 2015). More so, some Chinese factories on the continent process some raw materials, this provides employment for Africans. In addition, the Asians have contributed to human capital development on the continent by training about 36,000 professionals of African origin between 2010 and 2012 (Ayodele & Sotola, 2014; Konings, 2007).

On the other hand, Chinese investments, loans and aids to African states are gradually creating the culture of economic dependency, as these countries are hooked to Chinese for funding of so many projects in their budgetary allocations. This is a change from one master to the other, the danger of economic dependency is enormous and severally discussed in terms of experience with the West. Repeating such a relationship with China means that the well-being of these economies depends on the decisions, actions and reactions of the Asians in the future (Kelly, 2012; Ncube et al., 2010). Similarly, Chinese loan to the continent is increasing the debt profile of some countries on the continent. The import of this among others is the danger of 'debt trap'. Many countries on the continent are already struggling with heavy 'debt burden' owed to Western institutions; therefore, accumulated Chinese debt should be analysed in terms of its impact on the future economic security of the continent. This is important, given the recent rumour of Chinese takeover of Zambia Electricity Company due to debt default. If this is true, then Africa is gradually lured into Chinese colonialism (French, 2014; Zheng, 2010;). Another threat to economic security is Chinese retail outlets on the continent where Chinese goods are sold at cheaper price. These have led to job lost by African retailers and increase the unemployment on the continent. Again, the dumping of cheap Chinese goods on the continent has resulted in de-industrialization and the consequent loss of employment with its inherent impact on the economy of these states and region. Also worrisome, is the employment of large contingent of Chinese in areas where Africans have the competence to work. This does not only deny employment opportunities to Africans but also abort technological transfer (Helstrom, 2009; Park, 2009; Thrall, 2015).

Political Security

Chinese contributions to political security on the continent in terms of checkmating political repression and promotion of human rights are low. Indeed, the five principles of peaceful existence enunciated in 1953 by the Chinese to guide their engagement with the outside world resonate in its relations with Africa, especially mutual respect for sovereignty and territorial integrity, and 'noninterference in each other's internal affairs' (Helstrom, 2009: 7). The import of these among others is the refusal of the Chinese to influence the political direction of African states in terms of democratic governance, as well as its norms and values as prescribed by the West. Thus, human rights abuse and political repression in African states are not seen as diplomatic issues as they remain within the internal affairs of African states. The lackadaisical attitude of Beijing to democratic governance emboldens African sit-tight leaders and dictators to perpetuate atrocities since China has emerged as a willing partner to buy their resources and finance their government without any conditionality on internal governance (Gonzalez, 2010; Moore, 2014; Ncube, 2013). These explain Sudan, Zimbabwe and DR Congo romance with the Asians in spite of egregious human rights abuses, political repression, corruption and authoritarianism. Similarly, Beijing supply of military hardware and equipment to African states are threats to political security on the continent since these arms are sometimes used against perceived political opposition and in suppression of legitimate protest by the citizens. For instance, Beijing supplied, Sudan and Zimbabwe with assorted armaments such as artillery pieces, battle tanks, air defence weapons, amour fighting vehicles, trainer and fighter aircrafts, small arms and light weapons at different times. Specifically, the Asians provided Mugabe administration with anti-riot equipment, short ware radio jamming equipment in order to check public protest and jam perceived offensive broadcast of the opposition and foreign radio stations in the run up to the 2005 Presidential Elections (Bhola, 2007; Chang, 2007). The impact of these logistics on the outcome of the elections and subsequent elections were evidently antithetical to political security on the continent (Kriger, 2008; Moore, 2014; Ncube, 2013).

Community Security

The participation of Chinese Armed Forces in peacekeeping on the continent has contributed to the security of communities and regions affected by violent conflicts. For instance, it has over 4000 troops in Sudan to protect some oil facilities. It has also participated in the UN peacekeeping in Darfur, Sudan, Cote d'Ivoire, Liberia and Congo. Notably, a Chinese general was the UN Force Commander in Western Sahara in 2007, and Beijing has the highest number of troops on UN missions in Africa when compared to other permanent members of the UN Security Council. Chinese navy has been patrolling the East African water to contain the threat of piracy (Helstrom, 2009; McDonald, 2008).

Paradoxically, Chinese sales of military equipment to resources rich countries on the continent are detrimental to community security in the mineral producing areas. Most of these governments use these weapons to suppress the agitation of the minerals producing communities over pollution and marginalization. Niger Delta and Sudanese conflicts are illustrative (Akpabio & Akpan, 2010; Barnes, 2005). More glaring was the role of Chinese weapons in the Darfur genocide since Western countries had placed arms embargo on Sudan (Ayabei, 2017; Large, 2008). Similarly, the Chinese were willing to supply arms to both sides of the Libyan conflict during the 'Arab Spring'. More so, Chinese' small arms and light weapons (SALW) is a major contributor to ethno-religious conflicts and banditry on the continent, since they are cheaper to acquire by communities and groups (Ajala, 2016; Ngang, 2007; Thrall, 2015).

Environmental Security

There is no doubt, Chinese construction of roads, rails, drainages and hydro-power facilities among others have improved environmental management in Africa. The landscaping of the project sites has also beautified the environment. The drainages support erosion and flood controls which are central to environmental preservation and management. More so, the construction of housing for Angolan leaders has added value to the capital city and improved the physical and environmental layout of the city (Dollar, 2016; Edinger & Pistorius, 2011; Kelly, 2012; Konings, 2007).

On the other hand, no Chinese institution is a signatory to 'Equator Principles' (EPs): a global framework adopted by financial institutions to assess, determine and manage environmental and social risk in project design, finance and execution across the globe. Consequently, Beijing is not transparent in carrying out Environmental Impact Assessment (EIA) on projects before their execution. This is exacerbated by the corrupt nature of African institutions saddle with the responsibility of enforcing desirable environmental laws and policies within their domain. This is illustrative in the controversy over the Gabonese and Sudanese hydropower dam projects (Alves, 2008; Helstrom, 2009; Thrall, 2015). Related to this, is the sector of Chinese interest in Africa. Oil and other mineral deposits are non-renewable resources which are depleting as the extraction takes place. The import of this among others is that the current rate exploitation cannot sustain future generations. Consequently, the continent is threatened by resource depletion (Alden & Alves, 2009; Cherp & Jewell, 2014). More so, the extraction of mineral resources comes with enormous environmental pollution and degradation which affect the livelihood of communities, destroyed the ecosystem with its flora and fauna, dislocate communities and lead to violent conflicts which further destroy the environment in a cyclical manner as experienced in Niger Delta, Angola, Sudan, DR Congo among others. These are direct threat to environmental security on the continent (Ajala, 2016; Gonzalez, 2010; International Crisis Group, 2002; Rodriguez et al., 2014).

Health Security

Chinese has contributed to health security on the continent through the organization of conferences and seminar on the prevention of some diseases. This was illustrated on its 'roll back malaria' and HIV/AIDS prevention program in Nigeria. Besides, the Chinese have also boosted health facilities on the continent with the construction of Orotta Hospital in Asmara Eritrea, 32 hospitals and 145 health centres in the DR Congo (Anshan 2007; Eisenman & Kurtantizik, 2006).

Paradoxically, the Chinese resource policy has tremendously threatened human security in Africa. Studies in Nigeria revealed the health implication of oil exploration in Africa. Firstly, the air quality of the regions is polluted with Alkanes, Alkenes, BTEX, carbon monoxide, hydrogen sulphide, nitro oxide, sulphur dioxide among others. The health hazard of these substances includes skin infections, itching, lung swelling, vomiting, cancer, heart and brain damage, poor development of foetus and children, miscarriage, convulsion, mucus membrane and respiratory tract irritation. Others are spasms, swelling of upper respiratory tract, fluid build-up in lungs and death, breathing difficulties and acute airway obstruction, shortness of breath, rampant diarrhoea from the consumption of fish and seafood (Gobo et al., 2010; Yakubu, 2017). Secondly, waste water and hazardous chemicals pollute the environment and affect water quality in the region. For instance, produce water, spent drilling mud and drilling cutting are generated from the exploration and production of crude oil. These substances contain heavy metals, organic and inorganic hazardous waste such as naturally occurring radioactive materials (NORMS) which pollute and contaminate sources of potable water and waterways. The discharge of these substances perpetually gain access to the underground water, contaminate it and spread to streams, wells, boreholes and other sources of water in the surrounding environment (Andrade et al., 2010; Clinton et al., 2009, Telleza et al., 2002; Yakubu, 2017). These waters therefore threaten human health and other lives in the environment.

Similar studies in Krugersdorp, Blesbok spruit, Kilip and Wonderfontein in South Africa; Blanket Mine, Iron Duke Mine in Gwanda District and Mazowe Valley in Zimbabwe; and three rivers (Shinkolobwe, Lwisha and Kansonga) in Katanga region and Artisanal gold mining in DR Congo revealed similar threats to health security in the regions. In South Africa, Acid Mine Drainage (AMD) generated by the exposure of pyrite bearing rock to oxygenated water from rainfall, when descanted to natural water course—river or stream contaminated and undermined the quality of water in the studied areas. This reduces the sources of table water, at this time that the population is increasing and the demand is correspondently rising (McCathy, 2011; Ochieng et al., 2010). Moreover, the presence of heavy metals, such as cadmium, copper, iron, lead manganese, mercury, molybdenum, selenium and zinc among others in mining regions across the country, lead to diarrhoea, mental disorder, cardiovascular disease, gastrointestinal tract inflammation Wilson's disease, Parkinson's disease and immune disorder (Ebenebe et al., 2017). In Zimbabwe, mining activities in Blanket Mine have altered the physical and chemical components of the ecosystem in Gwanda District, while Iron Duke Mine in Mazowe Valley releases its highly acidic wastewater into two evaporation bonds on the north-eastern side of the mine. This leads to the acidification of the groundwater and its contamination with Iron, copper, nickel, cobalt, lead, zinc and sulphuric oxide. The health implication of these substances is similar to what is obtainable in the Niger Delta region in Nigeria and mining regions in South Africa (Mathe & Phiri, 2016; Ravengai et al., 2005). Similarly, the health security of the inhabitants of Katanga in the Eastern Democratic Republic of Congo is threatened as a study on water in the three rivers (Shinkolobwe, Lwisha and Kansonga) showed unacceptable level of leads and cadmium concentrations, and the Artisanal gold mine degrades the landscape. At both mining sites, the environment is heavily polluted, ecosystem altered and they were complaining of metabolic disorder, burning sensation, certain tumours and short-term sterility (Butuzi & Some, 2016; Kalonda et al., 2017). Besides, Chinese flooding of Africa with substandard equipments, foods and drugs comes with health hazard. Substandard equipment, such as generators and other machines, increases the risk of accident, while substandard foods and drugs complicate illnesses and sometimes lead to death (African Press Organization, 2015; Agbaraji et al., 2012; Aminu & Gwarzo, 2017).

Food Security

Chinese have invested in the agriculture sector in Africa, by acquiring land for commercial farming which has boosted food production and promotes food security. Moreover, the construction of roads, rails, irrigation and other infrastructure has enhanced farming and the evacuation of farm produce from farms to marketing centres. These have increased connectivity between buyers and sellers, and indeed promote the availability of food to final consumers. It has also increased the profit of farming and the income of farmers on the continent. In addition, irrigation and other technologies innovated by the Chinese have improved the knowledge of some farmers on the continent. Many farmers have also benefitted from the improved seedlings and inputs brought in by the Chinese. The net effect of these activities is some innovation in agriculture techniques on the continent which increases food production and enhances food security (Alden & Alves, 2009; Cheru & Modi, 2013;).

Scholars have also identified the threat of Chinese resources extraction on food security on the continent. The negative impact of oil exploration and mining activities in terms of soil pollution reduces soil fertility. It also contaminates the crops which reduces the consumption value of food produced in the affected region. For instance, there is a reduction in minerals and vitamins content of green leaves and vegetables, as well as protein content of cassava in oil polluted communities in Niger Delta (Clinton et al., 2009; Gobo et al., 2010). Related here, is the threat of potable water shortage in some mining regions in South Africa where the surface water is persistently contaminated by Acid Mine Drainage (AMD). The import of this among others is the dearth of water for irrigation, fish farming and livestock production which affects food their availability and supply. Besides these contaminated water and air affect the health of the inhabitants of these communities and thus affect their productivities as farmers. This further threatens food production on the continent (Anshan, 2007; Butuzi & Some, 2016; Ebenebe et al., 2017; Mathe & Phiri, 2016). In the same vein, land grabbing for Chinese acquisition dislocates communities which hitherto depend on these land for subsistence living and agriculture. This does not only reduce their food productivity but also force them to depend on others for food and other basic needs. Besides, the growing population of Chinese on the continent estimated at 1 million, means that the continent has more mouth to feed. This puts additional pressure on food and other consumables and threatens food security (Askouri, 2007; Cheru & Modi, 2013; French, 2014; Park, 2009).

Personal Security

The support of the Chinese in equipping the arms bearing security services in Africa has promoted personal security, as these services are better equipped to contain violent threats by criminal elements on the continent. This has reduced the menace of crime, terrorism, ethnic and religious violent which hitherto threatened individual liberty and choice of action and location on the continent. In addition, by enhancing the logistic capacity of the UN peacekeeping mission on the continent and participating in some missions, Chinese have contributed immensely to personal security by containing the spread of those threats (Helstrom, 2009; McDonald, 2008).

On the other end, the Asians' activities that threaten every component of human security discussed earlier on also threaten personal security, since individuals are the objects of security in the paradigm. The consequences of the 'debt trap' to the Chinese and subtle colonialism would increase the crime rate due to the loss of jobs. Such development would require increment in security expenditure which further deprives the critical sector of the required funding, thereby perpetuating poverty, conflicts and crime in a cyclical manner on the continent (Helstrom, 2009; Zheng, 2010). Similarly, the Asian mantra of 'non-interference' in the internal affairs of African states has emboldened states backed terrorism/killings and ethnic cleansing, as well as political repression as witnessed in Darfur, Zimbabwe and Gabon. Besides, Chinese arms and equipments are used in these heinous crimes against personal security (Ayabei, 2017; Schaefer & Tkacik, 2008). Related to these are the environmental terrorism caused by the pollution of air, water and soil through the Asian extractive activities. This leads to sickness and death, internal displacement, loss of livelihood, contaminated food and water and decrease in crops yield; these factors permeatively threaten individual existence in mineral-rich regions in a genocidal magnitude (Ajala, 2016, Mathe & Phirii, 2016, Yakubu, 2017). Furthermore, Chinese labour practices on the continent are debasing to the extent that it encourages criminality. Casualization of workers in order to reduce wage bill and avoid placing workers on pension deprives Africans of job security and decent living which sometimes leads to crime and loss of interest in such job. Similarly, Africans in Chinese companies work under the terrible and inhuman conditions without regard to safety. For instance, many Nigerian factory workers died in overnight inferno in Ikorodu, a suburb of Lagos in September 2012, because they were locked up overnight in the building by a Chinese foreman.

Conclusion

The study focuses on Chinese resource policy and its strengthening and threat of human security in Africa. It reviews the pattern of outside influence on human security in Africa from the slave trade, era to the post-colonial milieu which were antithetical to human security. It highlights the impacts of Chinese scrambling for African resources in the new millennium and the contribution of the engagements to human security on the continent which reveals that while there are positive economic growth, financial inflow and infrastructural development from Chinese dealings with the continent, there are enormous threats to human security from these dealings. The threat includes debt trap and subtle colonialism, strengthening an authoritarian regime which represses communities, institutions and individuals, environmental terrorism which does not only threatens the health and food security of the present generation but also the existence of subsequent generations on the continent. To this end, African leaders need to evolve a common environmental policy on mineral resource extraction which would contained the menace of environmental terrorism and enhance sustainable development. There is a mandatory need for resource-rich countries on the continent to establish Generational Trust fund which would save a good percentage of current revenue earned from resources for future generation, since these resources are depleting and non-renewable. Besides, African Civil Society Organizations (CSOs) need to challenge the excesses of the Asians in terms of casualization of workers, weapons supply and tacit support for authoritarianism government and human rights abuses, among other in order to safeguard human security on the continent. Above all, there is a need for increase in inter African trade and investment, as well as intra-continental technology transfer which would facilitate the processing of African resources within the continent and promote the delinking of Africa from exploitative relations with the rest of the world.

References

African Economic Outlook. (2011). *Africa and its emerging partners*. Paris: OECD.

African Press Organization. (2015). *Survey on electrical counterfeiting in Africa*. Rueil-Malmaison: Schneider Electric.

Agbaraji, E., Ochulor, D., & Ezeh, G. (2012). Food and counterfeiting in the developing nations: The implications and way-out. *Academic Research International, 3*(2), 24–31.

Ajala, O. (2016). Human security in the Niger Delta: Exploring the interplay of resource governance, community structure and conflict. *Journal of Sustainable Development, Law and Policy, 7*(2), 81–103.

Akpabio, E., & Akpan, N. (2010). Governance and oil politics in Nigeria's Niger Delta: The question of distributive equity. *Journal of Human Ecology, 30*(2), 111–121.

Alden, C., & Alves, C. (2009). *China and Africa's natural resources: The challenges and implications. Occasional Paper* No-41. Johannesburg: South African Institute of International Affairs.

Alkines. (2003). A conceptual framework for human security, *CRISE Working Paper* 2. Oxford: Centre for Research in Inequality, Security and Ethnicity.

Alves, A. (2008). China & Gabon, China in Africa. *Programme Policy Reports*. Johannesburg: South Africa Institute of International Affairs.

Aminu, N., & Gwarzo, M. (2017). The eminent threats of counterfeit drugs to quality health care delivery in Africa: Updates on consequences and way forward. *Asian Journal of Pharmaceutical and Clinical Research, 10*(7), 82–86.

Andrade, V., Andrade, B., Costa, B., Pereira, O., & Dezohi, M. (2010). Toxicity assessment of oil field produced water treated by evaporative processes to produce water for irrigation. *Water Science Technology, 62*, 693–700.

Anshan, L. (2007). China and Africa: Policy and challenges. *China Security, 3*(3), 69–93.

Askouri, A. (2007). China's investment in Sudan: Displacing villages and destroying communities. In F. Manji & S Marks (Eds.), *African perspectives on China in Africa*. Cape Town; Nairobi, Oxford: Fahamu-Networks for social Justice.

Ayabei, C. (2017). The rise of China and conflicts in Africa: The case of Sudan. *African Journal of Political Science and International Relations, 11*(2), 29–35.

Ayodele, T., & Sotola, O. (2014). *China in Africa: An evaluation of Chinese investment*. Lagos: IPPA Working Paper Series.

Barnes, S. (2005). Global glows: Terror, oil and strategic philanthropy. *African Studies Review, 48*(1), 1–22.

Bhola, G. (2007). *China and India battle for influence in Africa: Part 4.* http://www.gimmiethescoop.com/China-and-India-battleforinfluence-in-Africa-part-4 (accessed November 8, 2018).

Brautigam, D. (2011). *China in Africa: What can Western donors learn?* Oslo: Norfund.

Butuzi, S., & Some, I. (2016). *Environmental assessment of mercury pollution in two artisanal gold mining site in Eastern Democratic Republic of Congo.* Nairobi: United Nations Environmental Programme.

Chang, E. (2007). Chinese arms and African oil. *Space Daily* http://www.spacedaily.com/reports/analysisChinesearmsandAfricanoil999.html (accessed November, 7, 2018).

Cherp, A., & Jewell, J. (2014). The concept of energy security: Beyond the four as. *Energy Policy, 75,* 415–421.

Cheru, F., & Modi, R. (eds) (2013). *Agricultural development and food security in Africa: The impact of Chinese, Indians and Brazilians investment.* London: Zed Books.

Cheunng, Y., & Xinnwang, Q. (2009). Empirics of China's outward direct investment. *Pacific Economic Review, 14*(3), 312–341.

CHS. (2003). *Human security now: Final report.* New York: Commission for Human Security.

Clinton, H., Ujagwung, G., & Horsefall, M. (2009). Evaluation of total hydrocarbon levels in some aquatic media in oil polluted mangrove wetland in Niger Delta. *Applied Ecology and Environmental Research, 7*, 101–120.

Collins, O., & Burns, J. (2007). *A history of sub-saharan Africa.* Cambridge: Cambridge University Press.

De' Lovenzo, M. (2007). African perspectives on China-American enterprise. *Institute for policy Research,* October 4.

Dike, K. (1956). *Trade and politics in Niger Delta.* Oxford: Oxford University Press.

Dollar, D. (2016). *China's engagement with Africa: From natural resources to human resources,* Washington, DC: The John Li Thornton China Centre at Brookings.

Ebenebe, P., Shale, K., Sedibe, M., Tikilili, P., & Achilonu, M. (2017). South African mine effluents: Heavy metal pollution and impact on the ecosystem. *International Journal of Chemical Science Research, 15*(4), 198.

Edinger, H., & Pistorius, C. (2011). Aspects of Chinese investment in the African resources sector. *The Journal of the Southern African Institute of Mining and Metallurgy, 111,* 501–510.

Eisenman, J., & Kurlantziek, J. (2006). China's Africa strategy. *Current History, 105*(691), 219–224.

French, H. (2014). *China's second continent: How a million migrants are building a new empire in Africa*. New York: Knopf Double-day Publishing Group.
Gobo, A., Richard, G., & Ubong, I. (2010). Health impact of gas flares on Igwuruta/Umuechem communities in Rivers state. *Journal of Applied Science and Environmental Management, 13*, 27–33.
Gonzalez, A. (2010). Petroleum and its impact on three wars in Angola, Nigeria and Sudan. *Journal of Peace, Conflict and Development,16*, 58–86.
Hellstrom, J. (2009). *China's emerging role in Africa A strategic overview, FOI Studies in African security*. Stockholm: Swedish Defence Research Agency
Hodges, C. (1932). *The background of international relations*. New York: John Wiley and Sons.
Hull, C., & Derblom, M. (2010). Abandoning frontline trenches? Capabilities for peace and security in SADC region. *FOI Report No- f01-R-2768-SE.FO1* Swedish Research Agency.
International Crisis Group. (2002) *God, oil and country: Changing the logic of war in Sudan*. Brussels: International Crisis Group.
Kalonda, D., Tshikongo, A., Kule-Koto, F., Numbi, O., Busambwa, C., Kalonda, D., Bwalya, C. H., Otshudi, A., & Kalala, Z. (2017). Impact of mining on water of the rivers Shinkolobwe, Lwisha & Kansonga in the province of Katanga (DRC). *The Journal of Medical Research, 3*(2), 71–73.
Kelly, J. (2012). China in Africa: Curing the resource curse with infrastructure and modernization. *Sustainable Development Law and Policy, 12*(3), 35–41, 57–60.
Kobylinski, K. (2012). Chinese Investment in Africa; checking the facts and figure, *Association for international Affairs, Briefing Paper*, July.
Konings, P. (2007). China and Africa: Building a strategic partnership. *Journal of Developing Societies, 23*(3), 341–367.
Kothari, C. (2004). *Research methodology: Methods and techniques* (Second ed.). New Delhi: New Age International Publishers.
Kriger, N. (2008). Zimbabwe's Parliamentary Election of 2005: The myth of new electoral laws. *Journal of Southern African Studies, 34*(2), 359–378.
Large, D. (2008). China and the contradictions of 'non-interference' in Sudan. *Review of African Political Economy, 35*(175), 93–106.
Mathe, M., & Phiri, A. (2016). The impact of mining on the environment in Gwanda District Zimbabwe; A case study of Blanket Mine. *Imperial Journal of Interdisciplinary Research, 2*(5), 503–512.
McCathy, T. (2011). The impact of acid mine drainage in South Africa. *South African Journal of Science, 107*(5–6), 1–7.
McDonald, M. (2008). Chinese warships sail: Loaded for pirates. *New York Times*, December 26.

Mentan, T. (2002). Exiting the whirlpool? Pan Africanism caught in the crossfire of identity and globalization. *Africa Journal of International Affairs, 5*(1&2), 73–140.

Moore, D. (2014). Death or dearth of democracy in Zimbabwe? *Africa Spectrum, 49*(1), 101–114.

Morgan Than, H. (1978). *Politics among nations: The struggle for power and peace* (5th ed.). New York: Alfred A Knopf.

Morrison, K. (1978). Domestic politics and industrialization in China: The foreign trade factor. *Asian Survey, xviii*(7), 690–700.

Muntschik, J. (2011). *Picky regional security integration in Southern Africa Development Community: Longshadow of table mountains and the alps*, 41st UACES Conference Exchanging ideas on Europe 2011, Cambridge, September 5–7.

Ncube, C. (2013). The 2013 Elections in Zimbabwe: End of an era for Human Rights discourse as a counter-hegemonic strategy? *Africa Spectrum, 48*(3), 99–110.

Ncube, M., Lufumpa, C., & Ndikumana, L. (2010). Chinese trade and investment activities in Africa, African Development Bank Group. *Policy Brief, 1*(4), 11.

Ngang, D. (2007). *Small arms and light weapons: The role of small arms and light weapons in conflict and security in sub-Saharan Africa*. Austria: EUCPS.

Ochieng, G., Seanago, E., & Nkwonta, O. (2010). Impacts of mining on water resources in South Africa: A review. *Scientific Research and Essay, 5*(22), 3351–3357.

Okon, E., & Esin, M. (2018). Democracy and conflict in Africa: Conceptions and theoretical perspectives. *African Strategic Survey, 1*(2), 122–141.

Okon, E., & Ojakorotu, V. (2018). Imperialism and contemporary Africa: An analysis of continuity and change. *Journal of African Foreign Affairs, 5*(2), 227–449.

Park, Y. (2009). Chinese migration in Africa, China in Africa project *Occasional Paper No- 24*. Johannesburg: South African Institute of International Affairs.

Ravengai, S., Love, D., Love, I., Gratwicke, B., Mandingaisa, O., & Owen, R. (2005). Impact of Iron Duke pyrite mine on water chemistry and aquatic life-Mazowe valley, Zimbabwe. *Water SA, 31*(2), 219–228.

Reid, R. (2014). Horror, hubris and humanities: The international engagement with Africa, 1914-2014. *International Affairs, 90*(1), 143–165.

Rodney, W. (1972). *How Europe underdeveloped Africa*. New York: Howard University Press.

Rodriguez, J., Rodriguez, F., Gutierrez, C., & Major, S. (2004). Oil, poverty and environment in Angola. *Bolelinde la Associacion de Geografos Esparnoles, 64*, 427–432.

Schaefer, B., & Tkacik, J. (2008). Zimbabwe's enabler: How Chinese arms keep Mugabe in power, the heritage foundation. http://www.heritage.org/research/Africa/wm1997.cfm/ (accessed November 28, 2018).
Shalmon, D., & Lee, H. (2008). Searching for oil: China's oil strategies in Africa. In R. Rotberg (Ed.), *China into Africa; Trade, aid and influence*. Washington, DC: Brookings Institution.
Takamine, T. (2006) *Japan's development aid to China: The long running foreign policy of engagement*. New York: Routledge.
Telleza, G., Nirmalakhandan, N., & Gardea-Torresday, J. (2002). Performance evaluation of an activated sludge system for removing petroleum hydrocarbons from oil field produced water. *Advance Environmental Research, 6*, 455–470.
Thrall, I. (2015). *China's expanding African relations: Implications for national security*. Santa Monica, CA: Rand Corporation
UNDP. (2004). *Human security report: New dimension of human security*. New York: the United Nations.
United Nations. (2009). *Human security in theory and practice: Application of human security concept and the UN Trust Fund for human security*. New York: United Nations.
USGS. (2008). *Mineral commodity summaries*. Washington, DC: US Geological Survey.
van Nieuwkerk, A. (2012). *Towards peace and security in Southern Africa*. Maputo: Friederich Ebert Stiftung.
Wallerstein, I. (1967). *The modern world system*. New York: Vintage Books.
Whewell, D. (2008). China to seal 9bn US Dollars DR Congo deal, *BBC News*. http://news.bbc.co.uk/2/hi/programmes/newsnight/7343060.stm (accessed November 4, 2018).
Yakubu, O. (2017). Addressing environmental health problems in Ogoniland through the implementation of United Nations Environment Programme recommendations; environmental management strategies. *Environments, 4*(28), 1–19.
Yergin, D. (2006). Ensuring energy security. *Foreign Affairs, 85*(2), 69–82.
Zheng, L. (2010). Neo-colonialism, ideology or just business: China's perception of Africa. *Global Media and Communication, 6*(3), 271–276.

CHAPTER 3

Sustainable Human Security in Africa: Exploring the Effects of Diminishing Natural Resources and Low Sovereign Wealth Funds

Uche Nwali

Introduction

Part of the optimism that heralded political independence in most African states was the hope that the hard-won freedom would translate to greater use of the abundant natural resources to advance societal development and the general good. Several decades after, Africa's natural resources have not yielded the expected shared prosperity. Instead, they have produced a paradox of plenty. Decades of mining the continent's natural resources have enriched only a privileged few while deepening poverty and expanding the frontiers of conflict amid resource depletion, rising sovereign debts and decaying development infrastructures. What is more, despite billions of dollars accruing from natural resources annually, only a few countries in Africa have Sovereign Wealth Funds (SWFs) for the future. And even for such countries, there is a growing debate in recent

U. Nwali (✉)
University of Lagos, Lagos, Nigeria

K. J. Ani et al. (eds.), *Political Economy of Resource, Human Security and Environmental Conflicts in Africa*,
https://doi.org/10.1007/978-981-16-2036-2_3

years over the merit of saving for future generations when the present generation is still languishing in penury. This paper argues in the affirmative, pointing out that both goals are not mutually exclusive. However, there is a threat (shifting natural resource use and value) that could hinder human security in Africa in future—a threat that seems underestimated and is less widely analysed, yet troubling. Future generations will have fewer natural resources to meet their human security needs even if climate change is rolled back. This will be caused not just by depletion as a result of resource exploitation, but also by technology driven alternatives that may emerge and render some natural resources redundant and consequently threaten human security in natural resource-dependent countries. This study investigates the push and pull effect of resources on human security in Africa.

Human security, which represents a new dimension of security that emphasizes political, social, economic, and environmental well-being of the people, has continued to resonate in the twentyfirst-century security discourse around the world. This, perhaps, is because of the increasing recognition that the traditional notion of security that limits its scope to the protection of state's territorial integrity against external aggression using military force is inadequate for understanding and for curbing internal conflicts, and economic challenges such as poverty and the vulnerability they unleash, which could make the citizenry susceptible to acts that could also undermine national security. Thus, it is not surprising that there is quite impressive interest in and literature on human security, especially in Africa, where there seems to be a linkage between extreme poverty and rising national insecurity.

However, despite this growing interest by scholars and policymakers on the continent and beyond, it seems the scope of human security has been limited to meeting the socio-economic needs of the present as only a little attention has been given to the need to protect future generations against fear and socio-economic deprivations. Again, some of the threats that will encumber sustainable human security in future are conspicuously underestimated in the extant literature even when human security is among the integral themes of the global development and security frameworks such as Sustainable Development blueprint which advocates for a "development that meets the needs of today without compromising the ability of future generations to meet their own needs". Human Security Now report of the Commission on Human Security extends the scope of security beyond the state's territorial integrity to people's economic, political, social and environmental safety. It also captures the Millennium Development Goals (MDGs) which elapsed in 2015 and the Sustainable Development Goals (SDGs) whose agenda is to among other things, by 2030, eradicate global poverty and hunger and lack of access to good healthcare, quality education, potable water and sanitation, affordable and clean energy and to conserve natural resources and mitigate climate change (see UNDP, 2015; Tavanti, 2013; Easterly, 2007).

Essentially, there are three major threats to sustainable human security in Africa. The first is the resource governance deficit epitomized by natural resource exploitation and political corruption. It is on record that the quest by "European powers to capture and exploit African resources played a key role in the transformative process of colonialism" (Murombedzi, 2016: 59). Colonialism was all about natural resource exploitation and domination, and many of the inequalities on the continent today are caused by the unequal access to the continent's natural resources (Maloba, 2017; Onimode, 1982; Ake, 1981, 1996). This exploitation is reinforced through low pricing and under-invoicing of Africa's natural resources by the industrialized world, a practice that has lasted through the ages. Africa's political elites are also a party to this conspiracy: rather than the public good, they are driven by self-interest, and so they connive with and collect kickbacks from the exploiters of Africa's natural resources. The traditional exploiters are the West but in recent years the list is widening as China and other emerging economies joined the scramble for African resources. The elites also engage in outright embezzlement of proceeds of natural resource sales. According to the report of the High-Level Panel (HLP) on "Illicit Financial Flows from Africa" chaired by the former South African President—Thabo Mbeki, Africa loses over US$50 billion annually to illicit financial flows, and between 1970 and 2008 over US$800 billion has been siphoned. The amount ballooned to over 1 trillion dollars in the last 50 years. A significant portion of these monies were the proceeds of the continent's natural resources. Oil exporting countries accounted for the largest share and Nigeria is on the lead with 30.5% of total illicit flows between 1970 and 2008 (AU/UNECA, 2016; AU/ECA, 2015). In fact, African economies lose through corruption and tax evasion more than 10 times what they receive in aid (Labour Party cited in Cross, 2017: 353). The consequences of this have been protracted infrastructure deficit, extreme poverty and the accompanying social vices and conflicts. The "paradox of plenty" cum the "resource curse" hypothesis is still very true of Africa—the "blood diamond" as we saw in Liberia, Sierra-Leone, and even Congo, and the "blood oil" in the case of Nigeria and Sudan/South Sudan are some of its manifest praxis.

The second threat is climate change. It is common knowledge that global warming is causing desertification in some parts of the world and flooding in others, all of which could restrict access to and/or diminish available resources. And this can induce conflicts and impact human security.

The third threat is the diminishing natural resources not only in terms of declining reserves but also shifting global resource use and demand that could render some natural resources redundant in future. Both the first and second threats have been sufficiently interrogated in the extant literature (Sawe, 2018; Murombedzi, 2016; Oyama, 2014; Obi, 2010; Nwosu, 2010; Watts, 2008; Collier, 2007; Ibeanu, 2005; Ross, 2004; UN Commission on Human Security, 2003). But the third threat appears to have attracted little attention except in energy security discourse where emerging clean energy and energy switch (e.g. from oil to solar/wind, and also from oil to natural gas) and the impact on global economy and oil states' foreign earnings dominate debate: the debate is rarely about the consequences of these changes on job and human security.

Also, because human security is not being met in Africa, it is often difficult on the continent, especially in sub-Saharan Africa, to extend thoughts and policies on human security beyond the present to the future. Nonetheless, protecting future generations from socio-economic and environmental deprivations are a sine quo non for a secure future, particularly for Africa which is highly dependent on natural resources that are now diminishing, thus raising concerns about the ability of future generations to meet their own needs. Africa is a treasure trove of natural resources, accounting for about 10% of global freshwater resources, 17% of global forest cover, a quarter of mammal species and a fifth of bird and plant species (United Nations, 2008: 29). Its hydrocarbon resource is huge and its gift of precious stones such as gold, diamond, and many others, remains unmatched. While African governments rely on export of these resources to meet their revenue needs, households rely on them for job, income, nutrition, health and energy.

Many years of intense and predatory exploitation of natural resources of most African countries have triggered resource depletion. For instance, it is projected that Nigeria's crude oil reserves of 37 billion barrels would exhaust in the next three decades, by 2048 to be precise (Calcuttawala, 2017; Maurice cited in Vanguard, 2011). According to the Ghana Chamber of Mines, and International Council on Mining & Metals 2015 Report, Ghana, the second largest gold producer in Africa is projected to witness a continuous decline in gold production at the rate of 4.6% per year due to some factors among which is the aging life cycle of its gold reserves and mines. South Africa's situation is not that different: its available gold resource reserves will run out in the next 39 years although its reserves of Platinum Group Metals (PGM) has 335 years to depletion counting from 2014 (Statistics South Africa, 2017: 17–21). But even the PGM faces some challenges too—sudden fluctuation in price and decline in demand in future.

Given the aforementioned realities, Africa's present is bleak and its future seems even bleaker. From the north of Africa to the south, east to the west, resource-endowed countries face similar challenge of diminishing reserves and export revenue, and this has implication for human security on the continent. Several factors account for the diminishing resources: non-renewable nature of these resources, poor resource governance, indiscriminate and predatory exploitation and climate change.

But beyond these factors, there is also the challenge of shifting global use and demand of natural resources driven mainly by the fast-evolving technologies that are altering not only the automobile industry and the entire energy landscape with the invention of fuel-efficient cars and electric vehicles (EVs) cum alternative eco-friendly energy (e.g. wind and solar), but also genetically modified organisms (GMOs) and recycling of used goods—all of which are increasingly rendering fossil fuel and conventional natural resources (including raw materials such as cash crops) less useful. So if Africa's natural resources are to be conserved, in a few decades to come, their global use and demand may still decline and so will government and individual revenue.

In the midst of these challenges are expanding frontiers of conflict, mounting sovereign debts, decaying infrastructures, and low Sovereign Wealth Funds, which also have consequences for human security in the present and in future. Usually, how these factors will collectively affect the future of human security in Africa has either been underestimated or not given adequate attention in the extant literature. It is this gap that this paper seeks to bridge by bringing to the fore these evolving challenges and by suggesting the need to mainstream them into the contemporary security discourse in order to develop a comprehensive and sustainable human security architecture that meets today's socio-economic needs of the people while creating a promising prospect that will augment the needs of the humans of tomorrow.

Understanding Sustainable Human Security in Africa

At the United Nations Millennium Summit in 2000, Kofi Annan, then Secretary General of the UN outlined six shared values that reflect the spirit of the UN Charter and which are of utmost relevance to twentyfirst-century intra and international relations and these include freedom; equity and solidarity; tolerance; non-violence; respect for nature; and shared responsibility (UN, 2000). These values are increasingly threatened in our world today and it seems the threat will continue for the foreseeable future. Hence, it is not surprising therefore that the world is talking about "human security now"—access to income, food, health, education and of course environmental and personal safety. But what about human security for the unborn, especially in Africa, where most countries are dependent on natural resources which are finite and facing depletion? No doubt, challenge such as this has prompted some talks about economic diversification on the continent. For example, in Nigeria, the government in recent years has been talking about "Nigeria Beyond Oil" which is a phrase that captures government's ambition to diversify Nigeria's economy from oil to agriculture and solid minerals. But the problem with such diversification is that it is from one exhaustible natural resource to another or to cash crops whose production is dependent on limited natural resources such as land and water, which are also facing threat. These resources will continue to diminish as the population increases irrespective of whether the climate change is rolled back or not. Again, such transition from one resource to another threatens human security in terms of job security. Although a transition from oil economy to agriculture is a noble idea, it portends job loss for those who work in the oil industry.

So, the question that still arises is how do we make human security sustainable in Africa given that future generations will likely have fewer natural resources to meet their needs and will equally face the consequences of technologically induced change? The answer you will get depends on who you ask. For a farmer, the likely answer is: eradicate acts that undermine farmlands so that farming can continue for eternity. A fisherman probably would want an end to pollution, and the streams/rivers/seas/oceans to remain habitable for fishes. A hunter who is dependent on the game may demand an end to activities that threaten the forest resource so that hunting can continue in perpetuity. For those who work in the oil industry, it is by tapping and developing oil resources. Everyone wants to keep their means of livelihood and probably conserve and save for their children. But it is inevitable that some of these means of livelihood will give way not to climate change which can be controlled, but to civilization with its intended and unintended consequences: infinitely unleashing technological breakthroughs/celebration and at the same destruction.

Take oil jobs for instance, as wind and solar power ascend the energy spectrum and become the dominant source of power to homes, schools and industries, the demand for fossil fuels will decrease and so will conventional oil jobs—this process has already started. Traditional occupation like hunting is yet another example. Forest resource is being eroded by other uses of land like urbanization and industrialization such that in the next century, the world will be left with fewer forests; most, if not all of which would be game reserves where hunting cannot even take place. In some places this could lead to conflict, which ultimately will undermine human security. Already in Africa, competition for land resources is fueling inter-tribal and intra-communal conflicts. In Nigeria for instance, access to land is at the centre of the farmers-herders' crisis, which has claimed thousands of lives and caused huge economic loss and hardship (Adelakun et al., 2015; Oyama, 2014).

As a solution to resource depletion and/or technology induced threats to human security, some may suggest; in the case of oil industry for example, re-train the oil workers so that they can fit in the emerging alternative energy industry or elsewhere, and for hunters, give them a different means of livelihood. While this may sound sensible and seem promising, the fact remains that the growing technology revolution in various fields of human endeavour creates fewer jobs. In fact, it seems the main driving force of the latest inventions and innovations is; more profit through more productivity and efficiency with less hands. Artificial intelligence cum the emergence of human-like robots that can perform human tasks even faster and more efficiently is another typical example. Such technology takes away jobs from people and this is largely why despite many recent breakthroughs in inventions and innovations around the world, the global unemployment rate seems to be growing and more people are losing their jobs, even in industrialized countries. Then the question that arises is, do we treat technology as one of the many threats to sustainable human security, and as we celebrate the latest technological achievement, are we doing enough to factor in its likely fallout, into human security policies and discourse? Perhaps the answer is no. A scan of human security literature and even national and international policy documents reveals this deficiency.

Different notions of the concept of security have evolved through time to the twenty-first century. In ancient times, and traditionally, security was conceived through the prism of the physical protection of people and communities. With the emergence of the modern state, the notion of security shifted to the state's territorial integrity and its protection against internal and external aggression using military might. The traditional focus of security on the state was partly because the fundamental purpose of the state is to protect its citizens. But the erosion of the state capacity to offer protection, by factors such as economic challenges, globalization, and bad governance has triggered a refocus of security beyond the state to individual human beings and international system in order to compensate for state failure (Axworthy, 2001). Security issues today include insecurities driven by non-military challenges (Poku et al., 2007). This refocuses which gained increased momentum in the post-Cold War era gave birth to the concept of human security—a concept, which represents a shift in the understanding of security from state-centred to people-centred.

The idea of human security was introduced in 1994 by the UNDP Human Development Report which described it as security beyond security from physical violence and which encompasses other types of securities such as income, food, health, environmental, community and political safety (UNDP, 1994). This idea was further consolidated by the Commission on Human Security Report which states that human security does not seek to displace national security, but rather to complement it (Commission on Human Security, 2003). Thus, human security is about freedom from fear which emphasizes the protection of victims of armed conflict which was the original idea, and it is also about freedom from want which seeks to ensure the socio-economic well-being of the people (Gasper, 2005; Hampson & Daudelin, 2002). There are about seven types of human insecurities that could cause fear and socio-economic deprivation (see Fig. 3.1).

Human security has three major pillars, namely, freedom from fear; freedom from want and freedom to live in dignity (United Nations, 2016:

Type of Insecurity	Root Causes
Economic insecurity	Poverty, unemployment, lack of access to credit and other economic opportunities
Food insecurity	Hunger, famine, sudden rise in food prices
Health insecurity	Epidemics, malnutrition, poor sanitation, lack of access to basic health care
Environmental insecurity	Environmental degradation, resource depletion, natural disasters
Personal insecurity	Physical violence in all its forms, human trafficking, child labour
Community insecurity	Inter-ethnic, religious and other identity-based tensions, crime, terrorism
Political insecurity	Political repression, human rights violations, lack of rule of law and justice

Fig. 3.1 Types of human insecurities and possible root causes (*Source* United Nations [2016] and UNDP Human Development Report [1994])

4). Achieving these pillars has been difficult, especially in sub-Saharan Africa. But even more difficult is their sustainability, hence the emergence of the notion of sustainable human security. The notion is a paradigm that captures the most contemporary knowledge on human security, and it emerged from about three decades of reflections on sustainable development, human security human development, human dignity and human sustainability (Tavanti, 2013).

There have been attempts to integrate these new security concerns into security policies at regional and sub-regional levels, and this is very visible in Africa. In this regard, Tieku (2007) contends that human security concerns in Africa informed the transition of the Organisation of African Unity (OAU) to African Union (AU). At its 2000 Summit, the AU took human security into account in its African security policy. Factors such as poverty, conflicts, terrorism and climate have been identified as the major threats to human security in Africa. Protection from physical danger and economic lack is also among the core principles of New Partnership for Africa's Development (NEPAD) and African Peer Review Mechanism (APRM) which is a brainchild of NEPAD (Colliers, 2004). In West Africa, ECOWAS has also done the same by incorporating human security into its strategy of building an efficient regional security system. This is demonstrated by the Organisation's increasing emphasis on crisis prevention, peace-making and peacebuilding as well as economic and political rights in order to ensure greater social inclusion, through its Supplementary Protocol on Democracy and Good Governance (Sahel and West Africa Club/OECD 2006; Hussein et al. 2004).

No doubt national and regional governments in Africa have designed good policies aimed at achieving human security, but these policies have yielded meagre return. Abutudu (2005) blames this on neo-liberal agenda which advocates for market fundamentalism and non-interference of state in production and distribution of goods and services, hence the decline of welfare state and the rise of liberal policies such as privatization and the removal of state subsidies from various social and productive sectors (education, health and agriculture), all of which encumber the economic security of people in post-colonial Africa. Yet, "nothing can be a greater threat to security than being excluded from life supporting economic activities" (Ojo, 1999: 6). Economic well-being particularly food security is essential for sustainable human development (Conceição et al., 2016). Unfortunately, millions of people in sub-Saharan Africa still suffer acute hunger and starvation (UNDP, 2012).

The failure of both national security and human security in Africa is largely why the continent is negatively stereotyped and portrayed in the media and at international fora as a hotbed of wars, violence, hunger, diseases and death (Arthur, 2017). These challenges have contributed to Africa's vulnerability to even a more dangerous problem—terrorism. From the countries in the horn of Africa to those in the oil-rich Gulf of Guinea, particularly Nigeria, Islamic extremism and terrorism are on the rise as the continent increasingly becomes a safe haven for pockets of terrorist organisations (e.g. Boko Haram) affiliated to global terrorist networks such as Al Qaeda and ISIS. This appalling development has helped create, reinforce and transplant transnational threats to other parts of the world and that is why more than ever, Africa is now a serious concern for Western countries such as the United States and those in Europe who are usually the main targets of transnational terrorism (Harris, 2017).

For Ball et al. (2003) as well as Poku et al. (2007), lack of good governance at state level and in security organisations is responsible for the poor physical and human security situation in some African states. This has led to a strain in state-society relations as the citizens seem to no longer trust their states' ability to provide them physical and socio-economic safety. Similarly, Picard and Lelei (2015) posit that governance is the missing link in efforts towards meeting human security on the continent.

Although institution and governance lacuna and also neo-colonialism are indeed huge challenges for human security in Africa, there are other challenges. Clove (2005) highlights some of these challenges with emphasis on resource and environment related problems such as lack of access to resources, the growing pressure on the natural resource base and loss of biodiversity as a result of degradation of arable land, over-fishing and deforestation. Thomas and Wilkin (1999) observe how the globalization of world politics is affecting human security in Africa by expanding both the scope of security issues and the actors. This is true in that globalization has triggered collective global response that is helping Africa deal with such challenges which are some of the consequences of climate change that is now threatening people in different ways with those in Africa being the most hit. But the globalization of trade, finance and investment could also impede human security by deepening inequality (Thomas, 2005). It widens not only the economic gap between the North and the South, but also income disparity within nations particularly in the South with many countries in Africa being the most affected victims (Khor, 2000).

From the foregoing, it is obvious that the literature on human security is quite remarkable. Nonetheless, what seems to be missing is the negative impact that technology (notwithstanding its inherent opportunities and benefits) and shifting global resource use and demand will have on the continent in future. Surprisingly, these threats are also underestimated by the United Nations who, MacFarlane and Khong (2006) rightly observe, has played a major role in extending the notion of security beyond its traditional meaning and scope to include development, economic, environmental, social and political safety. In specific cases (like the Human Development Report 1994, and the 2003 Report of Commission on Human Security titled "Human Security Now"), where human security dominated global discourse on development and security, the major focus has always been on resource sustainability and reduction in human vulnerability by eradicating poverty and mitigating environmental degradation in order to slow down climate change. Technology induced resource-related threats to human security such as shifting resource use and demand as well as the recycling of used goods are often missing or underestimated. How job loss from technology driven transition (e.g. fossil fuels to wind and solar energy) and the accompanying low demand for certain natural resources and decline in government revenues, will affect household income and community's life and states' capacity to provide human security, and the need to dedicate policies, research and resources to mitigating such effect, are the gap in the literature. The decline in government revenue as a result of energy switch reduces the capacity of the state to pay workers' salaries, provide basic amenities and enforce human rights. Millions of working people around the world will be pulled below the poverty line as they lose their jobs due to resource or the energy switch.

Africa's Vast Natural resources—A Source of Power, Insecurity and Poverty

Africa is richly endowed with numerous precious natural resources ranging from crude oil to solid minerals and timber. With 12.5% of the world total oil production and 9.5% of estimated global crude oil discovery, Africa accounts for the world's third largest oil reserves, ahead of South and Central America (8.5%) but behind the Middle East (61%) and North America (11.6%). Nigeria, Libya, Algeria and Angola are leading oil producers in the continent (Alden & Alves, 2009: 6). In terms of solid minerals, Africa is home to world's rarest gems and base metals. Available records show that Africa holds a significant proportion of global reserves accounting to 30% of bauxite, 60% of manganese, 75% of phosphates, 85% of platinum, 80% of chrome, 60% of cobalt, 30% of titanium, 75% of diamonds and nearly 40% of gold. Sub-Saharan Africa produces 7% of global oil production and known reserves are of a similar magnitude (Inter-ministerial Committee for International Cooperation and Development—CICID, 2008).

South Africa seems to be an undisputed leader in the solid mineral sector, accounting for 80% of world's total production and 90% of world reserves of platinum and 75% of world reserves of manganese and the second largest gold producer in the world: only behind Australia. The Democratic Republic of Congo (DRC) is the leading producer of cobalt at 36% of world's total production, and possesses half of the world's known reserves, and also produces a significant amount of diamond. The DRC, South Africa and Botswana together forms the global diamond triangle as they account for over half of world's diamond output and 60% of known deposits. Zambia also sits on large deposits of copper and iron ore. Zimbabwe has diamond and platinum, Gabon has manganese, and Angola boasts of diamond, copper and iron ore (Alden & Alves, 2009: 6).

Most African countries depend on natural resources for employment and revenue. In the solid mineral sector alone, about five to six million people in Africa (20 million in the world) engage in small-scale mining, aside larger millions of people in the formal employment of mining companies (CICID, 2008). In some countries, natural resources account for over 80% of government income. In 2012 alone sub-Saharan Africa revenue from natural resource exports was about $300 billion accounting for 75% of its total exports (World Bank cited in IBIS, 2015). But, despite these huge earnings, most countries in Africa are still in abject poverty. Political corruption, inadequate resource governance, exploitation and political instability are some of the challenges that make many of them to derive little benefits from their natural resources (Sawe, 2018; Diamond, 1988; Ekeh, 1975).

Quite a number of consequences have accompanied the mining of Africa's natural resources. Apart from the fact that many of these resources are non-renewable, extracting them from their location usually alters the topography of the soil, leading to pollution of the environment which in some instances impedes the traditional means of livelihood (such as fishing and farming) of the host communities. And because socio-political institutions and resource governance in Africa are weak, these consequences are often the norm rather than an exception. Thus, inadequate environment impact assessment, oil spillage and gas flaring are common and sometimes deliberately committed by the mining companies (most of which are foreign transnational corporations) in the pursuit of profit although there have been cases of sabotage by other vested interests like the militant groups operating in the host communities.

The "paradox of plenty" and "resource curse" are still very much tenable on the continent. Africa's vast natural resources have yielded only little benefits for the populace and have become more of a burden than a blessing. Corruption, primitive accumulation, poverty, resource-induced conflicts and environmental degradation are the defining features of resource-rich African states (Watts, 2008; Collier, 2007; Ross, 2004). For instance, in Nigeria's oil-rich Niger Delta, oil extraction has "dispossessed" and "impoverished" the local population, thus fueled popular violent resistance in one hand and counter-state violence on the other hand (Obi, 2010:219; Nwosu, 2010; Ibeanu, 2005). Needless to say that human security suffers under such atmosphere of popular violence and counter-violence by the state.

The hypothesis that the Nigerian experience as shown above proved true is the resource-power-violence-state correlation. Indeed, "there is a deep structural link between the use and control of resources and the organisation and exercise of power. Control over resources is the ultimate source of power" (Shivji cited in Murombedzi, 2016: 60) and leasing cause of state repression. The "high premium on state power" is largely because it guarantees access to resources (Ake, 1996). Access to natural resources is also driving the struggle for power in the international system between the old industrialized world superpowers (Europe, North America and Japan) and the emerging world superpowers (e.g. China). The increasing appetite of emerging economies for raw materials is putting pressure on supplies, leading to "rush for resources that are known to be finite, Africa is the object of flattering attention" (CICID, 2008: 27–28). The rush for African natural resources is pushing ever deeper into pristine, sensitive and remote areas that were (until recently) difficult to access and largely untouched (Hobbs, 2012: 2). China, though a latecomer and perhaps, the newest actor in the scramble for natural resources in Africa, is making waves in the unfolding resource rush. Given its industrialization and dramatic rise in the last two decades that made it the world's third largest economy, and the accompanying growing appetite for hydrocarbons and other precious minerals and timber, China has in recent decades made a foray into resources exploitation in Africa (Alden & Alves, 2009). China's presence in Africa's resource industry is enormous: it has progressed from "a status of no position in the resource market in 1995 to a standing as a significant player today with oil leases from Angola to Sudan and mining concessions from the Democratic Republic of the Congo (DRC) to South Africa" (Alden & Alves, 2009: 4).

However, what is unbecoming of a nation that prides itself as "communist" is the rapacity that China displays in exploiting Africa, a rapacity that in some instances parallels or surpasses that of Africa's traditional exploiters—the West. China seems to have perfected what some scholars described as "debt trap diplomacy", in which it offers "predatory loans" to poor and corrupt countries, particularly in Africa suffering capital crunch and infrastructure deficit knowing full well that those countries won't be able to repay the loans. And when any of them defaults on repayment as is often the case, China capitalizes on it to take over key national assets such as port or valuable natural resources (Shattuck, 2018: 3). From Zambia where it has succeeded in using "debt trap" to gain access to critical national assets (e.g. Zambia Electricity Company) and also the minerals (e.g. cobalt and copper), to Nigeria and elsewhere where it seems to be an ever willing party to shady contracts with the corrupt governments, to Sudan where it engages in illegal mining of oil, China's predatory activities in Africa's natural resource industry are quite alarming.

Russia, though a stealth accomplice, is another key player in the web of predators of Africa's natural resources by being one of the major suppliers of weapons used by some militant groups in Africa contending for power and control of one natural resource or the other. One typical example is the role of Russia in the going crisis in the Central African Republic where Russia is believed to be supplying arms to both the government and the rebels (The Economist, 2018).

Given these realities and environmental degradation that have also become ones of the defining features of resource exploitation in Africa, it would appear that there is a global conspiracy, from the West to the East, to strip Africa of her precious resources and leave behind a legacy of ruins. Meanwhile, in the global resource market, every country is a selfish player. And perhaps there is no objective way to determine who is right and who is wrong. The losers today probably would have indulged in the same acts they accuse the winners of if they were the winners. And the winners would have become the accuser if they were the losers.

Nonetheless, to blame only the West and China for Africa's resource predicament will amount to half-truths. The political class in Africa benefits from the kickbacks that are used to oil the web of patronage and looting that characterize resource governance and exploitation in the continent. This is largely why in the midst of declining national wealth and growing poverty in Africa, the number of billionaires on the continent has continued to increase. This is so for even those countries with extreme cases of economic deprivation and depleting natural resources. More often than not, many of the African billionaires are mostly state-made as they often emerge from shady mining deals (e.g. cronyism in resource allocation and granting of mining license), handling of government contracts or from government's preferential treatment such as waiver on importation of essential scarce commodities like rice, cement, salt, etc.

Outright embezzlement of rents from Africa's natural resources is a norm in Africa. It is on record that over half century of mining Africa's natural resources has yielded several billions of dollars in government revenues. But significant portion of these monies has either been mismanaged or siphoned by the African elites (Watts, 2008). Take crude oil for instance: based on the projected oil price of $50 per barrel, it is estimated that between 2006 and 2020 Nigeria alone could generate more than $750 billion in oil revenue and the whole of West Africa, more than $1 trillion, most of which are likely to be embezzled (Lubeck et al., 2007). With few exceptions like Botswana, the story is the same across resource-rich African countries.

Equally worrisome is the fact that despite the huge revenue accruing from natural resources, Africa's governing elites have continued to borrow foreign loans (like in the past, such loans are often mismanaged or embezzled), leading to a situation where after few years that debt relief was granted to heavily indebted countries in Africa, some of these countries such as Nigeria have slipped back into debt burden (Okeke & Nwali, 2015). For example, in 2018, Nigerian government spent over 2 trillion naira on debt servicing (The Cable, 2018), an amount that is well above the annual budgetary allocation for capital projects. According to recent report by International Monetary Fund (IMF), Nigeria's revenue ratio to debt is very high and unsustainable: over 63% of revenue is spent on debt servicing alone (IMF cited in The Sun, 2018). Just as heavy debt encumbers human security in the present by consuming resources that would have gone into provision of social infrastructure, so will it affect human security in future by saddling future generations with debt burden.

Another likely threat to sustainable human security is natural resource depletion and technology induced shift in resource use and demand. Logically, as humankind exploits natural resources to meets its needs and in some instances maximize profit, resource depletion occurs even if the environment is not degraded and the climate change is mitigated. Moreover, as inventions and innovations (e.g. alternative energy sources like solar and wind, EVs, GMOs, to mention but a few) drive civilization but also "destruction" around the world, there is a gradual shift in global resource use and demand which over time will render some natural resources redundant or even valueless. Take crude oil for instance, its global demand is plunging and it is projected the dominance of fossil fuels as the major source of energy will begin to decline drastically from 2040 as the demand for solar and wind energy as well as EVs accelerates (Purvis,

2018; Ghouri, 2018). Similar fate awaits other resources including solid minerals as their use diminishes or their alternatives emerge. Resources including manpower, whose value and demand can be reduced by artificial intelligence, will equally be affected. Also, efficient use of goods in the form of recycling of used products will be "painful" for some natural resource-dependent countries since it will lead to decrease in demand for natural resources that serve as raw materials for such products. All these will have severe consequences for sustainable human security in future. And it is not only Africa that will feel the effects but Africa will be most affected because it is heavily dependent on natural resources.

Sovereign Wealth Funds: A Choice or a Necessity?

From an economic perspective, one would expect that natural resource-endowed nations would be leaders not only in developing infrastructures and poverty reduction but also savings in terms of Sovereign Wealth Funds (SWFs). Regrettably, this is not the case in resource-rich Africa. Unlike Europe (e.g. Norway) and some Middle East countries (e.g. Saudi Arabia, Qatar, and UAE), where natural resources have served the purpose of creating functional social infrastructures and robust SWFs, most resource-rich African countries have low national savings (Gilpin, 2016). Although a few African countries have created SWFs and some others are considering establishing one, the continent's SWFs are still low and account for a tiny fraction of the global SWFs (Hove, 2016; Diallo et al., 2016).

As at August 2018, the total value of the global SWFs stood at 8.1 trillion dollars out of which 4.4 trillion dollars is from oil and gas-related resources. Africa owns meagre 2.7% of the global SWFs compared to other resource-rich region like the Middle East which owns about 40% mainly from oil resources (Sovereign Wealth Fund Institute—SWFI 2018). Little wonder Uche Orji—the ex-Chief Executive of Nigeria's SWFs—Nigerian Sovereign Investment Authority, once lamented that if the sovereign wealth of some countries (see Fig. 3.2 and Fig. 3.3) were shared out among its citizens at present, every citizen of Botswana would get a chunky $2,400, every Nigerian will get less than $7 whereas each Norwegian will get about $170,000 (The Economist, 2017).

This low share and ranking of Africa in the global SWFs may not be unconnected with the continent's historical corruption, profligacy and wastes that have characteriszed resource governance over the years. Rather

Country	Fund Name	Assets (in in $US)	Year Established	Source Resources
Libya	Libya Investment Authority	66 billion	2006	Oil
Algeria	Fund for the regulations of receipts	56.7 billion	2000	Oil
Botswana	Pula Fund	5.5 billion	1994	Diamond
Angola	Fundo Soberano de Angola	4.6 billion	2012	Oil
Nigeria	Nigerian Sovereign Investment Authority	1.4 billion	2011	Oil
Senegal	Senegal FONSIS	1 billion	2012	Non-Commodity
Rwanda	Crystal Ventures	.5 billion	2009	Mineral & Agriculture.
Mauritania	Fonds National des Revenus des Hydrocarbures	.3 billion	2006	Oil and Gas
Ghana	Ghana Petroleum Funds	.045 billion	2012	Oil

Fig. 3.2 Top Sovereign Wealth Funds in Africa (As at August 2018) (*Source* Adapted from Sovereign Wealth Funds Institute [2018] and Hove [2016])

than save proceeds of natural resource exports, African political leaders tend to squander such proceeds. The continent's little savings in the SWFs are often vulnerable to the waste appetite of the political leaders. For example, in 2017, a government minister in Ghana argued that the government should empty the money in the country's SWFs for future generations and use it to fund projects for the present generation. Such is the type of "dilemma" that is common in sub-Saharan Africa which discourages saving as most political leaders are willing to spend but never to save. It is not surprising, therefore, that the region has only a dozen Sovereign Wealth Funds—most of the funds were established in the past two decades (The Economist, 2017; The Royal Institute of International Affairs, 2016).

Accordingly, Anthony Venables and Samuel Wills of the Oxford Centre for the Analysis of Resource-Rich Economies posited that Africa's SWFs should focus on two roles: first is that since a sudden windfall can

Country	Fund Name	Assets (in $US)	Year Established	Source
Norway	Government Pension Fund – Global	1.058trillion	1990	Oil
China	China Investment Corporation	941.4 billion	2007	Non-Commodity
UAE	Abu Dhabi Investment Authority	683	1976	Oil
Saudi Arabia	SAMA Foreign Holdings	515.6	1952	Oil
Singapore	Government of Singapore Investment Corporation	390	1981	Non-Commodity
Qatar	Qatar Investment Authority	320	2005	Oil and Gas
South Korea	Korea Investment Corporation	134.1	2005	Non-Commodity
Australia	Australia Future Fund	107.7	2006	Non-Commodity
Iran	National Development Fund of Iran	91	2011	Oil and Gas
Russia	National Welfare Fund	77.2	2008	Oil

Fig. 3.3 Top Sovereign Wealth Funds in the World (As at August 2018) (*Source* Adapted from Sovereign Wealth Funds Institute [2018])

trigger inefficient spending, it makes sense to save and invest the windfall abroad until capacity is built. Second is that such funds invested in liquid assets can be deployed to stabilize the national budget when resource commodity prices fall (Venables; Wills, cited in The Economist, 2017). Moreover, a country can help its future generations benefit from exhaustible natural resources such as fossil fuels by investing their proceeds in productive capital and in transportation, water and sanitation infrastructures as well as human resource capital (Hanneson, 1998). Having SWFs can facilitate the achievement of aim such as this.

Again, challenges facing human security in Africa today are numerous: Africa suffers from extreme poverty; the greatest shortfall in infrastructure; fast population growth and urbanization amid rising unemployment. To meet the infrastructure gap which is critical to human security on the continent will require about 40 billion dollars of annual investment in infrastructures over the coming decade and another 40 billion dollars to maintain the existing infrastructures (Infrastructure Consortium for Africa cited in NEPAD-OECD African Development Initiative, 2008: 2). To bridge this infrastructural deficit will require saving and then investment in social amenities. In other words, SWFs in Africa can be used for economic stabilization, intergenerational savings accumulation, buffers against economic shocks and wealth diversification and domestic investment in infrastructure (Hove, 2016: 11).

By and large, most African households particularly those in rural areas rely on natural resources to cater for their nutrition, health and energy needs. If without these resources the present generation cannot meet their needs, it then becomes an ethical obligation that these resources should be conserved since without them the future generation cannot also meet their needs. And if the predatory exploitation as is presently the case, could make some of these resources go extinct in future, resource injustice demands that actions should be taken to prevent this from happening and/or at least save part of the proceeds made from exploiting these exhaustible resources as a heritage for future generations.

However, having SWFs is one thing while managing the funds properly is another. Just like the case of natural resources, poor governance has crept into SWFs administration in Africa such that in some countries (e.g. Nigeria) "the boards are appointed by the government, usually as political favours. Unsurprisingly, the competence and efficacy of these boards are questionable and oversight is lax" (Gilpin, 2016: 2). Nigeria's experience with the Excess Crude Account which was marred by political interference and mismanagement shows that it is not enough to have SWFs: good governance plays important role in the success of any SWFs (Dixon & Monk, 2011: 1).

Conclusion

The culture of building roads and railways as well as other development infrastructures including spare capacity in electricity generation, not for the immediate use but for the future as could be seen in some industrialized and emerging economies in North America (e.g. Canada), Asia (e.g. China) and so on, is non-existent in Africa. Sovereign saving and futuristic investment are not a popular culture either, hence the low Sovereign Wealth Funds of most African countries. All these factors coupled with diminishing natural resources, technology induced shifting global resource use and demand, and mounting sovereign debts, are variables that will affect and determine the trajectory of human security in Africa in future. Therefore, it is important that these variables are taken cognizance of when mapping out policy, legal and institutional frameworks and dedicating resources to address the challenge of human security on the continent. For it is in doing so that sustainable human security which meets people's needs today and lays secure foundation for future generations can be achieved. Putting in place mechanisms and social infrastructure that will improve human security of future generations could as well enhance people's well-being in the present.

Creating and growing robust SWFs and investment in functional social infrastructure will be right steps in the right direction. While investment in infrastructure will serve as catalyst that can trigger and sustain socio-economic development that is needed to save the present population and the unborn from hunger and extreme poverty, the SWFs will act as buffer against shocks arising from natural resource depletion, shifting resource use and demand and plummeting earnings as well as climate change and the boom and burst that characterize the global capitalist economy. SWFs can withstand these shocks since they will be invested in diverse strong businesses (including the big transnational corporations) across the industrialized economies in different continents of the world. One inherent contradiction of the global capitalist economy that makes it somehow beneficial to everyone including the exploited worker, and the dominated periphery is that it rewards capital (even more than human labour) irrespective of who owns it and where it comes from. Creating and investing SWFs in transnational companies will ensure that Africa benefits from the surplus values accruing from global capitalism, thus reduce its loss from resource exploitation cum the accompanying capital flight which currently defines Africa-industrialized world relations.

African countries searching for SWFs model(s) to follow can adapt Norway's model in which only certain percentage of the profit yields from the SWFs are legally allowed to be taken and shared by the government in times of fiscal emergency, whereas the principal amount and the remaining part of the profit are retained and re-invested. Some form of cooperation among SWFs already exists. Norway's SWF provides expertise advice and training to countries that want to build wealth management capacity (Santiso, 2008). The Nigerian government can tap from such expertise resource. This model is imperative for African countries whose political leaders live on corruption and seem to delight in siphoning the commonwealth. The model will reduce the possibility of a rogue government coming to power and squandering savings and investments that are dedicated to future generations.

Also important is the need for investment in research and technology, especially those that can add value to Africa's natural resources and equally aid the development of alternatives that will help Africa to not only withstand technology = induced transition, but also to move from a natural resource-dependent continent to become a technology = driven economy.

References

Abutudu, M. (2005). Human security in Africa: Challenges and prospects. CLACSO.

Adelakun, O. E., B. Adurogbangba and L. A. Akinbile (2015). Socioeconomic effects of farmer-pastoralist conflict on agricultural extension service delivery in Oyo State, Nigeria. *Journal of Agricultural Extension*. Vol.19 (2), pp. 59–70.

Ake, C. (1981). *A political economy of Africa*. Nigeria: Longman Nigeria Plc.

Ake, C. (1996). *Democracy and development in Africa*. Ibadan: Spectrum Books Limited.

Alden, C. and A. C. Alves (2009). China and Africa's naturalresources: The challenges and implications for development and governance. Governance of African Resource Programme, Occasional Paper No.41, Johannesburg: South African Institute for International Affairs.

Annan, K. A. (2000). *We the peoples: The role of the United Nations in the 21st century*. New York: United Nations, Department of Public Information.

Arthur, P. (2017). Promoting security in Africa through Regional Economic Communities (RECs) and the African Union's African Peace and Security Architecture (APSA). *Insight on Africa*. Vol.9 (1), pp. 1–21.

AU/ECA. (2015). Report of the High Level Panel on Illicit Financial Flows from Africa. African Union and Economic Commission for Africa Conference of Ministers of Finance, Planning and Economic Development.

AU/UNECA. (2016). Progress Report on the Implementation of the Recommendations of the High-Level Panel on Illicit Financial Flows from Africa and the Special declaration of the Assembly on Illicit Financial Flows from Africa. United Nations Economic Commission for Africa and African Union.

Axworthy, L. (2001). Human security and global governance: putting people first. *Global Governance: A Review of Multilateralism and International Organizations*. Vol.7 (1), pp. 19–23.

Ball, N., J. K. Fayemi, F. Olonisakin and R. Williams (2003). *Security sector governance in Africa: A handbook*. Lagos, Pretoria and Washington, DC: Centre for Democracy and Development, Institute for Security Studies and the Centre for International Policies.

Calcuttawala, Z. (2017). Nigeria to switch to gas as oil reserves set to dry up in 25 years. June 28. https://oilprice.com/Latest-Energy-News/World-News/Nigeria-To-Switch-To-Gas-As-Oil-Reserves-Set-To-Dry-Up-In-25-Years.html.

Collier, P. (2007). *The bottom billion: Why the poorest countries are failing and what can be done about it*. New York: Oxford University Press.

Colliers, J. (2004). Human Security in Africa: A conceptual framework for review. A Monograph for the African Human Security Initiative.

Commission on Human Security. (2003). *Human security now*. New York: United Nations Publication

Conceição, P., S. Levine, M. Lipton and A. Warren-Rodríguez (2016). Toward a food secure future: Ensuring food security for sustainable human development in Sub-Saharan Africa. *Food Policy*. Vol.60, pp. 1–9.

Cross, H. (2017). Neoliberalism, labour power and democracy—The sense of an ending. *Review of African Political Economy*. Vol.44 (153), pp. 353–357.

Diallo, B., F. T. Tchana and A. G. Zeufack (2016). Sovereign wealth funds and long-term investments in sub-Saharan Africa. Macroeconomics and Fiscal Management Global Practice Group and the Office of the Chief Economist, Africa Region. Policy Research Working Paper 7903.

Diamond, L. (1988). *Class, ethnicity and democracy in Nigeria: The failure of the First-Republic*. Basingstoke and London: Macmillan.

Dixon, A. D. and A. H. B. Monk (2011). What role for sovereign wealth funds in Africa's development? Centre for Global Development Oil-to-Cash Initiative Background Paper.

Easterly, W. (2007). How the millennium development goals are unfair to Africa. Brookings Global Economy and Development, Working Paper No.14.

Ekeh, P. P. (1975). Colonialism and the two publics in Africa: A theoretical statement. *Comparative Studies in Society and History*. Vol.17 (1), pp. 91–112.

Gasper, D. (2005). Securing humanity: Situating "human security" as concept and discourse. *Journal of Human Development*. Vol.6 (2), 221–245.

Ghouri, S. (2018). How will fossil fuels fare in 2040? Retrieved from https://oilprice.com/Energy/Energy-General/How-Will-Fossil-Fuels-Fare-In-2040.html.

Gilpin, R. (2016). Policy brief: Whither sovereign wealth funds in Africa? The Brown Capital Management African Forum. Wilson Center Paper No.4.

Hampson, F. O. and J. Daudelin (2002). *Madness in the multitude: human security and world disorder*. Don Mills, ON: Oxford University Press.

Hanneson, R. (1998). *Petroleum economics: Issues and strategies of oil and natural gas production*. Quorum Books: Westport, CO.

Harris, G. T. (2017). Why Africa matters to US National security. Atlantic Council Africa Center.

Hobbs, J. (2012). Upstreaming environment into investment Decisions. IMF Conference on Management of Natural Resources in Sub-Saharan Africa held in Kinshasa, DRC, March 21.
Hove, S. (2016). Sovereign wealth funds and infrastructure development in Africa. QGRL *Working Paper No. 02*. Switzerland: Quantum Global Research Lab.
Hussein, K., D. Gnisci, and J. Wanjiru (2004). Security and human security: An overview of concepts and initiatives. What implications for Africa? Sahel and West Africa Club/OECD.
Ibeanu, O. (2005). Our mothers' courage silenced all guns: Women and conflict in the Niger Delta. *University of Nigeria Journal of Political Economy*. Vol.1 (1), pp. 52–73.
IBIS (2015). Natural resource watch. Report on Sub-Saharan Africa.
Infrastructure Consortium for Africa cited in NEPAD-OECD African Development Initiative (2008). Emerging public and sovereign fund investors in Africa's infrastructure: Challenges and Perspectives. The Expert Roundtable on Investment on Infrastructure, December 11.
Inter-ministerial Committee for International Cooperation and Development CICID—(2008). Mineral resourcesand development in Africa. Strategic Guideline Document.
Khor, M. (2000). *Globalization and the south: Some critical issues.* Ibadan: Nigeria.
Lubeck, P. M., M. J. Watts, and R. Lipschutz (2007). Convergent interests: U.S. energy security and the "securing of Nigerian democracy". Centre for International Policy Report.
MacFarlane, S. N. and Y. F. Khong (2006). *Human security and the UN a critical history*. Bloomington: Indiana University Press.
Maloba, W. O. (2017). *The anatomy of neo-colonialism in Kenya: British imperialism and Kenyatta, 1963-1978.* African Histories and Modernities. Cham, Switzerland: Springer International Publishing Ag; Palgrave Macmillan.
Murombedzi, J. C. (2016). Inequality and natural resources in Africa. World Social ScienceReport 2016. Paris: UNESCO and the ISSC.
Nwosu, B. U. (2010). Oil conflicts and security in the Niger Delta: Exploring the dynamics of conflicts and search for peace. *Nigerian Journal of International Affairs*. Vol.36 (1), pp. 114–129.
Obi, C. I. (2010). Oil extraction, dispossession, resistance, and conflict in Nigeria's oil-rich Niger Delta. *Canadian Journal of Development Studies/Revue canadienne d'études du développement*. Vol.30 (1–2), pp. 219–236.
Ojo, O. (1999). Economic underpinnings of security in Africa. Port Harcourt: CASS Monograph, No. 12.

Okeke, G. S. M. and U. Nwali (2015). Debt management and servicing in Nigeria: A political analysis of post-debt relief. *Nigerian Journal of Business and Social Sciences*. Vol.8 (2), pp. 77–94.

Onimode, B. (1982). *Imperialism and under-development in Nigeria: The dialectics of mass poverty*. London: Zed Books Ltd.

Oyama, S. (2014). Farmer-herder conflict, land rehabilitation and conflict prevention in the Sahel region of West Africa. Center for African Area Studies, Kyoto University.*African Study Monographs*. Suppl.50, pp.103–122.

Picard, L. A. and M. C. Lelei (2015). Achieving sustainable development in Africa: A good governance perspective. In L. A. Picard, T. F. Buss, T. B. Seybolt and M. C. Lelei (eds.), *Sustainable development and human security in Africa: Governance as the missing link*. New York: Routledge, pp. 1–20.

Poku, N. K, N. Renwick and J. G. Porto (2007). Human security and development in Africa. *Royal Institute of International Affairs*. Vol.83 (6), pp. 1155–1170.

Purvis, D. (2018). The rapid acceleration towards peak oil demand. Retrieved from https://oilprice.com/Energy/Crude-Oil/The-Rapid-Acceleration-Towards-Peak-Oil-Demand.html.

Ross, M. L (2004). How does natural resource wealth influence civil wars? Evidence from thirteen cases. *International Organization*. Vol.58 (1), pp. 35–67.

Sahel and West Africa Club/OECD (2006). Human security in West Africa: Challenges, synergies and action for a regional agenda. Workshop organised by Sahel and West Africa Club/OECD at Lome, Togo, March 26–28. Volume 1, Summary Report.

Santiso, J. (2008). Sovereign development funds: Key financial actors of the shifting wealth of nations. OECD Development Center, Emerging Markets Network Working Paper.

Sawe, B. E. (2018). Which continent is the richest in natural resources? Africa is endowed with great natural wealth. Worldatlas.com Retrieved from https://www.worldatlas.com/articles/which-continent-is-the-richest-in-natural-resources.html.

Shattuck, T. J. (2018). How China dictates the rules of the game. United States of America: Foreign Policy Research Institute (FPRI).

Sovereign Wealth Fund Institute—SWFI (2018). Sovereign wealth fund rankings. Retrieved from https://www.swfinstitute.org/sovereign-wealth-fund-rankings/.

Statistics South Africa—Stats SA (2017). Environmental Economic Accounts Compendium Report, No. 04–05–20.

Tavanti, M. (2013). The basics of sustainable human security. World Engagement Institute.

The Cable. (2018). N2.2trn on debt service, fresh N1.6trn loan, rising oil dependence—7 troubling facts about 2018 budget. Retrieved from https://www.thecable.ng/n2-2trn-debt-servicing-borrow-fresh-n1-6trn-rising-oil-dependence-7-troubling-facts-2018-budget.

The Economist (2017). Buried treasure: Sovereign-wealth funds catch on in Africa, but countries disagree about how to use them. March 16.

The Economist (2018). Russia se to strengthen its presence in Africa. October 11. http://country.eiu.com/article.aspx?articleid=1917234575&Country=Russia&topic=Politics&subtopic=R3.

The Ghana Chamber of Mines and International Council on Mining & Metals Report (2015). Mining in Ghana—What future can we expect? https://www.icmm.com/website/publications/pdfs/mining-partnerships-for-development/mining-in-ghana_what-future-can-we-expect.

The Royal Institute of International Affairs. (2016). Africa's sovereignwealth fundsdemand, development and delivery Africa. Chatham House, Programme Conference Paper Summary, September 2014

The Sun. (2018). Nigeria's debt service obligations too high, unsustainable—IMF. October 11. Retrieved from http://sunnewsonline.com/nigerias-debt-service-obligations-too-high-unsustainable-imf/.

Thomas, C. (2005). *Global governance, development and human security: the challenge of poverty and inequality*. London: Pluto Press.

Thomas, C. and P. Wilkin (1999). *Globalization, human security, and the African experience*. Boulder, CO: Lynne Rienner Publishers.

Tieku, T. K. (2007). African Union promotion of human security in Africa. *African Security Review*. Vol.16 (2), pp. 26–37.

United Nations—UN. (2000). World leaders adopt United Nations Millennium Declaration at conclusion of Extraordinary Three-Day Summit. Press Release GA/9758.

United Nations (2008). Innovation for sustainable development: Local case studies from Africa. New York: United Nations Publication.

United Nations. (2016). *Human security handbook: An integrated approach for the realization of the Sustainable Development Goals and the priority areas of the international community and the United Nations system*. New York: Human Security Unit, United Nations.

United Nations Development Programme—UNDP. (2012). *Africa human development report 2012: Towards a food secure future*. New York: UNDP.

United Nations Development Programme—UNDP. (2015). Sustainable development goals. UNDP.

United Nations Development Programme—UNDP *Human Development Report. (1994).* New dimensions of human security. New York: Oxford University Press for the UNDP.

Vanguard. (2011). Nigeria's crude oil to dry up in 37 years, except... November 30. https://www.vanguardngr.com/2011/11/nigeria's-crude-oil-to-dry-up-in-37-years.

Watts, M. (2008). Imperial oil: The anatomy of a Nigerian oil insurgency. *Erdkunde*. Vol.62 (1), pp. 27–39.

CHAPTER 4

The Dynamics and Complexities of Natural Resources and Conflicts in Angola

Kelvin Bribena

Introduction

The process of natural resources extraction qualifies as the most visible cause of conflicts and crises around the world. This is quite understandable given that a resource is a gift of nature; and nature is that phenomenon that every human, group and nation claims to represent, or, believe to represent them. Natural resources therefore are considered as the resources of and for all. However, following the social conflicts that emerged after the period of homoeostatic equilibrium and subsequent commencement of ownership of private property, alienation has overtaken natural resources that used to belong to all, at least theoretically, and both the state and non-state actors have been culpable in alienating others from the resource of nature. Actors include the state, indigenes and multinational companies and so on, and conflicts often emerge when there is clash of interest among them.

K. Bribena (✉)
Faculty of Law, Niger Delta University, Yenagoa, Nigeria

K. J. Ani et al. (eds.), *Political Economy of Resource, Human Security and Environmental Conflicts in Africa*,
https://doi.org/10.1007/978-981-16-2036-2_4

Thus, in Africa, for example, natural resources have generated war and conflicts in Nigeria, Democratic Republic of Congo, South Africa and Angola to mention a few. These conflicts have led to loss of lives, internal displacement of huge parts of populations, refugees and asylum seekers that have become burdens on other nations around the world, as well as many international organizations. The natural resources related conflicts can be seen to be pronounced in Africa, its effects and consequences are intertwined among nations of the world. Even multinational companies that deal in them, from what their name implies, are representatives of the business interests of many nations and are often not neutral in wars and conflicts generated by natural resources. Thus, this chapter intends to focus on the dynamics and complexities associated with natural resources in Angola.

Historical Overview of Angola

Angola is the second largest country in the South of Sahara Africa, with purportedly the largest landmass. It covers 1,25 msqkm and has 18 provinces. This includes the oil-rich Cabinda which is separated from the rest of the country by a slim coastal strip at the mouth of Congo. It shares border to East with Zambia, to the South with Namibia, to the North-East with DR Congo and to the West with the Atlantic Ocean. It has an estimated population of about 29.78 million as at 2017 (IUCN, 1993). Angola has a large Bantu population and has large amount of ethnicities. The major ethnic groups are Ovimbundu which is the largest with 37%, Kimbundu with 25%, Bankongo with 13%, Mesticos mixed of African/European constitute 2%, European constitute 1% and others make up for the remaining 22%. Notwithstanding the ethnic conglomeration of the country, like most African countries, Angola is a marriage between ethnic groups which were not consulted at its formation, but were forced at gunpoint to be Angolans (Davidson, 1992).

Historically, Angola was originally inhabited by the Pigmoids and Khoikhoi population before the beginning of the first century in the modern era. However, massive migration of Bantus from West and Central Africa change the population to Bantu dominance which was illustrated with the emergence of the Bantu Kingdom of Ndongo, with Ngola as its king. Angola, therefore, is said to derive its name from the title of the Bantu king (Birmingham, 1966).

Traditionally, the inhabitants of modern day Angola were farmers and hunters. However, there was trade between kingdoms before the arrival of the Portuguese navigator, Diego Cao in 1482. His arrival was significant in opening Angola to the outside world and eventually to the iniquitous slave trade. Millions of Angolans were sold into slavery and carted away by the Portuguese to Brazil in the America, where they work in plantations. The impact of this rape of manpower on the Angolan society was enormous. Besides this, the traditional economic structure was dislocated and reconstructed to fit the demands and desires of the Portuguese (Klein, 1972; Miller, 1988; Ferreira, 2012).

The centuries long relations between Angola and Portugal were effectively concretized by the Berlin Conference of 1884/1885 and it became part of the Portuguese African colonies till 1975 when the Post World war II dynamics outdated colonialism and encouraged liberation war across the continent. Portuguese colonialism in Angola was oppressive. Force labour and other exploitative practices were common. No effort was made to develop the indigenous communities, but so much was done to repatriate the resources of the colony to Portugal and other parts of the world as dictated by the commercial interest of the colonizers (Candido, 2013; Marcum, 1976; Rodney, 1972).

Consequently, the delay or unwillingness by the Portuguese to negotiate for peaceful transfer of power to Angolans as were done by Britain and France in 1950s and 1960s attracted global criticism. Besides, it led to armed insurrection against the colonialist.

Notwithstanding the explosion of resistance in the 1960s, anti-colonial movements in Angola started as early as 1910, when urban-based Assimilados and Mesticos in Luanda and Benguela formed the 'Angolan League' and Let's Discover Angola *(Vamos Descobrir Angola)* movement in 1940s. Union of the peoples of Angola was founded in Northern Angola (UPA) as a Kongo movement but transformed itself to the FNLA with a wider objective of political independence for the Angolan people. MPLA was founded by Viviato de Cruz and others who were in Let's Discover Angola, and UNITA was founded in 1966 by Jonas Savambi who broke away from FNLA (Meijer and Birmigham, 2004). Some scholars identified ethnic and religious leaning of the liberation movement: MPLA was identified with the Mbundu and Mesticos, as well as a Roman Catholic or Methodist, the FNLA was linked to Baptist Bakongo and UNITA was related to Congregational Ovimbundu. However, FNLA had the deepest affinity, to ethnic Kongo in Angola and the DR Congo, since its activities were more prominent within the community of over 700,000, Kikongo-speaking (Brinkmang, 2003; Fromont, 2014).

In the first half of 1974, there was remarkable change in Portugal following the ousting of Salazau Caetano by the Movement of the Armed Forces (MFA), a group of junior officer who resented Caetano's totalitarianism and unwillingness to negotiate independence for the colonies. Effort was, therefore, made to ensure peaceful transition to Angolan rule in the country. This led to a meeting of the three rebel movement and the Portuguese government in Alvor in January 1975. The meeting ended with an agreement between the parties and provided for a constitution, transitional government, elections and independence. The rebel movements did not allow the Alvor Accord to work since they tried to outsmart one another in the competition to control Luanda. In the mid of this political tension and widespread protest against colonialism in Angola, the MPLA seized the capital Luanda and declared the independence of Angola on November 11. It also chose and sworn-in Agostinho Neto as the president of new state. This decision of MPLA in the midst of uncertainty over the political future of Angola had its challenges, as the new government had to deal with the Portuguese colonial army, as well as UNITA and FNLA were in this mix. At first, Holden Roberto's FNLA was the strongest of rebel movements and operated from the North with the support of late president Mobutu of DR Congo, the United States and China. It almost took charge of Luanda earlier in the year. Similarly, Jonas Savimbi's UNITA operating from the South and Central with the support of South African defence force almost took control of Luanda, if not for the intervention of Cuban and Soviet troops sent to support the MPLA. Thus, the new MPLA government excluded both UNITA and FNLA in Angola and was threatened from every side within and outside Angola, which became the theatre of Cold War contest between the two blocs (Meijer and Birmingham, 2004; Bender, 1978; Bissonett, 2008).

From 1975–2002, Angola fought a civil war orchestrated by opposing forces of the Cold War, Western bloc supported UNITA and the Eastern bloc as well as African countries supported the MPLA which gained global recognition. By 1976, Angola was declared a Republic by President Agostinho Neto. He died and was succeeded by Jose Eduardo dos Santos in 1979 as the president (PICSIM, 2005). Efforts were made to negotiate peace between the MPLA and UNITA; and this led to a multiparty election in 1992. UNITA, however, rejected the electoral outcome which gave victory to the MPLA. Savimbi took up armed resistance again and had a control of almost 70% at the end of 1993. The MPLA government fought back and by 1994, both parties signed a peace deal which provided for a government of national unity in 1997 and UNITA accepted governmental positions. In 1998, Savimbi quit the government and resumed armed struggle until his assassination in 2002. His death paved the way for the transformation of UNITA into a political party and participation in political processes as an opposition party (Ferreira, 2006).

A critical question arose as to what drove and sustained the conflicts in Angola throughout its history? An answer to this question includes the role of Angolan resources in fueling and sustaining conflicts since the arrival of the Portuguese to the country. Its rich human resources were responsible for concentration of slave trade on its coast by the Portuguese, and its fertile land sustained plantation farming and forced labour (Fromont, 2014; Candido, 2013; Heywood, 2009). Similarly, the post-colonial conflicts were motivated by the desire of external and internal forces to control and exploit the natural resources of Angola. The country is rich in bauxite, feldspar, phosphates, iron ore, lumber, uranium, fish, diamond and petroleum. It has proven reserves of gypsum, granite, beryllium and cement as well as undeveloped reserves of wolfram, vanadium, uranium, tungsten, quartz, silver, nickel, phosphate rock, manganese, lignite, gold, copper, clay and iron ore. While uranium is strategic in terms of nuclear energy and weaponry, diamond and crude oil are high on global demand. Angola produces 11% of the global output of diamond in the world, the third largest producer on the continent. Besides, it is second largest crude oil exporter in sub-Saharan after, coming second to Nigeria. It is also a member of the Organization of Petroleum Exporting Countries (Thomas, 2012; James, 2011; Ferreira, 2006). Indeed, the proceeds from the sale of these resources and the prospect to control them are central to the interest of all actors in fueling and sustaining the wars (Anderson et al., 2017; Frynas and Wood, 2001; Gonzalez, 2010; Mathias and Wegenast, 2009; Ndumbe and Cole, 2005).

Resource Curse Syndrome

In recent time, the concept and what constitute resource curse has led to series of debates in the developing and developed societies. The Natural Resource Governance Institute (NRGI) (2015) describes resource curse as the inability of resource-rich states to utilize the natural resource to develop and uplift the welfare of the state. This concept has been known as the paradox of plenty that further connotes the failure of highly endowed states to maximize and benefit from the natural resources. The dichotomy of resource curse is premised on a drastic socioeconomic and political development after sudden discoveries of natural resources in a country. That is, natural resources as one of the leading products in the international political economy system, especially gold, crude oil, bitumen and others attract high revenue to countries that possess it in quantum. Conversely, studies in this regard have revealed negative developmental pattern and retrogression (Natural Resource Governance Institute, 2015). This has been tied on the leadership failure that is embedded in illicit deals of government officials with companies that explore these resources, as well as pervasive illegal mining and exploration by the local people due to institutional failures; vandalism of companies' properties who explore these resources without the need for corporate social responsibility. These factors among others have caused retrogressive development, and led to the deplorable conditions that some resource-rich developing states experience of which Angola is inclusive.

The concept or characteristics of resource curse entails challenges arising mainly from social, economic and political spheres that are peculiar to states that are vast in crude oil and other natural resources. The concept also unravelled the discourse why states failed to experience holistic development in the midst of oil boom that should attract huge revenue to the endowed oil state. Most of these states are identified with authoritarian tendencies that frequently experience conflict, fragile economic system compares to states that are not endowed with such natural resources. Series of research have suggested that the ruling elites should identify workable policies and developmental plan to avoid some of the negative consequences of extraction and maximize the benefits (Natural Resource Governance Institute, 2015).

However, the argument on resource curse has moved beyond leadership failure to the other dimensions or theories that tend to justify the reason why countries that are vast in natural resources still experience backwardness and huge economic crisis (Amundsen, 2014). Social scientists within the purview of politics and economics have revealed that wealth that emanates from crude oil, mineral and gas is distinctively different from wealth from secondary production or services due to its large upfront costs, long production timeline, site-specific nature, scale (also known as large *rents*), price and production volatility, non-renewable nature, and the secrecy of the industry (Natural Resource Governance Institute, 2015). The observations below buttressed the notion of resource curse from theoretical perspectives.

Theories of Resource Curse

The debates on what resource curse constitute and its cause has generated schools of thought leading to formation of theories and explanations (Natural Resource Governance Institute, 2015).

The economic explanations also called the *Dutch disease* express a progressive increase of revenues from natural resources that escalate the exchange rate and reduce other sectors relatively less competitive and that the volatility of commodity prices is disruptive. Here, the bad price effect and a diminishing investments "crowds out" manufacturing and agriculture (Amundsen, 2014). In other words, a sudden leap of natural resource revenue can stampede other sectors of the economy, especially the manufacturing industries. That is, creation of inflation or exchange rate rise and distorting the movement of the factors of production like labour and capital from the non-resource sector to the resource sector. The negative impact of inflation and exchange rate rise can harm the economy for years if not decades. This economy theory has manifested in countries like Iran, Russia, Trinidad and Tobago and Venezuela. These impacts can be minimized if the country has the absorptive capacity to transform resource revenue inflows into tangible investments, such as roads and electricity; the government uses resource revenues to make investments in the economy that generates non-resource sector growth; or the government places a portion of its resource revenues in foreign assets. Over the last 25 years, Chile, Indonesia, Norway and the UAE have largely managed to overcome Dutch disease (Natural Resource Governance Institute, 2015).

The authoritarian and democratic dichotomy theory is another perspective to explaining resource curse. This view reveals that natural endowment creating boom for a country tends to deepen authoritarian tendencies. That is, the general belief is that citizen seems to be unaware of the inflow arising from oil wealth than the transparency on taxation. This view has been championed by political scientists who argued that the ruling elites are more proactive, responsive to the country in the context of the tenets of democracy and citizens in particular when income emanates from taxation. In other words, a country whose huge revenue comes from oil such as the case of Angola; the quest to retrieve taxes from citizens will be diminished. This will automatically lead to low investment on national budget by the entire population in a country. Under natural resource-led economy, political leadership is weakened and the ruling elites and politicians will very likely demonstrate ineptitude in relations to the demands of the citizens. Consequently, the atmosphere of secrecy upon the amount accrued to the state as a result of mining and exploring of the natural resources normally make the citizens experience parochial cultural norms.

The Angola experience buttressed the explanation above, that is, democratic deficiencies of Angola's institutions have made them unable to prevent the capture of the rents by the ruling elite and unable to preclude it from misusing the state apparatus for its power and rent seeking. Angola cannot be considered either free or democratic because of its low human and political rights record (Amundsen, 2014). It is a country with severe human rights abuses, where dividends of democracy and civil liberties are openly denied to the citizens. Since Angola gained independence from the Portuguese colonial empire, the power struggles ensued between three liberation parties with strong international links have diminished democratization of the country.

The proponents of this argument believe that the presence of democracy that gives citizens participation, free and fair electoral process and transparency in governance can mitigate and defy the essences of resource curse (Natural Resource Governance Institute, 2015). Moreover, the involvement of citizens on budgeting debates and direct (re)distribution of wealth. In support of this theory, Amundsen (2014) argues that blocked democratization is the main indicator of a resource curse in Angola. He revealed that there are no effective checks and balances, a separation of powers does not exist, elections are postponed and never held, and the president is Africa's longest serving. Political power is centralized and monopolized, and the ruling elite seems entrenched (Amundsen, 2014).

Political upheaval and protracted conflict are another dimension or thought or theory on resource curse. The point here is that natural resources or mineral deposit can instigate communal crisis and elites struggle over a particular resources leading to lack or none implementation of pro-people capital and infrastructural projects. This notion is very pronouncing in the governance of Angola in relation to her oil-rich region (Cabinda). To buttress the theory, studies have identified that right from 1990 to date, oil-rich nations have experience protracted communal clashes and civil war due to the act of injustices and lack of transparency in the management of the oil wealth. This notion is uncommon in non-oil states that rely on taxation, secondary production or services. The Angola case is a reflection of this notion and countries like Democratic Republic of the Congo, the Niger Delta in Nigeria, Iraq and Libya depict this tendency (Natural Resource Governance Institute, 2015).

The above view can be likened to the excessive power of the presidency which more often is deployed in an undemocratic manner. That is, the situation whereby the Presidency is particularly "too strong" in Angola. The President of the Republic serves as the head of state, government, army and ruling party; he has extensive powers over nominations and resource allocations and faces few constitutional constraints and no real checks and balances. The national petroleum company, Sonangol, is the basic rentier tool for the ruling elite. It has served well as an oil company, regulator, and tax collector, and this "golden goose" has been protected and kept intact as an island of competence and efficiency, to pay for the regime's survival, protection, and protection and prosperity (Amundsen, 2014).

Wasteful, Inefficient spending and borrowing, this can lead to huge debt trap and debt crisis. It arises when a particular government loses focus on investment, especially education and capital project, this can cause a chain reaction that will cripple the entire system or sectors in country. When there is the presence of certain kind of inflation which may create doubt in government expenditure, the certainty to effectively and efficiently utilize or spend fluctuating and unpredictable revenue is rare. In this case, most governments experience artificial trapped economy in the form of boom-bust cycles which put so much pressure on legacy and self-acclaimed projects (in the expense of national interests) like airports, erecting unproductive statues and monuments as a result of revenues increases. Then, when revenue declines, horrible and painful economic deduction or cuts defines the whole processes.

Another defining characteristic of the above notion is excessive spending on recurrent expenditure, building of massive monuments and non-result oriented subsidization of certain products as a result of abundance natural resource wealth. While items that fall within social amenities such as health, education and other essential social services suffer. Because of personal interest and self-aggrandizement of elites when they are in government, the quest to empty the national purse and engage in the act of borrowing has led most African states to debt crises. This occurs when there is existence of longer term flows of wealth that peak from the natural resource (oil), but when the law of diminishing returns sets in, debt crisis become an issue. Angola in various facets depicted this analysis and countries like Mexico, Nigeria and Venezuela as at the 1980s also experienced this situation.

The theory of weak leadership and institutional underdevelopment can create resource curse. This view argues that weak leaders and institutions can lead to underdevelopment in the mist of abundance natural resources. This theory expresses that when a country relies on one product such as oil, which is run or managed outside the budgetary allocation process. There is the likelihood for it to be misuse and thereby result in state capture by the selfish elites for their personal interest at large. For instance, the instrument that enables elites to hijack revenue is premised on sovereign wealth funds, national investment on oil organisations and contract award on mining and explorations. This will warrant the ruling elites to have less interest in investing in capital project that will drive the economy and produce job for the citizens, but rather they will be engrossed with *rent-seeking*, that is, fight for control of these resources. The Angola's case serves as point of reference where the elites fight over the oil region's natural resources to just own the rents from them. In some cases, politicians or government officials have also purposefully dismantled societal checks or created new regulations to get access to these resources or to provide access to friends or family members and this process is nicknamed *rent-seizing*.

Bringing the above explanation to the Angolan scenario, it identified that the Angola courts have not able to pin down any judgment on any single case within the realm of social litigation, in other words, a court case that tries to settle a dispute that has to do with a violation of social or economic rights in the sphere of government responsibility. Besides, the tribunal is very inadequate in terms of independence. The court president and judges are nominated by the President of the Republic and not subject to parliamentary oversights at the level of appointment. Moreover, the government is not obliged to submit the general state accounts to the tribunals/courts for audits. Also, the tribunal does not handle high-level political cases, except for those that serve a political purpose, on demand (Amundsen, 2014).

Deplorable social condition and environmental damage have been advance as part of the dimensions or theory of resource curse. The burden of argument falls on the mining and oil exploration companies that have failed in their corporate social responsibilities. The process of allocating capital project to communities and investment can create envy and enemy between and among communities leading to destruction of properties and lives. This situation gets worsen when the ruling elites obtain the fund meant for the development of the communities and use it for personal needs. Also, environmental issues such as dust from mining, scarring of the landscape, noise from process operation, contamination of hydric sources from waste rock and tailing disposal, massive use of water in the extractive process, gas flaring causing health problems and wasteful CO_2 emissions and seismic disturbances. In addition, many of the political and economic problems outlined above constitute or can result in the violation of human rights. The contract between the government and the extraction company could address these issues and clarify whose responsibility it is to manage these impacts.

In a nutshell, societies that are rich in oil fall into the trap of the problem of managing the immediate communities and welfare of the state as a whole which created a big challenge to oil states but not necessarily mean resource curse. Recent studies like NRG (2015) have demonstrated that low-income states are more prone to resource curse challenges. As there is an increasing number of new discoveries in low-income countries, it is useful for policymakers to be aware of these trends so that they can respond appropriately.

Angola's Natural Resource Curse and Conflicts

The extractions of oil and diamond natural resources in Angola have been distinctive in the conflicts that engulf the country. Most scholarships on Angola's national crises link every violent eruption to three constituents interconnected with natural resource excavation. According to Maphosa (2012), civil strife, dysfunctional economy, and illegitimacy of political leadership are the three major ingredients that worsen the role natural resources such as oil and diamond play to fuel violence in Angola and other African nations. The Angolan crises and violence are mostly bedevilled by these three dimensions. Protracted fighting between the Popular Movement for the Liberation of Angola (MPLA) and the National Union for the Total Independence of Angola (UNITA) cannot be separated from these dimensions over control of revenues from oil and diamond in Angola.

Under the rule of MPLA's President Jose Eduardo dos Santos, the combative attacks against the Angolan Armed Forces (FAA) by the UNITA-led Jonas Savimbi group had links to perceived political illegitimacy of the state and woeful economic existence of Angolans. In the view of Taylor (n.d.), the quest for control of Angola's oil and diamond resources led to failure of every peacebuilding and peacekeeping attempt. The resumption of hostilities between UNITA and FAA in December 1998 was the fallout and breakdown of the Lusaka Peace Accord that relatively had everything to do with contestations over the control of the natural resources of the country. The persistent battles over who should control Angola's oil and diamond wealth played out too in the 1992 elections which entertained large scale claims of illegitimacy of the MPLA's victory, especially from the militia UNITA group.

Crude oil income and revenues from diamond on both sides were more often militarized and deployed to fortify and consolidate armed engagement by the two warring actors (Andersen, 2003). Hence, Andersen's contention that returns from extracting oil and diamond legally or otherwise in Angola is a critical reason of conflict in the country. By conservative estimates, it is believed that UNITA made an estimated 3.7 billion US dollars between 1992 and 1998 from especially illegal diamond deals according to the survey of Global Witness (cited in Taylor, n.d.). In the same vein, the Angolan government is projected to have earned between one and three billion dollars in the 1990s from crude oil alone (ibid., Taylor, n.d.). The in-fighting between FAA and UNITA thus had linkages to the extraction of rents from the proceeds from natural resources. Ultimately, the revenues emanating from Angola's natural resources increased the dehumanization of the state rather than enhanced human security. This outcome, as it were, underscores the resource curse thesis as a model for explaining Africa's underdevelopment amid plenty natural endowments of which Angola typifies (Maphosa, 2012).

According to United Nations (UN), 40% of civil strife and civil wars in Africa in the last six decades have familiarities with natural resource ventures with no bearing on the continent's human development (cf. Rice and Patrick, 2008). While for instance, within this same period, Angola's oil production rose astronomically, but it's ranking on the UN Human Development Index (UN-HDI) diminished from 73 out of 174 countries to the position of 160 (Taylor, n.d.). In the Angolan oil and diamond resource exploitation situation, the abysmal economic gain from the sector is one important factor why armed conflict persists there. The decadent economy of the Angolan people is implanted in many respects to the "grievance narrative" which sustained the bifurcation of citizens into those for AMPL and those army-willing for UNITA (Andersen, 2003). Indeed, conflict in Angola by no means has one basic motivation which is self-economy of the key actors in the conflict than national well-being of citizens. It is doubtless that UNITA as a group did not engage in armed conflict out of the desire to use proceed from diamonds to satisfy pecuniary wants of its members and their associates too, aside procuring arms.

Angola's civil war which by estimation lasted almost 30 years was more a war over the control of natural resources, especially rents from oil and diamonds. Andersen's (2003) research found that the presence of diamond and oil in the political governance matrix of Angola between 1975 and 2002 (the estimated period that Angola's civil war lasted) made every attempt at peaceful settlement between UNITA and FAA elusive. The fighting over diamond and oil rents in Angola is all about exerting control to superintend over the state apparatus. On the one hand is the FAA which is the armed wing of the MPLA. The other side is UNITA, which according to literature exposition depends greatly on natural resources rents to sustain its irredentism against the Angolan state apparatus of government (Humphreys, 2005). It has been observed that the MPLA through its subsidiary FAA sustained its armed conflict against the rebel UNITA group by its control of off-shore oil activities while UNITA endured its armed struggle through illicit diamond mining (Harsch, 2007). It is evident, as the Global Witness Report indicates, that "blood diamonds" were a significant retooling source of financing for the rebel UNITA group to stockpile its armoury with much intensity. The foregoing point is the reason Taylor (n.d.) holds that blood diamonds reinforced UNITA's disregard of the 1992 election outcome which favoured MPLA and emboldened it to undermine the Lusaka Peace Protocol.

Because the Angolan apparatus for natural resources governance is widely de-legitimated by conflicts, Mehlum et al.'s (2002) notion of "grabber friendly institutions" comes out apt as a model to explain the Angolan resource curse theory. "Grabber friendly institutions" as conceived by Mehlum, Moene and Torvik (2002: 1) alludes to state apparatuses of conflict management indulging in diverting natural resources rents to "unproductive activities as a result of resource abundance". In Angola, for sure, wide spread corruption and massive pillaging of the wealth from her natural endowments retains the resource curse theory in the polity. A 2011 Human Rights Watch report projected that the Angolan state could not account for $32 billion in government revenues. The Global Financial Integrity (GFI) 2011 Report says $6billion constituted illicit financial flows out of Angola and that Angolan government could not give account of $8.45 billion (i.e. 23% of GDP) between 1997 and 2001 (Ovadia, 2014). Calls for transparency, therefore, in the governance and management of the oil and diamond endowments of Angola by MPLA stalwarts have been actually mere paper talk.

Rice and Patrick (2008) highlight and underscore the international dimension to the conflict situation through the involvement of transnational/multinational corporations and other foreign actors, indicative of the weakness of the Angola nation to properly mitigate its resource curse syndrome. The power bifurcation of control—FAA to oil and UNITA to diamond—in Angola remain so because, in a way, foreign actors through their multinational corporation were benefiting from the absence of transparency in Angola's extractive sector and ineffectual stringent governmental regulation was lacking. Given that most African nations lack optimum technical and administrative know-how to exploit their natural resources, transnational and multinational corporations were hopefully expected to make up for that lacuna. However, the UNDP July 16 report, that declared that Africa's natural resources have "barely touched people's lives", is an indictment also on foreign operators in the Angolan oil and diamond explorative terrain (Harsch, 2007; Ovadia, 2014).

Literatures on the resource curse theory hold that weak institutions and state incapacity not only undermine effective natural resource governance but enables international partners to destabilize society. Angola, like other resource endowed underdeveloped nations symbolize the thesis that resource abundance is a driver of conflict and political tension through domestic collaboration with outsiders due to their dysfunctional public administration systems (Maphosa, 2012). Resource curse theorists such as Mehlum, Moene and Torvik (2002) believe that a linkage does exist between public administration's institutional incapacity and incapability and conflict cum underdevelopment in nations blessed with huge natural means. The example is made of economic growth of not-to-rich resource countries like Korea, Singapore, Israel, among others as against the stunted growth of resource-rich countries like Angola, Venezuela, Nigeria, etc. (see Ovadia, 2016; Humphreys, 2005; Auty, 2001).

According to David Keen (1998), clashes that emanate from natural resources business reveal the underlying motif of "profit and power" (cited from *New Scientists Daily Newsletter online*, 2002).

Thus, the Angola natural resource conflicts cannot be disentangled from the pecuniary socio-political and economic desires of the political actors in the MPLA, FAA and UNITA as fortified by the profit motive of some international players. The game theory is therefore valuable to uncover why conflict persisted in Angola's natural resource extractive sector by the role foreign state actors, as well as other multinational/transnational corporations play.

What is being stressed is that the conflict in Angola, as other crisis-prone resource-rich country, is a product of both the game and structure-functionalism theories. The game theory assumes that brinkmanship underlies every move and activities of every stakeholder in the diamond and oil mining business in Angola. Whereas the inauguration of the Diamond Development Initiative (DDI) in 2005 by civil society groups (Global Witness and Partnership Africa Canada) in collaboration with two transnational ventures in gold, diamond and other precious stones, De Beers and Rapaport, relate to the structural-functionalist dimension of conflict flowing from resource curse. In a synopsis, this article situates both the game and structure-functionalism theories as pertinent in understanding the Angolan conflict and resource curse. Analysis of Angola's conflict and warmongering is a spirited game of rivalry between MPLA backed by its military wing, FAA, in contradiction of rebel cum insurgent groups of which UNITA is most significant. And to the government, multinational corporations operating in Angola, the Angolan military as well as the rebel groups, conflict has been structuralized as a function of expression of grievances against the activities of the two warring competitors. Owing to this, Angola continues to remain a fragile state at the edge of failure or even collapse. As a consequence of the Angolan conflict over natural resources, incapacity of public administration to deliver good governance and modern public utilities linger. Empirically, Angola's resource curse-conflict nexus captures graphically the Hobbesian state of nature whereby governance in Angola is still at the level of being "harsh, brutish and nasty".

Consequences of Resource Curse Conflicts on Angolans

Natural resources endowment has for long been tagged as one of the driving forces for conflict in Africa. Angola is not doubt one of the potentially richest African countries with striking oil reserves and diamond deposits. However, the Republic of Angola is ranked among the poorest countries in the continent, despite the country‘s immense wealth of oil, gas and other mineral resources deposits.

Natural resources in Angola are crucial part of the country's economic mainstay. They constitute the primary generators of income, and identities to most of the developing countries such as Angola. It is of no doubt that natural resources constitute an integral part in the understanding the nature of conflict in Angola as a result of the role they play in such conflicts. The extraction of natural resources has resulted in conflicts in many African counties including Angola. Examples of such countries include Nigeria, Angola, Liberia, Sudan, and Democratic Republic of Congo and so on. Over time, the conflicts involving natural resources have escalated and wedged overwhelming consequences and brought misfortune to many countries in Africa, especially in terms of stability and peacebuilding.

A number of countries among which is Angola have gone through varying levels of conflicts as a result of mineral deposits. Conflicts resulting from natural resources in the last few decades have claimed lives of many innocent citizens including children, men and women. A United Nation (UN) survey shows that Africa's death ratio in the last 60 years is connected by about 40% to the conflicts ensuing from the resource curse syndrome. In the case of Angola, resources conflicts have aggravated inequality in the country, as the income in thriving sectors such as oil and diamond only go into the pockets of few wealthy ones, while the vast majority of people are driven to the very edge of poverty and many others pushed beyond starvation.

Natural resource conflicts have had profound negative impact on the people of Angola. The natural resource conflicts have impeded Angolans‘ ability to enjoy their economic, social and cultural rights. It has denied them the ability of having sufficient funding for essential social services including healthcare and quality education. As a result, millions of Angola continue to live without access to hospital services and quality education.

In recent years, as oil revenues surged, the Angolan government has refused to provide information about the use of public funds to its population, undermining their right to information. It has failed to establish hundreds of courts and allowed the judiciary to become dysfunctional, undermining Angolan's ability to hold government officials and others accountable. And it has not fully committed to free and fair elections, thus removing another avenue of accountability.

Had the government properly accounted for and managed the disappeared funds? It is likely that more funds would have been allocated to the fulfilment of economic, social and cultural rights, such as increased spending on education, health and other social services.

The impacts of natural resources have played negatively on the people of Angola in all spheres of society. Despite the fact that Angola is excessively blessed with natural resources, Angola remains one of the poorest countries in Africa. The country has a literacy rate not at par with its national income which ought to reflect in the budgetary allocation to the education sector. The implication of this is that, many Angolans cannot make sense of contents in books, how much more to understand how to go about demanding for accountability, probity and secure their human rights. Although, in Africa today, Angola's literacy rate falls below average, it is far better than what is obtained in countries such as Burkina Faso and Burundi. However, in Angola, quality education, especially that of a girl-child continues to be a major problem.

According to the UNDP Human Development Multidimensional Poverty Index developed by Oxford University, Angola remains one of the poorest countries in Africa, with at least 55% of its people living below poverty line. Life expectancy of the total population of Angola remains around 38–76 years, a figure which happens to be the worst in Africa and in the world.

Even though sex education and other youth education programs are helping to fight against HIV/AIDS, in 2009, about 200,000 Angolans were living with the deadly disease with about 11,000 deaths recorded in the same year. In other words, HIV/AIDS continues to threaten the peace of the country. Diseases such as malaria and water-borne diseases including typhoid fever, protozoan and bacteria diarrhoea continue to be a threat to the lives of Angolans.

Concluding Remarks

From the forgoing analysis, if Angola is a fragile state, then it is of no surprise. The effect of protracted crises and conflicts naturally is bound to disable the state's institution to be able to address and overcome the forces that aggravate the resource curse syndrome in the country. Unfortunately, the warring parties in the Angolan natural resource extractive environment and process are themselves not benefactors of the nature-endowed blessings of the society by the combats. Amid these plentiful conflict imbroglios, even the MPLA, UNITA, FAA, multinational corporations, international war collaborators and equally Angola's entire public administration infrastructure cannot claim to be at peace in their affairs. Ultimately, it is the ordinary Angolans that are the worst-hit victims of the resource curse disease that is embedded today in the psycho-social mentality of the superstructure of the Angolan society.

It is obvious that self-aggrandizement and pursuit of pecuniary desires have underpinned the operations of the actors in the Angolan natural resources conflicts.

Because of Angola's historical conjecture—its colonial dynamics leading to the pseudo-democratic election in 1992—this article point of departure on the players and supposed game changers in the Angolan conflict condition is that they could not have been anything close to being nationalistic or statesmanlike. This view is premised on the belief that post-colonial Angolan state was very likely to be teleological to the mentality of her colonizers. As earlier noted in the paper, Angola's colonial experience was one of overt pillage, oppression and dehumanization from the Portuguese colonial administration (Candido, 2013; Marcum, 1976; Rodney, 1972). And a common trench of colonialism in Africa was that at Independence, the colonizers were likely to handover to a petty bourgeoisie class groomed to sustain the interest of the metropolitan state (in this context, interest of Portugal and the other European allies). By definition, a petty bourgeoisie class is one whose ideological leanings resemble that of their masters and teachers whom are the colonial overlords.

Thus, whether for good or for bad, those who Angola was handed over to at Independence obviously inherited the mindset to pillage the state's natural endowments as the colonial state did. Surprisingly, however, is the extent to which the petty bourgeoisie Angolans themselves who assumed the takeover of power from Portugal relegated the interest of the state and

Angolans in enjoying their God-given natural resources. A hard-fought resumption of political power at Independence was meant to be for the benefit of the people. But it turned out to be a "Greek gift of a Trojan horse". More than ever, the battles for control and management of rents from oil and diamond and other natural resources did not in any way consolidate Angola's Independence. Instead, it merely shifted the focus of the struggle away from the colonizers to a greater devastating dimension of ethnic mutual suspicion, ethnic hatred, killings and disintegration of the state eventually.

Self-interest of the international players in the natural resource venture of Angola did not also help to abate the deepening of the resource curse syndrome in Angola. In one breathe was the effects of the ideological festers of the Cold War as championed by America's capitalism versus the Russian brand of communist socialism as it affected the ideological foundation itself of Angola. In another breathe was the ideological impositions brought to bear on the different key actors in Angola's natural resources extraction scenery by ethnic, political, cultural and religious ideas.

As earlier noted in the article, ethnicity and religious inclinations were fundamental factors that stirred the bifurcation of Angola's resource curse struggles. Literature exposition reveals that that the MPLA tilts more to the Mbundu and Mesticos cultural propensities as well as to the belief system of the Roman Catholic and Methodist Churches. While UNITA was akin to the Ovimbundu ethnic leanings, as well as to the idea of state-religion interaction of the Baptist Church. Also, at the level of operations of the multinational extractive corporations too in Angola were evidences of an extension of the capitalism-socialism dichotomy. What all these ideological bifurcations meant in our discourse herein, and what they stress in the article is that international actors too, through different means entangled the Angolan state to where she is today in terms of socio-political and economic underdevelopment despite the country's rich and huge natural resources reserves.

The picture painted from the foregoing analysis, and broadly speaking, it is inconceivable that Angola would not suffer resource curse. It was likely to be the case because all the colonial, political, social, economic, ideological and bilateral/multilateral encrustations on the Angolan state were not geared towards establishing and building a capable Angolan state. Evidence of an iota of such aspiration may be somewhat difficult to decipher from our analytic scrutiny of the natural resource curse of Angola. In fact, when public administration system of a country has been debased, like that of Angola, from the colonial into the post-colonial epoch, the Angolan people cum Angolan nation is most likely to always remain at the margin of state collapse. This Angolan situation is also worsened by the international political economy system of natural resources extraction. Until advanced countries de-emphasise the urgings for the natural resources of less and developing economies like Angola, international and domestic vested interests would always ensure that sanity, transparency and accountability do not reign in Angola's public administration operations.

On a final note, only Angolans and their leaders can truly reverse the resource curse syndrome besieging the country. And the first step to achieve this is to institute a truly democratic government whose ascendancy to political power results from a widely acclaimed legitimate election process. Only a truly democratic government can deliver accountability and fast track the process of reformation of the superstructure of the Angolan nation as well as stop the armed irredentism of the militia insurgent groups confronting the state through its government. With adherence to the democratic principles in play in the governance process, the Angolan people can be said to now be partaking in their governance. The democratic government hence, having enjoyed legitimacy, can be assured of the people's support for reform mechanisms that will be constructed to address the illegalities and absurdities surrounding the exploitation and extraction of the nation's natural resources.

A vital way too to address grievances of the different interests in Angola's conflict crises is to institute a government that is perceived as not bias against the interest of any of the parties. If we suggest a government of national unity encompassing all the various interests, such may not really archive the goal of national unity for the country. This may be so because the grievances that exacerbate the resource curse problem of Angola are deep-rooted and ethnically clothed. In such a scene, the process to instituting a government is as important, if not far more important, than just the formation of a government of unity. In the light of this, a proportional representation system is advocated. The proportional system of representation should take cognizance about representation of all the various ethnicities, local interests and marginalized groups such as the aged, handicapped and the women-folks. The government that evolves from such proportional representation system must embrace decentralization of powers, privileges and functions in the area of natural resource governance. Adequate constitutional safeguards should be erected to ensure that centre/national executive arm of government is not extremely too powerful. By implication, the parliament must enjoy substantial power of oversight to ensure that the executive arm does not run *ultra vires* the constitutional powers allotted to the office. On this note, this article proposes that Angola move from its unitary-presidential constitutional governance mode to a federal-presidential system. Consociational federal policies like rotational presidency, ethnic balancing in political appointment, federal character and quota system in the distribution of public properties of any kind and affirmative programmes for advancing the aspirations of marginalized ethnic groups would be valuable to eliminating natural resources extraction related conflicts in Angola.

The judiciary also needs to be allowed requisite independence and latitude to operate. Ouster clauses should be non-existent in the jurisprudential laws of Angola. Ouster clauses that disallow judicial review of expenditure of the executive of the revenues from natural resources in Angola worsen the conflicts and deepen the resource curse. The courts should have the power to hear queries from bureaucrats over the financial expenses of the rulers at all the levels of government. Reforms to established independent-minded policing structures needed to be instituted too in Angola as a way to checkmate the powers of the executive and legislatures. By implication, public policy reforms in line with strengthening the adjudicatory institutions and other members of the Temple of Justice are sacrosanct for Angola to eradicate natural resources extraction related conflicts.

In the same vein, policy reforms are therefore necessary to delineate the rules of engagement of multinational corporations operating in Angola's extractive sector. Allocation of mining or drilling rights must be open and accountable to the people eventually. Here, the bureaucratic arm responsible for overseeing mining and oil drilling ventures should from time to time make public its audit of the activities of businesses, whether indigenous or foreign, in the natural resources extraction circle. Apart from this, civil society organizations needed to be wooed by the government and collaborated with to provide insights, expose illegalities and proffer solutions to advance accountability, environmental protection and anti-corruption emanating from the sector. The civil societies should be encouraged to collaborate with village, town and municipal community development organizations to get feedbacks about the activities of mining and other business ventures that relate to Angola's natural resource exploration. In this regard, local groups and organizations are valuable sources of information on the degradation to their environment that these ventures portend.

What the above thinking implies is that Angola needs to have a Freedom of Information Law in place to enable for more openness and transparency in government. The challenge of free and easy access to information on the goings-on in the nation's extractive sector is one of the banes to why Angolans are not reaping bountifully from their God-given natural resources. Secrecy by government officials in the dealings of the sector have encouraged public corruption rather than abated it. With such a law in existence, the public can equally track the materialism inclinations of those entrusted to supervise the earning and expenditure of revenues from the natural resources endowments of Angola.

One suggested direction for the future democratic regime by this article is to ensure to diversify the Angolan economy. Surely, the Dutch disease—a situation whereby too much focus is given to one sector (in this context, natural resources mining) at the expense of other tangible revenue sources which eventually cause stunted economic growth—is empirically the case in Angola. A radical shift of the economic mainstay of Angola from oil and diamond rents to other sectors like agriculture, tourism, industrialization and entertainment would most possibly discourage young Angolans from taking to armed struggles. Economically, diversification of the Angolan economy will dissuade further recruitment of youths into conflicts as well as stimulate advances in the education sector. From comparative perspective, successful diversification of economy policies goes hand-in-hand with educational sector development.

By extension, Angola's economic diversification will lead to further drop in the illiteracy rate, and as is well known in military circles that an educated mind is less prone to armed combat and highly prone to use initiative positively. It is not to be disregarded too that diversification of the Angolan economy will abate poverty, reduce mortality and morbidity rates of the country. The policy will aid to create massive employment opportunities as the less the idle hands in Angola exists, the less in-fighting that is likely to happen. Economy diversification too will reduce government's reliance as natural resources rents and blossom revenue generation from such other sectors like taxation, manufacturing, agri-business and a host of others. A well-known fact is that resource curse is prevalent in a mono-economy that is solely reliant on natural resources rents. Hence, to diversify the Angolan economy is tantamount to a vital strategy of peacebuilding and peacekeeping.

To cap all these suggested measures to be put in place by a democratically appointed government in Angola upon being inaugurated, government must endeavour to return all parties in the armed combats back to the peacebuilding negotiation table. In view of this, Angola needs to institute a Peace and Reconciliation Commission to help hasten the process of peacebuilding. Here, the international community with Africa's main continental organ, the African Union (AU), can be valuable as a mediator of the peace process. The instituted democratic government must establish its impartiality to entrenching peace in Angola by sitting at such table as an interested party and not as the arbitrator. This, it can do, by authorizing both international and continental mediators to preside over the process. This democratically legitimated Angolan government must, however, make sure that those engaged to mediate for sustainable peacebuilding, whether within Africa or outside the continent, are impartial dramatis personae or better still neutral actors in the natural resources matrix of the country.

References

Amundsen, I. (2014). Drowning in Oil: Angola's Institutions and the "Resource Curse". *Comparative Politics, 46*(2), 169–189. Retrieved on May 6, 2019, from https://www.jstor.org/stable/43664097.

Andersen, J., Nordvik, F. & Tesei, A. (2017). *Oil and civil conflict: On and off (shore)*. CAMP Working Paper Series, No. 1.

Andersen, K. H. (2003). *Resources and conflict in Angola: An economic conflict analysis*. Published Online Master Thesis, University of Oslo, Norway. Retrieved from https://www.duo.uio.no/handle/10852/16966, Permanent link: http://urn.nb.no/URN:NBN:no-6302.

Auty, R. M. (2001). *Resource abundance and economic development*. Oxford: Oxford University Press.

Bender, G. (1978). *Angola under the Portuguese—Myth and reality*. Berkeley, CA: University of California.

Birmingham, D. (1966). *Trade and conflict in Angola: The Imbundu and their neighbours under the influence of the Portuguese*. Clarendon Press.

Bissonette, B. (2008). *The Angolan proxy war: A study of foreign intervention and its impact on the fighting*.

Brinkman, I. (2003). War and identity in Angola: Two case-studies. *Lusotopie, 10*(1), 195–221.

Candido, M. (2013). *An African slaving port and the Atlantic West: Benguela and its Hinterland*. Cambridge: Cambridge University Press.

Davidson, B. (1992). *The Blackman's burden: Africa and the curse of the nation state*. Nairobi: Times Book.

David Keen. (1998). *The economic function of violence in civil wars*. Oxford: Oxford University Press.

Ferreira, M. (2006). Angola: Conflict and development, 1961–2002. *The Economics of Peace and Security Journal, 1*(1), 24–28.

Ferreira, R. (2012). *Cross cultural trade in the Atlantic world: Angola and Brazil in the Era of Slave Trade*. Cambridge: Cambridge University Press.

Fromont, C. (2014). *The art of conversion: Christian visual culture in the Kingdom of Kongo*. Chapel Hill, NC: University of North Carolina Press.

Frynas, J. & Wood, G. (2001). Oil and war in Angola. *Review of African Political Economy, 28*(90), 587–606.

Gonzalez, A. (2010). Petroleum and its impact on three wars in Africa: Angola, Nigeria and Sudan. *Journal of Peace, Conflict and Development, 16*, 58–86. Retrieved from www.peacestudiesjournal.org.uk.

Harsch, E. (2007). Conflict resources: From 'curse' to blessing. *Africa Renewal: African News and Analysis from the United Nations Online*. Retrieved on May 10, 2019, from https://www.un.org/africarenewal/magazine/.../conflict-resources-'curse'-blessing.

Heywood, L. (2009). Slaving and its transformation in the Kingdom of Kongo 1491–1800. *Journal of African History, 50*(1), 1–22.

Humphreys, M. (2005). Natural resources, conflict, and conflict resolution: Uncovering the mechanisms. *Journal of Conflict Resolution, 49*(4), 510.

James, W. (2011). *A political history war in Angola, 1974–1990*. Piscataway, NJ: Transaction Publishers.

Klein, H. (1972). The Portuguese slave trade from Angolan in the eighteen century. *The Journal of Economic History, 32*(4), 984–918.

Maphosa, S. B. (2012). Natural resources and conflict: Unlocking the economic dimension of peace-building in Africa. *Policy Brief: Africa Institute of South Africa. Africa.Org, Portal online*, No. 74, March, Retrieved on May 9, 2019, from https://www.africaportal.org/publications/natural-resources-and-conflict-unlocking-the-economic-dimension-of-peace-building-in-africa/.

Marcum, J. (1976). Angola: Background to the conflict. *Mawazo, 4*(4), 5–12.

Marthias, B. & Wegenast, T. (2009). Oil and diamonds as causes of civil war in Sub-Saharan Africa. *Columbia International, 70*, 35–59.

Meijer, G. & Birmingham, D. (2004). Angola from past to present. In G. Meijer (ed.), *Accord: Military peace to social justice*. The Angolan peace process. London: Conciliation Resources.

Mehlum, H., Moene, K. & Torvik, R. (2002). *Institutions and the resource curse*. Working Paper Memorandum, Department of Economics, University of Oslo.

No. 29, pp. 1–20. Retrieved on May 10, 2019, from https://www.econstor.eu/bitstream/10419/63059/1/354828169.pdf.

Miller, J. (1988). *Way of death: Merchant capitalism and the Angolan slave trade, 1730–1830*. Wisconsin: University of Wisconsin.

Natural Resource Governance Institute (NRGI). (2015). *The resource curse: The political and economic challenges of natural resource wealth*. Retrieved on May 6, 2019, from www.resourcegovernance.org.

Ndumbey, A. & Cole, B. (2005). The illicit diamond trades civil conflicts and terrorism in Africa. *Mediterranean Quarterly, 16*(2), 52–65.

New Scientists Daily News online. (2002, June 29). Blood diamonds and oil. Retrieved from https://www.newscientist.com/article/mg17423495-200-blood-diamonds-and-oil/.

Ovadia, J. S. (2014). Local content and natural resource governance: The case of Angola and Nigeria. *The Extractive Industries and Society, 1*(2), 137–146. Retrieved on May 10, 2019, from eprint.ncl.ac.uk/file_store/.../93ECC058-DE0D-4AA8–93BA-01412A533FFA.pdf.

Ovadia, J. S. (2016). *The petro-developmental state in Africa: Making oil work in Angola, Nigeria and the Gulf of Guinea*. London: Hurst Publishers.

PICSIM (2005). *Republic of Angola*. Princeton: International Relations Council, Princeton University.

Rice, S. E. & Patrick, S. (2008). *Index of state weakness in the developing world*, p. 3. Washington, DC: The Brookings Institute.

Rodney, W. (1972). *How Europe underdeveloped Africa*. London: Bogle-L'Quventure Publications.

Taylor, S. (undated). Natural Resources and Corporate Responsibility: The case of Angola's war. *HPN Humanitarian Practice Network Online*. Retrieved on May 9, 2019, from https://odihpn.org/magazine/natural-resources-and-corporate-responsibility-the-case-of-angola%C2%92s-war/.

Thomas, G. (2012). *Angola: Mining, minerals and resources*. Retrieved form http://www.azomining.com/article.aspx?ArticleID=86.

UICN. (1993). *Environmental synopsis: Angola, Gland: International Union for Conservation of Nature*.

CHAPTER 5

An Eco-Marxist Critique of Capitalism in Africa

Victor Ojakorotu and Bamidele Olajide

Introduction

This chapter considers an Eco-Marxist critique of capitalism using its environmental effects arising from the exploitation of resources such as oil and gas, gold, copper and timber in Africa. This is to the extent that there is an environmental conspiracy between Multinational Corporations and the local bourgeoisie against Africa through activities such as extraction and mining and logging of timber, among other environmentally dangerous economic activities. Capitalism is the main driver of the formation of modern Africa. This is because the urge to satisfy the demands of the ever-expanding market for capitalist production along

V. Ojakorotu (✉) · B. Olajide
Department of Politics and International Relations, North West University, Mafikeng, South Africa

K. J. Ani et al. (eds.), *Political Economy of Resource, Human Security and Environmental Conflicts in Africa*,
https://doi.org/10.1007/978-981-16-2036-2_5

with the sourcing of raw materials inspired the balkanization of the continent among European powers (Rodney 1973). Hence, the influence of capitalism on Africa and its development looms large and six decades into independent nationhood, the political economy of Africa is simply a discourse on the dynamics of capitalism. The historical trajectory of Africa from the pre-colonial times through colonialism and neocolonial aftermath cannot be divorced from the onslaught of capitalism on the continent. Colonialism was informed by the need for an institutional approach for sourcing primary products for European markets.

Through colonialism, Africa was thrusted into the global trade orbit which was and is still controlled by Western capitalist forces. This has produced capitalist contradictions as African countries were at various stages of development before colonialism. Thrusting them into the capitalist orbit has led to the economic crisis of the most chronic type especially since the advent of independence (Onimode 1988). Beyond the economic crisis that is rocking the continent on account of Western capitalist incursion and consolidation, the situation of the continent as the site for raw materials has also led to a serious environmental crisis. The reality of environmental crises such as drought, erosion and coastal inundation, pollution, desertification, disruption of local and indigenous economies, poverty and alienation from ancestral lands among others has compounded economic crisis for the masses of African peoples.

Eco-Marxism holds that the profit-orientation of capitalism ultimately leads to a metabolic rift, a mismatch between the goals of capitalism and the need for nature to cleanse and replenish itself as was predicted by Marx. This is the resultant effect of the aggressive quest for profit, which is the defining feature of capitalism (Foster 2015). Eco-Marxism considers the environmental consequences of the philosophy of capitalism. In Africa, the activities of local and Multinational extractive companies are responsible for the metabolic rift in the continent. The metabolic rift is seen in the accidental and or wilful spillage of extractive wastes leading to the pollution of water supply to the people, the degradation of land and other environmental issues. In timber-rich African countries, aggressive logging for profit predisposes these countries to desertification with two of the fastest-growing deserts in the world, Sahara and Kalahari, in the continent.

The chapter is structured into seven sections. Section one serves as the introduction to the chapter while section two is a theoretical discourse on Eco-Marxism. Section three is an overview of capitalism in Africa. Section four considers the dialectical relationship between capitalism, nature and environment as section five engages in the employment of Eco-Marxism as an approach for the criticism of capitalism in Africa. Section six looks at possible ways of mediating the metabolic rift, the crisis that arises out of the incongruence between the profit aggression of capitalism and nature in Africa. Lastly, section seven contains the concluding remarks for the chapter.

Eco-Marxism—A Theoretical Discourse

The ideas of Marx on the consumption of resources for profit by a few have significant implications across the facets of human life. One of such is the impact of capitalism on nature and the environment. Hence, Eco-Marxism becomes a theoretical lens for examining this impact. Eco-Marxism is an adaptation of the Marxian paradigm to issues of nature and environment. The exploitation of nature to the advantage of a few and to the exclusion of the majority which is reduced to traders of labour-power has dominated the trajectory of Marxian thought over a long period while the ecological side of the Marxian coin has also been attracting intellectual attention. Nature is an important aspect of production and as such Marxist analysis of the society cannot be complete without the inclusion of the impact of capitalist production on it. This is because the history of the development of society is that of the relation between the economic process and nature (Deleage 1989).

The Marxian analysis of surplus-value starts with the affirmation of a spectrum involving the exertion of labour-power which starts and ends with nature. This happens in two ways, it extracts resources for production from nature and afterwards directs waste from production back to nature. Hence, the production of surplus-value means the depletion and pollution of nature. Eco-Marxism notes that the advent of capitalism more than any economic epoch has had the greatest impact on nature. Nature and its resources are treated as inexhaustible. This capitalist orientation portends not an only economic crisis to the society, it also comes with an unprecedented ecological crisis (Deleage 1989). This position is also affirmed by Wallis (2010) cited in Carter-Roberts (2019: 2) that "capitalism abuses the soil as much as it exploits the worker". Eco-Marxism dwells fundamentally on the critique of capitalism by Marx and the damage it does to nature and indirectly to man. It is a combination of the Marxist doctrine of anti-capitalism, ecology, anti-globalization and pro-environmental policies (Ntuli 2018). The theory also dwells on the fulcrum of Marx's Materialist Conception of History (MCH) to properly situate the place of nature in the production of material wealth.

Foster (2015) argues that relations between socialism and ecology have been complex, interdependent and dialectical. He argues that the link between Marxism and ecology is a way of merging two traditions with distinct history and logic. While the former deals with class and class relations, the other deals with relations of man with the environment. As a result, the ecological content of the Marxian paradigm continues to elicit considerable interest. Marxism, therefore, serves as a tool for making sense of the ecological dynamics of the society in relation to capitalism. Ecology has limited tools on its own to offer a social explanation of the environmental crisis facing the world. The dialectical method of analysis offered by Marxism lays bare the contradictions between capital and nature.

In view of the arguments and position on the ecological sterility of the Marxian paradigm, a good number of important works have been published to establish the ecological content of Marxism. Works of scholars like John Bellamy Foster, Paul Burkett, Michael Lowy and David Harvey, among others have come to put Eco-Marxism as the social theory of ecology. Foster developed the idea of 'metabolic rift' from Marx's metabolism between man and nature to describe what Lievens (2010) describes as the 'Marxisisation' of ecology and 'ecologisation' of Marxism. Eco-Marxism shows major ways in which capitalist constitutes a threat and or destroying nature. One, there is an economic crisis in the form of resource scarcities which throws up the cost of resources, two, the ecological crisis which finds major expression in 'Metabolic Rift'.

The concept as theorized by Eco-Marxists gives historical materialism a clearer picture of the contemporary ecological crisis facing the world at the hands of capitalism. It offers dialectical analysis and a vivid description of the social relations of the production system to nature. Marx believes "labour is the father of material wealth; the earth is the mother" (Ntuli 2018). Historical materialism portends successive changes in the relationship between humans and nature. The trajectory of metabolism reached an injurious pitch with capitalism that changed the value of nature in the relations of production. Nature is the source of production, labour exerts its power on it. Hence, the separation of labour from nature results in dire consequences between humans and nature in which there is "exhaustion of labour-power and robbery of natural resources" (Saito 2017, p. 290).

Metabolic rift portends that nature has been depleted to such a level that it cannot support or replenish itself. It is a situation of ecological crisis never hitherto known in history. It deals with the alienation of man from nature through labour (Ntuli 2018). The result of the separation of man from nature is that the latter is depleted and sapped of energy and nutrients. Marx argues that the extraction of minerals from the veins of nature and the subsequent attempt at artificial replenishing of its amount to the irreparability of the rift between man and nature.

Environmental problems facing the world today are products of the metabolic rift as nature's reserves have been drained through the exploits of capitalism. In a sense, the assertion of Marx that "man, through his actions, mediates, regulates and controls the metabolism between himself and nature" (Foster 2015, p. 2) shows that at a point the metabolism ran counter of its self. As such the processes between man and nature could not be sustained which implies that nature and labour interdependency is not at equilibrium. Metabolic rift occurs once nature has been treated in the way of elasticity of capital and polluted. Once the pollution is much to the extent that it exceeds the self-cleansing power of nature, the environment is degraded (Akashi 2016). This disequilibrium between man and nature gave rise to the need to make forays into different areas of the world to shore up the production by nature. This is known as ecological imperialism. Ecological imperialism is the unequal ecological exchange between two regions or ecological exploitation of weaker regions by advanced capitalist nations (Foster 2015).

Eco-Marxist view of capitalism is such that the latter harbours ambivalence between use value and exchange value. Marx's ecological approach is thus a critique of production, in which nature is ascribed little or no value. Marx argues that "there is an antagonistic tension between use value and exchange value as important to both internal contradictions of capitalism and its conflict with its natural environment" (Foster 2015, p. 6). Capitalism downplays the ecological and social cost of production. It has as crucial content the idea of 'free nature' that can be appropriated and used freely save with the exertion of labour. Capitalism constitutes the private appropriation of the commons. This creates economic class between industrial agriculturalists and mining moguls who turn nature into private property and as a result create what Hardin (1968) describes as 'Tragedy of the Commons'.

Capitalism in Africa: An Overview

Colonialism made incursions into the African continent centuries before formal partitioning of the continent's kingdoms and civilizations into among European powers. In the view of Rodney (1973) the roots of Africa's current situation can be traced back to the centuries fifteenth century when the continent was involved in asymmetrical trade relations with the West. African economic relations with the West did not start with free trade. In Rodney's view, the slave trade that went on for several centuries in which European merchants came to Africa to amass manpower for their plantations in Europe and the Americas did not involve the exchange of values between Africans and Europeans, it was rather through "warfare, trickery, banditry and kidnapping" (Rodney 1973: 144). This served to deplete the African labour force owing to the whisking away of able-bodied Africans out of the continent. In effect, the African continent started its relations with the West on a backfoot from which it has not recovered several centuries afterwards.

The Berlin Conference of 1884/1985 served to officially transplant the capitalist system into Africa. Following centuries of trade, commodity and slave trade, the advent of industrialization in Europe necessitated the annexation of Africa by European powers (Odukoya 2018). This was the beginning of the modern exploitation of Africa. The nature and character of colonialism in Africa were such that Africa served as the site for sourcing of raw materials for European industrial production. Colonialism as the political face of capitalism meant that European merchants and businesses dominated trade and the production of raw materials both in agriculture and mining. This justifies Marx and Engels cited in Odukoya (2018: 173) in that "Colonialism presented capitalism in naked form, stripped of decorous clothing of European bourgeois society". Colonial governments across Africa supervised the pillaging of Africa for cheap resources for Europe.

Colonialism had little to do with African development. In terms of the development of critical infrastructure, colonial powers only developed enabling infrastructure for the movement of raw materials from their source-locations to the points of repatriation to the European industrial centres. For example, in Nigeria, rail lines were constructed to link important trade centres such as Ibadan, Kano Enugu among others to ports facilities in Port Harcourt and Lagos (Adeyemo 2019). In Ghana, the railway was constructed in 1901 to link Kumasi and Takoradi, to pave way for easier movement of raw materials (Elbra 2017). Colonial powers in the continent developed transportation and other infrastructure simply for the exploitation of Africa and its resources (Oshin 1988). In the same vein, colonial laws and policies were facilitatory to Africa's colonial pillage. In Cameroon and Sierra Leone, facilitatory Ordinances were made by colonialists on land to facilitate the exploitation of mineral resources (Njoh and Akiwumi 2012). Ayoade (2010) criticized the British House of Commons for spending "a mere twenty-nine minutes" to deliberate on the Richards constitution of 1946 but spent quality time on and passed into law four Ordinances, three of which were 'the Minerals Ordinance, the Public Lands Acquisition Ordinance, and the Crown Lands Ordinance', which were all relevant to resource exploitation in Nigeria by Britain.

Independence and post-colonialism did not present any respite for Africa in relation to capitalist exploitation. That is why it is contested that African states should rather be referred to as neocolonial states instead of post-colonial states (Ndlovu-Gatsheni 2013). In neocolonial Africa, having been thrusted into the global capitalist orbit, African countries continue to battle with the vagaries of past. One of the most important features of the neocolonial capitalist onslaught on Africa is activities of the Multinational Corporations which are exploring and exploiting resources in the continent. The post-independence economy of African countries has been dominated by Multinational Corporations many of which have a monopoly in their areas of business (Onimode 1978; Udofia 1984). These foreign businesses continued the resource exploitation and subsequently capital repatriation from Africa to the metropolitan centres of the West. Economic strategies by some African countries to ensure that foreign economic interests in the continent respond to local economic needs such as nationalization resulting in partnerships between Multinational Corporations and public entreprises didn't stop the siphoning of surplus offshore and other undue advantages for the former (Shivji 1973).

Another feature of capitalism in neocolonial Africa concerns the activities of the comprador bourgeoisie. These are Africans who serve as facilitators and local agents for foreign economic interests in the continent (Ake 1976). As an inverted capitalist system, the absence of homegrown capitalists meant that the system had to depend on the activities of the comprador bourgeoisie. The emergent petty or national bourgeoisie at independence became compradorized owing to a lack of independent capital (Shivji 2003). Through the comprador bourgeoisie, the West continued its economic carnage on Africa. Without the requisite capital to run the system, the comprador bourgeoisie which is well represented in the political class undermined economic development of their countries. This is at the heart of the failure of attempts of socio-economic rebirth by Africa countries as alluded to by Shivji (1973). The emergence of comprador bourgeoisie ensured surplus appropriation from Africa by another means and this time, the West in collusion with the leadership of African countries robbed the continent of its resources and effected created even wider development between the continent and the West (Ake 1976).

The import of capitalism in Africa in the pre-colonial, colonial and neocolonial epochs is that the continent has been effectively robbed of resources, human and capital. While it is true that Africa has lost immensely through capitalism in its relations to the West, there is yet another angle to its loss. It is the environmental damage of capitalist activities in the continent. Mineral resources exploration has left indelible environmental damage in many resource-bearing communities across the continent. The Multinational Corporations are still the champion of the reality ably assisted by their African appendages who continue to be members of the political class in the continent. Hence, from outside and within the continent, capitalism continues to deal a massive environmental blow to the people. The next session shows case studies of capitalism's environmental carnage on Africa through Multinational Corporations and their local agents.

Capitalism, Nature and Environment in Africa

Capitalism is both an economic and environmental threat to Africa. While there is a historical economic siege on the continent by the West through the economic and political instruments of capitalism, it is also necessary to see how capitalism has led to environmental damage in the continent. As home to 30% of the world's natural resources, it is apparent that the whole continent is facing one environmental travail or the other due to unbridled exploration and exploitation of resources (Ojakorotu & Olajide 2019). This served to bring a critical look at extractive activities by industrial concerns across the continent. It shows a terrible reality of environmental damage. For this paper, environmental impacts of extraction and exploitation of oil and gas, gold, copper and timber are considered.

Oil and gas are arguably the most environmentally abused natural resource in Africa. Africa is home to 7.5 of the world's oil reserves and 7.5% of the natural gas reserves (Research and Markets 2019). It is instructive to note that oil and gas exploration in the continent has been led by Western oil majors since colonial days. The environmental imprints of oil and gas exploration and exploitation leave much to be desired in oil-producing countries such as Nigeria, Angola, Gabon, Chad, Sudan, Equatorial Guinea, Republic of Congo and Cameroon among others. The activities of oil Corporations have left oil-bearing communities across the continent with massive environmental damage.

The unhealthy focus of profit for oil companies and rents accrual for African governments relegate environmental impacts of oil and gas activities to the background (Badgley 2014; Nanok and Onyango 2017; Legge and Zhibo 2018). In the Niger Delta region on Nigeria, for example, home to Africa's largest oil deposit, the environmental damage arising oil and gas exploration and exploitation have effectively compromised the biodiversity of the region. Chuks-Ezike (2018) argues that from 9 to 13 million barrels of oil have into the Niger Delta within 53 years. Oil spillage across the region has ruined the indigenous economies of the people as land and water for farming and fishing have been contaminated. The complicity of Oil Multinationals in the environmental damage in the region comes to the fore in the Ogoni oil spill for which the community sued Shell Petroleum in a Dutch court (Friend of the Earth International 2019).

Africa has a vast gold deposit with about 30% of the global production of the mineral (Mbendi 2018). Gold is mined in 34 sub-Saharan African countries with Ghana and South Africa as the leading ones (Elbra 2017; Mbendi 2018). Gold mining is one of the earliest mining activities on the continent. While gold mining has a history of over 1000 years, modern mining started in Ghana with the opening of the Obuasi Goldfields in 1895. The case of gold mining explains the rationale of settler colonialism in South Africa which began commercial gold mining in 1886 (Odukoya 2018; Mineral Council South Africa, 2019). Commercial gold mining in the continent is led by Multinational mining companies. The environmental effects or 'The Cost of Gold' as described by the Harvard Law School International Human Rights Clinic (2016) has been enormous. This is arguably due to the fact that gold produces more waste than other minerals (Elbra, 2017).

In Ghana, for example, gold mining is a major cause of water pollution through "acid mine drainage, heavy metal contamination and leaching, processing chemicals pollution and erosion and sedimentation" (Emmanuel et al. 2018, p. 46). Other environmental impacts of gold mining include loss of agricultural land and vegetation and depletion of agricultural resources, air pollution and noise pollution (Emmanuel et al. 2018). Ghana has a history of cyanide spills on account of gold extraction. In 1996, there was leakage of 36 million litres of cyanide solution into the Angonaben stream which destroyed cocoa and cause skill ailments for the people. In 2001, there were two spills of cyanide in Wassa West District of the Western Region from a mined owned by Ghana Goldfields. Other forms of pollution in Ghana include spilling of mining reagents and spent chemicals which have been found to cause land degradation in the country (Hilson and Haselip 2004).

A number of African countries have large deposits of copper, led by the Democratic Republic of Congo (DRC) and Zambia. Other countries with large deposits of copper include Botswana, Namibia, South Africa and Uganda. The majority of the copper deposits of the countries is found in the Copperbelt region of Central and Southern Africa (The Editors of Encyclopaedia Britannica 2014). Commercial mining of copper in the DRC commenced with the establishment of the Union Minère de Haut-Katanga in 1906 and 1928 with the opening of the Roan Antelope Mine in Zambia (Lungu 2008; The Editors of Encyclopaedia Britannica 2014). Like other resources, copper mining in Africa is dominated by foreign mining companies, albeit the nationalization of copper production between 1969 and late 1990s in Zambia when it was managed by Zambia Consolidated Copper Mines (ZCCM) (Lungu 2008; Limpitlaw 2011).

The environmental impacts of copper mining in the DRC and Zambia are horrendous. Due to the recent copper boom in Africa, it has been established that the boom has produced linkages between mining and forestry in DRC and Zambia. The establishment of new mines in Lubumbashi and Chingola in the two countries have led to increased deforestation, forest degradation and decrease in non-timber forest products among other issues (Mwitwa et al. 2012). Copper mining in Zambia is also linked with food insecurity in the country as it causes land degradation thereby affecting crop yields from farming (Jakobsson 2019). Copper mining in Zambia brings the environmental damage of extractive capitalism to the fore with the legal battle between about 2000 people of Shimulala, Hippo, Hellen and Kakosa villages in the Chingola Region sued Konkola Copper Mines, a subsidiary of UK-based mining Conglomerates, Vedanta Resources for pollution of a Kafue River, a major source of water supply to the villages in 2006 (Vidal 2019; Gayle 2015).

Africa has very rich forests. The forest cover of the continent stands at 650 million hectares, representing 17% of the world's forest cover (Nix 2019). Industrial and artisanal logging occurs across the continent with attendant environmental consequences. According to Statista (2020), Africa's forest cover reduced from 674.4 million hectares in 2010 to 624 million hectares in 2015 while those of Europe and North and Central America experience an increase in forest cover over the same period. Logging of timber is arguably one of the most abused resource exploitation in Africa (Global Witness 2015). In forest-rich countries across the continent, indiscriminate and illegal logging continues to put the environment in danger. Issues such as deforestation, loss of biodiversity, soil erosion, soil compaction, disruption of the hydrological cycle and desertification arise as a result of the almost unrestrained logging going on in the continent (Fuwape 2003).

The dynamics of logging the DRC bring into clearer perspective the malaise of timber management and exploitation in Africa. The DRC is home to the second-largest block of tropical forest in the world, standing at 145 million hectares, representing 62% of the country's territory (Samndong and Nhantumbo 2015). Due to long years of civil strife and weak institutional controls in the country, logging has been carried on illegally with impunity. Timber from the DRC makes their way to the international market. While this has been blamed on artisanal logging, there are findings that there is massive illegal industrial logging in the DRC (Global Witness 2015). Logging concessions have been found to be fraught with issues such as corruption, non-payment of taxes, logging outside permitted areas, logging in excess of permitted volumes and rules flouting by industrial loggers (Global Witness 2015). Timber find its way outside of the DRC to the global industrial centres leaving the people to bear the environmental brunt of the blind quest for profit.

Eco-Marxist Critique of Capitalism in Africa

The capitalist onslaught on nature in Africa is a historical process. Based on this fact, it suffices to assert that the history of capitalism in Africa is the history of the exploitation and depletion of nature. Right from the pre-colonial to the neocolonial era of the African-capitalism interface, the issues of the depletion of nature and degradation of the environment in the continent have come to the fore. Beyond the capital flight to Western and now Chinese metropoles, Africans are made to face the environmental brunts of the quest for the profit of the 'investors'. The ecological dynamics of Africa are such that the capitalists and their African appendages cart away societal resources and leave the people with polluted and degraded land, which in turn increases the intensity of poverty in the continent.

Colonialism portended little regard for African interests including the environment. The realpolitik of colonialism lied in the quest for sourcing cheap raw materials and markets for surplus goods produced in the West (Ayoade 2010). Hence, across the continent, colonial powers passed enabling laws for the exploitation of raw materials. The neocolonial phase of capitalism in Africa has dealt more harm to the environment more than any era in the history of Africa (Mazrui 2002). While it is true that a good number of African countries pursued economic policies that gave them full control of extractive sectors of their economies, the eventual ascent of capitalism flowing from the neoliberal pressures of the Washington Consensus brought nature and environment under unprecedented and unfettered exploitation. Hence, Ghana, Zambia and other countries that privatized their mines and became open to the opening more mines by foreign mining countries (Lungu 2008; Carter-Roberts 2019). Even countries that did not nationalize their extractive industries like Nigeria had to liberalize the more and allowed more Western extractive majors into the country (Ekanade 2014).

Carter-Roberts (2019) notes the elements of the capitalist onslaught on African environment as including globalization, the transnational structure and the repressive state. Globalization which arose following the end of the Cold War brought about economic interdependence never seen before in the world. One feature of the economics of globalization is its short-term focus (Carter-Roberts 2019). As a result, resource exploitation received a new impetus with the setting up of new mining facilities thereby increasing the lucrativeness of the extractive business on the continent. The transnationality of mining businesses added more force to the quest for global profit-seeking with Africa as a major source of raw commodity. This situation brought out more pollution and waste on the continent as the cases of industrial pollution of mining companies grew since the advent of globalization (Mazrui 2002). Efforts of resource-bearing communities to speak to the desecration of have been met with repression by the State. In the case of the Ogoni oil spill by Shell and the rest of the Niger Delta, the Nigerian state resorted to state violence. It led to the execution of the Ogoni Nine, led by Ken Saro-Wiwa in 1995. In Africa, the state which officials are largely the local appendages of international and transnational mining businesses would rather use state apparatus to quell protests from resource-bearing communities to keep the rents flowing in and the profits flying out to the home countries of the Multinational Corporations (Osaghae 1998; Anifowose 2011).

The exploitation of resources and the attendance environmental issues in Africa speak crucially to the thesis of 'metabolic rift'. In the exploitation of natural resources in Africa, the quest to appropriate surplus for profit by mining companies makes them care the least about nature and environment. There is arguably no mineral extraction in the continent that does not leave behind sad environmental tales in the resource-bearing communities. Foster (2015) and Akashi (2016) contend that metabolic rift is the resultant imbalance between capital and nature to the extent that the former treats the latter as an infinite factor of production. In Africa, the proliferation of Multinational extractive companies meant that the quest for profit relegates the nature and environment to the background. This explains the pollution arising from spillage of extractive poisonous residues across the continent. From Ghana to Nigeria to Zambia, to the DRC and even South Africa and the rest of the continent, the desecration of nature by capital is massive. The Ogoni oil spillage in Nigeria and the celebrated legal tussle between Konkola Copper Mines and its parent company, Vedanta Resources on account of pollution of the Kafue River bring this into perspective.

Capitalism also succeeded in creating a false sense of development in the continent. This comes with the establishment of new urban centres around mining areas. It is apposite to state that these urban centres lack the necessary ambience of urbanity. They are just locations of abode for modern-day peasants close to enough to the mines and the rigs. The impacts of extraction include land degradation, desertification, erosion, food insecurity, unplanned and uncoordinated spatial extension and urbanization, resource conflicts, health hazards, extirpation of rare species of flora and fauna and a total inability of land to replenish and regenerate itself and a complete loss of biodiversity. In the Niger Delta region of Nigeria, due to long years of oil exploitation and gas flaring, the region has been described as an ecological wasteland and wreck (Kafada, 2012; Tyokumbur, 2014). Pollution from oil spills in that region is responsible for the decline of fish stocks (Osuagwu and Olaifa 2018). In Zambia, due to lead mining, the town of Kabwe in the Copperbelt Region has been deemed the most toxic town in the world. The mass lead poisoning of the town has been found to have damaged the brains and other organs of many generations of children (Carrington 2017).

Capitalism as the harbinger of the metabolic rift in Africa is not about to abate. Rather than abating, the structures of capitalism are webbing. This is to the extent that in the present century, African countries are growing more powerless and acquiescent to capitalist ethos. The African situation is better captured with the soliciting for 'investors' who are given liberal concessions and conditions to exploit resources from the continent. The import of this is that the more the number of 'investors' African countries can attract, the higher what accrues to the comprador bourgeoisie. In essence, this leads to a higher degradation of the environment and a fiercer metabolic rift between capital and nature on the continent.

Mediating the Metabolic Rift: Need for the Abolition of Private Property in Africa's Extractive Industry

How does Africa mediate the metabolic rift between capital and nature? The historical impacts of colonialism as seen through the exploitation of natural resources with countries of the continent becoming members of and signatories to international instruments to solve ecological problems. This is rather part of what Foster et al. (2011) referred to as the managerial approach to the global ecological crisis. It is also apposite to state that the ecological crisis in Africa has not responded to the managerial approach because of the intensification of the capitalist exploitation of nature and its resources on the continent. What is Africa's antidote to capitalism and its environmental carnage?

The metabolic rift raging in Africa requires revolutionary interventions. The goal of Eco-Marxism is to undo the structures that facilitate capitalist exploitation of the continent. According to Carter-Roberts (2019), there is a need to reconsider the ideas surrounding use value and exchange value as it applies to Africa. This is at the heart of mediating the metabolic rift in the continent. The import of this is to undo private property as the activities of transnational and local mining companies are to the privatization of the commons. The evaluation of the ecological cost resource of exploration should come before profit, which is a reversal of the logic of capitalism. Hence, mediating the metabolic rift is a revolution against capitalism, its structures and promoters on the continent.

Mediating the metabolic rift requires some revolutionary interventions that seek to ensure that African resources are used for the development without constituting injury to nature and the environment. A cardinal aspect of these interventions is the nationalization of the extractive sector of African economies. This means the abolition of private property as African countries have either sold or concessioned the resource-bearing communities to the Multinational and local extractive companies. In oil-producing countries, for example, oil wells have been allocated to Multinational Oil Corporations such as Shell, Chevron, Total, Agip, etc. The non-oil resources across the continent are also been led by these companies. Hence, the nationalization of natural resource exploration will reverse the short-term orientation of capitalism that focuses on profit to the detriment of the environment. The nationalization will come as the second wave of nationalization in Africa as it might be argued that past efforts at nationalization did not work, ultimately leading to liberalization.

Historically, social, economic and political dynamics of the world has come in phases. This historical fact is buttressed in the work of Huntington (1993), describing the late-twentieth-century global acceptance of democratization as the "Third Wave" of the phenomenon. Before then, the first and second waves occurred in from 1828 to 1926 and 1943 to 1962, respectively. Klein (2015) also used the idea of waves to suggest solutions to capitalism's mindlessness that is causing global warming. For her, waves of popular movements in the history of the world have achieved social change. She cited examples of social movements against the slave trade, racial discrimination in the United States and the more recent Arab Spring. Africa's first wave of nationalization was the years between the years following independence to the rise of the neoliberalism from the 1980s to 1990s. For example, Zambia nationalized its copper production between 1969 and 2000. In Southern Africa, Angola, Mozambique and Tanzania also nationalized several sectors of their economies (Kongwa 1990). Other countries that adopted the policy included Ghana, Guinea, Zaïre (The DRC), Sierra Leone, Morocco and Togo among others (Aleksandrovskaia et al. 1976).

Another criticism of the that might be levelled against the nationalization of the extractive industries of African countries is that in a number of African countries such as Benin, Burkina Faso, Cape Verde, Gambia,

Guinea Bissau, Mali, Nigeria and Senegal among others the land belongs to the state, including resource-rich ones. Hence, the land has already been nationalized (United Nations Economic Commission for Africa 2011; Chouquer 2011). State ownership of land is not nationalization because officially there is no nationalization policy operational and African states still allocate lands to Multinational and local capitalists to exploit resources. Once the allocation is done, these businesses treat the allocated lands as private property. The new nationalization policy will retrieve all lands for the commonwealth and the exploration of resources will be done without the aggressive search for profit by capitalism which depletes resources and degrades nature and the environment in the continent.

As a revolutionary act, the nationalization of resource exploration in Africa is a first step in the mediation of the metabolic rift in Africa. For African countries to be able to do this, there is also a need to come up with policies that revert the land to the people. The hitherto alienation of the people from the land encourage irresponsible governance by comprador-led political class across the continent. A people's revolution will ensure that the second wave of nationalization in the continent does not go the way of the previous experience. The African political class needs to be swept off by the people to pave way for the nationalization process. The environmental carnage of capitalism on the continent can then be checked as resources are owned by the people and their exploration will be for the people instead of the reality of absentee ownership that siphons African surplus to the metropoles across the world.

Conclusion

Africa has been subjected to resource-rape and ecological crisis by colonial and neocolonial forces over several centuries. It is a rich continent that houses the world's most impoverished people whose resources have been used to feed development elsewhere around the world. Eco-Marxism is a struggle against this ugly reality to undo the structures that prioritise profit over ecological ambience. The entrenchment of capitalist values and structures have received tremendous support from the comprador bourgeoisie which is used as the openings for Western economist interests in the continent. Being members of the political class, comprador bourgeoisie seeks to protect its interests leading the reinforcement of capitalist structures, which in turn have grave environmental effects on the people, their ways of life and livelihoods.

The metabolic rift arising from the foregoing accounts for the ecological events since the twentieth century. The consolidation of capitalism on a global scale has come to affirm the warnings of Marx of the ecological perils of capitalism. Today, ecological crises such as drought, rainfall variability, flooding and coastal inundation, resources scarcity and conflicts, global warming and climate change have come to assert the ecological contradictions of capitalism. Hence, for Africa, the nationalization of natural resource exploration will ensure that natural resources belong to the people and its exploration are for their benefit. This will eliminate the mindlessness with which Multinational Corporations and local mining companies pursue profit to the detriment of nature. It will also serve to arrest power from the comprador-dominated political class which through its privileged position facilitate resource exploitation for pecuniary gains and profits for their metropolitan masters.

References

Adeyemo, B. A. (2019). Colonial transport system in Africa: Motives, challenges and impact. *African Journal of History and Archaeology, 4*(1), 14–26.

Akashi, H. (2016). The elasticity of capital and ecological crisis. *Marx-Engels Jahrbuch, 2015*(1), 45–58.

Ake, C. (1976, March). Explanatory notes on the political economy of Africa. *The Journal of Modern African Studies, 14*(1), 1–23.

Aleksandrovskaia, L., Matsenko, I., & Schultz, A. (1976). Experience and problems of nationalization in African countries. *International Journal of Politics, 6*(4), 66–86.

Anifowose, R. (2011). *Violence and politics in Nigeria: The Tiv, Yoruba and Niger Delta Experiences*. Lagos: Sam Ironausi Publishers

Ayoade, J. (2010). Nigeria: Positive pessimism and negative optimism. *Valedictory Lecture, Faculty of the Social Sciences, University of Ibadan, Nigeria, September, 17*.

Badgley, C. (2014, May 19). West Africa oil boom overlooks tattered environmental safety net. *The Centre for Public Integrity*. Retrieved from https://publicintegrity.org/accountability/west-africa-oil-boom-overlooks-tattered-environmental-safety-net/. Accessed May 14, 2019.

Carrington, D. (2017, May 28). The world's most toxic town: The terrible legacy of Zambia's lead mines. *The Guardian: Environment-Pollution*. Retrieved from https://www.theguardian.com/environment/2017/may/28/the-worlds-most-toxic-town-the-terrible-legacy-of-zambias-lead-mines. Accessed June 16, 2019.

Carter-Roberts, A. (2019, February 4). *A critical assessment of Eco-Marxism: A Ghanaian case study*. Retrieved from https://www.e-ir.info/2019/02/04/a-critical-assessment-of-eco-marxism-a-ghanaian-case-study/. Accessed June 18, 2019.

Chouquer, G. (2011). Aspects and characteristics of State-owned land in West Africa. Online Knowledge Base: Natural Resources Governance around the World. Retrieved from https://www.agter.org/bdf/en/pages/page-10.html. Accessed June 21, 2019.

Chuks-Ezike, C. (2018). Environmental crime liability of the Nigerian government in its oil pollution menace. *Environmental Risk Assessment and Remediation*, *2*(2), 1–7.

Deleage, J. P. (1989). Eco-Marxist critique of Political economy. *Capitalism Nature Socialism, 1*(3), 15–31.

Elbra, A. (2017). A history of Gold mining in South Africa, Ghana and Tanzania. In *Governing African gold mining* (pp. 67–103). London: Palgrave Macmillan.

Ekanade, O. V. (2014). The dynamics of forced neoliberalism in Nigeria since the 1980s. *Journal of Retracing Africa, 1*(1), 1–24.

Emmanuel, A. Y., Jerry, C. S., & Dzigbodi, D. A. (2018). Review of environmental and health impacts of mining in Ghana. *Journal of Health and Pollution*, *8*(17), 43–52.

Foster, J. B., Clark, B., & York, R. (2011). *The Ecological Rift: Capitalism's War on the Earth*. NYU Press.

Foster, J. B. (2015). Marxism and ecology: Common fonts of a great Ttransition. *Monthly Review, 67*(7), 1–13.

Friends of the Earth International (2019, May 17). A journey through the oil spills of Ogoniland. *News*. Retrieved from https://www.foei.org/news/oil-spills-ogoniland-nigeria-shell [Accessed May 13, 2019]

Fuwape, J. A. (2003). *The impacts of forest industries and wood utilization on the environment*. Paper submitted to the XII World Forestry Congress 2003, Quebec City, Canada. Retrieved from http://www.fao.org/3/XII/0122-A2.htm#P28_106. Accessed August 4, 2019.

Gayle, J. (2015, August 1). I drank the water and ate the fish. We all did. The acid has damaged me permanently. *The Guardian: Global Development*.

Retrieved from https://www.theguardian.com/global-development/2015/aug/01/zambia-vedanta-pollution-village-copper-mine. Accessed June 18, 2019.

Global Witness (2015, June). *Exporting impunity: How Congo's rainforest is illegally logged for international markets*. London: Global witness Limited.

Hardin, G. (1968). The tragedy of the commons. *Science*, *162*(3859), 1243–1248.

Havard Law School International Human Rights Clinic. (2016). *The cost of Gold: Environmental, health and human rights consequences of Gold mining in South Africa's West and Central Rand*. Retrieved from https://hrp.law.harvard.edu/wp-content/uploads/2016/11/The-Cost-of-Gold-Full-Report-Final.pdf. Accessed June 14, 2018.

Hilson, G., & Haselip, J. (2004). The environmental and socioeconomic performance of multinational mining companies in the developing world economy. *Minerals & Energy-Raw Materials Report*, *19*(3), 25-47.

Huntington, S. P. (1993). *The third wave: Democratization in the late twentieth century* (Vol. 4). University of Oklahoma Press.

Jakobsson, L. S. (2019, May 6). *Copper With A Cost-Human rights and environmental risks in the mineral supply chains of ICT: A case study from Zambia*. (Report No. 94). Swedwatch. Retrieved from https://swedwatch.org/wp-content/uploads/2019/05/94_Zambia_190429_enkelsidor.pdf. Accessed June 14, 2019.

Kadafa, A. A. (2012). Environmental impacts of oil exploration and exploitation in the Niger Delta of Nigeria. *Global Journal of Science Frontier Research Environment & Earth Sciences*, *12*(3), 19–28.

Klein, N. (2015). *This changes everything: Capitalism vs. the climate*. Simon and Schuster.

Kongwa, S. (1990). Nationalization: Lessons from Southern Africa. *Africa Insight*, *20*(3), 189–193.

Legge, L. E. L. & Zhibo, L. (2018). The environmental and social impacts of oil exploration and production on Melut basin of South Sudan. *International Journal of Scientific and Research Publications*, *8*(10), 197–209.

Lievens, M. (2010). Towards an Eco-Marxism. *Radical Philosophy Review*, *13*(1), 1–17.

Limpitlaw, D. (2011). Nationalization and mining: Lessons from Zambia. *Journal of the Southern African Institute of Mining and Metallurgy*, *111*(10), 737–737.

Lungu, J. (2008). Copper mining agreements in Zambia: renegotiation or law reform? *Review of African Political Economy*, *35*(117), 403–415.

Mazrui, A. A. (2002). Nkrumahism and the triple heritage in the Shadow of globalization. *Draft Lecture, Mar*.

Mbendi. (2018). *Africa: Gold Mining*. Retrieved from https://mbendi.co.za/indy/ming/mingmrau.htm. Accessed June 9, 2019.

Mining Council South Africa (2019). Brief history of Gold mining in South Africa. *Mining For Schools*. Retrieved from https://www.miningforschools.co.za/lets-explore/gold/brief-history-of-gold-mining-in-sa. Accessed August 13, 2019.

Mwitwa, J., German, L., Muimba-Kankolongo, A., & Puntodewo, A. (2012). Governance and sustainability challenges in landscapes shaped by mining: Mining-forestry linkages and impacts in the Copper Belt of Zambia and the DR Congo. *Forest Policy and Economics*, *25*, 19-30.

Nanok, J. K., & Onyango, C. O. (2017). A socio-economic and environmental analysis of the EFFECTS of oil exploration on the local community in Lokichar, Turkana County, Kenya. *International Journal of Management, Economics and Social Sciences*, 6(3), 144–156

Ndlovu-Gatsheni, S. J. (2013). *Coloniality of power in postcolonial Africa*. African Books Collective.

Nix, S. (2019, March 21). Maps of the world's forests: World forest cover maps and natural tree ranges. *ThoughtCo., Animal and Nature*. Retrieved from https://thoughtco.com/maps-of-the-worlds-forests-1343036. Accessed August 4, 2019.

Njoh, A. J. & Akiwumi, F. (2012). Colonial legacies, land policies and the millennium development goals: Lessons from Cameroon and Sierra Leone. *Habitat International*, *36*, 210–218.

Ntuli, M. (2018, May 24). *Eco-marxism and deforestation*. Pambazuka News-Land and Environment. Retrieved from https://www.pambazuka.org/land-environment/eco-marxism-and-deforestation. Accessed March 6, 2019.

Odukoya, A. O. (2018). Settler and non-settler colonialism in Africa. In S. O. Oloruntoba, & T. Falola (Eds.), *The Palgrave handbook of African politics, governance and development* (pp. 173–186). New York: Palgrave Macmillan.

Ojakorotu, V., & Olajide, B. (2019). Ubuntu and nature: Towards reversing resource curse in Africa. *Ubuntu: Journal of Conflict and Social Transformation*. Special Issue September 2019, 25–46.

Onimode, B. (1988). *A political economy of the African crisis*. London, NJ: Zed Books with the Institute for African Alternatives.

Onimode, B. (1978, December). Imperialism and multinational corporations: A case study of Nigeria. *Journal of Black Studies*, *9*(2), 207–232

Osaghae, E. E. (1998). *Nigeria since independence: Crippled Giant*. London: Hurst & Company.

Oshin, O. (1988). Developing infrastructure of exploitation: The example of colonial transport on the Bauchi Tin Fields, 1902–1914. *Transafrican Journal of History*, *17*, 123–138.

Osuagwu, E. S., & Olaifa, E. (2018). Effects of oil spills on fish production in the Niger Delta. *PloS one*, *13*(10).

Research and Markets (2019, April). *Africa oil and gas sector Report 2019/2020*. Retrieved from https://www.researchandmarkets.com/reports/4771797/africa-oil-and-gas-sector-report-20192020?utm_source=BW&utm_medium=PressRelease&utm_code=lfl9vn&utm_campaign=1248653+-+Africa%27s+Oil+%26+Gas+Market+2019%2f2020&utm_exec=joca220prd. Accessed May 13, 2019.

Rodney, W. (1973). *How Europe underdeveloped Africa*. Dar es Salaam: Tanzanian Publishing House.

Saito, K. (2017). Marx in the anthropocene: Value, metabolic rift, and the non-cartesian dualism. *Zeitschrift für kritische Sozialtheorie und Philosophie*, *4*(1–2), 276–295.

Samndong, R. A., & Nhantumbo, I. (2015). *Natural resources governance in the Democratic Republic of Congo Breaking sector walls for sustainable land use investments*. International Institute for Environment and Development, Country Report February 2015. Retrieved from https://pubs.iied.org/pdfs/13578IIED.pdf. Accessed August 4, 2019.

Shivji, I. G. (2003, October 29–31). *The rise, the fall, and the insurrection of nationalism in Africa*. Address to the CODESRIA East African Regional Conference held in Addis Ababa, Ethiopia. Retrieved from http://ccs.ukzn.ac.za/files/shivji.pdf. Accessed June 6, 2018.

Shivji, I. G. (1973). Capitalism unlimited: Public corporations in partnership with multinational corporations. *Africa Review*, 3(3), 359–381

Statista (2020). Forest area worldwide in 2005, 2010 and 2015, by continent (in million hectares). *Statista: Agriculture-Forestry*. Retrieved from https://www.statista.com/statistics/264665/world-forest-area-by-continent/. Accessed August 4, 2019.

The Editors of Encyclopaedia Britannica. (2014, January 6). Copperbelt. *Encyclopedia Britannica*. Retrieved from https://www.britannica.com/place/Copperbelt-region-Africa. Accessed June 13, 2019.

Tyokumbur, E. T. (2014). Review of ecological effects of oil exploration in the Niger-Delta, Nigeria. *International Journal of Agricultural Sciences and Natural Resources, 1*(4), 76–80.

Udofia, O. E. (1984, March). Imperialism in Africa: A case of multinational corporations. *Journal of Black Studies, 14*(3), 353–368.

United Nations. Economic Commission for Africa. (2011). Land policy in Africa: West Africa regional assessment.

Vidal, D. (2019, April 10). Zambians can pursue mining pollution claim in English courts. *The Guardian: Law*. Retrieved from https://www.theguardian.com/law/2019/apr/10/zambians-can-pursue-mining-pollution-claim-in-english-courts. Accessed June 18, 2019.

CHAPTER 6

Theoretical Postulation of National Integration and the Roles of Political Parties: A Reflection on African and Asian Countries

Nelson Goldpin Obah-Akpowoghaha and *Victor Ojakorotu*

Introduction

It has been known that most nation-states in Asia and Africa had been under colonial subjugation for years before leaping into freedom. At the onset of the post-independence years, these countries were tied with vast array of problems which need to be tackled and among one of them which needs to be solved at the outset was the problem of national integration. These countries also inherited from the colonial rule certain features of administrative and legal system, forms of government and fixed territory, which help in their efforts to build or mar their state and nation (Haokip, 2011: 228).

N. G. Obah-Akpowoghaha (✉)
School of Arts and Sciences, Division of Humanities and Social Sciences, University of The Gambia, Gambia, Gambia

V. Ojakorotu
Department of Politics and International Relations, North West University, Mafikeng, South Africa

K. J. Ani et al. (eds.), *Political Economy of Resource, Human Security and Environmental Conflicts in Africa*,
https://doi.org/10.1007/978-981-16-2036-2_6

The havoc of colonization upon African and Asian countries led to the proliferation of democratic ideals as recipe for national development. Concepts like free market economy, political participation, periodic elections and so on have been advocated in this regard. And political parties have been seen as vehicle to deepen these ideals, and studies that were produced after post-colonial era focused on political parties and democracy without much interest in the role of national integration vis-à-vis political parties in African and Asian states. While many articles on democratic theories have been dedicated to resolving diverse crises developing countries are facing especially in Africa and Asia (Udofia, 1981; Schlesinger,1984; Wiseman, 1990; Joseph, 1991; Przeworski & Limongi, 1997; Schedler, 1998 cited in Obah-Akpowoghaha, 2013), still, the problem of national integration is yet to be tame. There are proportional cases of civil war, communal clashes, farmers and herdsmen clashes, kidnapping, destruction of state's properties, uncontrollable gender inequality, the raise of ethnic militias and insurgencies under democratic governance (Ime et al., 2007; Anifowose, 1998; Aziza et al., 2010; Haokip, 2011). However, the essence of this piece is to interrogate national integration theories and political parties as a base to solve issues in African and Asian countries. Compatibilities of these theories will be assessed along with political occurrences in Africa and Asia in order to proffer objective answers, thoughts or theories that will create a path for national integration in these two continents. This piece reflects on the works of Claude Ake; Amitai Etzioni; Coleman and Rosberg; Huntington; Osei-Kwame; Karl Deutsch; and other theorists that serve as mythological approaches in this investigation.

The aforementioned issues upon colonization have created mechanistic states in Africa and Asia, and attempt to manage issues bedevilling modern states in these two continents after colonial extinction has led to series of researches and policies leading to programmes, state creation and in general, integrative mechanisms. The quest for unitary system, federalism, quota system, federal character, unity schools, power rotation, bicameral legislature, periodic elections, among others have been incorporated to intensify national integration in African and Asian countries. While these mechanisms have relatively strengthened national cohesions in some states, yet the quest for national integration in these continents has dominated the polity due to the act of political violence; youths unrest, the rise of ethnic militias and militancy, insurgencies, terrorism, farmer and herdsmen clashes, communal clashes, that be fell communities in Africa (Bandyopadhyay & Green, 2009; Obah-Akpowoghaha, 2018). However, political parties as an agent of national integration through their functions and programmes have revealed that political parties can tame and mitigate crisis bedevilling heterogeneous states especially those that emerged after decades of colonization (Etzioni, 1962; 1963). The functional role of national integration, interest articulation and aggregation performed by political parties serve as unifying mechanisms for resolving sharp ethnic groups within a country. The configurations of modern political parties entail selections, scientific elections and image representations of all groups that exist within a country. That is, party programmes, aspirations, logos, image, ideology and so on should represent all groups that exist within the country as against parochial or primordial interests. A clear-cut ideology that promotes majority interests and makes provision for the minority is part and parcel of the ideals of modern political parties which intensify national integration.

The quest for national integration is a multidimensional goal that political leaders and societal elites strive to attain, and good leadership in any country arises from elites' compromise towards building national interest. In other words, national development and integration are functional roles of every citizen not just political parties and its elites. Other elite aside political parties are constitutionally mandated to vote as well as educate other citizens and show huge interest in contributing to national issues (Norris, 2005; Obah-Akpowoghaha, 2018). Consequently, series of literature have revealed that while attempt has been made by political parties in Africa and Asia in building viable states and attracting investors for economic and social development, still, the rate of political violence and the drive for secession have risen in recent times in most African and Asian countries (Ojakorotu, 2015; Ikelegbe, 2014). Studies have identified these issues from different perspectives such as democracy and political parties (Jinadu, 2014; Lijphart, 1977) and this current paper will evaluate it from the dimension of theoretical postulation of national integration and political parties in Africa and Asia. The main thrust of the work is to examine the problems of national integration and efforts to put together the different theories of national integration by some countries in Africa and Asia.

Statement of Problem

With the gaining of independence by countries of Asia and Africa during the middle of the twentieth century, the task of nation-building has been left with these countries. The first and foremost problem encountered by them was the issue of integrating the vast chunk of people who had been loosely administered with varying degrees by the colonial powers. In large and multinational nation-states, the problem of integrating people inhabiting different regions with varied language, religion, culture and ethnic communities, the task is an arduous one. As Leonard Binder, while analysing the crisis of political development in new nation-states, pointed out: "the greatest task facing the new nation will be to build a nation out of a collection of tribes or of isolated communities" (Binder 1971: 46 cited in Haokip, 2011). Scholarly works after World War II and early post-colonial systems have been dedicated to policies of political integration especially re-habitation and reconstruction, yet the issues of national integration have resurfaced in several national discourse in the international politics and developmental studies—hence this study.

Research Methodology

This research is designed to investigate theories of national integration sometimes called political integration. The primary source of data upon this research was derived from online scholarly publications that extensively discussed the subject matter. This work is premised on cases in Asian and African countries and attempts to put together the different theories of national integration. And selections were based on purposive sampling procedures, although the research perception was motivated by pluralistic tendencies of countries mainly created by external forces. The basis of data analysis is expounded on deduction and content analysis in relation to thematic pattern. National or political integration theories serve as basis for illustration.

Methodological and Theoretical Considerations

It has been noted that the thrust of political integration lies in the existence of political culture. In a similar notation, Sidney Verba (1965: 513 cited in Haokip, 2011) identified patterns of scientific beliefs, demonstration of symbols and values orientations which describe the nature of political action in a given environment. He revealed that the subject of beliefs in social or behavioural sciences is not all crucial to the discourse of political culture; but rather the area that has impactful mechanisms on politics in an important way. In another discourse, it has been stress that the theories or models of political integration by most scholarly theses have been argued on cultural homogeneity on the grounds of homogeneous political culture. And which has been often termed as a precondition for political or national integration and leading to political cohesion and stability, particularly in emergent democracies (Lijphart 1971: 4–5 cited in Haokip, 2011). Also, the place or interplay of shared cultural values and norms does not impact strategically or serves as a main mechanism for unification but rather a notable variable that aids the system before the entire system can be deepened for the project of integration. Similarly, Claude Ake advises on the permutation and the inputs of each entity or member of the political system to cede their loyalty to the centre and build the foundation of sincerity (trust) to one another. He further stressed that a society without the foundation of trust among members of sovereign state in its dealings and relations "there can be no stable expectations about the modes of acquisition and exercise of political power, no coherence and predictability in political life" (Ake 1967: 487). In other words, the existence of diverse cultural entities in a plural state is overwhelmingly dissimilar that an interaction with one another is cumbersome. Hence, the quest for integration in the context of common interest, trust and the need of national identity will be a waste of efforts. Corroborating the above analyses, Karl Deutsch noted that the elementary stage of political integration falls within the purview of widening and increasing social communication system. The enhancement of the communicative instrument of the emerging states emanates from social mobilization mechanisms. That is, an expectation whereby major collections of old mode of interactions, demand and supply, and psychological attachment progressively withered away or segmented, and while entities or individual(s) strive to embrace new patterns of socialization and behaviour that are derived from the centre (Deutsch 1961). Most Asian and African countries experienced difficulties arising from the act of social mobilisation that captured enormous primordial attachment of existing bodies which most times generate tensions and political upheaval.

National Integration and Brief Reflection on Nigeria: Ethiopia; and South Africa

Nigeria is a sovereign state that existed within West African region that came to be as in 1960 after subsequent battle for independence by the locals popularly called nationalists. This event was informed by series of injustices received by original inhabitants of the present-day Nigeria from the colonial master, the British administrators. Prior to the advent of colonial rule, the land mass (Nigeria) was ruled by kings, queens and princes, and the system of administrations fell on certain nobles and diviners. Political stability and cohesion rest upon absolute loyalty to the nobles (Emirs or Kings or Queens) which normally intensified through the genuineness of the nobles towards the people. As in 1906, a colony has been built and the inhabitants have been subjugated to foreign norms and culture indirectly. In 1914, proper governance that depicts the system of the colonial master was made visible before the people, and the incorporation of the Northern entities and the Southern entities known as protectorates emerged. This was done out of British interest and scramble in line with the 1885/1886 Berlin Conference as mechanism to acquire more territories in the world. Various systems of government introduced by the colonial masters disfavoured the inhabitants of the present-day Nigeria from 1906 to 1960.

The voting systems were limited and the original inhabitants were seen as second fellow and strangers in their fatherland. This arouses the interests of those that were privileged to experience Western culture and values (education) to liberate themselves and their territories from the stronghold of colonial masters. Education was a force and mechanism that aided the struggle for self-determination coupled with United Nations policy of decolonization. At the period of Lyttleton constitutional development of 1954 and its emergence, there was relative integration among the elites on the course of independence and the occupation of the land by the true inhabitants. By this period, the inhabitants of the land mass (Nigeria) have realized the importance of governance and the need to institutionalize political parties. But at the period of 1960 to 1966, the political parties that existed were formed along ethnic lines, and the foremost nationalists rally around their ethnic fraternity as a mechanism of dominion. Fear of dominion among minority nationalities heralded the Nigerian political system and the need for national integration was out of place. The system was bedevilled with animosity propelled with hate speeches and electoral fraud which motivated the Nigerian military to overthrown the then democratic elected government in 1966. Out of this dilemma, the system of ethno-religiosity and ethnic attachment reign in the political climate which made the then military to introduce unitary system of government as an integrative mechanism to tame disintegration viruses against the Nigerian state. The system of federalism then gives much power to the existing regions and the possibility of successful secession was not far fetched because of the hatred among ethnic nationalities. As in 1967, the Nigerian military that came as messiah to salvage the political system further deepened primordial interests and hatred among Nigerians which culminated in civil war of three years.

This phenomenon was also present in the second republic as in 1979/1983, a period that ushered economic possibility of development due to enormous wealth brought about by the sale of crude oil as a result of the high price of the product. A notable criticism in this era happened to be the issue of corruption and ethno-regional politics. The political parties that existed during the first republic whose roots come from ethnic associations still existed in the second republic, and there were changes of nomenclature. The Northern People Congress took the title of the National Party of Nigeria though get few support from the eastern part of Nigeria. The Action Group gave birth to United Party of Nigeria (UPN) headed by Chief Awolowo, and the Nigerian People's Party an offshoot of NCNC which was headed by Dr. Nnamdi Azikiwe. The NPP and the NPC formed a coalition government, but there were a lot of conflicts and disagreements among the politicians leading to weak government. Issues that beset the second republic were enormous and it weakens the need for political integration. To start with the menace of corrupt leaders that attracted international communities tilted the development of the country into state of diminishing return. Among the allegation that was levelled upon politicians are as follows: the cement scandal of the beginning of 1970s; the Festival of African Culture (FESTAC) in Lagos; Federal Housing Scheme; the Federal Mortgage Bank; Central Bank of Nigeria; National Youth Service Corps; the Nigerian Supply Company; the Nigerian External Telecommunication; and the construction of a new federal capital territory, Abuja. Eventually, all governmental institutions were involved in one form of criminal allegation or the other. A notable politician like Umaru Dikko was alleged in the act of corruption. Umaru Dikko was involved in series of scandals such as issuance of licenses to import rice and other. These and among others threatened national integration which later invited the military into active party politics after the notable electoral fraud levelled against NPN.

Another bitter scenario that nearly collapsed the Nigerian state was the Annulment of the presidential election of 1993 that the acclaimed winner was not declared in the person of Chief M.K.O Abiola. The third republic was smashed by the then ruling dictator, Major General Ibrahim Badamasi Babangida (IBB) and in the course of Chief M. K. O. Abiola seeking for restoration of his mandate, death visited him. His death was seen as conspiracy and deliberates against the Yoruba race in the country. The beating drums of secession (like Oduduwa State) and imaginable crises engulfed the political climate of the country which was worsened when Northern Military elites were alternating the leadership of the country among themselves. This was visible when the then military dictator Major General Sani Abacha floated political parties that adopted him as the sole candidate for another election after the extinction of the Social Democratic Party (SDP) and National Republican Convention (NRP). Prior to the emergence of Sani Abacha as the head of state in the country, the then SDP and NRC brought hope to the country. The SDP and NRC as political parties brought Nigerians into two umbrellas for proper political engagement and national re-engineering upon serious national discourse. These parties possess distinctive political issues (ideologies), that is, one to the left and the other to the right built on certain developmental agenda. But the then military dictator (IBB) has his plan against national interest that was unknown to most Nigerians. At the end of the whole process, IBB technically handed over power to another dictator (Sani Abacha) (through Ernest Shonekan interim government) who constituted baseless political parties that adopted him. Within this political intrigues and military conspiracy against Nigerians, Major General Sani Abacha died along the process and another version and set of political parties came to be through the leadership of Abdulsami Abubakar. Somehow there were three major political parties that existed and possess the strength to integrate Nigerians except the challenge of Alliance for Democracy that was little bit engrossed with Yorubas that seems to be regional or ethnic party. The victory of a Yorubaman in the election brought a sense of togetherness and forgiveness upon the annulment of June 12, 1993 presidential election in the country. The Fourth Republic signalled a lot of prospects and hopes to Nigerians locally and internationally upon the removal of various sanctions against the country and couple with debt cancellation that was accrued from wasteful spending in the past.

Against this sensational hope for all and the fourth republic fell short of expectations of Nigerians. Most notable acrimony and events that characterized this republic were electoral fraud, bureaucratic and political corruption, and leadership failure in different levels. This creation diverted elites' interests from politics of national integration to politics of self-aggrandisement and hate speeches. This phenomenon has continued till date.

Again, recent activities in Nigerian party politics upon the winner takes it all have intensified the politics of bitterness and less inclusiveness which have nullified the beliefs that political party is a platform that unites individuals from diverse ethnic groups. This is because most of these parties lack internal party democracy, political ideology and that has led to loss of focus towards national integration in Nigeria's political system. Literature on party politics in Nigeria has argued that due to the aforementioned variables, intra-/inter-party activities have been driven by divisive politics like voting along ethnic lines, sponsoring of ethnic militias and politics of hate speech, politics of patronage, etc., which have caused big challenge for political parties and elites in the quest for national integration in the country (Ikelegbe, 2014; Pogoson 2014; ICIR 2016 cited in Obah-Akpowoghaha, 2018). Other entrenched factors that have been identified in literature within Nigerian party politics to be against national integration are elite's regional alliance and ethnic party politics. Other issues that have threatened national integration are: the rise of ethnic militias; militancy; regional foot soldiers; unemployment rate; and inflation.

The quest for national integration in modern-day Ethiopia which was formally known as Abyssinian should be seen as an easy task and free of colonial entrapment unlike Nigeria and South Africa whose activities have been directly or indirectly manipulated by former colonial masters. In line with this thought, Ethiopia happened to have stayed aloof from direct world powers during the reign of economic and political subjugation, that is, the 1884/1885 Berlin Conference leading to scramble for African countries. Upon its strategic strength in the continent, studies have shown that Ethiopia still faces the problem of national integration that a lot of leaders tend to seek for foreign strength through acquisition of weapons and invitation of external powers to curb and subdue internal opponents. This was evidently demonstrated by Emperor Menelik II when he sent a circular letter to European power asserting his allegiance in 1891 and upon his quest and ambition to acquire more territories. Some of the challenges that befell modern-day Ethiopia in the past can be seen from her pluralistic nature and migration, leading to the superiority of one ethnic group over the other (UNHCR, 2016; Gemtessa, 2014; Belay, 2013).

It is a known fact that South Africa harboured sharp and antagonistic groups and races which has served as a huge barrier to national integration in the past. Studies on the context of the South African people have shown that its policies and agenda on national cohesion past and present centre on people-oriented approach and de-emphasize state-centred approach with specific issue items like individual liberty from physical threat of any kind and functional environmental system devoid of mechanical hazard that upholds human dignity and standard of living (Landsberg, 2009; Mukwedeya, 2016).

South Africa has been anchored on social cohesion and nation-building which has been informed due to her historical background that has been premised on taming inequality and racism. Right from the inception of 1994 democratic process, various South African governments have initiated programmes and doctrines: like Delivery Agreement of Outcome 12; National Social Cohesion Summit; the Electoral Commission of South Africa; Electoral Act No. 73 of 1998; Kampala Document Human security approach integrated by Southern Africa Development (SADC); the Nelson Mandela and Botha peace pact of 1985 and among others (South Africa, n.d; Electoral Commission of South Africa National and Provincial Elections 22 April 2009) that were aimed at promoting social cohesion and national integration.

In a dialogue paper presented by Mukwedeya (2016), he identified issues facing African countries after independence. Countries like Tanzania, Kenya, South Africa and Namibia have experienced proportional challenges against the backdrop of nation-building. Laying claims on evidences in literature, the study revealed that there is disparity and uneven development vis-à-vis nation integration in the continent. It further asserted that inequality has threatened South African and Namibia bill for national integration. In taming these menaces, he identified that sense of belonging individual countries should be re-engineered and emphasized, "based on shared experiences of exclusion and marginalization that cut across ethnic and religious differences".

Theoretical Postulation

National integration is anchored on the building of a close interdependence between and among federating units of a state leading to loyalties to the national government and its agencies. Contemporary and classical literature on national integration has crystallized conditions necessary for sustaining and consolidating national integration. According to Leonard Binder, he observed the formation of cultural-ideological consensus of a very high degree of inclusiveness. Amital Etzioni identified the ability of the state to own, possess and control instrument of violence. For Carl Rosberg, Paden and Edward Soja, they maintain that elites and masses experience dichotomy, the gradual narrowing of the elite-mass gap that is entrenched in modern states, that is, the vertical plane (and reduction of cultural and regional tensions and discontinuities) and on the horizontal plane in the process of forging a homogenous territorial political community will to national integration. Myron Weiner built his analyses on the policies of assimilation and associations in favour of national identity, bringing culturally and socially discrete groups into a single territorial nationality that over-shadows or eliminates subordinate parochial loyalties (Deutsch 1957, 1964; Etzioni, 1962; Jacob & Teune, 1964; Weiner, 1965; Coleman & Rosberg, 1964; Hass, 1964 cited in Clark, 2000; Zolberg, 1967, cited in Peretomode, 1985). Consequently, the concept of national integration centres on elites' compromise in relation to the whole interest against the parts. The whole is more than the parts and it is the whole that gives meaning to the parts and the parts can only live and exist when the whole is functioning. In other words, the state is the massive group that exists in every society and all other groups such as political parties, mass media and pressure groups can only make meaningful impact when the whole is active. Scholars such as Authur F. Bentley and David Truman have identified the need for every group in a society to strive to build the whole as sustaining device that leads to the fulfilment of the existence of various parts (Varma, 2006). This notion from group theories seems to be incompatible with political institutions in Africa whereby state resources have been hijacked and used for primordial and personal interests (Ikelegbe, 2014; Ojakorotu, 2015; Obah-Akpowoghaha, 2018). However, this paper will attempt to reveal some cases of political institutions that have been engrossed with personal interest against Burk's conceptualization of political party.

Approaches to National Integration and State Strategies

In a study, Bandyopadhyay and Green (2009) identified the crises that post-colonial government faced after the departure of the colonial master. In a bill to solve these crises, countries tuned to certain integrative models towards ensuring peaceful coexistence in their domains. The change of nomenclature of countries' name buttressed this observation, for instance, Gold Coast to Ghana, Dahomey to Benin, Gilbert Islands to Kiribati, Abyssinia to Ethiopia and aside this, state creation, quota system, adoption of federal system, unitary system, federal character, zoning, multi-partism and so on were aimed to promote national integration. Other studies have as well indicated that these integrative mechanisms and policies fell short of expectations; some of these policies aggravated disunity and heavy threat to national integration. Scholars like (Alapiki, 2005; Obah-Akpowoghaha, 2018) have argued that these mechanisms or policies are ploy by some elites to consolidate their political and economic ascendency within the polity. The model of creating or caving state from state or provinces, zoning, federal character and quota, multi-partism by African leaders especially in Nigeria, Kenya, South Africa and Ethiopia are calculated mechanisms designed by them to strengthen their political reign. The integration crisis facing African states particularly Nigeria, South Africa and Ethiopia manifests in the minority question, ethnic politics, inequality, religious fundamentalism and conflicts. The entire social matrix in these countries has been motivated to focus on a self-centred elite interest leading to inter- and intra-community, inter- and intra-ethnic, and inter- and intra-religious strife.

Integration and Formation of States in Africa

Studies have revealed that colonial administrators were not concerned with inventing good leadership in uniting Africans but rather implanting cells of rancour among Africans. At the peak of their political scheme, the act of bringing sharp ethnic groups to form a country as route to extend neo-colonialism was purported and initiated. Prior to their final departure, there was the absence of the educated elites in formation of government and they decided to choose non-educated elites like the community chiefs and rulers who are not familiar with the natural resources in their domain. This nature of configuration set educated elites against community chiefs, and the bases, foundations of disunity and cord of national disintegration were engrafted in African politics. While the educated elites were conscious of this scheme, the consciousness of ethnic domination heralded African politics whose leadership was built on ethnicity and primordial interest. Formation of political parties was derived from ethnic associations and inclinations, and this among other crushed and reprimanded the need for national integration (Peretomode, 1985). At the zenith of ethnic politics, the military institutions considered it as a duty to salvage the society from ethnic driven leaders. Political institutions were put aside and coup d'état set the continent ablaze. This was another bad omen that diminished the progress and the quest for national integration in continent; the military deepened ethnic configuration and swayed the African continent into a pit of underdevelopment.

However, democratic advocacies and human right activists seen it as abnormal for the military to be involved in leadership. This quickens the military to hand over political leadership to civilians for active politics and leadership in Africa. But the politics of ethnicity and self-centredness were still much endowed in African leaders, and in the need to resolve this, policies and designs were formulated yet countries in Africa suffered from integration problem which led some countries to civil war and communal clashes.

Tenets of National Integrations and the African States

The basics of national integration have to be consciously incorporated by nation's builders and that entail integrating elites in each region, tribe, ethnic group and institutions. It is at this point of realization that formidable states and institutions come to fruition. But state formation in Africa at the eve of colonial extinction was premised on taking over leadership without anticipating what it entails. That is, most African leaders were tired of the white-man rule over them and their lands, and the clamour for self-determination and freedom overtook the political climate of the continent. Africans were relatively united in the course of independence against the colonial masters, but studies have unveiled that those that took the mantle of leadership abysmally failed in the act of governance in their various territories. This failure can be associated with lack of certain basic tenets of national integration that may be described as theories of national integration. Evidently in Nigeria, tribal sentiment and the fear of dominion were at its peak after the departure of the white men among the three major ethnics groups: the Igbo, Yorubas and Fulani/Hausas. And that politics of bitterness and hate speech defined the political scene of Nigerian politics which later attracted the military into politics and led the country into a colossal civil war, a heavy mark of national disintegration. And other African countries like DR Congo, Sudan, Angola, South Africa (majority Blacks and minority White) and Ethiopia also witnessed ethnic bitterness and hate speeches against each other in their territories leading to loss of lives and properties (Carbone, 2007; Peretomode, 1985). In these countries, there are still pockets of ethnic and communal violence that leadership ineptitude and corruption have exacerbated. National integration demands the act of sacrifice purported by the ruling elites to eliminate ethnic propagation towards building a national identity that caters for all. The act makes every elite to derive his or her aspiration from the national identity, an identity that empowers and gives directions for ethic fulfilment and self-attainment within the polity.

From the thesis of Geertz (1963 cited in Obah-Akpowoghaha, 2018), two general policy options that help a heterogeneous society in the bill for national integration include: the act of collapsing diverse and multi-ethnic groups into an agreed national cultural body that caters for the interest of all, a seemly construct of general will; the recognition of a general identity by all that gives chance for subunits or tribes to coexist in single state; and programmes or policies that ensure and guarantee unity among diverse people (in languages, traits, traditions, norms, culture and tales) that create a centre for coordination and supervision of existing regions or group in a federation. In a similar version from Deutsch (1966), he sees it from the perspective of nation-building that has similar connotations with national integration, an artificial creation by architecture that is set on certain model spearheaded by leadership, desires and the goal of the designer. In another construct, Emerson (1966) argued that nation-building arises when inhabitants of a place (citizens) pledge their full loyalty to sovereign state without having a primordial interest or double loyalty. In line with these thoughts, national integration in third world countries existed when segmented territories that are not self-sufficient were brought together mechanically to form a union; this union has to be negotiated and rebranded to suit the intents, desires and aspirations of the people after the departure of the white man. But the major hindrance to this (re)negotiation and rebranding policy option by post-colonial or independence states is that there exist asymmetric relations among states in the global politics that have skewed African states to dependency position. And whose decisions are primarily directed by economic and political policies of the North against the South such as the failed Structural Adjustment Programmes (SAP) (Obah-Akpowoghaha, 2018).

Within this atmosphere of international system, there is need for emergent states in Africa to reshape territories and have formidable fronts to deepen certain agreeable national culture that motivates the holistic development of groups towards a national identity. This act will set the stage for economic, sociocultural and political rejuvenation and development, making federating units viable. Existing institutions and the elites in each region need to negotiate for national symbols and codes such as national days, flags, national stadium, language, national airlines, national worship centre, national myths and so on, without giving priority to one group over the other.

Another point to note vividly is that national integration is affair of trouble states whether homogenous or heterogeneous. These identities can witness conflicts and regional political rivalries. The Rwandan genocide case and the incessant conflict in Sudan demonstrated the lack of religious, ethnic and racial affinity within the nation. Findings have revealed that states with similar origin and historical lineage also face intense disintegration tendencies. Whereas a remarkable example such as Cameroon existed, the pitfalls like Senegambia Confederation show the difficulties of bringing together French- and English-speaking countries (Dobbins et al., 2007).

National integration or nation-building has also been seen from the angle of institutionalization of democracy after mitigation of political upheaval in country by the arm-forces. The study that was carried out by James Dobbins as in 2003 in conjunction with RAND corporation perceived nation-building or integration in the aforementioned conceptualization. The study was built on the cases of Germany, Japan, Somalia, Haiti, Bosnia, Kosovo and Afghanistan which led to the invitation of the American military force to plant democracy as a balancing currency to bring about integration of every unit into national interest (Dobbins et al., 2007). The notion of external forces as mechanism to bring about national integration seems to be contradictory against other scholarly definitions of nation-building or integration especially countries that have experienced colonization. And the tenets of democracy attract multiparty system that gives unequal balance in a polity. In most African countries, the syndrome of winners take all has fuelled insecurity, the politics of bitterness and hatred (hate speeches). National integration or nation-building arises when state's apparatus and institutions work in conjunction with elites in different regions and professions in a sovereign state. Initiations and policies that emanate within the inhabitants of a trouble state, the need for economic, sociocultural, political and psycho-sociological gains and otherwise are some of goals that a troubled state aims to intensify in order national integration or nation-building. A country like Nigeria has large population, natural resources, military and the beauty of cultural diversity which are some of the striking elements that force the elites (successive governments) in the country to introduce integrative mechanisms such as establishment of Unity School, the National Youth Service Corp (NYSC), Quota system and federal character to foster national integration (Clark, 2000; Wallerstein, 1960). But studies have identified that federal character and quota system have deepened the mark of discrimination and ethnic marginalization in the country (Obah-Akpowoghaha, 2018). This result differs from countries that have adopted similar mechanisms in Western and European countries like regional or state creation, quota system and proportional representation. Like in United States, states or regions are acquired for economic and political domination.

The point of dichotomy stems from societal forces and sincerity of purpose among the elites and the initiators of the national agenda. In Africa, corruption has been domesticated in some institutions and the political will or scientific mechanisms to detect or put out such menace are low, which has crippled the course for nation-building. Resources meant to fulfil certain promises have been out-rightly embezzled and wasted in primordial and frivolous affairs. Unlike corruption in Western and European countries, there are scientific mechanisms that monitor and fish-out corrupt officers or citizens such as workable constitutions, strict observation of ethical conducts, the presence of CCTV, judicial and legislative independence, acquisition of states or regions (for economic and political expansion), and so on. This orientation is different from the practice in African countries that unethical practice is very pervasive and corrosive to the system (Cheteni & Shindika, 2017; Mahmood, 2008).

The Asian Case: Malaysia

Malaysia is a plural state with the existence of sharp ethnic groups and multi-religions that rested in Southeast Asia. As a multicultural nation, the country has faced diverse issues of national integration which entails racial configuration. Although studies have been conducted in the past in respect of the subject matter in the country as in 1993 and 2007 that suggested the path of policy options (Aziza et al., 2010). Consequently, policy initiated by the government to intensify integration was misinterpreted by the inhabitants due to the number of quotas given to the Malays against the Indians and Chinese that were relatively higher in terms of schooling (Lee, 2004; Pong 1993 cited Azizi et al., 2010).

In a study, Aziza et al. (2010) identified certain influx of immigrants into the land of Malaysia formally called Malaya from another Asian axis. The study was built on descriptive and inferential statistics and explained through integrative model. The study revealed integration was feasible at the third level showing a lower score within the Chinese groups among the domains, while the Malays got the highest score in the cognitive domain. And affective domain goes to the Indians in its highest form, and it is further noted that upon these indications still there is need for improvement.

Consequently, the study adopted three basic ideas as a theoretical framework: integration constructs; bloom's individual development domains; and levels of integration. The cardinal constructs that buttressed the analyses were social distance, ethnocentrism and national identity. These constructs were for measuring elements of integration which referred to peaceful living, integration being committed to national identity as well as being loyal to the nation. From the study, it was revealed that Malaysia from under British administration for many years and in order for them to extend their colonial rule. There was need for the policy of divide and rule that led to the agenda of free immigrations without strict policies. This was as a result of mining areas and the development of rubber estates that attracted the Sikhs that serve as policemen and take care of security—Indians to serve as clerical, technical staff and the need for road building and laying railway lines (Zulhilmi & Rohani, 2003 cited in Aziza et al., 2010). The study further noted that British occupation for so many years led to sharp cultural divide in terms of localization of residence; career and education among the inhabitants, the Malays,

Chinese and Indians (Zainal, 1986 cited in Aziza et al., 2010); and interactions mainly happen in the offices, workplace and the market places which intensified attitudes of prejudice and strengthened ethnic identities leading to a weak social relation (Mahli, 1988; Azmah, 2001 cited in Aziza et al., 2010). But above all the situations were not ignored due to the anticipated political upheaval; rather, there was need for coexistence among them (Zahid, 1997 cited in Aziza et al., 2010).

Aziza et al. (2010) strongly argued that the act of national integration in a plural society is germane to the development and survival of modern plural states that Malaysia is not an exception that captured the Malays, Chinese, Indians and other ethnic groups. And that the question of relying on external diplomacy and helps is outdated process of national integration. That existing government and cultural groups should identify issues and workout plausible mechanisms within the context of existing economic, socio-political and cultural dynamics that are intrinsic and extrinsic in nature in the country. Aziza et al. (2010) point out policy implication and what Malaysia as country needs to do to intensify integration.

On point of policy implementation and the need for national cohesion, one of the Malaysian prime ministers (Datuk Seri Najib Tun Razak) as in April 2009 buttressed issue of national cohesion on bases of 'One Malaysia'. Accountability and transparency, service to all, respect and fairness in public discourse, accessible educational system and job for all on the grounds of performances and merit are sacrosanct to the development and unity of country (Azizi et al., 2010).

Party Politics in Malaysia

The Malaysia's political parties have been driven by her pluralism and socioeconomic activities particularly the interests of the Malay; Chinese; and Indian population. The political parties exist out of these three configurations of ethnic fraternity. The United Malays National Organization (UMNO), the Malaysian Chinese Association (MCA) and the Malaysian Indian Congress (MIC); and the configuration give birth to a strong alliance called Perikatan and later assumed a different name to Barisan National (National Front) as in 1973. This political fellowship of groups in Malaysia led Barisan configurations won the various elections and was able to demonstrate high level of legitimacy before the populace in the area of complex Malay quests for securing the privileges of the

Malay majority, insuring Chinese business activities and improving India's demand for socioeconomic change (Case, 1995; Khalid, 2014). In other words, the quest for national integration in Malaysia was built on the formation of a national group that comprises the existing ethnic groups which identified area of interests and challenges among the groups. In a historical review, Case (1995; Khalid, 2014) identified that the Malaysian political parties existed in three epochs (1969, 1970, 1980). He points out that the Malays who seem to be the original inhabitants of the land with slight population of over 50% were noted for administrative and bureaucratic power, and the Chinese immigrants were in charge of credit and merchandize in the cities. Indians invest and controlled rubber plantations in the system.

At the onset of this creation, the Malays were uncomfortable with the economy system and this act of indifferent affected UMNO, and the Chinese were active in party politics within the Democratic Action Party (DAP) and involved in assemblies organized by GERAKAN (People's Movement Party). This intensified the grievances of the Malays in an unprecedented sharp ethnic violence, but preventive measure from the national political group tames the menace (Case, 1995; Khalid, 2014). The Barisan political alliance intensified her efforts during the second era as in 1970 by assuring the populace an economy boom and equality for all and harmony across ethnic divides. This was particularly directed towards the Malays in order to integrate them economically. Yet the Chinese's businesses grow unprecedentedly due to uninterrupted law that made the Barisan political alliance to sustain its dominance for a long period (Case, 1995; Khalid, 2014). Above all the Barisan political alliance contributed to the unity and national integration of Malaysia and they were aided by the leadership of the country, especially the prime ministers like Tunku Abdul Rahman; Tun Abdul Razak; Tun Hussein Onn; Dr Mahathir Mohamed; Abdullah Ahmad Badawi (Khalid, 2014). The point here for a country to succeed and galvanize the minds of the citizen in ensuring their interests sincere and altruistic leaders are needed. Malaysian prime ministers have demonstrated to a large extent the strength of uniting and integrating the Malaysian people in different epoch.

The above qualities of leadership and the efforts of alliance seem to be different in most African states whereby leaders concentrate development and wealth into their personal empires. Political parties' alliance most times glorifies ethnic elites and creates more sharp antagonistic attendances among the masses of different ethnic configurations (Obah-Apkpowoghaha, 2013, 2018).

The Asian Case: India

The idea of national integration in India cut beyond creating a centre for coexistence of different groups, but rather stimulating the spirit of patriotism towards building the state. In India, there is existence of sharp different beliefs and ideals but the thrust of national issues demands the support of all. And Indians have recognized different integrative mechanisms towards ensuring the quest for patriotism such as the composition of their National Anthem and others. This has given India a profound success story of a nation that has managed multicultural groups and the mechanisms of development are in place and not distorted. Issues of national development are matter of concern to Indians that are propelled by the leaders whose integrity is unquestionable. The principle of truth and equal status is part of leadership styles that have galvanized the country's political system. The country comprises dominant religions that are quite different from each other such as the Hinduism, Sikhism, Buddhism, Jainism, Islam and Christianity which are allowed freely to exist, and the fundamentalists. India has demonstrated what is called *Sarva Dharma Samabhava*, that is, a sense of equity and dignity for every individual's faith or ideals. For instance, Hinduism is a religion that consists of variety of creeds and faiths, which are further divided among many castes, sects and sub-sects.

Yet, the place of patriotism on national issues takes priority over other ideals. Another important mechanism put in place by India has to do with the creation of centre of worships for various groups such as holy shrines and pilgrimages. India as a country also experienced certain disintegrative tendencies after the departure of the colonial master (Britain) that led to two different identities mostly princely kingdoms which were seeking for autonomy of its own and while the dominant one seeks for an integrated state of India. Some princely kingdoms purported to join Pakistan or Burma to form a country but not with the current entity called India. In order to avoid this action, there was the creation of states department that was controlled by the leadership of Sardar Vallabhbhai Patel and V.P. Menon. And whose duties are to design enduring integrative mechanisms of uniting the over six hundred princely states to the general entity and to prevent balkanization of the country or create an avenue for other princely states to join Pakistan or Burma (Menon 1956 cited in Haokip, 2011).

At the eve of British departure, there were several princely states left loose to decide the union that is suitable for them. States like Hyderabad and Manipur aligned with India after some political intrigues. The integration process of over six hundred princely states took techniques of baits and threats of mass pressure that were tactically done. The central roles of bait were to engage in generous gifts and rewards which also involve making some of the princes as Governors or Rajpramukhs (Sarkar 1983 cited in Haokip, 2011). A notable strategic challenge encountered along the process was that of the compromise of uniting neighbouring provinces towards the centre. Consequently, as on August 15, 1947, the Congress has successfully attempted to sign an Instrument of Accession with the existence of the princely states with India and acknowledge central authority over the three areas of defence, external affairs and communications. And by January 26, 1950, a constitution was derived upon the Indian Republic that fully integrated all the princely states and stating their rights of operations. The coming together of these states was "a culmination of long-drawn, multi-stream process of transformation, unification and integration of the Indian people into one political entity" (Nag, 1999: 74 cited in Haokip, 2011).

Notable among the success of India's national integration is ascribed to the efforts of Sardar Vallabhbhai Patel and the Indian nationalism struggle for freedom especially in the areas of integrating different religions, languages and cultures into a single political entity. In nutshell, Haokip's work revealed that the acts of integration were premised on negotiations, promises, baits and even relatively coercion. The configuration of over six hundred princely states and other loosely administered areas enjoying varying degrees of autonomy was initially a great challenge to the new government, and it poses serious obstacle to the unity, cohesion and stability. The thesis of Claude Ake (1967) alluded to the fact that the process of integration took radical measure of force especially the north-eastern states. After independence, yet relative insurgent acts from some nationalities like the Kuki (Kuki National Assembly) vigorously asked for an entity under the purview of the Indian government leading to submission of copious memoranda to the Central Government (Haokip, 2011). It shows that the project of national integration is a process and an end in itself.

Party politics in India after the extinction of colonial system were driven by the existence of diverse groups that strongly interact with political parties. Most political parties seek electoral supports on the basis of religion, caste, creed and region undermining national interests. This has been described as an act of national disintegration. The essence of political parties is to create an atmosphere of good life for the citizenry and political consciousness

A study carried out by Asif nurjaman (2014) identified certain alarming features that pose threat to national integration in India. He described national integration as psychological binding or a sense of feeling of oneness among different multicultural groups in country. However, the study revealed variables like regionalism, linguism, caste, communalism, which have led to politics of minorities, backward classes, agitation, rallies and violence, secession and the act of terrorism.

The Nexus Between Political Parties, National Integration and Ethnicity

Classical studies on ethnicity have justified certain elements that aid national integration. In a study that was carried out in West Africa by Wallerstein Immanuel, he pointed out that ethnicity served as platform whereby individuals are linked with other groups in party politics and the act of re-socialization, which helps in preservation of class structure, is fluid and avoid the reintroduction of caste, while promoting political tensions. He noted that in modern states, the act of loyalty to ethnic cycle interferes less with national integration than loyalty to external family and ethnic groups are more service oriented and conscious to the people than external family. In another thought, ethnicity can as well play a dysfunctional role when the elites are rent seeking and motivated by personal aggrandizement. In the study, the drive for national political parties can tame ethnic bitter politics and thereby create a system of housing interests (Wallerstein, 1960). But against the notions and claims by Wallerstein, current statistics in relation to ethnic politics seem that ethnicity has no value of any sort to address national issues and the question of national party as can be seen in the case of sixteen years of Peoples' Democratic Party (PDP) reign in Nigeria. Politicians in the eastern part of Nigeria decried of margination and the onset of the PDP leadership in Fourth Republic. The quest for resource control by the minority ethnic groups was pronounced that oil violence eclipsed the region (Iledarei & Suberu, 2010; Ojakorotu, 2015), yet the PDP was seen as national party. And the integrative mechanisms put in place then deepened ethnic lines and invented politics of bitterness (Obah-Apkpowoghaha, 2013, 2018).

In another investigation by Omodia (2018), he identified classical input and output functions of political parties formulated by Almond and Powell, and argued that the input function involves political education through the use of rallies, campaign and so on. But these roles are played by few political parties in most African states in sectional motives and others are just for constitutional representation. Most of them only surface during election in order to claim subventions from the central government, and after elections, duties of political parties become forbidden affairs. African political parties' move towards national integration can be subsumed into two parts: state formation and manifestation of integrative actions in the bill to promote statehood, and nature of post-colonial state that affect national integration. Political party as democratic institution in an emerging state has been ethnicized and engrossed with tribal and regional issues, evidently found in the multiplicity of political parties which has narrowed and affected their functions vis-à-vis national integration (Omodia, 2018).

From the analyses given by Carbone (2007) in respect of the institutionalization of political parties in Africa. Most of these scholarly studies centre on democratization and democracy in line with Western indices. Political parties have been emphasized as device that exists along with democracy and the point of national integration as a role to bridge the gap of ethnic and primordial interests is scanty. Post-colonial states experience dysfunctional process due to decades of slavery and colonial system, and the implantation of democracy as a platform for empowerment and development has not shown concrete evidence for over many years of independence in most African states. Rather, the resultant effect of most scholarly works concerning the performer of political institution has been premised on lack of institution due to cultural deficits and ethnic attachment. On these bases, categorization and typology of party system and party formation have defined the analyses of most Western and European scholars. These typologies have been used as a model to judge the strength and direction of African political parties against what constitutes the origin culture of the African people. Tables 6.1 and 6.2 accentuate the thought of Gunther and Diamond which has been seen as mirror to capture African politics. While these models and other Western typologies have given meaning to the nature of political parties in Africa, literature on national integration and the place of political parties have been marginally overlooked. This can be associated with the norms of democracy as the reigning currency of ascendency which has economic bearings

Table 6.1 African political regimes in 1989. Brief description of African Political parties and Party System

Military regimes	*One-party regimes*	*Inclusive multipartism*	*Racial Oligarchies*
Burkina Faso, Burundi, Chad, Ghana, Guinea, Lesotho, Liberia, Mauritania, Nigeria, Sudan, Uganda	Angola, Benin, Cameroon, Cape Verde, Central African Republic, Comoros, Congo, Djibuti, Equatorial Guinea, Ethiopia, Gabon, GuineaBissau, Ivory Coast, Kenya, Madagascar, Malawi, Mali, Mozambique, Niger, Rwanda, São Tomé, Seychelles, Sierra Leone, Somalia, Swaziland, Tanzania, Togo, Zaire, Zambia	Botswana, Senegal, Mauritius, The Gambia, Zimbabwe	South Africa
$N = 11$	$N = 29$	$N = 5$	$N = 1$

Source Bratton–van de Walle (1997:77 cited in Carbone, 2007)

with capitalism, and this system of economic development has been alien to the African people that are familiar with socialist and communal systems.

Integration Theory

Integration theory has been relevant in most post-colonial states as a device of achieving political cohesion and national development. Southern Africa down to West African countries is characterized by states that possess pluralistic nature. And the use of integration theory to reduce ethnic crises is most recommended by recent literature in African states. Approaches like functionalist, the federalist and the cybernetic are instrumental in resolving ethnic misunderstanding and crises. The functionalist analyses identify with issues of cultural, economic, linguistic and religious heterogeneity. The quest to harmonize these variables towards prompting citizens into a homogenous entity that leads to civil participatory governmental system and the place of socialization by political parties

Table 6.2 Species of political parties

Parties	*Pluralist*	*Proto-hegemonic*	*Racial Oligarchies*
Elite Base		Traditional Local Notable Clientelistic	
Mass Base *Ideological/socialist* *Ideological/nationalist religious*	Class-Mass Pluralist-nationalist denominational	Botswana, Senegal, Mauritius, The Gambia, Zimbabwe	Leninist Ultranationalist Fundamentalist
Ethnicity	Ethnic congress		
Electoral	Catch-all Programmatic Personalistic		
Movement	Left-Libertarian post-industrial extreme-right		

Source Gunther and Diamond (2003:173 cited in Carbone, 2007) is vital in the course of the whole process (Hass, 1964 cited in Clark, 2000). And for the federalist system, it preaches the putting in place of central coordinating structure over other subordinate units while the cybernetic analysis, a derivation from communication theory, emphasizes the building of network of interactions that entail the sender, channel, receiver and feedback made available for citizens to comprehend. It gives the citizens an atmosphere of web of interaction of understanding how the system operates and evolves which fosters political unification of the constituent parts into one national body.

A visit to Weiner (1965), variables like territorial, value, elite-mass and integrative behaviour are strategic in the quest for national integration. For him, national integration dwells on the contending issue of creating sense of territorial nationality that overrides or is superior to primordial interests or loyalty. The unification of dissimilar socioeconomic, religious, ethnic and geographic variables within the purview of national interests popularly called homogenous entity, the Greek city state in the days of Plato served as a referent point. This formation emanates from arrogating power to the centre whose aim embodied the interest of all which will catalyse the citizens to pledge their loyalty into the national government. This general entity serves as a body of realizing live goals for the entire citizens; this was the practice in the polis in the Greek city state.

In another version of national integration, the pluralist interpretation takes much space in modern political science debate. It supports the cross-fertilization of diverse groups or cross-cutting affiliation between and among different growths. Osei-Kwame preached about cultural accommodation and tolerance model as a *sin qua non* for national integration, and second, the elimination doctrine popularly called assimilationist. Osei-Kwame described this model as *cultural displacement model* which revealed that primordial and civil bonds are structurally exclusive. And the bill for national integration subsumed all other groups into game theory of zero sum that eventually leads to the manifestation of homogeneous state (Zolberg, 1967, cited in Peretomode, 1985). In other words, intra-group cohesion and loyalties are eliminated but there exists loyalty to the national body that eclipsed formidable social classes. Elucidation of these integration theses gives comprehensive antidote of taming crises that bedevilled plural states in modern states.

Theory of Charismatic Leadership

As the name implies, the thought here emphasized the oratory and gifted nature of a person in a community that will attract other members within the communities to buy into his or her views. The individual serves as an embodiment of harmony and unity with territory, he/she serves as the spoke man. He/she remains the interpreter and is likened to be better informed among other persons within a region. The charismatic leaders possess enormous gifts that bring people of different tribes and localities. Respect and loyalty serve as his or her benefits; hence, the quest for national integration is made simple and easy when the doctrine of charismatic leadership is employed. This thought has been advanced in the works of Ake (1969), Apter (1963); Wallerstein (1961), Weber (1957), Runciman (1963) and Horowitz (1963) who are known as the versatile proponents. In other works of political integration analyses, Friedrich (1961) identified the weakness of the doctrine arguing that it speaks about power but it lacks governance principles. He stressed that the connotation of leadership aside diffusion of power is meaningless and charisma is at point of antithesis where power assumed a power; it can doubt what charismatic leader can do in course of governance (Ake, 1967). Enmet (1958 cited in Peretomode, 1985) argued that the thought of Weber on charisma falls within myopic analyses of what constitutes leadership and which cannot capture other variables in human society. She suggests that "charisma is more applicable to inspirational leadership than to the 'hypnotic' leadership which Weber describes".

The Political Party Brokerage Theory

As an integration theory, it placed emphasis on the legitimation of an authority anchored upon a person. In other words, national integration can be made known when citizens accept the ruler-ship of a state. Scholars like Wallerstein, Emerson, Sklar, LaPolombara and Weiner, Stokes, Coleman and Rosberg, and Burnham are strong proponents of the theory. Wallerstein (1961) believes that national integration occurs when citizen legitimizes a state; that is, elections by majority are *sin qua non* for national integration. This entails conscious attempt to get all individuals that constitute citizens of a state to be loyal. According to Wallerstein, variables like mass participation and active involvement propel and intensify national integration, when the choice of the masses reflects the outcome of an election or a process. In another thought, Osei-Kwame (1980) made two basic assumptions that are tied to this theory. Political parties need to extend the hand of fellowship to all levels in the society as a mechanism of votes capturing through entertaining parochial interests into their national manifestos. The point of embracing ethnic interests and other primordial feelings makes the party to be rooted within the grassroots level, thereby consolidating the quest for national integration arising from the feelings of belonging as against alienation and marginalization.

The Elite-Mass Gap Doctrine

This scientific thesis arises out of the system that existed in history that emanated from classes especially within the capitalist permutation. The essence of this theory is upon the need to narrow the socioeconomic and cultural lifestyle that leadership and certain economies have put in place that has led the masses into deplorable conditions. Subscribers to this thesis like Binder (1964) and Shils (1958) have extensively written on it. The point of emphasis is that national disintegration or crisis that modern societies face results from the high level of socioeconomic and cultural gap that entrapped countries. Coleman and Rosberg (1964) view national integration from the perspective of political dynamism, as the bridging of the elite-mass gap in the vertical plane in a bill to develop an integrated political process and play active part in politics (civil political culture). The scientific taming of cultural and regional pressures and discontinuities on the horizontal plane overall entails bridging elite-mass gap and forging a system of territorial cohesion. However, the pitfalls of this doctrine lie in the point of tribalism and primordial attachment that scholars of elite-mass gap did not take cognisance of. Primordial indices in state can destabilize development and collapse the bill of national integration. Narrowing the socioeconomic and cultural gap between the elites and masses indicates a different thought in a political system which demarcates the beliefs of the people. Studies have shown that sometimes the masses and elites may not be fashioned in the atmosphere of homogeneity, and this theory may not sound superb like Nigeria that harboured over 200 tribes that are lumped together as the Nigerian masses may be Hausas, Ibos, Yorubas, (Ijaws, Urhobos, Itshekiris, Binis, Ishans), or TIV, Catholics, Protestants, Muslims, or Animists, peasants or urban labourers (Ake, 1967).

The Free Market Model

The popular proponents of this theory are Hass and Schmitter (1967). They argued that the quest of national integration can only be achieved when political leaders base their goals on rationality of distribution and service delivery. The act of maximizing resources in achieving certain gain upon an individual participant is germane towards the path for national integration. This theory has been labelled and tied to international relations doctrine among states. It has been pointed out that "there exists an inferential jump in the postulation that the pursuit of individual calculations, as defined, will automatically lead to the creation of an integrated community" (Dudley, 1976).

The Structural-Functionalist

In a liberal format, Osei-Kwame (1980 cited in Peretomode, 1985) believes that when a state bought into the forces of modernization like the mode of wages, employment, industrialization, commercialization, urban residence, migration, mass media, formal education and increased political participation, it tends to mitigate and put off traditional particularistic and which will foster integration. The works of Coleman (1955), Lerner (1958), Mitchell (1956), Almond and Verba (1963), Parsons (1964), Eisenstadt (1966) and Cohen (1974) cited in Obah-Akpwoghaha (2018) supported this theory. The basis of this theory is anchored on the belief that low economic atmosphere will weaken national integration, thereby instigating political upheaval. This thesis has been used side by side with most African countries in an empirical analysis (Unchedu 1970; Bates 1973 cited in Peretomode, 1985).

Social Communications-Transactional Theory by Karl Deutsch (1957, 1964 cited in Obah-Akpowoghaha, 2018) buttressed issues on the level of interactions that a nation engaged. A thesis engendered the sender, receiver, channels, messages and feedback mechanisms which are linked with transactions and social communication as a ploy for integration in a given political setting. The thrust of theory lies on the political cohesiveness of individuals in a political arrangement which tends to affects relationship in the settings. The underlining logic is that the higher the volume of transactions among members in a social setting, the greater integration the tendencies will penetrate. He further mentioned typologies of interactions that entail interactions that involve the interchange of messages like emails, telephone, radio, television, and so on; business that has to do with exchange of goods and services; and mobility which delves into the movement of individuals and the occurrences or number of contacts. Against this thought, Huntington (1967 cited in Obah-Akpowoghaha, 2018) argued that communities' awareness as result of information dissemination can intensify the demands of the citizens against the state and further create intense politics which can instigate violence. In his words: 'increased communication may generate demands for more 'modernity' than can be delivered (by the political system). It may also stimulate a reaction against modernity and activate traditional forces'.

The Cross-Pressure Theory

The Equitable or Balanced Development Approach

This doctrine manifested in most part of the African states, but the weakness of this thesis lies on how and what mechanisms to be adopted for equitable distribution that will lead to satisfaction of all ethnic groups and balanced development. According to Busia (1967), a former Prime Minister of Ghana and sociologist, he articulated that when there is the existence of equal development in a state and the citizens strive on the laws of justice as a code to distribute wealth adequately without prejudice in a political setting, the disease of tribalism and ethnic politicking will cease to exist; hence, atmosphere of national integration will be intensified.

Consociational Democratic Theory

This theory was championed by Apter (1961), Lehmbruch (1967), Bluhn (1970), Idem (1971, 1975) and Lijphart (1968, 1969, 1971, 1975, 1977, 1979) cited in Obah-Akpowoghaha, (2018). Apter (1961) embraced the term 'consociational democracy' to buttressed politics in Africa. He was of the view that democracy will nurture diverse feelings and norms in heterogeneous states leading to a viable society that promotes unity. He narrowed his point on the system of compromise and ethnic accommodation. In another thought, Lijphart (1969) concept of consociational democracy engendered the creation of certain political variables that preach non-divisiveness and tolerance in order to mitigate crisis that bedevilled plural societies, "while recognizing the necessity of transcending cleavage lines on some critical occasions". He further asserted that building a stable polity in heterogeneous states did not require any special arrangement as the all-encompassing cooperation at the elite class to offset the centrifugal inclinations of societal settings. In his book, four major characteristics or principles of consociational democracy were noticed: a political compromise that steers from the atmosphere of grand coalition political rulers of the segments of the heterogeneous society; the absolute power conferred on certain elites (veto) or the choices of the majority rule; the act of proportional representation as a leading standard in appointments especially civil service, and distribution of state's resources; and relative degree of autonomy for each constituency to enable for its internal dealings.

Concluding Remarks

This paper has revealed that the task of national integration among states in Asia and Africa has passed through struggle for retaining certain identities and nationalities against the fear of dominion by major ethnic groups. Asian countries like Malaysia and India adopted a skilful means in incorporating sharp identities into central government. India utilizes negotiations, coerce, juice appointment and rewards in tactical manner towards integrating all nationalities into the centre. In Malaysia, there was the need for accountability, transparency and fairness in politics and other sections in the country. The policy of one Malaysia and one people dominates the political climate of the country. Politics or political parties were central in the Asian political integration, especially demonstrating good leadership qualities that captured the entire population towards working for the state.

The quest for national integration in Africa has been tough and challenge in countries like Nigeria and South Africa. Nigeria due to her sharp ethnic history and elites' interests in the activities of national integration seems to be fragile and unrealistic. Integrative mechanisms such as quota system, federalism, unitary system, unity schools and so on have been put in place in most African states that integrate the multi-ethnic groups in individual countries. Yet, there are cases of violence resulting from the syndrome of hate speech and electoral fraud. These and among others have made most states in Africa to be fragile and in a disintegrative path.

Also, this piece has identified the roles of political parties from the prism of liberal perspectives and centred it on capturing the interest of the voters in order to participate and control the government. Classical scholars have seen political parties as the institution that facilitates national interest upon democratic norms. For Gabriel Almond and Powell whose work on political parties has attracted policymakers and political leaders, and accentuated the functions of political parties from the dimension of input and output analyses, yet, the application of these thoughts in African and Asian countries has not yielded concrete national development (integration). Consequently, the paper has entertained series of national integration theories against the proliferation of democratic ideals as a recipe for national development. While most African and Asian countries bought into the concept of democracy and political parties as a viable instrument for political cohesion and development. Yet, this piece has discovered in works of other scholars that Asian and African countries have experienced marginal crises under democratic governance. Democratic ideals have been utilized at expense of these two continents' (Asian and African culture) beliefs. Most of these theories adopted were in conformity with European and Western thoughts against the nature and beliefs of the African and Asian societies. Hence, this piece suggests and recommends that the path for national integration should be defined within multidimensional theories that will appropriate the African and Asian beliefs, nature and sensitive to her configurations.

References

Ake, C. (1967). Political integration and political stability: A hypothesis. *World Politics, 19*(3), 468–499.

Alapiki, E. (2005). State creation in Nigeria: Failed approaches to national integration and local autonomy. *African Studies Review, 48*(3), 49–65.

Anifowose, R. (1998). Theoretical explanation of political violence. *Violence and politics in Nigeria: The Tiv and Yoruba experience* (pp. 1–30). Enugu, Nigeria: Nok Publishers International.

Aziza, Z., Salleha, A., & Ribua, H. E., (2010). A study of national integration: Impact of multicultural values. *Procedia Social and Behavioural Sciences, 7*(C), 691–700. http://www.sciencedirect.com. Accessed 23 April 2018

Bandyopadhyay, S., & Green, E. (2009). *Nation-building and conflict in modern Africa*. Houghton Street, London: Suntory and Toyota International Centres for Economics and Related Disciplines and London School of Economics and Political Science.

Belay, G. F. (2013). *A review of ethiopia's security challenges in The Horn of Africa*. Ministry of National Defense, Ethiopia, United States Army War College. Accessed 25 February 2019.

Binder, L. (1964). National integration and political development. *American Political Science Review, 8*(3), 630.

Busia, K. A. (1967). *Ethnicity, religion and nationality—Methodist Heritage* (p. 9). London: Routledge and Kegan Paul. Accessed 3 April 2019.

Carbone, G. M. (2007). Political parties and party systems in Africa: Themes and research perspectives. *World Political Science Review, 3*(3).

Case, W. (1995). Malaysia: Aspects and audiences of legitimacy. ln Muthiah Alagappa (Ed.), *Political legitimacy in Southeast Asia*. California: Stanford University Press.

Cheteni, P., & Shindika, E. S. (2017). Ethical Leadership in South Africa and Botswana. http://www.anpad.org.br/bar.

Clark, H. U. (2000). *An evaluation of the effectiveness of the National Youth Service Corps Scheme as an instrument for promoting National integration in Nigeria* (PhD thesis Department of Public Administration). Ahmadu Bello University, Zaria

Coleman, J. S., & Rosberg, C. G. (1964). *Political parties and national integration in tropical Africa*. University of California Press.

Dobbins, J., Jones, S. G., Crane, K., & Degrasse, B. C. (2007). *Beginner's guide to national-building*. Published by the RAND Corporation. http://www.rand.org/.

Dudley, B. J. (1976). Military government and national integration in Nigeria. In David R. Smock & K. Bentsil-Enchill (Eds.), *The search for national integration in Africa*. New York: The Free Press.

Electoral Commission of South Africa National and Provincial Elections 22 April 2009

Emerson, R. (1966). Parties and national integration in Africa. In Joseph LaPalombara & Myron Weiner (Eds.), *Political parties and political development* (pp. 267–302). Princeton: Princeton University Press.

Etzioni, A. (1962). A paradigm of the study of political unification. *World Politics, 15*.

Etzioni, A. (1963). *Political unifications*. New York: Holt, Rhinehort and Winston.

Gemtessa, G. (2014). *State formation and national state-building project: Comparative approach*. Department of Political Science University of Oslo. Accessed 25 February 2019.

Haokip, T. (2011). Theoretical considerations of political integration and the Indian experience. *International Journal of South Asian Studies(IJSAS), 4*(1), 221–234. Society for South Asian Studies. Pondicherry University.

Hass, E. B. & Schmitter, P. C. (1967). Economic and differential patterns of integration: Projections about unity in Latin America. *International Organization, 18*(4), 327–328.

Ikelegbe, A. (2014). Political parties and violence. In O. Obafemi, S. Egwu, O. Ibeanu & J. Ibrahim (Eds), *Political parties and democracy in Nigeria* (pp. 314–339). Kuru, Nigeria: National Institute for Policy and Strategic Studies (NIPSS).

Iledarei, W., & Suberu, R (2010). *Oil and gas in the Federal Republic of Nigeria.* Conference on Oil and Gas in Federal Systems. Washington, DC: World Bank Headquarters, Black Auditorium, USA.

Jinadu, A. (2014). Political parties and democracy in Nigeria. In O. Obafemi, S. Egwu, O. Ibeanu & J. Ibrahim (Eds), *Political parties and democracy in Nigeria* (pp. 19–41). Kuru, Nigeria: National Institute for Policy and Strategic Studies (NIPSS).

John, I. A., Mohammed, A. Z., Pinto, A. D., & Nkanta, C. A. (2007). Gun violence in Nigeria: A focus on ethno-religious conflict in Kano. *Journal of Public Health Policy, 28*(4).

Khalid, K. A. T. (2014). *Moderation and power sharing in Malaysia: Accommodating concept and practice.* Ethnic Studies Paper Series. No. 33. KITA, UKM. Bangi.

Landsberg, C. (2009). *South Africa's "African agenda": Challenges of policy and implementation University of Johannesburg.* Prepared for the Presidency Fifteen Year Review Project. http://www.europarl.europa.eu/meetdocs/2009_2014/documents/d-za/dv/3_african_agen/3_african_agenda.pdf. Accessed 3 April 2019.

Lijphart, A. (1977). *Democracy in plural societies; a comparative exploration.* New Haven: Yale University Press.

Mason, A. (2010). Integration, cohesion and national identity: Theoretical reflections on recent British policy. *British Journal of Political Science, 40*(4), 857–874.

Mahmood, S., (2008). *Corporate governance and business ethics for SMEs in developing countries: Challenges and way forward*, viewed 20 May 2011, from http://www.kantakji.com/fiqh/files/companies/w111.pdf.

Mukwedeya, T. G. (2016). *Nation building in Africa: Post-colonial experiences and lessons from Tanzania, Kenya, South Africa And Namibia.* Mandela Institute For Development Studies Youth Dialogue Dar Es Salaam, Tanzania, University of The Witwatersrand.

Norris, P (2005). *Political parties and democracy in theoretical and practical perspective.* U.S.A. National Democratic Institute for International Affairs.

nurjaman, M. A. (2014). *Nature of Indian politics Vis-à-vis the challenges to national integration: An analytical study.*

Obah-Apkpowoghaha, G. N. (2013). *The impact of political recruitment on democratic consolidation in Nigeria (1999 to 2007)* (Unpublished M.Sc thesis). Department of Political Science, Faculty of Social Sciences, Obafemi Awolowo University, Ile-ife, Osun State, Nigeria.

Obah-Akpowoghaha, G. N. (2018). *Party politics and the challenge of national integration in Nigeria's Fourth Republic* (Unpublished PhD Dissertation). Department of Political Science, Faculty of Social Sciences, Obafemi Awolowo University, Ile-ife, Osun State, Nigeria.

Ojakorotu, V. (2015). *Curing the affliction from the "oil curse" to sustainable development in Africa's "Petro-States" Inaugural Lecture*. Published by the Office of the Vice-Rector (Academic) North-West University, Mafikeng Campus, South Africa. Accessed 4 March 2019.

Omodia, S. M. (2018). Political parties and national integration in emerging democracies: A focus on the Nigerian state.*Mediterranean Journal of Social Sciences, 6*(9). http://creativecommons.org/licenses/by-nc-nd/3.0/.

Peretomode, V. F. (1985). *Political parties and problems of national integration: A case study of the Federal Republic of Nigeria* (Ph.D Thesis). Faculty of the Graduate College of the Oklahoma State University, OK, USA.

Shils, E. A. (1958). The intellectuals and the powers: Some perspectives for comparative analysis. *Comparative Studies in Society and History, 1*(1), 5–22.

UNHCR. (2016). Comprehensive refugee response framework: From the New York declaration to a global compact on refugees. http://www.regionaldss.org. Accessed 25 February 2019.

Varma, S. P. (2006) *Modern political theory* (pp 143–173). New Delhi:Vikas Publishing House.

Weiner, M. (1971). Political integration and political development. In J. L. Finkle & R. W. Gable (Eds.), *Political development and social change*. New York: John Wiley and Sons.

Weiner, M. (1965, March). New nations: The problem of political development (pp. 52–64). *Annals of the American Academy of Politcal and Social Science*, 358. Cited in Emmanual O. Oritsejafor. (2009). National integration in Liberia: An evolving Pursuit (pp. 96–120). In. *The Journal of Pan African Studies, 3*(1).

Wallerstein, I. (1960). Ethnicity and National Integration in West Africa. In *Cahiers d'études africaines, 1*(3), 129–139. https://www.persee.fr/doc/cea_0008-51960.

CHAPTER 7

Peace-Making, Government and Communal Conflict in Nigeria: Evidences from Ife-Modakeke Crisis

Kazeem Oyedele Lamidi

Introduction

Communal violence is a common occurrence in Africa. It comes in a variety of shapes and sizes. Racial cleavages continue to be a major obstacle to nationhood development, and violence erupts often between ethnic groups. These disputes have developed a trend, leading scholars to blame greed, power and wealth sharing for their origins (Lamidi, 2019c). Consequences of the crises resulted in deaths of many civilians, people's migration and property devastation, among other things. As a result, the issue of preserving balance and peace-making among opposing parties by a third party is the greatest challenge confronting Nigeria's conflict resolution process, Nigeria inclusive.

Effectiveness of peace-making therefore depends on the ability of government to find an impartial balance on the majority of these

K. O. Lamidi (✉)
Obafemi Awolowo University, Ife, Nigeria

K. J. Ani et al. (eds.), *Political Economy of Resource, Human Security and Environmental Conflicts in Africa*,
https://doi.org/10.1007/978-981-16-2036-2_7

contentious topics as an institutional mediator. To this end, the government acts as a correlational link between the independent and contingent variables of peace-making and communal violence. The dispassionate equilibrium, on the other hand, can only be achieved if the source(s) of the conflict(s) are identified and dealt with equally. According to this report, the Ife-Modakeke crisis is a strong case study due to its political significance in Yoruba culture, as well as its potential for dispute settlement in Nigeria and beyond.

In that it applies to a mechanism aimed at settling racial tensions by positive means, dispute resolution is multi-faceted. In certain instances, judicial committees were established to resolve communal clashes that determine the root causes of the dispute and fix issues by mutually acceptable, as well as enduring remedies (Raimi, 2010). However, the Ife-Modakeke crisis, despite its origin and duration, makes an exception by 'ideal' government interference. According to Asiyanbola (2007), the Ife-Modakeke crisis is Nigeria's longest intra-ethnic conflict, among others, confirming it as an obvious case study with intricate information on the subject matter.

Nigerian peacebuilding is also in its early stages. The Ife-Modakeke crisis has much, if not any, of the same escalation characteristics as other crises. Though the Ife-Modakeke crisis has been a long-standing phenomenon in these conflicts, it seems to be amenable to the implementation of an adaptive dispute resolution model that will prevent conflict from escalating.

Contextual Discourse

Both the Ife and the Modakeke are Yoruba people from Osun State in southwest Nigeria. Both are said to be descendants of Oduduwa, the Yoruba people's progenitor, according to oral history. The two cultures' sociocultural and political structures are almost similar, and their regional distribution overlaps significantly. However, through their close kinship, Ife and Modakeke have been at odds for many decades (Toriola, 2001; Raimi, 2010). In Ife, the Modakekes are regarded as outsiders, renters and refugees. The Ife citizens, on the other hand, consider themselves as the 'landlords' of Modakeke.

According to historical accounts, the inhabitants of Modakeke fled to Ile-Ife after the fall of the Old Oyo Kingdom in the nineteenth century, resulting in migration crisis to the south and the occupation of their current site. As a result, two separate groups of people emerged: initial settlers (landlords) and migrants, renters, farmhands and a resettled population referred to as refugees (Modakeke). The distant origins of the conflicts between the two parties are these categorizations (Oladoyin, 2001; Toriola, 2001; Asiyanbola, 2007).

It is widely acknowledged that the reasons for dispute between the Ife and Modakeke people are many and diverse. To this end, the Nigerian government's actions at all levels were not in vain in addressing these sets of crises, lending credence to their resolution at the time. In this context, government is described as constituted authorities at the city, state and federal levels working together to improve stability. Government's intervention lines are primarily to mediate conflicts and cross-examine disputant parties, and vice versa. These activities direct the formation of government, making it easier for it to play a major role in peace-making. The government policies and efforts on mediation, arbitration and peace-making in these long-standing crises are deserving of exploration for other societies to try as such disputes arise in their environments.

Conceptual Issues

Peace-making is a preventive exercise which underlines the cardinal function of government in the resolution of communal conflict. These three (3) concepts are interconnected in the sense that they depict the existentialism of government towards its essential function of peace and security provisions. This remains any government's single-mindedness among other attentions due to conflict inevitability in societal spheres. Ellis (1996) emphasized that the inability of post-colonial states to meet the economic demands of their citizens could make conflict more violent in African states. The government's position is called into question since most tensions in African societies are tribal. This is due to the fact that the disputes are of the two communal types (Olaleye, 2016). Salim (1997), on the other hand, argued that, considering the existence of their localizations, the wars pose a danger to regional and global stability.

Regardless, this explains the deterioration of what is said to be communally inclined. Nigeria remains clearly one among the few affected countries in terms of inter-ethnic, rivalry and other forms of conflict (Albert, 2007). Communities in Nigeria have been violent based in terms of tribal disputes, as shown by the indiscriminate use of sophisticated firearms during communal conflicts, and most prominent is the Ife-Modakeke crisis (Lamidi, 2019c). The continuation of these tensions necessitates a redefinition of the government's position, as well as the inclusion of peacekeeping as one of its social themes (Lamidi, 2021). As a result, government at every level is seen as an administrative authority with a strong focus on communal problems and the ability to handle all types of communal violence until it escalates.

This, in turn, underlines the essence of peace-making which aims at forestalling crisis. The operation is mainly preventive-oriented. The quest of social philosophers underscores the varied approaches of peace-making. These are clear in Mahatma Gandhi's and Martin Luther King's writings. The duo's agreement is to resolve conflicts before they become explosive by avoiding the use of violent means (Noll, 2013; Lamidi, 2020). In today's jargon, peace-making entails preventing any kind of confrontation from escalating (Dawson, 2004). However, it is not entirely effective, necessitating the need for peacekeeping. But, in the best-case scenario, a confrontation is settled before it escalates.

Multiple aspects of peace-making influence the dynamics of conflict. Each of the aspects reveals the uniqueness of peace-making that is not comprehensive. To put it another way, if peace-making is a latent variable, it is better to reframe the problem in terms of conflict outcome rather than operationalization. For instance, regardless of how peace-making is defined, significant evidence suggests that it promotes peace's long-term sustainability. Similarly, to encourage regional control of conflict, reliable results are published. Any researchers also conclude that some missions help to create stability, although this depends on the form of mandate (Albert, 2007; Noll, 2013; Dixon, 2016). Peace-maker capability has shown to be effective in preventing conflict on a local level, although it has a lesser impact on the length of local peace.

This places a high premium on peace-making than other mechanisms of peacebuilding. The context of peace-making is worthwhile in governance process as it assists in returning normalcy and economic prosperity. In South Africa, for example, Desmond Tutu's movement sought to make peace through struggles against oppression, thereby leading to social changes within the political and economic landscape (Best, 2005; Albert, 2007; Cajvaneanu, 2011). In clear terms, peace-making is a pre-conflict resolution mechanism which tends to give no room for conflict occurrence. It is a holistic mechanism to be deployed to face the challenges posed by the general insecurity in Nigerian states (Olaleye, 2016).

Therefore, peace-making turns out not only imperative, but instructive to enhance peaceful coexistence.

In view of the contested nature of concepts in conflict studies, it is necessary to show the meaning of conflict in this study so as to situate it in proper perspective. Conflict can be perceived in form of catakata, wahala in Yoruba parlance, quarrel and so on (Ayokunle et al., 2004). Coser (2006: 8) states that "struggle over ideals and claims to scarce rank, influence, and assets in which opponents seek to neutralize, kill, or destroy their adversaries". "Conflict is intended to reveal divergent dualism and achieve certain kinds of disunity, even though it is by the annihilation of one of the conflict parties", Park and Burgess (2011: 574) concluded.

The definition illustrates the fact that conflicts emanate over divergent views. It also tells us that the resolution of the divergent views may be problematic which may necessitate one of the parties to seek means to annihilate the other party. The definition helps us to understand the nature of conflicts that occur across communities in Africa, especially on land and chieftaincy issues among other communal issues. In congruence, this conflict space should not be given—hence the need for government, as the coordinating agency, to institute peace-making mechanisms in place. In lieu of the above, this paper explores the government roles towards peace-making on communal conflict with insight from Ife-Modakeke crisis.

Existing Studies on Conflict and Communal Resolution

Babbie (2009) concluded that conflict is more often seen via the prism of sociocultural beliefs, and non-rational reactions are more likely, which Boulding (2002) has previously described as 'inner heart' values, special epistemologies formed by perceptions of who we are, how we classify ourselves in the social world, and how others have reacted to us in that universe of complicated conflict comprehension. Deep-seated tension is likely to arise where low-power communities believe that dominant power-individuals or groups have breached collectively understood standards of justice, either expressly or indirectly. Low-power cultural groups, which have generally been excluded from the negotiation table, view disagreement from the perspective of beliefs that have historically influenced their interactions with the mainstream society. They add diverse perspectives to the negotiation table that don't all fit into the interest-based bargaining framework, and then other parties from opposing viewpoints weigh in; the agreement gets more complicated and challenging.

The issue outlined above, according to this report, will only be solved if studies pay greater attention to discovering the cultural material used by communities in dispute management and resolution. The uniqueness and difficulty of group disputes, as well as the people involved, have made it difficult to develop universally applicable theory (Svensson, 2007). The problematic nature is seen in workshop and conference mechanism with its simulated processes that sometimes does not accommodate the idiosyncrasies of the local people. The position helps us to understand the complexity of public policymaking in a community composed of two distinct groups. In this situation, discovering cultural values that sustain the differentiated identity in one community becomes a viable means of managing conflicts in such community. It also requires that a study can be carried out during peace time unlike studies initiated only when crisis has broken out in such communities.

Murray (1993) concluded that dispute resolution scholars and professionals working in two environments do not often embrace metaphysical moods without questioning them, nor do they adapt such hypotheses without tailoring them to particular circumstances. The work further opined that the task for theorist is to use the work of practitioners to shape and reshape their theories much like astronomers and physicists are now using the results of space travel and satellite technology to restructure their views of the universe. The obstacles facing conflict resolution practitioners in handling this task are many: the demands for confidentiality by parties; the difficulty in creating control groups or laboratory conditions; lengthy gestation periods for most conflicts; complexity of the personalities or actors; strategies and motivations involved; and the different skills necessary for practitioners.

The fact that dispute resolution is a multidisciplinary area means that its philosophy is woven with threads of other disciplines across the three main faculties: namely, arts, sciences and social sciences. Conflict resolution theory, on the other hand, has been fundamental because it has provided practitioners outside the community where the conflict occurred with skills and techniques. Despite the scarcity of rigorous comparative literature on communal dispute resolution, several case studies have attempted to clarify the outcome in specific situations. Otite and Albert (1999) examined a variety of Nigerian disputes and concluded that the best prospects for stability are found in an interconnected context in which state and non-state players organize their activities. State tactics, on the other hand, have a poor track record. It is more difficult to maintain lasting peace in situations where 'public' actors have historically used indiscriminate aggression in response to the conflict, according to Cox (2016). Others demonstrated how political actions have often struggled to address disputes due to a lack of involvement or awareness of the local context. While the quick availability of small arms in troubled countries often fuels local unrest.

Many studies have centred on non-state peace processes, especially in areas where national structures are fragile or absent, due to the inability of many states to avoid and settle local conflicts. In Africa, there is a call for revived interest in various ways of traditional dispute resolution, which normally include cultural-driven arrangements for mediating or deliberating (Bevan, 2008; Lamidi, 2020). Numerous case studies looked at many trials and attempted to draw larger conclusions from them. Several studies, for example, have reported effective local dispute settlement using traditional mechanisms (Frank, 2002; Chapman & Kagaha, 2009). Also, Farah (1999) proposed that sustainable peacebuilding in Somaliland was due to a voluntary, bottom-up strategy.

Customary institutions can fill the void (Boege, 2006; Menkhaus, 2008). Since customary organizations are headed by local players, they could be best positioned to design a mechanism that is tailored to the local environment, as well as adapt far more quickly than state-led programmes (Imobighe, 2003). While the need for grass-roots-based dispute resolution is acknowledged, and several promising examples can be found, there is no study that contrasts results and shortcomings to determine the extent and drawbacks of customary mediation.

Non-Governmental Organisations (NGOs), religious associations and Community-Based Organizations (CBOs) are often active in resolving communal tension, in addition to the state and customary authorities. In several nations, the number of NGOs participating in peacebuilding has increased dramatically in modern times. Local communities also view such organizations as impartial and trustworthy, and they are seen to be effective mediators and politically autonomous (Elfversson, 2015), as it was demonstrated in an extraordinarily violent communal dispute in Kumasi, Ghana.

However, the part that NGOs can play is often limited by financial and realistic constraints (Abdulrahman & Tar, 2008). Eaton (2008) has chastised non-governmental organizations (NGOs) participating in the "business of reconciliation" for their inability to dissect the complexities of tensions surrounding communal conflict. Mkutu (2008) raised related concerns about the position of NGOs, adding that although a good number of NGOs is performing above average. Some might have negative consequences, owing to their operational rationale not matching local realities (Ikelegbe, 2006; Lamidi, 2021; Kamat, 2003). Albert (1999) proposed that religious organizations are indeed strategic in resolving inter-ethnic tensions, just that their effectiveness could be contingent on the conflicting groups having common views.

Furthermore, conflict processes remain underappreciated in the current literature. First, it's unclear if mission phases should be addressed in the same manner as disputes are. Systematically identifying steps of peacekeeping operations will offer fascinating insights into the key processes that the most active missions go through. Second, no comprehensive study of the effect of project length on violence has yet been conducted. But current peace-making research does not investigate the optimal duration of active missions (Lamidi, 2019b). This pattern is the product of wider contexts as well as obligations and commitments.

It is impossible to say which missions are more successful at various stages of a war or which are actually best suited to respond to rapid changes between them. In the scientific study of peace-making, explicit modelling of conflict processes is also lacking. Dixon (2016) recognized that world conflicts are complex, and that crisis periods can be followed by changes in action strategies. Despite the fact that his study covers a wide range of initiatives, his idea of escalatory test to assess success is highly commendable. Furthermore, particularly in conflicts that are more prone to escalation, study of the evolution of the communal conflict can be a significant criterion for evaluating success. More importantly, it is theoretically feasible to establish an optimal starting point of peace-makers which will decrease risk of confrontation and encourage peace-making tasks.

Conflict trajectory is an important and unexpected absentee of conflict-driven facets that are being overlooked in the literature. Indeed, in the conflict mediation literature, the timing of third-party strategies is critical since each conflict process necessitates tailored responses and allows for narrow goals (Lamidi, 2019a). It is a well-designed and effective resolution effort which will occur when disputes are at the optimal for action, according to the literature on conflict management (Collier & Sambanis,

2002). Thinking through confrontation phases and identifying the interventions which are most likely to work are potentially more useful in each scenario.

There is currently no agreement on a "gold standard" for evaluating the success of peacekeeping, and the need for ultimate standard is debatable. A mission's success is determined by its mandate, so there are as many criteria as mandates. On the other hand, it necessitates limiting mission evaluations to a more limited range of results than those discussed here. However, the standard or collection of parameters chosen does not contribute to the conclusion that other results are unimportant in gaining a better understanding of peace-making as a method.

Limiting the appraisal of effectiveness to the ability of peace-makers to preserve peace and mitigate military conflicts, for example, does not mean that civilian security is less essential. Peacekeeping activities are complicated, and they have an effect on the violence within countries at different levels (e.g. tribal populations, separatists and political elites) and size. Although various definitions of efficacy have been suggested in the literature, facets of the complex relations between peace operations and war have attracted less consideration but can have homogeneous impact.

To summarize, recent literature on communal dispute resolution has identified a wide variety of situations and generated a substantial body of empirical data. There is support from case studies that non-state mediators are best suited than state actors to discuss and settle the roots of conflict, and that they will also assist the parties in reaching long-term peace negotiations. However, there is little comparative research that explicitly analyses the conditions for success, and the interaction between different actors, central and local involved in local peace-making is understudied. Thus, this implies little about under what circumstances mediators can contribute to sustainable peace. In the subsequent section, this paper discusses government in non-partisan mediation perspective, as well as the condition for non-state mediation.

Theoretical Perspective

This section therefore attempts to examine theoretical underpinnings on conflict and its resolutions with assumptions from peace-making perspectives. According to Osaghae (2006), the intractable nature of ethnic conflicts has presented a significant challenge to conflict management theory and practice, especially given the apparent lack of traditional processes and instrumentality. He pointed at the failures of international or national processes of adjudication (Murdie & David, 2010), negotiation (Boulding, 2002: 119), mediation (Moore, 1996; Bevan, 2008) and all the ad-hoc military and police strategies adopted for conflict management and resolution. Astor (1991) and Boulle (1996) argued that the failure of the conventional method of conflict management is linked to the bias motive of the intervening agencies.

In the Rhodesia/Zimbabwe mediation in 1976–1979, the Africans' believe that Britain and US sympathy was to the white Rhodesians. Also, US interest has always been established strongly in the intervention between Israel and Arab neighbours. The most effective strategy also relies on studies into how organizations can resolve problems on their own, how they can become involved in dispute resolution, and how they can become facilitators. Astor (1994) and Imobighe (2003) had pointed to the difficulties associated with formal procedures of conflict management and resolution and argued that mediation, conciliation, arbitration, problem-solving, workshop, counselling and other forms of intervention in conflicts are widespread. However, the increasing reliance upon the Alternative Dispute Resolution (ADR) procedure is because the courts are overcrowded and inaccessible. Legal procedures for handling disputes are costly and often raise the level of contentions between the parties. Therefore, there is sense that better resolution of conflict can be obtained through the alternative means of conflict resolution.

On this note, Scimecca (1993) argued on the insufficiency of the already existing theories and showed a great support for alternative dispute resolution strategy even in an environment which already has high level development in legal formalism. The approach aided the establishment of neighbourhood justice centres. Weber concluded that authority built purely on force is inefficient, and that society cannot stay stable until citizens see the power hierarchy as valid and those in positions of power as worthy of their positions. Therefore, ADR is designed to help the poor, the downtrodden—that is, those with no access to the expensive legal system and between conflicting parties with less emphasis on logicality but on morality accompanied with in-depth understanding of the issues in context.

Burton (1993) argued that theorist on this perspective should move from institution to persons as the units of analysis. The effect of dispute in question, whether at the micro- or macro-level, determines the efficiency of the problem-solving solution. In this case, success is described as playing an undeniable and significant role in the final resolution of the conflict or, at the very least, explicitly laying the groundwork for more formal talks that lead to a resolution of the conflict and the establishment of a new constructive partnership between former adversaries. According to Kamat (2003), Bevan (2008), Babbie (2009) and Dixon (2016), success is seen when the following factors are present: (1) where the task has an effect on the individual person in the sense that it affects their beliefs, images and attitudes; shifts their expectations; creates new conceptual possibilities and opportunities; and, in some instances, completely transforms the way they see the situation in front of them. (2) When the workshop's production, in the sense that at least some activities conclude with participants taking notes on concrete strategies.

Montville (1993) took a psychological look at the healing process of admittance of guilt, fault or mistakes by one of the parties in conflict. This is done to create a confidence building which prevents future conflicts or heals the wounds of victims no matter the type of injury inflicted during the conflict. He pointed to a comparative analysis of how confession, by a warring leader of a group, can lead to forgiveness or lead to the de-legitimization of stereotypic beliefs about an enemy. According to the position, ethnic and religious tensions are consistently the most vulnerable to conventional diplomatic or political mediation and negotiating techniques.

As a critique to confession as a healing process after a conflict situation, According to Menkhaus (2008), a rigorous analysis in persuasive mass persuasion reveals that it is more likely to reinforce rather than modifying currently existing beliefs. When it comes to societal views against opposed or distrusted individuals or countries, both sociological and psychological influences—such as social networks, belief structures and prominent politicians—and psychological factors—such as family and peer racial preferences—serve as roadblocks to new favourable evidence being received. It is important to add that experience has thought us that any repeat of an act already forgiven will lead to total disregard at another time (Lamidi, 2021).

Black and Avruch (1989) took a succinct analysis of how cultural differences can pose some difficulties for interveners or negotiators to resolve conflict within such settings. The problem has to do with the attempt to discover a universal set of valid theory, techniques, methodological and conceptual difficulties. A view of the world from the eyes of another society (one potential outcome of an intercultural encounter) reveals regions of obscurity (things we cannot see through clearly). More to this, when culture is associated with descriptions as traditional, stereotypical modes of behaviour, characteristic of some group, etiquette and custom, they are impervious to change through time. The conflict resolution practitioner is expected with his/her skill in culture analysis to transcend these cultural barriers in resolving conflicts in intercultural settings. The understanding is crucially important and should guide the fundamental techniques of the third-party interveners (governments).

Government and the Conditions for Non-state Mediation

Regardless of a state's institutional condition, governmental activities are critical to peace-making processes, which are either negotiated by either government or non-state actors. This paper used an actor-centred approach to clarify the criteria for effective communal dispute resolution, taking into account relations between the state, mediators and the main conflict groups. It has two major consequences: first, it limits the position of the adjudicators and damages the public legitimacy; second, it has notable impact on the views of conflict parties about the probability of getting results at the negotiating table. The government's conformation on the Isakole (Land Rent) dispute of 1946–1947 demonstrated this (Afolayan, 1998).

State actors have shown vested interests in some disputes owing to their need to reinforce or preserve their place of influence. Bias may arise from a person's interaction with the conflict players, as well as from local resources and the conflict's problems (Brosché, 2014; Lamidi, 2020). In terms of money, the dispute could be about a strategic or economic problem, or it could take place in a strategic or economic region. For example, according to Boone (2014), the economic value of the region where conflict occurs will influence state policies in relation to the conflict. The government's stance on a local dispute can vary depending on whether community groups are powerful political allies, dangerous critics or politically insignificant (Cederman et al., 2010; Wilkinson, 2006).

This was similar to the controversy on the creation of Olorunsogo Plank Market (Agbe, 2001) and the obstruction to self-help construction projects by a Modakeke Fund-Raising operation in 1980. (Albert, 2001). Such complexities are likely to be especially critical in a setting where election results are closely linked to ethnic voting. Supporting a party embroiled in a communal dispute, for example, perhaps an opportunity to show appreciation to the people of the town for their electoral supports (Allen, 1999). This highlights an important prerequisite for non-state actors to get involved in the peacebuilding process. The reflection of Kalyvas' elite interaction theory, on the other hand, should be discarded. The next segment, focused on the Ife-Modakeke experience, will address government's position in peace-making as well as its engagement issues.

Government and Peace-Making: Analysis from Ife-Modakeke Crisis

It is worth noting that Ooni Abeweila made the first effort to settle the Ife-Modakeke crisis in 1847, mostly with the aim of resettling the Modakeke people in another area. According to Akinjogbin (1992), this was based on the presumption that providing a large gap between the Modakeke and Ife people would certainly bring an end to the crises' insurgence. The second time was in 1886, when the Anglo-Yoruba Treaty was concluded, and the Modakeke leaders declined to sign it because the 1886 peace treaty had deceived and ignored them. This was due to clause 5 of the treaty, which specified that Modakeke town would be rebuilt on land between the Osun and Oba Rivers (Lamidi, 2019c). In 1909, Ooni Adelekan Olubuse signed this treaty, which resulted in the resettlement of some Modakeke villagers, who later returned after his death. This effort, once again, failed.

The rationale behind providing information on previous attempts by traditional and socio-political institutions was to underscore the fact that not only government is the sole formidable force on peace-making process. Efforts could, however, be taken by other semi-formal and informal institutions. Be that as it may, government holds legitimate positions, and it could be placed in a third party and more authoritarian position owing to its non-involvement in the crisis. Thus, it could be regarded as a potential institution for peace-making process. Against the backdrop of the failures of traditional institutions and socio-political group, the intervention of government has brought some noticeable changes, which are very much expected. One could acclaim that it is because the government is not a judge in her own case: it is instead a mediator with public interests on governance principles of equity, justice, accountability and transparency.

The government's position in peacekeeping, on the other hand, is primarily focused on communal conflicts. "Government has always been used to proffer responses to this recurring crisis", authored by Olayiwola and Okorie (2010: 953). Augsburger (1992), Albert (1999, 2001), Agbe (2001) and Asiyanbola (2007) all said that the government has only created "available" remedies that have largely improved peaceful coexistence until recently. Since understanding that the government has a privileged role in the peace-making process, it is critical to examine the rationalism underlying the use of committees as legislative instruments for peace. This usually receives administrative response from assigned authority. In addition, most conflicts have several dimensions: they may be sociocultural, political or economic upheavals. When responding to a problem resulting from each of these events, the government requires flexibility, inclusivity and scientific knowledge in order to have a clear understanding of the causes and potential solutions.

It is also worth noting that some religious organizations, humanitarian organizations and peace volunteers worked tirelessly to find a permanent solution to the deadly disputes and communal tensions. However, problems are not necessarily answered in the middle of all of this (Olayiwola & Okorie, 2010). In most cases, either the semi-formal groups' proposals are followed, or one of the warring parties accuses the bodies of being one-sided or refusing to concede something to their own side. Although there are some issues with some of the proposed proposals from time to time. A good example is the planned transfer of the Modakeke group to a new location by Anglo-Yoruba Treaty one of the semi-formal associations. This did not ultimately provide a lasting solution to the crisis. This raised question on peace sustenance: Could this recommendation put an absolute end to the crisis? What happens to the psychology, attitudes, affiliations, sociology and mindsets of Modakeke towards Ife people? What will happen to the already infringed crisis experiences, damages done so far and inter-generational stories? It was further suggested that semi-formal community recommendations are often carried out because they focus on the physical effects and associational aims of the solutions, undermining the complex undertones of communal confrontation.

Surprisingly, the government processed a big important and landmark effort to find a permanent solution to the age-old dispute between Ife and Modakeke with the help of USAID/OTI (Albert, 2001). According to Albert (2001), the government's efforts included a television drive, independent youth training and shared training on forgiveness, redemption and transformative leadership for the two groups. Furthermore, the government's position in promoting peace took into account the long-term viability of peaceful coexistence between the two groups. For the sake of peace, Agbe (2001), Toriola (2001), Babajimi (2003) and Asiyanbola (2007) stated that the Ife-Modakeke Inter-community Peace Advocacy Committee was formally inaugurated on September 16, 2000, at Oduduwa Hall, Obafemi Awolowo University, Ile-Ife, Nigeria. There is no doubt that this government effort was effective in restoring peace between the two communities, and members of both communities followed through with their pledges to keep the peace.

For this reason, the contribution of this paper to the body of knowledge is by providing an empirical detail on the role of government in peace-making process on communal conflict using Ife-Modakeke crisis as a reference point, and striving to offer a generalized principle of peace-making process by government in Nigeria and other developing countries. This becomes significance owing to the inevitable nature of conflict in local areas in developing world. Furthermore, existing research has looked into the past, triggers and implications of the Ife-Modakeke crisis (Albert, 1999; Aguda, 2001; Oladoyin 2001; Agbe, 2001; Toriola, 2001; Babajimi, 2003). However, the governmental position in the peace-making processes on communal violence has received little to no recognition, leaving chances for governments around the world to define their guiding principles on the tasks of peace-making processes using the government positions in the peace-making on the Ife-Modakeke crisis.

In view of the above, Asiyanbola (2007) asserted that the government's initial position in the peace-making process was aimed at investigating and clarifying the situation study of the communal dispute. The bond between Ife and Oyo people (Modakeke) was then discovered to be very cordial at first (Babajimi, 2003; Olayiwola & Okorie, 2010). They said that during the Owu War of 1825 and numerous Ijesha invasions, the Oyo refugees offered military assistance to the Ifes. However, Albert (2001) noted that government investigations into the reasons for the dispute so as not to regret their actions. They lost political and economic power over the Modakeke people as a result of this. Considering historical antecedents, descent, dynasty and cultural affiliation, this discovery served as a significant hint for the government to embark on Yoruba country oneness rather than the political idea of nation-state.

Furthermore, the government noted the rationalism behind the first two attacks initiated by the Ife citizens following Ooni Abeweila's death. The attacks were discovered to be staged in response to Ife people's displeasure with the deceased king's alleged collaboration with the Modakeke people, as well as the alleged killing of an Ife traditional figure in Ibadan. However, claims in favour of the Ife people's attacks were presented. According to Akinjogbin (1992), Ooni Abeweila was poisoned in 1849 and refused royal burial by the Ife people due to his cooperation with the Modakeke people. Also, after Ooni Abeweila's departure, Albert (1999) and Oladoyin (2001) stated that an Ife Chief, Okunade, the Maye who settled in Ibadan in the early nineteenth century, was an autocrat, despite being a brave warrior. He wielded so much power in Ibadan politics that the people of Ife began to see Ibadan as a satellite city. Some Oyo people in Ibadan questioned Okunade's autocracy. Later, he was reportedly executed, and the Oyo people seized control of Ibadan's political government, to the exclusion of their supporters (Olayiwola & Okorie, 2010). At this point, the government realized that the Ife people first vented their rage on the Modakeke people because of the Ooni Abeweila's apparent cooperation, and that the second attack was a revenge for the suspected killing of Chief Okunade in Ibadan by Oyo people, prompting the Ife people to vent their rage on the Modakeke people.

During the Ibadan and Ekitiparapo conflict, this situation resulted in trans-ethnic enmity, as shown by the fact that while Ife people allied with Ekitiparapo to fight the Ibadan, the Modakeke people allied with Ibadan to fight the Ekitiparapo. The explanations for the alignments may thus be deduced from a situational study of communal tension between the two groups. As a result of these studies, the government's position shifted to that of a historical observer, comparing the incalculable harm done to each other by the two groups, despite the fact that historical records claim that Ife and Modakeke indigenes are sons and daughters of the same parents. This historic fact that took the two warring sides together brought them to the same side, and they started to argue over the importance of peaceful coexistence. In a similar way, Asiyanbola (2010) asserted that racial attachment is a high index that any mediator can analyse and explain as a frontline of conduct in a peace-making mechanism involving communal violence or local crisis. His analysis of the Ife-Modakeke crisis showed how the government encouraged some mild inter-relationships between the two groups by launching a robust anti-ethnic connection drive and encouraging social integration. The study's findings imply that the less the focus on ethnic attachment, the stronger the inter-personal bond, as shown by the negative correlational analysis (r) of 0.91. As a result, the underlying presumption is that illuminating the central clarified source of conflict is a crucial government position in the Ife-Modakeke crisis peace-making process. This achievement is capable of being emulated by governments of other conflict-torn areas.

During the Cocoa Boom in 1946, there was a resurgence of this age-old situation. Ife landowners began to claim higher dividends (Ishakole) than they had previously agreed to. According to Albert (1999), Ife landowners began demanding Ishakole payments of up to 10% of the extracted Cocoa from the Modakeke. The Modakeke were against it and saw it as an exploitative measure, which they mentioned to the Ooni Adesoji Aderemi at the time. This crisis lasted until 1949, when the Modakeke was defeated by judicial decisions (Olayiwola & Okorie, 2010). Conflicts erupted in Modakeke on May 18, 1949, prior to the West African Court of Appeal hearing on this matter, resulting in separate factions within the Modakeke themselves (Albert, 1999; Babajimi, 2003).

In this case, the government recognized divisible interests among the Ife, Modakeke, and their different sociocultural classes in its reactionary steps to the crisis. The government's important position in the peace-making process can be thought of as bureaucratic implementation, which no other mediator, be it conventional organizations or local and international semi-formal groups, has the organizational power to do. The government's job was to include a peace settlement that would circumvent the split results from concerned quarters after observing the divisible interest. The then military government issued a Decree (institutional enforcement) that dislodged the Ishaloke collections. The government saw the need to circumvent divisible interests of communities on lands and borders, particularly the protracted land conflicts between Ife and Modakeke, by cancelling the impeding 'factor' that is normally different from one community to another, despite the Decree's strong purpose of tailored land use in Nigeria. The causal factor in the Ife-Modakeke crisis, however, was Ishakole, which was more of a conventional arrangement with little to no institutional specific rules and enforcements. The Land Use Decree of 1978, issued by Nigeria's then-Federal Military Government, effectively ended the Ishakole regime.

Furthermore, in the early 1980s, the political dimension of the Ife-Modakeke crisis became fully realized. This began in 1980. Modakeke held a fund-raising ceremony. It was interrupted by the agents of the State (policemen). Modakeke casted aspersion on the then Ooni of Ife despite having informed him. It was argued that Modakeke was not a separate town and, as a result, had no legal authority to collect funds for town construction (Albert, 1999; Lamidi, 2019c). The Modakeke began lobbying for their own local government council as a result of this. Yet, they were placed under Ife as normal, contrary to their expectations. As a result, in July 1983, a political squabble erupted between the Modakeke and UPN campaign teams. Of course, the government's position in mediating this political crisis was merely a campaign promise by the national ruling party (NPN). As opposed to the then-manageable crisis, this has a huge impact on the conquest of aggression that could have potentially ensued on a large-scale war level.

Another political factor is the 1996 establishment of a new council (Ife East). The Modakekes objected to the headquarters' location, claiming that the town deserved a local government of its own. The government seemed to be taking a holistic approach to peace reconciliation. Despite the fact that all interested parties and organizations were active in the peace-making process, the government acts as the dispute resolution exercise's coordinating body. At this point in the peace-making process, one of the most important roles played by the government was the systematic recognition of peace-making phases with the help of both local and international organizations.

Existing discourses showed that the mediator needs to help the conflict parties in order to find a mutually acceptable agreement about the conflict issue and promote long-term stability (Ramsbotham et al., 2006; Svensson, 2007; Lamidi, 2019b). The role of the mediators is affected by the broader political context. If the central government is biased in relation to a local conflict, state actors may try to manipulate the conflict resolution process to ensure an outcome in line with central interests. Within this context, it might deter the reigning peace in Ife and Modakeke environments. The mediating levels of government seemed not to be biased in processing series of meetings between the two towns.

Moreover, this will undermine the ability of non-state mediators to promote sustainable peace. Given that the resolution of the conflict will likely be strongly connected to structures and institutions under government control—the judicial system, land rights and border delimitations, economic policy, etc.—the central state has a strong ability to constrain the possibilities available to mediators. It can even block certain mediators from the peace process and select others more likely to promote an outcome in line with the government's interests (Lamidi, 2019c). Of course, the role of NGOs became limited in Ife-Modakeke crisis due to non-alignment of government with any of the conflicting parties either on interest or request.

Collocating with communal conflicts in Sudan, it found out that in cases where the government was biased it tended to manipulate local appointments and empower pro-government elites, undermining the legitimacy of potential peace-makers at the local level (Brosché, 2014; see also Cox, 2016). Ikelegbe noted that central powers, through clientelist networks, may co-opt civil society actors "such that they become conforming of the social order, legitimizing of prevailing state and corporate power and stabilizing of the status quo" (Ikelegbe, 2006; Lamidi, 2019c). In such situations, the neutrality and consequently the legitimacy of non-state mediators will be eroded.

Inter-group disputes are fuelled by the parties' confusion and concerns about the mediators' role, in which the government is a key player (Lake & Rothchild, 1996; Walter, 2004). However, the parties' views of the likelihood of resolving the dispute at the negotiation table will be influenced by the government's impartiality in relation to the conflict. To avoid stifling confidence between conflicting parties, government functions must be based on trust. This statement emphasizes the importance of government building trust as the first step in achieving peace. It is the foundation for all other mechanisms. This was the government's most notable involvement in the Ife-Modakeke crisis. Building trust goes beyond avoiding political prejudice and emotions (Lamidi, 2019c).

On the one hand, a group, that is disfavoured, may conclude that any agreement reached will not be tenable in the long run (unless it aligns with central political interests). A party with the backing of central leaders, on the other hand, could see no need to compromise in negotiations if a better agreement can be struck outside of it, with active or passive government support (Lamidi, 2019a). Hence, when political bias is present, this causes a commitment problem and it will be difficult to find a negotiated agreement reflecting the parties' underlying interests. A second issue with commitment concerns the central government's position in the implementation phase (Lake & Rothchild, 1996).

Brosché supports this argument by demonstrating how prejudice and selective impunity destroyed communal trust (Brosché, 2014). The same argument applies if the central government, rather than one side in the dispute, is skewed in favour of a particular solution. If any compromise reached represents core political interests, the primary parties would have little confidence in its long-term viability. To this end, one of the successive factors for building confidence and improving peace-making on communal conflict is the government's impartial stance.

Peace-Making Principle Adoptable by Government: Lessons from Ife-Modakeke Crisis

From the fore-going exploration, this paper further put forth the basic guidelines for peace-making processes which could be broadly adapted before interrogating the specific outlooks of communal conflict. Basically, it strives to offer generalized principles of peace-making process adoptable by government in developing countries. It becomes clear that to achieve this central goal, clarification of the conflict situation is imperative. Burton (1997) asserted that clarifying conflict situation facilitates four (4) main issues: scrutiny, getting facts about the conflict status quo, understanding the quests of the warring parties and reduction in emotional content. These issues cannot be left unattended to, to resolve any conflict.

Furthermore, the government's position as a coordinating mediator must not be compromised. Lines of action should be strictly followed, with a clear focus on the parties' agreement and validity. With the standing theory, the disputants' sentimental minds will be simplified. It will take some time for the concerned individuals or organizations to shape themselves into the mediation task. However, it will be most appreciated in the long run. Designing an overarching interest to evoke the separatist desires of the opposing parties is a more rational theory of peace-making. This can be accomplished with caution by combining all competing interests into a single target (Kalyas, 2003; Wilkinson, 2006; Boone, 2014). The underlying presumption is that the more important the target is to the disputants' search, the greater the chance of reducing conflict momentum. Others must be able to clearly distinguish the views in order to further solidify the integrative approach. Brosché (2014) claims that this prevents unnecessary reactions and increases the legitimacy of the resolution mechanisms. The show of dedication in all fonts is an attribute of the peace-making process. In addition, the course of action should be moderated to avoid making excessive commitments.

The champions of peace-making seldom preach violent conquest. It is regarded as forcing one's principles and objectives on another by force. Apart from its overall immorality, it can stoke anger, grievance and animosity, which can later erupt into more confrontation and abuse. Nonetheless, in certain extraordinary conflict circumstances, victory can be the only realistic or desired resolution: a test of power and the unmistakable brutal defeat of the opposing side—as in Hitler's Germany. To accept that all conflicts should be settled by arbitration, mediation or consensus. It encourages an aggressor to believe that what is his isn't negotiable, but what is yours is. If the aggressor so desires, resisting attack forces a test of values, skills and will. However, unlike conciliation or appeasement, this can be a smoother, less conflictual and less aggressive means of settling conflict, assesses various force reactions when fighting attack and does not immediately retaliate in kind when confronted with provocation. The most effective response is one that transfers control to bases that can be used more efficiently while reducing the possibility of escalation into violence. And you should answer proportionately. Overreacting to violence risks escalating into a longer and more intense confrontation, whereas underreacting seems weak and risks failure and continued aggression.

Regulation, like the 1978 land use decree, is successful in mitigating conflict but does not contribute substantially to the peacebuilding. Fortna (2003) adopts the categories to evaluate peacekeeping missions' success over time. Standard missions, unsurprisingly, have the greatest deterrent potential and reduce the likelihood of dispute recurrence. Observer and multidimensional missions suffer as a result of deterrence capability. Surprisingly, compliance missions are not linked to longer-lasting stability. These results contradict Cederman et al. (2010)'s conclusion that more UN troops (typically deployed in compliance missions) lead to more peaceful post-conflict conditions.

Concluding Remarks

This paper enumerated several main ideas of peace-making. In a case where relevant status quo expectations are broken, conflict arises from what the parties want. The factors of war, as well as peace-making, are situational attitudes, desires, preferences, capacities and will. Land, people, wealth, ports and borders are all just instruments or artefacts of dispute between cultures. Material factors, such as a country's topography or a state's mountainous frontier, only serve to frame and physically restrict confrontation. A clash of minds is the essence of war. The emotional field is the battleground. Its resolution is based on psychological concepts and guidelines.

Peace-making will strengthen human rights in host nations, but political mandates and activities in particular policy fields, as in other contexts, make the difference. Murdie and David (2010) concluded that peacemaking not only unconditionally aids in the settlement of communal disputes, but also encourages reconciliation efforts and relief missions, all of which have a positive impact on physical dignity rights. Although mediation strengthens the opposing communities' present and future human rights situations, humanitarian missions have a longer-term impact and can be harmful to physical stability in the short term. Peksen (2012) went on to say that the pro-government policies and interventions could increase human rights abuses. Hostile actions do not result in significant reductions in the forms of crimes committed; in reality, they lead to an increase in political incarceration in the affected region.

This paper established potential peace-making driving principles that could be operationalized by governments of other conflict-torn countries. It emphasized the importance of doing a situational study of the resulting disputes. It did, however, emphasize the importance of the government's indivisible values and the development of systemic overarching interests in the face of varied society and stakeholder interests. Government involvement in communal dispute resolution should be accompanied by institutional implementation that ensures the opposing parties' utmost compliance, and it is required that the government will have a comprehensive means of recognizing peace-making processes.

References

Abdulrahman, I., & Tar, U. A. (2008). Conflict Management and Peacebuilding in Africa: The Role of State and Non-state Agencies. *Information, Society and Justice* 1 (2): 185–202.

Afolayan, A. A. (1998). *Emigration Dynamics in Nigeria: Landlessness, Poverty, Ethnicity and Differential Responses*. USA: Ashgate Publishing Limited.

Agbe, A. G. (2001). The Ife Modakeke Crisis: An Insider View. *Ife Psychologia* 9(3): 14–20

Aguda, A. S. (2001). "The Effect of Communal Conflict and Violence on Urban Residential Segregation." A paper presented at the International Conference on Security, Segregation and Social Networks in West African Cities 19th to 20th centuries Organised by the French Institute for Research in Africa (IFRA) and Institute of African studies and Centre for Urban and Regional Planning, University of Ibadan, Ibadan Nigeria 29th to 31st October 2001.

Akinjogbin, I. A. (1992). "Ife: The Years of Travail 1793–1893", in I. A. Akinjogbin (ed.) *The Cradle of Race: Ife from Beginning to 1980*. Port Harcourt: Sunray Publications.

Akinteye, A., Wuye, J. M., & Ashafa, M. N. (2001). "Zango-Kataf Crisis: A Case Study", in A. Ogomudia (ed.) *Peace Support Operations, Command and Professionalism: Challenges for the Nigerian Armed Forces in the 21st Century and Beyond*. Ibadan: Gold Press Limited.

Albert, I. O. (1999). "Ife-Modakeke Crisis", in O. Otite, & I. O. Albert (eds.) *Community Conflict in Nigeria: Management, Resolution and Transformation*. Ibadan: Spectrum Books.

Albert, I. O. (2001). "USAID/OTI Nigeria Intervention in Ife-Modakeke Conflict", in I. O. Albert (ed.) *Building Peace, Advancing Democracy: Experience with Third-party Interventions in Nigeria's Conflicts*. Ibadan: John Archers (Pub.) Ltd.

Albert, I. O. (2007). "Concepts and Methods in Peace and Conflict Studies", in C. Bassey & O. Oshita (eds.) *Conflict Resolution, Identity Crisis and Development in Africa*. Lagos, Nigeria: Malthouse Press.

Allen, T. D. (1999). *Developing Effective Mentoring Relationships: Strategies from the Mentor's Viewpoint. The Career Development Quarterly* 49 (1): 59–73.

Asiyanbola, A. R. (2007). Urban-Ethno Communal Conflict in Africa: Nigeria. A paper submitted for presentation at the Union for Africa Population Studies (UAPS) Fifth African Population Conference, Arusha.

Asiyanbola, R. A. (2010). Ethnic Conflicts in Nigeria: A Case of *Ife-Modakeke* in Historical Perspective. *Journal of Humanities, Social Sciences and Creative Arts* 5 (1): 61–78.

Astor, H. (1991). Mediation and Violence Against Women. National Committee on Violence Against Women December 1991, ACT: CPN Publications.

Astor, H. (1994) Violence and Family Mediation Policy. *Australian-Journal of Family Law* 8: 3–21.

Augsburger, D. W. (1992). *Conflict Mediation Across Culture: Pathway and Pattern*. Alouisville, Kentucky: Westminister John Knox Press.

Ayokunle, F., Eze, B., & Okechukwu, I. (2004). *Conflict Monitoring in Nigeria: Developing Civil Society Action for Early Warning and Early Response*. Nigeria: West Africa Networks for Peacebuilding Nigeria.

Babajimi, P. (2003). "Ife-Modakeke Conflicts in Osun State", in T. A. Imobighe (ed.) *Civil Society and Ethnic Conflict Management in Nigeria*. Ibadan: Spectrum Books.

Babangida, I. B. (2002). "Ethnic Nationalities and the Nigerian State: The Dynamics and Challenges of Governance in a Plural Nigeria". A Distinguished Annual Lecture Delivered at National Institute for Policy and Strategic Studies, Kuru, Nigeria.

Babbie, E. (2009). *The Practice of Social Research*. Basingstoke: Palgrave Macmillan.

Best, S. G. (ed.) (2005). *Introduction to Peace and Conflict Studies in West Africa—A Reader*. Ibadan: Spectrum Books Ltd.

Bevan, N. (2008). Proceedings of Meaningful Measures: Valid Useful User Experience Measurement (VUUM), 5th COST294-MAUSE Open Workshop, 18th June 2008, Reykjavik, Iceland.

Black, L. & Avruch, H. (1989). *Governance and Development*. USA: Palgrave Macmillan.

Boege, V. (2006). Traditional Approaches to Conflict Transformation: Potential and Limits. Berghof Research Centre for Constructive Conflict Management. http://www.berghof-handbook.nd (Accessed on March 10, 2010).

Boone, C. (2014). *Property and Political Order in Africa: Land Rights and the Structure of Politics*. Cambridge: Cambridge University Press.

Boulding, E. (2002). A Journey into the Future: Imagining a Non-violent World, *Peace and Conflict Studies* 9 (1), Article 4

Boulle, L. (1996) *Mediation: Principles, Process and Practice*. Sydney: Butterworth.

Brosché, M. (2014). *Cultural Diversity in African Conflict*. Cambridge: Cambridge University Press.

Burton John W. (1993). "Conflict Resolution as a Political Philosophy", in Dennis J. D. Sandole & Hugo van der Merwe (eds.) *Conflict Resolution Theory and Practice: Integration and Application*. Manchester and New York: Manchester University Press.

Burton, J. (1997). *Violence Explained*. Manchester: University Press.

Cajvaneanu, E. F. (2011). *Resolving Public Conflict, Transforming Community and Governance*. New York: Manchester University Press

Cederman, L., Wimmer, A. & Min, B. (2010). Why Do Ethnic Groups Rebel? New Data and Analysis. *World Politics* 62 (1): 87–119.

Chapman, C. & Kagaha, A. (2009). *Resolving Conflicts using Traditional Mechanisms in the Karamoja and Teso regions of Uganda*. London: Minority Rights Group International.

Collier, P. & Sambanis, N. (2002). Understanding Civil War: A New Agenda. *Journal of Conflict Resolution* 46 (1): 3–12.

Coser, L. (2006). *The Function of Social Conflict: A Review.* New York: Free Press

Cox, J. P. (2016). *The Urban Order: An Introduction to Cities, Culture and Power*. USA: Blackwell.

Dawson, G. (2004). *Peacekeeping, Peacebuilding and Peacemaking: Concepts, Complications and Canadian's Role*. Canada: Parliamentary Research Branch.

Dixon, J. C. (2016). Nice to know you? Testing contact, cultural, and group threat theories of anti-black and anti-hispanic stereo-types. *Social Science Quarterly* 85, 257–280.

Eaton, D. (2008). 'The Business of Peace: Raiding and Peace Work Along the Kenya-Uganda Border' (Part I & II). *African Affairs* 107 (426–427): 89–110, 243–259.

Elfversson, E. (2015). Providing Security or Protecting Interests? Government Interventions in Violent Communal Conflicts in Africa. *Journal of Peace Research* 52 (6): 791–805.

Ellis, F. (1996). *Rural Livelihoods and Diversity in Developing Countries.* Oxford: Oxford University Press.

Farah, A. Y. (1999). Roots of Reconciliation: Local Level Peace Processes in Somaliland. Alliances for Africa Bulletin November.

Fortna, V. P. (2003). Inside and Out: Peacekeeping and the Duration of Peace After Civil and Interstate Wars. *International Studies Review* 5 (4): 97–114.

Frank, M. L. (2002). Organizational Commitment Across Three Sectors: Public, Non-Profit, and For-Profit. *Public Personnel Management* 31 (2). https://doi.org/10.1177/009102600203100206.

Ikelegbe, A. (2006). Beyond the Threshold of Civil Struggle: Youth Militancy and Militia-ization of the Resource Conflicts in the Niger Delta Region, Nigeria. *African Study Monograph* 27 (3).

Imobighe, A. T. (2003). "Ethnicity and Ethnic Conflicts in Nigeria: An Overview", in A. T. Imobighe (ed.) *Civil Society and Ethnic Conflict Management in Nigeria*. Ibadan: Spectrum.

Kalyas, C. (2003). A Theory of Joint Asset Ownership, *RAND Journal of Economics* 34 (1): 56–64.

Kamat, S. (2003). The NGO Phenomenon and Political Culture in the Third World. *Development* 46 (1): 88–93.

Lake, D. A. & Rothchild, D. (1996). Containing Fear: The Origins and Management of Ethnic Conflict. *International Security* 21 (2): 41–75.

Lamidi, K. O. (2019a). Challenges of Local Governance Institutions on Peace-building in Africa: Empirical Insights from Southwestern Nigeria. *Global Journal of Social Sciences.* Calabar, Nigeria. 18 (1): 95–106.

Lamidi, K. O. (2019b). Peacebuilding: Conceptual, Trajectory and Imperative Analyses in the Third World Countries. *Canadian Social Science* 15 (2): 53–64.

Lamidi, K. O. (2019c). Communal Conflict, Communal Peacemaking and Governmental Interventions: Lessons from the *Ife-Modakeke* Crisis. *African Journal on Conflict Resolution* 19 (2): 11–32.

Lamidi, K. O. (2020). Localism and Peacebuilding Mechanisms in African Countries. *Peace Studies Journal* 13 (2): 10–28.

Lamidi, K. O. (2021). An Evaluation of Peacebuilding Strategies in Southwestern Nigeria: Quantitative and Qualitative Examples. *Journal of African Conflict and Peace Studies* 4 (2): 7.

Menkhaus, K. (2008). "Somalia: Governance Versus State-Building", in T. Charles (ed.) *Building States to Build Peace*. Boulder, CO: Lynne Rienner.

Mkutu, K. (2008). *Guns & Governance in the Rift Valley: Pastoralist Conflict & Small Arms*. Oxford: James Currey.

Montville, J. V. (1993). "The Healing Function in Political Conflict Resolution", in Dennis J. D. Sandole & Hugo van der Merwe (eds.) *Conflict Resolution Theory and Practice Integration and Application*. Manchester and New York: Manchester University Press.

Moore, C. (1996). *The Mediation Process*. San Francisco: Jossey-Bass Publishers

Murdie, A. & David, R. D. (2010). Problematic Potential: The Human Rights Consequences of Peacekeeping Interventions in Civil Wars. *Human Rights Quarterly* 30 (1): 49–72.

Murray, C. B. (1993). Moral Reasoning in Social Context. *Journal of Social Issues* 49 (2): 185–200.

Noll, D. (2013). *What is Peacemaking?* Toronto: Centre for Urban and Community Studies

Oladoyin, A. M. (2001). State and Ethno-communal Violence in Nigeria: The Case of Ife-Modakeke. *African Development* 26: 195–223.

Olaleye, I. O. (2016). Traditional Institutions and Conflict Management in Ekiti State. Being a Thesis Submitted to the Department of Public Administration, Faculty of Administration, in Partial Fulfilment of the Requirements for the Award of Master of Science (M.Sc.) Degree in Public Administration, Obafemi Awolowo University, Ile-Ife, Nigeria.

Olayiwola, S., & Okorie, N. (2010). Integrated Education: An Instrument for Resolving Ife-Modakeke Conflict in Osun State, Nigeria. *Journal of Alternative Perspectives in the Social Sciences* 2: 953–965.

Osaghae, E. E. (2006). *Colonialism and Civil Society in Africa: The Perspective of Ekeh's Two Publics*. The Johns Hopkins University: International Society for Third-Sector Research.

Otite, O. & Albert, I. (1999). *Community conflict in Nigeria: Management, Resolution and Transformation*. Ibadan: Spectrum Books.

Park, R. E. & Burgess, E. W. (2011). *Introduction to the Science of Sociology: Redefined*. Chicago: University of Chicago Press

Peksen, D. (2012). Does Foreign Military Intervention Help Human Rights? *Political Research Quarterly* 65 (3).

Raimi, A. (2010). Identity Issues in Urban Ethno-Communal Conflict in Africa. An Empirical Study of Ife-Modakeke Crisis. *African Sociological Review* 8 (2): 45–57.

Ramsbotham, O., Woodhouse, T. & Maill, H. (2006). *Contemporary Conflict Resolution: The Prevention, Management and Transformation of Deadly Conflict*. Cambridge: Polity Press

Salim, S. A. (1997). Group Unveils Broad Restructuring. *AWSJ* 16 (July): 44.

Scimecca, J. A. (1993). Theory and Alternate Dispute Resolution: A Contradiction in Terms? In HRM 540 Theory of Conflict Resolution: Study Guide Module 1, (1998) Charles Sturt University.

Svensson, I. (2007). Fighting with Faith: Religion and Conflict Resolution in Civil Wars. *The Journal of Conflict Resolution* 51 (6): 930–949.

Toriola, O. J. (2001). The Ife-Modakeke Crisis: An Insider View. *Ife Psychologi* A9: 21–29.

Walter, B. F. (2004). Does Conflict Beget Conflict? Explaining Recurring Civil War. *Journal of Peace Research* 41 (3).

Wilkinson, R. G. (2006). Income Inequality and Population Health: A Review and Explanation of the Evidence. *Social Science & Medicine* 62 (7): 1768–1784.

CHAPTER 8

Indigene-Settler Dichotomy and Citizenship in Africa: Perspectives from Otuocha and Jos

Godwin Ezurike Uchegbu

Background to the Study

The affirmation of citizenship in Africa primarily on the basis of primordial characteristics of indigeneity breeds tension between natives and settlers in diverse ways that make the primary intents and purposes of citizenship blurred in favour of myths. Indigeneship is entrenched in the national life, making it the basis of engagement as the key and characteristic feature of the state. Indigeneship fragments the Nigerian people and propels, in most cases, group contestations in both urban and rural areas. The Nigerian state has always been organized on the basis of indigeneship, and over the years has attained a politicized status of a creed that has serious economic and socio-political implications. Indigeneship has become the basis for engagement in the Nigerian State as it precariously continues influencing the dynamics of events in the state (Bayart, 1993; Ake, 1985). Indigeneship portends struggle for state power, economic dominance, political ascendancy and belonging (Camilleri and Falk 1992). It

G. E. Uchegbu (✉)
University of Lagos, Lagos, Nigeria

K. J. Ani et al. (eds.), *Political Economy of Resource, Human Security and Environmental Conflicts in Africa*,
https://doi.org/10.1007/978-981-16-2036-2_8

also includes the redefinition of the content of citizenship and conditions of sovereignty (Marshall-Fratani, 2006; CODESRIA, 2005). It fragments Nigerian peoples and propels in most cases group contestations in both urban and rural areas. Indigeneship takes different forms in contexts and threatens state survival on a daily basis. Indigeneship in Africa, unarguably generate conflicts, pushed mainly by public claims of privileges (Geschiere, 2009). Indigeneship has become an overriding issue in politics in Africa and it fosters conflicts particularly in Congo DR, Sudan, Zambia, South Africa, Ivory Coast, Rwanda, Burundi and Uganda (Nzongola-Ntalaja, 2004). Given that Nigeria is the microcosm of Africa's promises and problems, it embodies the larger continental political crisis facing most African countries (Zambakari, 2011). Why does indigeneship with all its challenges appeal massively to a lot of Nigerians? Why is it so penetrative? How have Nigerians handled this problematic particularly in Otuocha and Jos?

According to Adesoji and Alao (2009), the indigene-settler dichotomy is an old problem. In pre-colonial times, indigenous people and settler groups in states, kingdoms and chiefdoms fused easily. In the colonial era, it was officially used for purposes of divide and rule North/South, Stranger/Native, Sabongaris and Tudunwadas to push imperial interests. The Nigerian colonial administrators profiled Nigerians and tenuously used the indigene-settler dialectic to sustain atomism that made exploitation flourish unhindered. Nigeria emerged from colonialism as a federation of mini-nations that laid the foundation for politicized indigeneship. In the contemporary times, it has assumed a more dangerous dimension for individual and group gains. Nigeria unarguably, in recent times, has witnessed how dichotomy breeds unbridled tensions in rural and urban areas between indigenes and settlers that constantly set the country into cycles of violent contestations. Today, it appears clearly that indigeneship has taken entrenched positions in the state by consistently dysfunctionalzing citizenship goals of integration and stability. Indigeneship frequently provokes contestations for community belongingness due mainly to its discriminatory tendency that gives indigenes differential access to state resources over settlers. Indigeneship circumscribes and negates citizenship as it makes it play second fiddle and these pose a threat to law and order. Indigeneship has functioned as a faulting line (enclosure) in Nigeria multicultural state, and grabbed and politicized, becomes a deadly weapon for dislocation and disempowerment.

Nigeria today is a federation of mini-nations (Jinadu, 2007; Osaghae and Suberu, 2005). The 1946 Richard's constitution formalized regionalism that led to the emergence of East, West and the North that set the path for ultra-competitive communalism in Nigeria. The regions crystallized into mini-nations with all manners of divisive tendencies. Later as states and local governments were created (1967, 1976, 1987, 1991 and 1996), the sectionalism and territorialization of rights imbued in the regions became more visible and localized.

There is a seeming agreement among Nigerians that indigeneship is traceable majorly to Nigerian State heritage (nature and character of the state, its constitution and extant laws, power politics of the elites—actions and inactions, land claims, identity masking and the cake-sharing mentality). These forces coalesce in making indigeneship the key and characteristic features of Nigeria.

The Nigerian constitution appears as the most potent source of power to indigeneship. The 1999 constitution states Nigerian citizenship in Section 25(1) where it deals with single Nigerian citizenship. It is acquired either by birth, marriage or naturalization. However, Section 318 (1) (a)–(b) and Section 14(3) define membership of 36 states through indigeneity and federal character. In one instance, it upholds single universal citizenship only to abridge it with indigeneship requirements, thereby leading to two classes of citizens. This constitutional somersault by default makes the constitution approbate and reprobate itself. The contradictions are between the formal provisions on citizenship rights and the constrictions by indigeneship clauses of federal character, quota, zoning that promote contestations. The lacuna in the constitution makes citizenship a second fiddle to indigeneship as it raises de-facto practices over de-jure and informal rules over bureaucratic principles. The skewed preference for indigeneity over the years has established its proclivity to de-accelerate cohesion and generate conflicts in every sphere of national life. State creations threw up frictions (Imo vs. Abia, Anambra vs. Enugu, Cross River vs. Akwa Ibom, Edo vs. Delta, Oyo vs. Osun, Kogi vs. Benue, Benue vs. Taraba, etc.) that are hard to forget. In some other situations, the struggle is within the same state (Aguleri vs. Umuleri, Zango vs. Kataf, Tiv vs. Jukun, Ife vs. Modakeke, and Hausa-Fulani vs. Berom/Anaguta/Afizere). These challenges confine Nigeria to persistent static disequilibria. There is no gainsaying the fact that indigeneship has tenuously generated contestations between and among groups (intra and inter) and it appears more precarious in the face of severe economic adjustments and dwindling political opportunities that make latent and existing conflicts become intensified within the locale. Before state creations, sectional and particularistic tendencies were more manageable as there were enough latitudes in the regions to absorb the differences. With state and local government creations, which reconfigured the ethnic and geopolitical spaces, every other thing of value changed in the same manner. With creation of each new state, local government or autonomous community, the number of Nigerians categorized as settlers continues to grow, dividing the population ethnically, empowering those considered indigenous (rights and privileges) and disempowering others considered non-indigenous, and this constrains citizenship. Today, it is a weapon in the hands of varying and willing groups to cause damages, depending on the level of available resources and competition. According to Alubo (2011, 2), no fewer than 80 major eruptions occurred in various sections of the country in the first 55 months of civilian rule since December 2003, and still on the rise. In Otuocha, the conflict between Aguleri and Umuleri has been raging intermittently since 1934, though they are people of common descent, yet deadly divided. In Jos, the contesting groups are the Hausa/Fulani vs. Berom/Anaguta/Afizere. In April 1994, the peace of Jos was shattered as violence erupted because the indigenes openly opposed the appointment of a settler, Aminu Mato, a Hausa, as chairman for the newly created Jos North LGA. The frustration in these places comes from the obstacles inherent in the contradictory notions in the Nigerian constitution that affirms differential rights on indigenes and settlers in the same country. In some other situations and times, dichotomy takes the form of nationality groups that harbour deep-seated grievances against the state (MASSOB, IPOB and other pro-Biafra groups in the East, Taliban groups in the North East, OPC in South West, and MEND, Avengers in Niger Delta, etc.). The manifestations indicate that the Nigerian State project is not only problematic, but has continued to show visible cracks over space and time. Today, indigeneship has become an exclusive form of property—an economic asset that gives some access to benefits that others cannot have. The clashes in the contested areas are about 'rights' and most times, assume dangerous proportions. The greater puzzle is that the communities in focus (Otuocha and Jos) had co-habited for a long time before becoming a theatre of crisis. Before the recent eruptions, Plateau has been described as the home of peace in Nigeria. It then becomes necessary to raise questions on why such communities that have been relatively peaceful turned to deadly struggles and have done so over the years without arriving at enduring solutions.

The Nigerian State has always been organized into the dichotomy of indigenes and settlers in spite of the constitution which provides for universal national citizenship. The Nigerian State has over time embraced indigeneship to the extent that once one is born outside of one's ancestral land, one remains a perpetual settler with abridged rights wherever one settles. This discrimination makes citizenship play second fiddle to indigeneship. Today, this arrangement has institutionalized difference, a huge fault line in the polity. Indigeneship deprives settlers' access to opportunities. Indigeneship promotes unhealthy rivalry that makes settlers suffer alienation and humiliation that most times transform into violent group conflicts. Consequently, Nigeria because of indigeneship has not been able to arrive at acceptable standards of citizenship, and this has harvested lots of problems that make citizenship the victim. It then becomes apparent that a lot of Nigerian citizens remain so-called through nomenclature while indigeneship continues to flourish, leaving citizens discriminated in terms of land ownership, economic and socio-political ascendancy. The state suffers as this practice vitiates its capacity to achieve internal cohesion. A state that is not cohesive lacks the capacity to develop and build internal effectiveness and hegemony necessary for state building. It is in order to address these problems that this research intends to explore indigene/settler dichotomy generally, paying greater attention to Otuocha and Jos crisis in order to give directions to policy frameworks that can help address indigeneship in Nigeria.

Research Questions and Scope

1. What role(s) did the state play in entrenching indigeneship in Otuocha and Jos?
2. How does land claims and politics push indigeneship in Jos and Otuocha?
3. What way(s) do renditions of history in Jos and Otuocha motivate indigeneship contestations?
4. What policy frameworks can we generate that can help resolve indigeneship?

The study focused on indigeneship as a derivative from state heritage, land claims, politics and identity masking. The study combines Otuocha and Jos (intra-ethnic and inter-ethnic groups) as a microcosm of Nigeria's situation. The study identifies indigeneship crisis in Otuocha and Jos as veritable mechanism applied by the state managers and elites in the furtherance of their hegemonic control through obfuscation and mystification of its content and practice. The study reveals that eco-political forces are the engines for the conflicts and the myths of ethnicity, and religious motivations bandied by the contending elites are mere covers for their particularistic eco-political interests in Otuocha and Jos.

Operational Definition of Terms and Literature Review

The following terms were deployed in this study and are defined as follows:

Differentiated Citizenship: This is the practice of labelling individuals in a state based on ancestral ties to communities considered indigenous to an area, either as indigene or settler. Fragmented, deregulated, categorized, fractured and differentiated were used interchangeably in this study.

Settler: Is a citizen that lives in a place other than his aboriginal place. In Nigeria, when a citizen lives outside of state of origin, he becomes a settler and is constrained in enjoying some rights. For example, an Igbo from Enugu state or a Yoruba from Osun decides to settle in Anambra and Lagos, respectively, automatically loses full benefits that citizenship confers. Settler is used to differentiate the locals from other citizens that reside in a locality.

Politics of Anxiety: This refers to the type of politics where there is massive distrust among political gladiators; each struggles to protect his enclave and must win at all cost irrespective of the methods adopted in achieving results.

Soft State: Are states run by selective rules that promote the vested interest of the managers and their protégées. It is highly mechanical and particularistic, and Nigeria appears to typify this condition.

Voluntarism: Any approach to human phenomenon that is not guided by objective laws of nature and economic conditions but based on the belief that it is the will of man that plays the decisive role in social development is voluntarism.

Citizenship is a concept that has influenced the trajectory of civilizations over space and time. From the rise of the state, citizenship attained a major political status and borrowing the words of Saddam Hussein, and it is the "mother" of all rights, implying the highest level of exchanges between the state and its members. It is characterized mostly in the ideal, as a bundle of obligations, privileges and rights that a state grants to its members. It confers legal status, agency, membership and participation in a political community (Ramaswamy, 2007; Olukoshi, 2002; Osaghae, 1995). In general terms, citizenship helps in limiting and defining the conditions of belonging (Johari, 2012; Nnoli, 1978; Ake, 1996). The ancient Greek civilization developed the modern concept of citizenship between 700 and 600 BC (Pattie et al., 2014). The Greek sees citizenship as a structured arrangement that allows members of the polis to rule and be ruled. The Romans used citizenship for incorporating the diverse peoples in their vast empire state and is the hallmark of civilization. Citizenship writings are found in the works of Aristotle, Tacitus, Cicero, Machiavelli, Hobbes, Locke, Rousseau, Montesquieu, Robespierre, Alexander Hamilton, F.W. Hegel, etc. Also of significance are the contributions of John Stuart Mills, the Jacobins in France during the French revolution of 1789, Thomas Paine, Charles Tilley, T.H Marshall, John Rawls, etc. These writers operated in distinct times and made contributions that constitute very useful philosophical fountainheads. Rawls (1973) and Marshall (1950) attract attention for their liberal theory of citizenship. In his theory of justice, Rawls (1973) presents a framework that explains the significance of political and personal liberties, equal opportunity and cooperative arrangements. He postulates that when cooperation between individuals is fair, justice can then be insured, and justice, in essence, becomes fairness. Rawls' citizenship is on the notions of equality and freedom, and these principles still constitute central concerns within citizenship debates. Marshall's theory is with particular reference to English history, and it stresses both rights and duties and sees citizenship as legal status associated with membership in a community. For lots of scholars, Marshall's theory of citizenship is at best qualified as a theory of social change which documents the growth of nationality through time. Due to the limitations inherent in the liberal view of citizenship, we take a look at the Marxists position. For the Marxists (Marx and Engels, 1848), citizenship is part of the bourgeois legal ideology of individualism that sustains false consciousness. Marxists treat the rights associated with citizenship as the product of bourgeois manipulation and observe that the idea of equal citizenship in a class-divided society is a sham, as it always protects the interest, privileges, rights and powers of the dominant economic classes. Marxists tend to dismiss the idea of citizenship rights as an individualistic bourgeois charade designed to obscure fundamental economic and social class divisions behind a veneer of equality. For Marxists, only in a classless society with collective ownership of the means of production that citizenship can transcend class distinctions and class divisions and be useful to humanity.

Continuing along the critical tradition of the Marxists, the feminists (Ruth Lister, Helga Hernes, Martha Fineman, Mary Beth Norton, etc.) hold the constricted citizenship status of women as an outcome of the skewed power arrangements in society. The feminists see inequality between women and men in society as a socially induced result generated in the public space based on the differential powers between the two groups. The feminist critique has provided the impetus to widen the search for alternative conceptions of citizenship and politics, and one of the emergent perspectives is the socio-psychological school. The socio-psychological school is basically of two strands—micro (individual) and macro (society). The micro-strands are cognitive engagement theory and general incentives theory, while macro-based are civic voluntarism, equity-fairness and the social capital model. The core ideas of micro-models are that understanding citizens' participation depends on the individual's access to information and on their ability and willingness to use them (Dalton, 2002). The micro-models are constrained by its over-emphasis on the importance of choice behaviours of individuals, which neglect structural determinants of citizenship emanating from the wider community rather than from personal choices. The macro-structured theories emphasize citizenship as a product of macro-level social forces rather than being the result of choices made by individuals. The civic voluntarism model of Sidney Verba and Norman Nie (1987) typifies the strands. The main idea of this model is that individuals with resources will participate, and these resources are the product of social structures, inherited characteristics from parents and educators. Just as the general incentives theory neglected structural factors, so the structural theories overlooked incentives. The macro-strands may contribute to explaining citizenship, but it is unlikely to provide the sole explanation of what makes a good citizen. In general, the limitation of the social-psychological theories is that they suit Eurocentric needs and less relevant to African challenges, particularly in grappling with the problems of fragmented citizenship. Another perspective that has made contributions to citizenship debate is the post-modernists.

Postmodernists argue that the process of globalization has eroded state sovereignty, resulting in the erosion of the political salience of regional, national identities and citizenship forms. Theorists within this persuasion envisage the replacement of national identities with citizenship forms that transcend national boundaries (Harty and Murphy, 2005; in Simon, 2012). A major contributor to this perspective is Kymlicka (1995) in his work 'Multinational Citizenship' Kymlicka (1995) and his school of thought envisages the need for additional rights for vulnerable minority groups, to sustain themselves amidst the dominant culture(s). Another contemporary portrayal of post-modernist citizenship is that forwarded by cosmopolitan citizenship (Habermas, 1996). The theoretical standpoint is that cosmopolitan citizenship transcends the boundaries of nation and state, yet fails to dispense with either. This perspective focuses on inclusion and the accommodation of difference and the 'advanced interconnectivity of cultures' that characterizes late-modern society. Cosmopolitan citizenship puts the notion of post-nationalism at the centre, and the key factor here is the residence. At the foundation of Habermas proposal is the notion of the dual existence of a constitutional order and a civil society characterized by a discursive democracy grounded in public spheres.

Apart from citizenship, indigeneship is another term that deserves attention. The concept 'indigene' has root on the Latin word, 'indigena', meaning native. In Nigeria, an indigene means "son of the soil" or "land owners". Kyernum and Agba (2013) assert that 'indigene' is used to describe an individual who can trace his or her ancestry to a particular place. Similarly, Plotnicov (1972) posits that "owners of the land" is used in Nigeria to describe indigenous peoples of an area, even when they are politically subordinate there, while "stranger" (settlers) covers people of alien origin who are permanently settled among indigenous people. In Nigeria, indigenes are essentially a group of people that have a common identity, common descent or lineage and cultural identity (Kyernum and Agba, 2013). The Plateau Peace Conference (2004) defined indigeneship as being peculiar to a people who were the first to have settled permanently in a particular area and who are often considered as 'natives'. Indigenes are tight in-groups whose characteristics are essentially primordial, immutable and non-transferable. Membership is claimed through one's parents or grandparents identifiable to a specific community that is indigenous to a state or local government, which, in effect, makes it a correlate to a local ethnic cum linguistic community. It is never acquired by residence, marriage or naturalization. They have rights to their lands, traditions, culture and politics. It is also used to confer special privileges which are beyond the reach of non-natives. Nigeria, like many other states in Africa (Congo DR, Sudan, Zambia, South Africa, Ivory Coast, Rwanda, Burundi, Uganda, etc.), has integrated indigeneship as an overriding issue in statecraft and politics (Nzongola-Ntalaja, 2004).

Indeed, contested citizenship has increasingly become relevant in the affairs of African states as shown in Ekeh (1975), Mamdani (1996) and Abubakar (2007). Ekeh's work, "Colonialism and the Two Publics in Africa: A Theoretical Statement", explains the 'unique' nature of African politics and citizenship. He identifies the contradictory notions of dissociation of rights and duties in the conception of citizenship in Africa as it promotes difference creating two publics: an amoral civic public from which right is expected, without duties; and a moral public regarding one's ethnic group, to which one's obligations are carried out without expecting any right. Ekeh (1975) sees the fractured social foundations of politics and citizenship in Africa as a product of informal policy and the disorientation of civil society, all of which explains the pathologies of state and politics emanating from the dynamics of internal social structures. These dialectics have a lot to do with contested citizenship, which is the essence of the national question in many countries which manifests in an endemic crisis of state ownership, and its associated problems of distorted social order and related pathological political, economic and social relations. In the same vein, Abubakar (2007) study, entitled "Rethinking State Failure: Identity, Citizenship and the Challenges of Democratization in Africa", gives a succinct treatise of the challenges facing most African countries in managing diversity in contentious areas. He argues that issues of identity and citizenship are critical in democratic consolidation in the continent. In some African countries such as Nigeria and Congo DR, central governments persist, but could not ensure peace, security and stability within remote territories. For Abubakar (2007), the feasible way of addressing state failure in Africa requires coherent historical analyses of state formation in the continent as well as incorporating unhindered citizenship rights in the democratization and nation-building projects. Just put; at the vortex of African crises is the question of identity and citizenship rights.

Mamdani (1996) work titled "Citizen and Subject: Contemporary Africa and the legacy of late Colonialism" turned out a groundbreaking work on African citizenship dilemma. He reflects on that aspect of the colonial political legacy that passes for common sense in the region of the African Great Lakes. Mamdani's work demonstrates how states can limit the possible modes of being a citizen and how African countries under colonialism and after give rise to the bifurcation of citizen and subject. He shows how the British adopted two approaches to ruling colonies like South Africa: direct control as a form of public civil power (which excluded natives) and indirect decentralized despotism through the tribal authorities as their principal answer to the 'native question'. In the study, he contextualizes three issues: citizenship, civil society and political majorities and minorities as outcomes of the democratic process. Perhaps it is important at this juncture to address succinctly the state of indigeneship in Nigeria. Adesoji and Alao (2009) maintain that indigene-settler dichotomy in Nigeria is an old problem. In pre-colonial times, indigenous peoples and settler groups in states, kingdoms and chiefdoms mixed peacefully, and a blend of autochthonous and migrant groups emerged. Indigeneship practice in colonial times (divide and rule) was deployed by colonial state to achieve hegemony (Nzongola-Ntalaja, 2004; Mamdani, 1996; Osaghae and Suberu, 2005). In the post-colonial and contemporary times, the game only got bigger and the players are more sophisticated. Today, myths are established to justify the divide between indigenes and settlers to reap gains. For Nnoli in Akinboye (2010), the post-colonial elites that inherited the state turned indigeneship into tool of 'divide and enrich' for self-interests (economic and political ascendancy) at the expense of the state and citizenry. Indeed, indigeneship contestations in Otuocha and Jos had attracted research attention. The bulk of the studies identified focused majorly on ethnicity and religion as prime motivators for the conflicts. This position is visible in the works of Ositen (2009), Ojukwu and Onifade (2010), Ogbeide and Joshua (2014), Toure-Kaza (2003), Obateru (2010), Ibeanu (2003), Egwu (1998) leaned more towards eco-political dimensions in illuminating contested citizenship. The reality today is that the indigeneship phenomenon is slippery as the dividing line between indigenes and settlers is very thin in the context of modern Nigeria. Puts it succinctly that Nigeria now provides the kind of example we need to understand the contradiction of a state without citizens; wretched people on rich land; paradox of a cowboy without milk; tale of a cloth maker who walks naked to market; and story of a butcher who eats bone for supper. Other climes are expanding the horizon of their citizenship using globalist reconstruction model; ours continue to shrink from Universalist to locale. This shrinkage of space has constrained our capacity for development. The lost space is now being idealized and converted to violence.

To correctly understand the situation, we turn to Reinhard Bendix in Osaghae (1990: 597) on functional and plebiscitarían principles of citizenship. Under the functional representation principle, there is no direct relationship between the individual and the state; the individual is a citizen because the group to which he belongs is a part of the state, and he is represented by those who rule or lead his society. Under the plebiscitarían principle, however, all powers intervening between the individual and the state must be destroyed so that all citizens as persons possess equal rights before the sovereign national authority. Applied to the Nigerian case, the injunction which assumes that all citizens are equal is plebiscitarían, while that which requires belonging to a group indigenous to Nigeria in order to benefit as a citizen is functional and this dialectic constitutes the base for the practice of indigeneship in Nigeria. With this practice, two levels of citizenship emerge—state and national. State citizenship is exclusive only to indigenes; national citizenship makes every member inclusive.

Indigeneship does not offer hope enough to the point that Nigeria is jocularly described as a state without citizens. Nigerians mostly have their allegiances and trust preferences in their ethnic groups. The Nigerian constitutions of 1979 and 1999 provided the legal architecture for indigeneship, especially Section 318(1) paragraph (VI) of the 1999 constitution. Every Nigerian is both an indigene and a settler as citizenship is substituted with indigeneship particularly when it comes to the issues of appointment, election or other benefits from the state. The indigene-settler dichotomy has been worsened due to the politicization of the Federal Character Principle as enshrined in the 1999 Nigerian Constitution. Section 147 (b) of the 1999 Constitution stipulates that the president shall appoint at least one minister from each State, who shall be an indigene of such State but fails to spell out the objective criteria for doing so. For Ibrahim and Igbozor (2002), these tendencies undermine the very essence of Nigerian citizenship. Nigerian citizenship is static and localized, and the reality is that any Nigerian that wishes full benefits of citizenship should remain in ancestral place. Otuocha and Jos debacles attract attention because of the persistence and intractable nature of the contestations, as they have lingered with no enduring solutions in sight.

Otuocha and Jos are not just boundary disputes nor inter-communal clashes but a much deeper contest that borders on who gets the 'soul' and the 'heart' of the places, especially who has the 'right' to 'rights' that guarantees monopoly to the exclusion of others. At this point, we can safely say that in the Nigerian citizenship agenda, integration was neither part of the imperial agenda nor part of post-colonial schemes and this manifest in what Bayart (1993) calls the 'Rhizome state' meaning that the real strength of the state exists invisibly below ground while exhibiting increasing social atomism among the people. Nigeria, as it stands today, approaches a concentric formation of ethnic enclaves with its attendant reactionary impacts.

Whatever meaning citizenship acquires in a given context, place and time, this review has demonstrated that citizenship is critical in defining the boundary of belonging while indigeneship is its dialectic. Within industrial societies, citizenship is a negotiated and constructed form, which allows individuals and groups to shape their histories and piece together multilayered identities that embody broad outlook that engenders greater scope for inclusion and genuinely engaged involvement. Indigeneship concerns itself with the provision of special rights to indigenes, and it has generated controversies, with regard to its implementation. Indigeneship constrains the emergence of a common political practice that strengthens the integrative function of citizenship. The danger of indigeneship is its recognition and institutionalization of difference that undermines the conditions that can make single citizenship. Experience in Africa, and Nigeria in particular (indigene-settler dichotomy), in whatever form or shape has divided the people with its proclivity to violent contestations, and this has vitiated the capacity of the state in every facet of life. In Nigeria, the mere inclusion of citizenship rights in the constitution and extant laws as basis of equality does not guarantee anything. Implementation becomes considerably constrained in dealing with the challenge of inherent diversity, inequality and change. The bulk of the studies come from a functionalist viewpoint, which attaches high premium on primordial values as core issues in the contestations. The functionalist perspective considers religion, culture, identity and ethnicity as critical factors in understanding the debacles in the contested areas. However, situations in society make material and political conditions impact citizenship vigorously, especially in how a community defines itself between local, state and national levels. This study moved away from this fixation to a more materialistic approach that places greater emphasis on economic and political dimensions as critical issues in social life. Material and political interests usually motivate people, and in the Nigerian environment, that is visibly motivated by pressing scarcity, predation and unbridled quest for accumulation (individuals as well as groups). This dialectic gets entrenched (Marx and Engels, 1848). The conflicts in Otuocha have been re-occurring intermittently for over a century even when the people are of common descent, religion and culture, and have lingered on (Ukoha, 2005). Published and unpublished works on Aguleri-Umuleri and Hausa-Fulani/Berom/Anaguta/Afizire conflicts focused selectively on aspects of the conflict depending on the interests of the researcher, and we noted that they majorly failed in giving adequate attention to material and political forces as the engine pushing the group conflicts.

Voluntaristic treatment of indigeneship dominated most of the studies identified in the review, and this raises Nigerian citizenship status to a myth. The position in this study is that the inability of these studies to majorly anchor on the material and political spheres weakened the studies. The primary roles placed on primordial factors (ethnicity, religion, identity narratives, etc.) in the affirmation of indigeneship appear teleological, and this typifies mystifications because, in Otuocha, ethnicity and religion did not prevent the battles between Aguleri and Umuleri. This study considered the primordial factors as useful, but not necessarily sufficient reasons for the persistence of the conflicts. It, therefore, placed more attention on the material basis of human lives, and the power relations that uphold them as critical issues in these struggles irrespective of the unit of contestations (intra-group, Otuocha, and inter-group, Jos) and this was the gap that this study filled.

Theoretical Framework

This study recognizes and appreciates the relevance of functionalism, while placing the highest premium on political economy as the guide for the study. Functionalism is built on the principle that society is made up of parts that are interdependently linked and simultaneously function for the general well-being of the whole. That if any part malfunctions, the system gets back to equilibrium by making use of its internal self-regulatory mechanisms to adjust itself to normalcy. This perspective was popularized by Emile Durkheim, Talcott Parsons, Robert Merton, etc. The outlook was popularized in political science by Gabriel Almond, David Easton, Verba and Coleman.

Functionalism, as applied, focuses on structure, particularly the difficulty in welding a united country from the multiplicity of ethnic groups. This approach is represented by the works of Billy Dudley (1978), Eghosa Osaghae and Suberu (2005), Onigu Otite (1990), Adele Jinadu (2007), and others that canvass the position that while attempts must continue to be made to forge a united country, the sheer number of ethnic groups in Nigeria makes this a difficult task. Marxian orientation addresses the struggles from the point of valued resources (economic and political) that determine access between individuals and among groups. This orientation informs this study. This perspective is canvassed in Nigeria by Claude Ake (1996), Bade Onimode (1988), Julius Ihonbvre and Okwudiba Nnoli (2010), Iyang Eteng (1999), Bala Usman (1987) and others.

Marxian Political Economy Approach: This study adopted the political economy approach by Karl Marx and Engels (1848) as its main theoretical framework as well as its research guide in understanding indigeneship challenges in Nigeria. It is a macro-based conflict theory that is holistic, in both content and character. Political economy approach is a theoretical tool that recognizes the intimate relationship of the substructure-economic) as the base and the superstructure-political and cultural factors, etc., in processes of development and change. This approach places a high premium on economic factors as the driving force in society, thereby making history and social life materially deterministic. Its aim is on how power and resources are contested and distributed in different situations and the implications for development outcomes. Economic and political factors shape the boundaries of what is feasible and possible in the matrix of citizenship politics.

This approach provides a broad spectrum for understanding the environment (indigeneship dilemma) in Nigeria. The understanding is particularly relevant in fragile and conflict-affected environments like Nigeria where the challenge of building a stable state and society is fundamentally political. By using this approach, it was possible to show how indigeneship promoted the politics of anxiety that vitiates the state.

Methodology

Methods: The study adopted a qualitative non-statistical approach. Qualitative method is an approach in research that pushes the insider perspective on the social action. King, Keohane and Verba (1994) in Onuoha (2011:12), as well as Creswell (2014) and Reynolds (2014), argue in favour of qualitative approach. The choice of qualitative method is based on the fact that they are not only good at probing into people's thought process situations; they are also suitable when the principal research interest is to understand the true nature of a complex phenomenon. The adoption of the qualitative approach is grounded in the logic that there is more to social action that can be adequately captured when structured surveys, social experiments or the quantitative methods are in use. The method favours the 'lived experience' of the subject and the meanings that subject attaches to the phenomena investigated and is not necessarily less scientific than quantitative methods.

Design: The study is a non-experimental qualitative design. According to Creswell (2014: 12), research designs are enquiries within qualitative, quantitative and mixed methods approaches that provide specific direction for procedures in research. Others have called them 'strategies of inquiry' (Denzin and Lincoln, 2011) in Creswell (2014: 12). The study makes use of field sources (primary) and library for secondary materials.

Study location: There are two study places, namely Otuocha and Jos. Otuocha (Aguleri vs. Umuleri) in Anambra East LGA, Anambra state in South East Geopolitical zone and Hausa-Fulani vs. Berom/Anaguta/Afizere in Jos (Jos North LGA), Plateau State, North Central Geopolitical zone.

The present-day Otuocha emanated from the "oche coasts" called otu oche, a strip for farming and fishing purposes. In late nineteenth century, due to the advent of colonialism, it gradually evolved into a commercial centre. Aguleri and Umuleri communities are located along the banks of River Omambala (Anambra), a tributary of River Niger at Onitsha, South East Geopolitical zone. Today, Aguleri and Umuleri are in Anambra East Local Government with headquarters in Otuocha, a strip of land that has been the bone of contention. Otuocha became a beehive for the legion of imperial companies and till date still retains its commercial character.

Jos is the capital of Plateau State and comprises of three local governments (Jos East, Jos South, and Jos North that is the case for this study). The area known as Jos today was inhabited sparsely by ethnic groups who were mostly farmers. Jos' early history is linked closely to the prosperity of the tin and columbite industry. Jos developed rapidly following the British mining of the vast tin deposits in the vicinity. Tin and columbite were mined extensively until the 1960s. Today, Jos North LGA is the core of the state capital and the area where most commercial activities of the state take place. The groups in conflict in Jos North are Hausa-Fulani (Jasawa) and Berom, Anaguta, Afizere. The study locations visibly are tense areas, though in Otuocha there has been some sort of peace after the 1999 crisis. In Jos, the atmosphere appears more volatile as fire still smoulders intermittently. Most respondents interviewed preferred anonymity for fear of possible backlash from their communities, which was consented by the researcher.

Data Collection and Analysis

The research technique is qualitative, and the data collection tools used are the key informant interview (KII) and non-participant observation for primary data. Secondary materials (library sourced materials—published and unpublished, anthropological and archival documents, petitions, memoranda, websites and media reports, as well as reports of governments) were also used. The use of (KII) interview advantages lay in the fact that the interviewees had the opportunity to freely express their opinions on different aspects of the phenomena. The responses were recorded in tapes and were carefully sorted, categorized and analysed into key themes for qualitative explanation. Necessary facts, quotations were used as illustrations to enhance interpretations of informants' level of understanding of the indigeneship contestations in Otuocha and Jos. The entire data were interpreted with the aid of relevant theories, concepts and textual materials. All the materials (primary and secondary data) were processed using content analysis technique that makes it possible to make valid inferences from data gathered. Information obtained from data was linked to literature to give empirical support to the qualitative deductions of the researcher (Rosenwasser & Stephen, 2000). The analysis captured the contested notion of the Nigerian indigeneship by dwelling extensively on reconstruction, interpretation and critique of deep-seated opinions, animosities and grievances in their economic and political contexts among other things.

Data: The researcher interviewed (community leaders, town unions/associations, women and youth leaders and some other members of communities (see Interview guide, Appendix A). Using purposive sampling technique, 24 informants were selected and interviewed across the two sites. Due to the nature of the research problem and the study universe, purposive sampling fitted best as precise representativeness is not necessary, and the researcher has adequate knowledge of the population, its elements and research aims Babbie (2006), Reynolds, (2014).

Interviews were undertaken in December 2016 and January 2017. Key informants used were attached as Appendix B. The researcher took notes and recorded the interviews electronically that facilitated safe keep of materials, which enhanced analysis and interpretations. The researcher also used the non-participant observation. Facts gathered from observation enriched the relevant issues investigated. Library-sourced materials; published and unpublished, anthropological and archival documents, petitions, memoranda, websites and media reports, as well as reports of governments among others, were examined to complement primary data.

The materials (primary and secondary data) were analysed using the content analysis technique that enhanced the contextualization and interpretation of meanings. We processed all the notes/recordings taken in the field interviews, observations and even secondary sources that facilitated interpretation of materials. Four research questions were thematically explained showing summary of findings with copious quotations from key informants. Other details were subsequently discussed in the findings. The research was organized and presented thematically with some quotations showing the informants' opinions, views and understandings.

Discussions

RESEARCH QUESTION 1: What role(s) did the state play in the entrenchment of indigeneship in Otuocha and Jos?

Citizenship by prerogative is a product of the state. Over time, generally, the state has shown it cannot meaningfully exist without citizens because the state–citizen relationship is bonded like a Siamese twin cojoined from birth. The informants' responses show that the bulk of the challenges in the contested areas crops up from heritage, the ambivalence and inadequate enforcement of the right to rights by the state. For the respondents, they expected a lot from the governments, but they don't do enough in taking measures to curb the menace until things degenerate into full battles, and in some cases, the government appears as a biased umpire in the affairs of contending interests in the state. For instance, in Otuocha, the then-chairman of the Anambra East Local Government, an Aguleri indigene, was indicted as biased manager in Otuocha in the 1995 crisis vide (ASG, 1995 panel report) the chairman-backed Aguleri. In Jos, the Federal Government accused the Plateau State Government of mismanaging the Jos crisis, leading to the suspension of Joshua Dariye as Governor for six months in 2004, which demonstrates the biased involvement of the governments in the crisis. The state in its traditional characteristics typically enjoys relative autonomy in the management of state affairs and therefore is expected to act as a neutral arbiter in the affairs of contending interests in the country.

The study shows that the Nigerian state structure, values and practices have tremendous reactionary impact on citizenship today. The investigation reveals that the informants consider the state quite responsible for the impactful contestations that are in place in the contested areas of Jos and Otuocha. The respondents majorly are in agreement that the problems in Otuocha and Jos are traceable to the penetrative imperialistic adventures of the British and the peripheralized power politics of Nigerian elites. The British brought with them ideas and values that changed Nigerians tremendously. The atomistic tendency of the Nigerian state was created and sustained by the divisive strategies of the British, which emphasized those things that divided Nigerians, so that in our various formations, we remained closed shops. In the territories Britain ruled, they installed multi-tier style of citizenship that promoted privileges, discriminations and the ethnic characters of African societies.

The differentiation and the consequent conflicts that prevail between Aguleri/Umuleri and the Hausa-Fulani/Berom/ Anaguta/Afizere were rooted in the state heritage of divide and rule and escalated by post-colonial elites that use indigeneship as a tool to divide and enrich themselves. The indigeneship policy is not gratuitous, but deliberate decisions which inform the basis of social engagement in Nigeria and over time has become an unproductive way of managing diversity in a globalizing world. The intrigues and conflicts generated by indigeneship clauses in the constitution, policies and de-facto political practices become salient with the possibility of groups acquiring authority that can be employed to further the interests of such groups. The heritage of indigeneship (inclusion and exclusion clauses in constitution) explains the cycle of violence in Otuocha and Jos as contestations propelled by the desire to establish group-exclusive ownership over land through the 'son of the soil' strategy. From observation and interviews, the state plays big role in the Otuocha and Jos conflicts. The failures in managing the conflicts stem from the inherent deficient actions or inactions of the state in dealing with issues mainly due to its character and nature that accentuates proclivity to unending struggles in Otuocha and Jos. The elites subtly and manifestly captured the state and drag it along by pursuing agendas that fulfilled its narrow-vested interests. The Nigerian state always involves itself in the struggles of social formations (classes and ethnic) that vitiate its capacity to mediate in the ordinary affairs of the state, such as indigene-settler fights. Rather than being a neutral arbiter, the state acts as a party to conflicts, and this explains the anxieties and apprehensions that often accompany the structure of state power in Africa (Osaghae, 1995: 22); thus, the state becomes a site for contestations (Ihonvbere, 2003). The groups engaged in the struggles in Otuocha and Jos to secure exclusive access to land and political dividends. Mamdani (1996), Osaghae and Suberu (2005), and Egwu (1998) are in agreement with the findings that social conditions in Otuocha and Jos were put in place in the nineteenth and early twentieth centuries by the British and escalated by post-colonial and contemporary elites. Today, indigeneship is partly an outcome of inherited values from the colonial arrangement and the additions imputed on it by post-colonial and contemporary practices.

RESEARCH QUESTION 2: How do land claims and enclave politics motivate indigeneship in Jos and Otuocha?

The material conditions of production and its relations in any society are vital to fulfilling its requirements for its members (Marx and Engels). The study shows that unbridled struggle for land is the springboard for all manner of contestations in the conflict areas. The land issue has always been a vexed one. Land is at the heart of the unresolved national challenges that contentiously drive politics in Nigeria. Land is such a prized asset in society that has attracted inestimable value. The premium placed on land has made contestations over it an attractive venture. People want to possess land and reap everything it can offer. Following the coming and the rise of mercantilist activities of the British in Nigeria, the status of Otuocha was elevated to a prime position of commercial and administrative centre in the Anambra River basin. The status triggered struggles over lands by individuals, organizations and communities. Jos also came into prominence with the discovery and mining of tin and columbite by the British. Based on the evidences (informants and literature), the pecuniary interest in Otuocha land escalated the conflicts because, from records, all the reported clashes and violent confrontations between Aguleri and Umuleri mostly followed outcomes of court litigations that severe the parties in the dispute. The moment it happens, the losing side mobilizes to negate the outcomes as none of them wants to lose Otuocha.

In 1933, the first court judgement was delivered that subsequently led to the first major clash in 1934 between Aguleri and Umuleri as a reaction to the decision of 1933. In Jos, the mining of tin pulled a lot of cheap labour from disparate groups that were ordinarily living their lives into the colonial enterprise that hastened communal struggles for land and political ascendancy to the detriment of the state. The struggles generated all kinds of narratives from Berom, Anaguta and Afizere to support 'first arrival' status to justify exclusive rights over Jos. It is the claims and counterclaims that drive the contestations in the areas as confirmed by informants. The indigeneship struggles in Jos keep throwing up from time to time, vitiating the state and the citizenry alike. From the responses, the most salient factor in the conflict matrix in the contested areas undoubtedly is the 'right to right' over land through claims of 'first' arrivals that automatically confer the 'son of the soil' monopoly rights that must be secured at all cost. The managers (politicians) who inherited the state escalated by default the burdened state with their dead weights, making the states unproductive and unviable through heavy reliance on primordiality. From literature, the colonial governments experimented with all manner of land policies it thought would serve its interest from private property, individual ownership of land and the attendant freedom of alienation of land which they thought would fast-track capitalist penetration, and by extension, the colonial experiment (Mbajekwe 2002). From informants' responses, the Otuocha conflicts escalated after key court judgements restrained access to Otuocha land that prevented the collection of rents and leases from the lands. The traditional Prime Minister (Onowu) from Umuleri stated the point succinctly when he said; my late father told me that time past, nobody ever sold land in our community. This idea of selling and buying land started when the white man came to rule over us. They taught our people the habit of selling land. If our people did not start to sell land, Aguleri and Umuleri would not be killing themselves today because these conflicts began when our people began to struggle for wealth through land sales.

The study shows that the attitude of governments did not help matters as they vacillated in putting up permanent solutions to Otuocha's problems. In Jos, the tactic was more precarious in the manner that land and indigeneship were tied together to enhance balkanization and hegemonization of society. In Jos, the colonial state tried all sorts of policies that left the areas divided. The British managed traditional institutions and other structures in Jos in such a way that left the areas perpetually divided. In Jos, chieftaincy and traditional authority were tailored to serve the overall interest of the colonial establishment, which was surreptitiously sustained by post-colonial and contemporary arrangements. The core issue is that for reasons of political expediency, the Nigerian state deliberately promotes indigeneship to enhance self-interests in society. For instance, if the colonial government had established projects on the land in Otuocha after the imperial companies have divested themselves, it would have taken control of it and obstructed the prospects of future struggles by the two communities. It failed to do so; unoccupied and undeveloped, the land became the source of continuous dispute between the communities. The differentiation and consequent conflicts that prevail between Aguleri/Umuleri, and the Hausa-Fulani/Berom/Anaguta/Afizere were rooted from colonialism and escalated by post-colonial elites that use indigeneship as a tool to divide and enrich themselves. The situation in Jos is aptly captured by the then commissioner of police in Plateau State, Mr. Akao, Olajide "the problem in Jos is all about land and politics, not ethnicity or religion" (Eagle-online edition of 6 March 2011: 1). This position is reinforced by interview and literature that shows that none of the upheavals in Jos (1994, 1998, 2000, 2002, 2004, 2010, 2012, 2014, etc.) till date is a direct fight emanating from religious or ethno-cultural infractions between Muslims and Christians, but elite perception of economic and political opportunities' 'marginalization'. In the North region of Nigeria, until the creation of states in 1967 and subsequent ones, the Hausa-Fulani constituted the hegemonic group with resentful animosities from the minority groups in the Jos area. Upon state creations and its reconfiguring of ethnic composition and identity, the minority groups latched on the opportunities state creations brought to press for their own access and control of their lands (indigeneship). The Jos debacle is aptly captured by a Berom man:

> These Hausa-Fulani are domineering. Majorly, they came from Bauchi area, they are not from Jos. hey have always troubled us even before the time of the British to independence. Now that state creations have restored our denied rights, we cannot any longer allow these usurping strangers to rub shoulders with us in Jos anymore.

The intrigues and manipulation generated by indigeneship conflicts become salient with the possibility of groups acquiring authority that can be employed to further the interests of such groups.

RESEARCH QUESTION 3: What way(s) does recourse to production of history in Jos and Otuocha drive indigeneship?

The finding is that the putative narratives of the groups in contestation were to establish their supremacy in order to reap gains. The logic of oligarchy is that there will always be elites in society. Elites are unavoidable segment in any state whose interests covertly and overtly influence groups. The informants' responses majorly show that the elites contribute to conflicts among citizens and between citizens especially over the question of individual and public rights and entitlements in communities. These conflicts of interests are the core and standard features in the contested areas. In the crisis areas, the power elites have demonstrated that 'interest', mainly economic and political, constitutes the base for actions. The elites do influence and dominate the direction of the superstructure (culture, religion, ethnic, etc.) that includes various narratives of 'first arrivals' in the areas. The interviewees complained that elites in their various communities over time smartly obscured the consciousness of people, making them believe that they have common gains to reap in the struggles while covertly they pursue their personal interests. Most of the reproductions of histories in the areas are generally deemed as the outcome of elite creations. There is the held view by majority of respondents that Aguleri and Umuleri elites engaged in the unhealthy rivalry and wars for control of the land because of monies from land leases, rents, contributions/levies by the communities to execute the land cases. Overtly, it appears as if the elites were obsessed with protecting the interest of the communities. In reality, they were self-seeking, motivated by their desires to appropriate the land and rents.

The elites in Otuocha engaged in physical combat and legal battles in the courts as they struggled to acquire and possess the land. In Jos, much of the violence witnessed in the town was stirred by the elites trying to recapture lost positions in inter-elite tussles. The losing elites usually fall back to ethnic demagoguery of 'marginalization' for reinventing their hegemonic controls. For instance, the troubles, dislocations and upheavals in Jos (1994, 1999, 2001, 2002, 2008, 2010, 2012, etc., till date) and even the herder/farmer clashes are traceable to interests that were foisted through ultra-ethnic narratives pursued by the respective elites. Anytime there was a shift in the power equation between the contending elites from the various ethnic enclaves, and the elites that feel disadvantaged from the power play smartly fall back to the pliable masses that follow the elites to their detriment. In Otuocha, the masking of interest was deployed effectively by the elites of the communities in the 1995 clash. The conflict, which ordinarily was an economic struggle between two property developers from the two communities, ended up as community war. According to Onwuzuruigbo (2011), the 1995 conflict was triggered by an attempt to construct a petrol filling station by elite from Umuleri, Chief Dan Ekwevi, alias 'Okwu oto ekene eze' (one who stands up while greeting the king). Ekwevi was said to have bought the land from a fellow Umuleri man known as Ikeli who had bought the land from Ngwuka, an Aguleri. Ekwevi, in 1995, began to develop the land. Aguleri elites who nursed interest in the land resented what they felt was unwarranted interference of Umuleri elite in Aguleri land. On September 30, 1995, Aguleri mobilized their youths, and they stormed the construction site, attacked the builders and later engaged Umuleri youths in a fight that quickly engulfed the two communities. Every group in the contestation has over the years crafted narratives/tales that separate them from others as indigenes while the rest must remain settlers perpetually. The colonial engagement produced Otuocha and Jos debacles because, before the invasion of the areas, land was part of the people's commonwealth, and ethnic differentiations were infrequent, minimal and peripheral. The heritage in terms of various land policies that were applied by the state alienated and disempowered the communities and created new sets of values and new modes of competitive communal struggles with the resulting anomie that has prevailed to date in the society. One key informant from Umuleri expressed his doubts:

> I have always wondered about 'distribution.' How are we going to share expected gains from the struggles? What will happen if at the end of the efforts we secure Otuocha? How will the lands be shared between and among members of the community equitably without creating grounds for internecine war amongst ourselves?

There were accusations of elites on both sides of embezzlement of community funds, rents and leases from Otuocha lands and expropriation of lands for personal enrichment, and these were covered under the guise of common interest of the communities. In Otuocha, elites were accused of converting part of the land in dispute to personal use. They were also accused of misappropriating rents from land leased; stealing and embezzling community funds set aside to prosecute Otuocha land cases. The enclaves were sustained by putative narratives for the war to continue to be beneficial primarily to the vested stakeholders in all the contesting groups. Following the carnage of the 1999 Otuocha crisis,

President Olusegun Obasanjo invited the leaders of the two communities to a meeting, and an agreement was reached that Otuocha does not belong to any of the warring groups; so today, there exist some forms of peace in Otuocha.

RESEARCH QUESTION 4: What policy frameworks can we reinvent to help resolve indigeneship?

The indigeneship legacy has a lasting impact on the development of Nigeria's post-colonial territorialized belonging. Nigeria practices differentiated citizenship, and over time, it has crystallized into secured closed shops, defended at all cost by the elites. Most of the state policies (regionalism, state of origin, quota, federal character, zoning, etc.) have ended up throwing up some unintended consequences (ethnicization syndrome) for the society. The trajectory of enclave politics was formally established with introduction of regionalism by the Richards' constitution of 1946. The regions that emerged were coterminous with identifiable primordial groupings that were sustained by mechanical solidarity for their pursuit of economic and political interests. Elites must not make inroads into territories that are not their ancestral bases. The structural frame and the emergent politics of closed shops enhance the continued segregation of Nigerians into camps that crystallises into permanent settlements that are prone to attacks by the settlers and indigenes, respectively (sabongari and tudunwada in the north). The enclosure politics subtly constitutes the ideological underpinnings behind the state policies of regionalism, federal character, quota, indigeneship, state of origin, zoning, among others as elite benefits.

This makes Nigeria an agglomeration of enclaves or closed shops (Post and Vickers, 1973; Joseph, 1991; Dudley, 1982; Eteng, 1999). Nigeria seemingly takes these policies as platforms to bring everybody on board but on the strength of diversity (ancestry, language, religion, etc.) that ends unintentionally to inchoate the society. The enclaves exist in the form of regions, states, local governments and diverse autonomous communities that are fertile grounds for all manners of agitations and conflicts. These enclave politics promote constant agitations for the creation of states and local governments. The interviewees from all the contesting groups displayed high level of understanding of the issues in conflict. The observations, discussions and informants' responses were distilled to reinvent threads for policy frameworks that can help eliminate indigene-settler dichotomy in Nigeria and elsewhere in similar situations.

We suggest the following as thread for citizenship policy frameworks. The state should inculcate the enforcement of residency rule—citizens' rights and rule of law by making them justiciable. Habermas, Onimode, Ake, Nnoli, Dudley and other scholars are in agreement that in the globalized world of today residence, the rule of law and enforcement of citizens' rights have become feasible means of affirming citizenship and eliminating discrimination inherent in indigeneship.

Summary of Findings

The study is an investigation into indigeneship; how it obstructs and frustrates the emergence of acceptable standards of citizenship by focusing on the Otuocha and Jos conflicts as a microcosm of the Nigerian state. The study provides a spectrum to understanding indigeneship and proffered solutions to the problems. In Otuocha, Aguleri and Umuleri are communities that are homogeneous in most social characteristics of ethnicity and religion (intra) but fiercely opposed to each other mainly because of indigeneship for land and political ascendancy. In Jos, inter-ethnic cleavages between Hausa-Fulani and Berom/Anaguta/Afizere also anchor on land and politics. The study reveals the tensions and conflicts in contested areas are consequences of mainly vested politicized decisions of state managers and elites, not necessarily of ethnic and cultural differences. The study establishes that the contestations in Jos and Otuocha are linked to the quest for ascendancy in land and political controls for individual and group gains through tenuous masked mobilization of ethno-religious and other related primordial identities. The study identifies that indigene-settler dichotomy diminishes the emergence of citizenship pursued through the deployment of various default public policies of inclusion/exclusion (regionalism, federal character, quota, zoning, state of origin, etc.) that favours indigenes over settlers.

The findings show that indigeneship obfuscates the understanding and practice of citizenship, and it generates the cycles of violence in contested areas (Otuocha and Jos) and it vitiates the state. The study established indigeneship as politicized fault line crafted by the state and elites for gains in Otuocha and Jos. The study identifies that people are likely to fight the moment their economic and political interests are jeopardized or threatened. The study successfully identified land and politics (ascendancy) as critical factors pushing the struggles in the contested areas irrespective of affiliation (intra- or inter-ethnic). The study identified ethnicity/religion;

putative narratives of the groups play instrumental roles as veneers/mask for mobilizations, not necessarily as ultimate reasons for the contestations in Otuocha and Jos. The study-generated policy threads (inclusive residence, rule of law and universal enforcement of citizens' rights) as guides that can help the making of policy frameworks to eliminate indigeneship and actualize citizenship in Nigeria and elsewhere in similar situations.

Recommendations

The study opines that citizenship conundrum in Nigeria needs to be addressed holistically by eliminating the contradictory notions in Nigerian citizenship (constricted rights, policies and practices) in the constitution, extant laws and de-facto politics by enforcement of the rule of law, citizens' rights and residency rights. The following are the recommendations for eliminating indigeneship and reinventing citizenship.

- Enforcement of single universal citizen rights throughout the length and breadth of the country across state, ethnic and religious lines in place of the multi-tier system of rights that portends uncivil tendencies for discriminations and conflicts.
- Nigeria collective identity should be on universal political and legal principles of human rights, the rule of law and practices moulded on the country's constitution and extant laws without any abridgement.
- De-territorialize belonging by de-emphasizing geographical factor (son of the soil/ethnic cum linguistic) labels that propel struggles. Government should take over contested lands to eliminate the agitations between and among communities (Otuocha and Jos).
- Promote civic engagement culture as counter-power to the hegemonic power of the power elites.
- Inclusive, residency-based citizenship is the feasible way of building and managing Nigeria.

Appendix A

Interview Guide

The State and Indigeneship Crisis in Otuocha and Jos

1. What would you say about the advent of the white man and its link to communal conflicts in your area?
2. What ways did the colonial rule impact indigeneship?
3. How do you see the state heritage of 'divided and rule' and the contestations in your area?
4. What is your perception of settlers restricted right in relation to indigene 'privilege' in your area?
5. What is your impression of the state practice of indigene-settler dichotomy (first to arrive) in a diverse Nigeria?
6. What is your opinion on the state actions or inactions in handling the disputed areas?

Land Claims, Politics and Indigenenship in Otuocha and Jos

7. We are the first to settle here, the lands belong exclusively to us. How do you react to this practice?
8. What is your impression towards the idea that settlers should remain settlers perpetually?
9. What is your impression of Government efforts on enforcement of rights especially on lands?
10. Does agitation for land affect the relations between communities?
11. How do you see the Nigerian state in the management of the indigeneship disputes?
12. Do you see the state as taking sides in the struggle of groups?
13. In your assessment, do you take state officials as fair to all parties in the crisis?
14. Is the state neutral in the ways it handles cleavages in the contested areas?
15. Do you share the opinion that the government is not decisive on issues until it degenerates to conflict (not proactive)?

Identity Renditions and Indigeneship Crisis in Otuocha and Jos

16. We are the first to settle here therefore the land is ours. How authentic is this claim?
17. Do you share the opinion that settler elites should restrict their involvement in politics to native places?
18. How do you see limiting of citizens' rights anywhere in the contested areas?
19. Please, who should enjoy full citizenship rights in the disputed area?
20. Settlers should not take appointive positions; it is for the sons of the soil. What is your impression?
21. Do religious and ethnic infractions really form the basis for group contestations?

Guides to Suggested Policy Frameworks That Can Help Actualize Citizenship

22. Do you see elite interests in the policy of indigeneship (Federal character, quota, zoning, etc.) as the motives for prosecution of conflicts?
23. Has the programs/policies of the state on indigeneship as it were, ameliorated group conflicts in the contested areas?
24. Is it proper to tie indigeneship to ethnicity in a diverse country?
25. Please give main reasons that you consider critical in the struggles of the contested areas.
26. Please make suggestions that can help in eliminating indigeneship and actualize citizenship.

Appendix B

Key Informants

Otuocha

1. H.R.H Igwe Nelson Okoye. Igwe Okebo 1 of Umuleri (Interviewed Umuleri 28 December 2016)
2. Mike Ekweonu Onowu, Iyasele of Umuleri (Traditional Prime Minister) Interviewed Umuleri 29 December 2016)

3. Hon. Pius Okonkwo (President General, Umuleri General Assembly) Interviewed Umuleri 29 December 2016)
4. HRH. Pius Idigo Igwe of Aguleri (Interviewed Aguleri 30 December 2016)
5. Eze Chukwuemeka Eri (Traditional prime minister) Aguleri (Interviewed Aguleri 31 December 2016)
6. Dr Sam Nnana Special Assistant to the Governor of Anambra State (Interviewed Aguleri 4 January 2017)
7. Chief Ignatius Akudolu—Community leader (Interviewed Aguleri 4 January 2017)
8. Mrs. Chinasa Ejinkeonye—Community leader (Interviewed Umuleri 5 January 2017)
9. Chief Chukwukandu Ikenna—Youth leader (Interviewed Umuleri 5 January 2017)
10. Chief Okoli Emeka (Interviewed Umuleri 5 January 2017)
11. Ikechukwu Anajere (Interviewed Aguleri 5 January 2017).

Jos

1. Jonathan Nyam, Spokesperson Anaguta Youth Movement (Interviewed Jos 13 January 2017)
2. Danityan Titus (Interviewed Jos 13 January 2017)
3. Chief Malachy Akwen (Interviewed 14 January 2017 Jos)
4. Prof. Danladi Atu (spokesperson for Afizere) (Interviewed Jos 14 January 2017)
5. Moses Gbande (Interviewed Jos 13 January 2017)
6. Ericson Fom (Spokesperson for Berom) (Interviewed Jos 15 January 2017)
7. John Nodza (Interviewed Jos 14 January 2017)
8. Ruth Akuh (Interviewed Jos 15 January 2017)
9. Aliyu Usman (Interviewed Jos 16 January 2017)
10. Haliru Garba (Interviewed Jos16 January 2017)
11. Dr Pindar Nelson (Interviewed Jos 16 January 2017)
12. kolo, Mamman (lnterviewed Jos 15 January 2017)
13. Haruna, Bello. (Interviewed Jos 16 January 2017).

References

Abubakar, D (2007). Rethinking state failure: Identity, citizenship and the crisis of the African State. Paper presented at the annual meeting of the International Studies Association 48th Annual convention Hilton, Chicago, IL.

Adesoji, A and Akin, A (2009). Indigeneship and citizenship in Nigeria: Myth and reality. Journal of an African Studies 2(9), March.

Ake, C (1985). A political economy of Nigeria. London: Longman.

Ake, C (1996). Is Africa democratizing? CASS Monograph. Lagos: Malthouse.

Alubo, O (2011). Ethnic conflicts and citizenship crises in Central Nigeria. Ibadan: PEFS Press.

Babbie, E (2006). The basics of social research. Belmont: Wardsworth.

Bayart, J. (1993). The state in Africa: the Politics of the belly. London and New York: Longman.

Camilleri, J, and Falk, J (1992). The end of sovereignty: The Politics of a shrinking and fragmenting, world England. Elgar publishers.

Creswell, J (2014). Research design: Qualitative, quantitative, and mixed methods approach. Thousand Oaks, California.

Dalton, R. (2002) Citizen Politics. New York Press.

Dudley, B. J. (1978). Instability and political order: Politics and crisis in Nigeria. Ibadan: University Press.

Dudley, B (1982). An introduction to Nigerian Government and politics. Macmillan Nigeria.

Eagle-online edition of March 6, 2011. https://theeagleonline.com.ng/.

Egwu, S (1998). Structural adjustment, agrarian change and rural ethnicity in Nigeria: Nordiska Afrikainstitutet research reports no 103.

Ekeh, P (1975). Colonialism and the two publics in Africa: A theoretical statement. Comparative Studies in Society and History 17 (1), 91–112.

Eteng, I (1999). Ethnic identity and the national question in Nigeria. Paper presented on 'civil society and Africa's democratic recovery' workshop, hosted by Nigeria-South Africa dialogue/initiative, held at Federal palace hotel, Victoria Island, Lagos, February 12–13.

Geschiere, P (2009). The perils of belonging: Autochthony between facts and norms: Contributions to a discourse theory of law and democracy, Rehg (trans.). Cambridge (MA): MIT press.

Habermas, J (1996). Globalization and citizenship: Report of the UNRISD International Conference, Geneva, December 9–11.

Ihonvbere, J (2003). Political liberalisation and democratisation in Africa: Lessons from country experiences. Amazon Publishers.

Ibeanu, O (2003). Aguleri/Umuleri conflicts in Anambra State. In Civil society and ethnic conflict management in Nigeria, Imobighe, T (ed.). Ibadan: Spectrum Books.

Ibrahim, J and Igbozor, O (2002). Memorandum submitted to the presidentila committee on provisions and practice of citizenship and rights in Nigeria. Lagos: CFCR.

Jinadu, A (2007). Managing and explaining ethnic conflicts in Africa: Towards a cultural theory of democracy. Claude Ake Memorial Papers no 1. Nordic Africa Institute, Uppsala University.

Johari, J (2012). Principles of modern political science. New Delhi, India, sterling, pp 638–652.

Joseph, R (1991). Democracy and prebendal politics in Nigeria. Ibadan: Spectrum.

Kyernum, N and Agba, A. S (2013). Indigenship question and its implication on the socio-economic development of Nigeria. Journal of Social Sciences and Public Policy 5 (2).

Kymlicka, W (1995). Multicultural citizenship. Oxford: Oxford University Press.

Mamdani, M (1996). Citizen and subject: Contemporary Africa and the legacy of late colonialism. Princeton, NJ: Princeton University Press.

Marshall, T (1950). Citizenship and social class. London, UK: Pluto Press.

Marshall-Fratani, R (2006). The war of who is who: Autochthony, nationalism, and citizenship in the Ivorian crisis. African Studies Review 49 (2), 9–43.

Marx, K and Engels, F (1848). The communist manifesto. Moscow.

Mbajekwe, P (2002). Debating land policy in colonial Nigeria. In Nigeria in the twenty-first century, Falola, T (ed). Durham NC: Academic Press, pp 263–279.

Multinational working group on citizenship and Identity in Africa CODESRIA (2005). Monographs series: Dakar, Senegal.

Nnoli, O (1978). Ethnic politics in Nigeria Enugu. Fourth Dimension Publishers.

Nnoli, O (2010). The tyranny of petty bourgeois political discourse in Fifty years of nationhood: State, society, and politics in Nigeria, Akinboye, S. Lagos Concept Publishers, pp 59–74.

Nzongola-Ntalaja, G (2004). Citizenship, political violence and democratization in Africa. Global Governance, 10, 403–409.

Obateru, Y (2010) Distress rule. Vanguard 3 (21), 9.

Ogbeide, F and Olatunji, J (2014). Between conflict resolution and conflict termination: A revisit *of the Ife-Modakeke crises.* Journal of Conflict Management in Africa and the Middle East (1), 001–008, July.

Ojukwu, C and Onifade, C (2010). Social capital, indigeneity and identity politics: The Jos crisis *in perspective African.* Journal of Political Science and International Relations 4 (5), 173–180, May.

Olukoshi, A (2002). Governing the African space for sustainable development: A reflection on NEPAD. Nairobi: Heinrich Boll Foundation.

Onimode, B (1988). A political economy of the African crisis. London: Zed Press.

Onuoha, G (2011). Challenging the state in Africa: MASSOB and the crisis of self-determination in Nigeria: Pretoria, African politics 4.

Onwuzuruigbo, I (2011). Horizontal inequalities: The case of Aguleri and Umuleri Communities in South Eastern Nigeria, Africa. The Journal of the International African Institute 81 (4).

Osaghae, E. (1990). The problems of citizenship in Nigeria: RI vista di studio e documentazion dell'ilstituto italiano Per l'Africa.Anno45, December 4 (pp 593–611) Published by ISIAO.

Osaghae, E (1995). Structural adjustment and ethnicity in Nigeria: Uppsala Scandinavian Institute of African Studies.

Osaghae, E. and Suberu, R (2005) A history of identities, violence, and stability in Nigeria: CRISE Working Paper, January 6.

Ostien, P (2009). Jonah Jang and the Jasawa: Ethno-religious conflict in Jos *Nigeria*. Muslim-Christian Relations in Africa, August.

Otite, O (1990). Ethnic pluralism and ethnicity in Nigeria. Ibadan: Shaneson Co. Ltd.

Pattie, C, Seyd, P and Whiteley, P. (2014). Citizenship in Britain: Values, participation and democracy. Cambridge: Cambridge University Press.

Plotnicov, L (1972). Who owns Jos? Ethnic ideology in Nigerian urban politics. Urban Anthropology, 1 (1), 1–13.

Post, K and Vickers, M (1973). Structure and conflict in Nigeria, 1960–1966. London: Heinemann.

Ramaswamy, S (2007). Political theory: Ideas and concept. India Macmillan, pp 208–229.

Rawls, J (1973). A theory of justice. Oxford: Oxford University Press.

Reynolds, P (2014). A primer in theory construction. Boston: Pearson.

Rosenwasser, D and Stephen, J (2000). Writing analytically. San Diego, CA: Harcourt Brace.

Sidney, V and Norman, N (1987). Participation in America political democracy and social equality. Chicago, IL: University of Chicago Press.

Simon, M (ed.) (2012). Development in the theory and practice of Citizenship. Cambridge, UK: Cambridge Scholar Publishing.

Toure-Kaza, T (2003). Ethno-religious conflicts in Kaduna. Human Rights Watch.

Ukoha, U (2005). The study of ethnicity in Nigeria. Oxford Development Studies 33 (1), 7–20.

Usman, B (1987). The manipulation of religion in Nigeria. Kaduna: Vanguard.

Zambakari, C (2011). South Sudan: Nation in the post-CPA era. Prospects and challenges. https://www.pambazuka.org. Retrieved July 28.

CHAPTER 9

Promoting Human Security in Nigeria: The Role of Tourism

O. O. Ajayi and J. O. Oyebade

Introduction

The West African sub-region, which Nigeria belongs to, is potentially among the richest globally due to the abundance of natural endowments (Aduloju & Pratt, 2014); it is however among the poorest mainly because of conflicts and irregularities over the years (Kaba, 2007). What remain as the aftermath of conflicts in the region is human security and developmental issues. Human security can be described as a people-oriented, integrated and comprehensive framework, addressing the questions of survival and the basic needs of life. It encompasses the concerns about continued existence, desires, wants, ease and improved life worth with the aim to attain the freedoms from fear, want and to live with self-esteem. Nigerian populace security is threatened by poverty, hunger, unemployment, injustice, inequality, dependence, health hazards, discrimination and ecological degradation which are topical issues in the country. In

O. O. Ajayi (✉) · J. O. Oyebade
Department of Hospitality Management and Tourism, University of Port Harcourt, Port Harcourt, Nigeria

K. J. Ani et al. (eds.), *Political Economy of Resource, Human Security and Environmental Conflicts in Africa*,
https://doi.org/10.1007/978-981-16-2036-2_9

addressing this, it has been advised that piecemeal policy and measures will not be sufficient rather a comprehensive development strategy is required; one of which is tourism.

Tourism is the most rapidly advancing industry worldwide with a yearly advancement rate of approximately 4%, 'comprising the activities of persons travelling to and staying in places outside their usual environment for not more than one consecutive year for leisure, business and other purposes not related to remuneration within the place visited' (UNWTO, 2014). The United Nations World Tourism Organization (2014) noted that tourism is among the strongest drivers of global economy, and as such is part of the approaches for reducing poverty in over eighty per cent of poor nations. In Nigeria, most touristic activities are centred around nature and culture. An interesting fact is that unlike the oil resources which the country greatly relies on and is located in greater abundance in the south-south geopolitical region than other regions, tourism resources are all round. All local government areas in the country possess one tourism attraction at the very least, which translates 774 potential tourism destinations (Esu, 2015), most of which are located in rural areas where issues of poverty, hunger and inequality are most raging.

While various scholars have linked various sectors to human security such as agriculture and energy, tourism has hardly been explored. This paper therefore took a theoretical approach in documenting the concept of human security, its current state in Nigeria, what tourism is and the types. Also, current status of Nigerian tourism and the notable tourism attractions in the six geopolitical zones of the country were also explored. The paper went further to explore the roles of tourism in promoting human security in Nigeria putting into perspectives the seven dimensions of human security; economic security, food security, health security, environmental security, personal security, community security and political security.

The Concept of Human Security

In order to have a good understanding of human security, what 'security' means needs to be addressed. According to Nwagboso (2012), security is defined as "being sheltered from damage or peril, the safeguard, assurance, and protection of qualities and the nonattendance of dangers to gained esteems". In other words, it involves the continued existence of humans and prevailing circumstances around them. It is the manifestation of maintaining peace and harmony within a defined geographical space (Adejumo, 2011). It also involves the maintenance of law and order as well as protection from unseen threats within a country (Nwagboso, 2012). Similarly, security was defined by Adebakin (2012) as "freedom from peril or risks, and the capacity of a country to ensure and create itself, advance and treasure esteems and honest to goodness premiums and upgrade the prosperity of its kind". In a nutshell, it can be said that security is a state whereby people live in a defined geographical space in a state of peace that is devoid of threats to lives and properties.

According to UNESCO (2002), the customary view about security is that which the government of a state is given to protecting their physical boundaries from external control and infiltration of various threats. That is, it was concerned with national security. Aduloju and Pratt (2014) noted that the tune has changed in the new global era where nations rather than wage wars against themselves are more interested in joining forces to develop policies that can aid individual nations in addressing peculiar challenges to them. Also, rather than focus on the protection of a nation's sovereignty and territories, there is a need to expand this to accommodate the safety and security of individuals, while additionally including non-military indices like poor quality of human lives, ailments and socio-political instability (UNESCO, 2002).

Human security as such has extended traditional impressions about security. Human security was first mentioned in the global arena in the middle of the late twentieth century, when new dimensions in explaining global practices were sought as well as the era of rigorous debates on the old and proposed concept of security, which will drive nation's activities in the coming century (UNESCO, 2005). The concept of human security is mostly linked to the Human Development Report on Human Security, whose drafting and championing was by MahbubulHaq in 1994, a past Finance Minister in Pakistan and with credible backing of AmartyaSen (Richard & Deepayan, 2006). While there is no universal definition of the concept as many scholars have framed their definitions differently, there is a general consensus on moving from the traditional scope of security to include one which focused on the people. It was further stressed human security aims at examining all aspects of human lives, and the probable dangers they may be exposed from various angles, rather than replacing national security (UNESCO, 2002). According to Aduloju and Pratt (2014), human security encompasses "a global approach linking security, governance, solidarity and development issues". It as such is focused on addressing security from an extensive angle including every socio-economic, political and environmental harms (Obasi, 2006).

The United Nations Development Programme (1994) defined human security as "how people live and breathe in a society, how freely they exercise their many choices, how much access they have to market and social opportunities and whether they live in conflict or in peace". It implies that anything which degrades the value of human lives whether socio-demography, lack of access to needed resources, etc., constitute a risk to security (Ramesh, 1997). On the other hand, whatever can improve the value of human existence such as undeniable right to access needed resources, socio-economic development, etc., means an increase in human security. The phenomenon thus manifests in two different angles (UNDP, 1994): first, protection from such aggressive dangers like starvation, illness and suppression. Second, it connotes safety from unexpected and upsetting happenings in the human environment. Haq (1995) concluded in their report that human security is not about weaponry rather it concerns the esteemed worth of human lives.

In the same light, the United Nations Commission on Human Security defined "human security as the effort by states and organizations to protect the vital core of all human lives in ways that enhance human freedoms and human fulfilment as well as empowering people to provide and care for them" (CHS, 2003). The two significant areas of human security addressed in the definition are those of safety and security as well as human empowerment (CHS, 2003). It means thus that individuals must exist without infringement of their human rights for them to be secured (UNESCO, 2005). The threats as identified by Prezelj (2008) include but not limited to "food threats, economic threats, health threats, environmental threats, personal threats, community threats, political threats, gender-based threats, demographic threats, crime in all forms, including terrorism, natural disasters, violent conflicts and wars, Genocide, anti-personnel mines, Small Arms and Light weapons (SALW)".

Pettman (2005) captured human security in a poem-like theme as being "about the young child that did not die of neglect, the serious epidemic that did not break out, the job that was not cut, the gun that was not run, the ethnic prejudice that did not result in violence, the dissident voice that was not made silent, the landmine that was not sold and installed, the woman who was not trafficked across state borders and sexually abused, the agricultural product that was not dumped to the detriment of the poor farmers, the short-term capital investment that was not allowed to wreck an infant industry, the addictive product that was not produced and shipped, the refugee that was not forced to flee and remain abroad and so on". There are seven dimensions to human security as identified by UNDP (1994). They are.

1. Economic security: assured fundamental earnings; job opportunities and accessibility of needed assets.
2. Food security: this means physical and economic access to food for all people at all times. A lot of people globally are faced daily with starvation due to the lack of food in their domains or the lack of the financial capacity to obtain food.
3. Health security: this entails accessibility of cures for ailments as well as enhanced health settings. The health security of individuals with lower income is generally less. As a result, communicable and scrounging diseases illnesses are the main culprits in mortality cases in developing nations.
4. Environmental security: this connotes access to viable biophysical surroundings devoid of environmental dangers such as desert encroachment and climate change which put human lives at risk.
5. Personal security: this refers to a person's safety from visible brutality. This can be from various dimensions such as local, national or international terrorization, intimidation from other ethnic set, threats from persons or gangs; terror specifically against the female folks and children due to their more vulnerable and dependency states; self-induced dangers such as suicide and drug abuse.
6. Community security: a lot of individuals achieve their sense of safety and security by being members of communal assemblage, whether household, society, associations, political gatherings, tribal set and so on. There is usually a lot of friction among the people because of heightened contest over inadequate assets and chances.
7. Political security: this entails existing in an environment where there is no threat nor infringement to people's fundamental liberties (Hussein & Glisci, 2004).

Human Security in Nigeria

Nigeria is popularly called the Giant of Africa, especially due to her massive population of over 190 million according to recent estimates, thus considered as Africa's most populous nation and the 7th largest globally. In 2015, Nigeria's economy is the twentieth biggest one with a value above $500 billion and $1 trillion in nominal gross domestic product and purchasing power parity (World Bank, 2016). The nation can however not pride herself as a giant in human security matters. This is because Nigeria has not been able to deliver the seven dimensions of human security.

Unemployment especially among youth and access to basic income remains an undiluted dilemma of the country. According to the reports of Trading Economics (2018), youth unemployment rate has been on the increase over the years. It averaged 21.73% from 2014 reaching a new high of 33.10% in the third quarter of 2017. According to the Food Security Portal (2012), an estimated 50 million Nigerian youths are unemployed. Up till now, the new national minimum wage proposed from #18,000 to #30,000 in 2018 has still not been actualized. Even as at #18,000, most state governments could not afford to meet the obligations to workers in the civil service. In the face of irregularity in salary payments, perpetual increase in costs of products and services, unstructured market environments, unemployment and/or under employment, economic security remains a wish for majority of the Nigerian populace.

Physical and economic assess to food at all times also remain a pertinent issue. Regardless of the abundance of natural endowments and fast trade and industry development, approximately seventy per cent of the nation's populace remains impoverished, living under the poverty index of $1.25 dollar per day (Naisbitt & Naisbitt, 2016). More so, Nigeria was positioned as the 40th of 79, and the 156th of 187 nations by the Global Hunger Index of 2012, and the UNDP Human Development Index, respectively. Lack of food and dearth of other resources are more prevalent issues in the non-urban areas of the country, with about eighty per cent living on below one US dollar daily (Food Security Portal, 2014). This is further compounded by lack of, or insufficient post-harvest machineries, meagre availability and dispersal of foodstuff, and unpredictable weather situations in rural Nigeria (Akinyele, 2009).

Nigeria was ranked as the highest producer of food like yam, cassava and beans globally by the International Fund for Agricultural Development (IFAD, 2012); she however still depends greatly on the import of farm animal products, fishes and grains. Despite the suitability of approximately seventy-five per cent of her land areas for agricultural practices, just forty per cent is being used (Omorogiuwa et al., 2014). The people in rural Nigeria are mainly involved in subsistence agriculture, characterized with high reliance on natural and seasonal precipitation, farming on small land areas especially meant for family survival (CSIS, 2018; Matemilola & Elegbede, 2017). Also, inaccessibility of much needed infrastructural facilities like roads has greatly affected the people and thus impoverishing them more, as farmers have restricted access to markets and are also deterred from obtaining farm input (IFAD, 2012). While food security has not always been the issue in the forties and early fifties as the agricultural system was sustainably practiced where different regions in the country specialize in selected foods, like cocoa, groundnut and rubber in the west, north and eastern regions, respectively (Ojo et al., 2012). The situation took a downward trend following the discovery of crude oil in the late fifties (IFAD, 2012).

Accessibility of cures for ailments as well as enhanced health settings is also a crucial issue especially in the rural areas of the country. There have been outbreaks of diseases such as cholera and yellow fever in the past. In recent times, lassa fever and ebola virus disease has left a landmark on the country. And of recent, is the COVID 19 pandemic. Major issue of concern is the lack of strong public health infrastructures and healthcare systems. Desert encroachment, massive destruction of forest areas, climate change issues and other environmental dangers also put the continued existence of the Nigerian populace at risk. Environmental security issues in Nigeria revolve around deforestation, desertification and attributed mostly to factors such as overpopulation, urbanization, pollution, flooding and inadequate planning. The annual forest areas deforested yearly in Nigeria according to the Food and Agricultural Organization (FAO) were approximately 1.5 million acres (Isife, 2012). Desertification is highly prominent in northern Nigeria. For instance, Lake Chad, the 6th biggest lake globally at some point (Gao et al., 2011), shrank from approximately 22,000 km^2 to about 300 km^2 from the 1960s to the 1980s (Singh et al., 2006), and now about 1/10 of its size in the 1960s (Alfa, 2008). This inadvertently affects the lives of people that are dependent on this lake for farm irrigation purposes.

Generally, it has also been observed that insecurity among persons, certain groups and communities exists in Nigeria which leads to group conflict and political instability. There has been increase in cases of kidnapping (e.g. Chibok school girls in 2015, ritual killings, kidnap in exchange for money, etc.), rape, drug use (in recent times codeine), civil unrest (e.g. Niger-Delta militancy), ethno-religious crisis (e.g. Boko Haram and Fulani Insurgency), land use fights (e.g. Fulani Herdsman), etc. Also, given the advent of democratic system of governance, there has been a change in the political scenery where forceful acts have become dominant in the nation's politicking. There is a great diffusion of weapons in the political environment, and as a result, small issues that could be resolved via peaceful means fast degenerate to aggressive situations where weapons are employed. On top of the list is the issue of corruption, a main factor implicated in human insecurity in the country.

What is Tourism?

Tourism is a global phenomenon and is praised as the largest and rapidly increasing sector globally. It has been defined by many scholars and experts, over the years. Mathieson and Wall (1982) defined it as "the temporary movement of people to destinations outside their normal places of work and residence, the activities undertaken during their stay in those destinations, and the facilities created to cater for their needs". Likewise, Macintosh and Goeldner (1986) defined it as "the sum of the phenomena and relationships arising from the interaction of tourists, business suppliers, host governments and host communities in the process of attracting and hosting these tourists and other visitors". It involves all actions which willingly and temporarily take individuals from their immediate environments so as to seek satisfaction of the needs of enjoyment, enthusiasm, experience, entertainment, rejuvenation, etc. (Ayodele, 2002). Da'Silva (2001) opined that tourism is the sign and act of businesses involving the attraction, transportation, accommodation and catering for visitors.

Zelenika (2005) also defined tourism as a composite of actions aimed at satisfying tourists needs while travelling and staying temporarily in selected which also has developmental implications on the socio-economy of the place visited. Likewise, NZU (2011) noted that "tourism is a collection of activities, services and industries that delivers a travel experience, including transportation, accommodations, eating and drinking establishments, retail shops, entertainment businesses, activity facilities and other hospitality services provided for individuals or groups traveling away from home". The most universally adopted definition is that of the United Nations World Tourism Organization (UNWTO) who defines it as "activities of persons travelling to and staying in places outside their usual environment for not more than one consecutive year for leisure, business, and other purposes not related to the exercise of an activity remunerated from within the places visited". In all of this, we define tourism as the temporal travel for leisure, business or other purposes. It is important to note that all travel is not tourism. In other for a travel to come under tourism, it must fulfil the following criteria:

1. Type of travel: Movement outside immediate environment: whether within the traveller's home country (domestic tourism) or outside his/her national borders (international).
2. Purpose: any purpose aside from earning income from the place visited. The purpose can also be multi-motivational (e.g. recreation and visiting family & friends).
3. Duration: maximum of one year. This defines the type of visitor that can either be an overnight visitors (tourists) or same-day visitors (excursionist).

The tourism industry has fast developed to become a crucial part of the economy worldwide (Esu, 2015). This is enhanced by increasing disposable earnings, higher free time advocacy coupled with viable international economies as a result of globalization, thus bringing about active competitiveness in the industry as well as obvious decline in cost of travel. As such, tourism is now a main instrument for economic development, job creation, revenue generation and foreign exchange earnings in a lot of nations (Basu, 2003). It is also seen to be a major instrument in developing rural financial system in less developed nations (Haller, 2012).

It was also established by the author that while the development of tourism cannot be detached from the development of international economies, the industry has also added tremendously to the development of international economies. This was further confirmed by the World Travel and Tourism Council (WTTC, 2017) which revealed travel and tourism contributed approximately ten per cent to global gross domestic product, a figure more than that of international economies for the 6th year consecutively while also employing one of every ten.

Types of Tourism

There are various types of tourism. Omonona and Kayode (2011) identified the following types of tourism:

Cultural or historical tourism: this is tourism based on places of historical and cultural interests. This involves journey undertaken to cultural or historical sites with the objectives of observing and appreciating the host, i.e. community culture or its historical sites with objectives of observing and appreciating the host, e.g. Lagos Black Heritage Festival.

Religious tourism: this involves religious visits to places such as the visit of Christians and Muslims pilgrims to Jerusalem and Mecca, respectively.

Ecological tourism: this involves tourism in natural environment like landscapes, waterfalls, beaches and protected area. It is a type of tourism that engines sustainability and responsible travel in its core.

Social tourism: this type of travel is sponsored by an employer or an agency to enable otherwise disadvantage workers to travel out to places and experience different social environment and social life.

Industrial tourism: this is tourism based on places of industrial interest like the Abeokuta Steel Rolling Mill and Kainji Dam in Niger state, Nigeria.

Recreational tourism: this involves travelling to destination offering various recreational facilities such as boat riding, water surfing, mountaineering.

In recent times, new tourism forms have emerged and become increasingly populous. They are:

Sport tourism: this involves travel to global, national or local sport event such as the FIFA World Cup, skiing, golf and scuba as a participant or an observer.

Food tourism: this is also called culinary tourism. It involves travel for the exploration of food as the purpose of tourism.

Wine tourism: this involves travel to destinations where wine is produced, wine festivals, and other comparable areas or events in order to consume or purchase wine.

Coastal/beach tourism: this is travel associated with the 3S: sun, sand and sea. It is born out of an inevitable attraction to the beach and coastal resorts for recreation purposes. It is one of the earliest forms of tourism.

Urban tourism: it describes travel in which the main destination and the place of interest is an urban area. While this form of tourism is relatively old, there has been increased attention in recent times.

Agri-tourism: this involves travel to agricultural destinations that helps in supporting rural farm economies.

Adventure tourism: this involves a tour of hardy environments, or to participate in audacious activities like mountain climbing and hiking.

Zoo-tourism: this is travel to experience animals in captive environments.

Dark tourism: this involves tour of destinations that have been connected with great fatality, mortality and anguish in previous times.

Medical tourism: this is a tour to receive medical care either better or more affordable in another area or country than in their own place.

Educational tourism: this is usually shortened to edu-Tourism and it involves travel for educational reasons in citadels of learning, or to other places simply for educational purpose.

Twin tourism: this is one of the newest trends in the tourism industry. It comes under the umbrella of cultural tourism but has been branded by the ambassadors as twin tourism. This was initiated by two Nigerian twins (the Oguntoye twins). It involves the travel of twins to a place associated with frequent twin births.

Other niche tourism includes wedding tourism, sex tourism, gambling tourism, etc.

Nigerian Tourism Outlook

Nigeria, being a nation located in the western coastal area of Africa, has abounding tourism potentials. The country is endowed with enormous endowments which qualify as tourism attractions. Nigeria was positioned as the 63rd, 68th and 98th of 140 African countries with regard to environmental sustainability, natural endowments and cultural resource in the Travel and Tourism Competitiveness Index (TTCI, 2013). The country according to Abiodun (2013) possesses at least one hundred and one natural and cultural tourism attractions that meets international standard and cut across the various extant regions.

An interesting fact is that unlike the oil resources which the country greatly relies on and is located in greater abundance in the south-south geopolitical region than other regions, tourism resources are all round. All local government areas in the country possess one tourism attraction at the very least, which translates 774 potential tourism destinations (Esu, 2015). The report of the Cross River Tourism Bureau (2012) shows that in Cross River State alone, one of the thirty-six states in Nigeria possesses at least eighty-five tourism resource; sixteen, forty-two, eleven and eleven of which are natural, culture-based, recreation-based and other categories, respectively.

According to the Hospitality Report Nigeria (2017), the country's economy is being enabled by development in the agricultural, communications and service sectors. However, the dominant export good is crude oil. The report also however revealed that the tourism industry contribution to gross domestic product was 1.7% while generating 0.7% of exports as well as 1.6% of jobs in 2015. Also, domestic travel spending experienced a 4.9% increase in 2016 over 3.2% recorded in 2015. The responsibility of formulation of policies, monitoring and maintenance of tourism is that of the Federal Ministry of Arts and Culture. In order to promote tourism in Nigeria, various actions have been put in place. For example, the National Tourism Policy was promulgated in 1990, followed by the establishment of the Nigeria Tourism Development Corporation (NTDC) in 1992, and subsequently the preparation of Nigeria Tourism Development Master Plan in 2005 in collaboration with UNWTO (Esu, 2015). While the master plan was designed to strengthen organizational capability of the county's tourism industry, few achievements have been recorded due to weak implementation of the plan. This is largely due to lack of strong political will as well inadequate tourism-inclined individuals in governmental offices (Esu, 2015).

Tourism impact on the country's economy with respect to jobs (2.8% share), gross domestic product (3.2% share), exports (3.5% growth per annum {2014–2024}) and capital investment (5.1% growth per annum {2014–2024}) has been dismally poor, when compared to other countries in African like Namibia, Tunisia, Kenya, Tanzania, etc. (WTTC, 2014). This poor performance is a resultant effect of various factors such as "inadequate investment, social and political instability, lack of integrated community-based natural resource management system, poverty, unemployment, dependency and indiscriminate hunting of wildlife, corruption, policy inconsistency, lack of proper implementation, project monitoring and transparency, and abandoned rural tourism projects" (Esu, 2015) (Table 9.1).

Tourism Attractions in Nigeria

Tourist attractions are classified into two major groups in Nigeria; Natural and Cultural/Historic Attractions, and these are found across all its states (Table 9.2).

Table 9.1 International tourist arrival and receipt in Nigeria (1995–2013)

Year	*Tourist arrival*	*Tourist receipt*
1995	656,000	$47,000,000
1996	822,000	$58,000,000
1997	611,000	$83,000,000
1998	739,000	$81,000,000
1999	776,000	$99,000,000
2000	813,000	$186,000,000
2001	850,000	$168,000,000
2002	887,000	$256,000,000
2003	924,000	$58,000,000
2004	962,000	$49,000,000
2005	1,010,000	$139,000,000
2006	1,111,000	$209,000,000
2007	1,212,000	$337,000,000
2008	1,313,000	$959,000,000
2009	1,414,000	$791,000,000
2010	1,555,000	$736,000,000
2011	715,000	$688,000,000
2012	486,000	$639,000,000
2013	600,000	$616,000,000

Source UNWTO (2014)

Table 9.2 Local cultural tourism attractions in Nigeria

Types of festival	*Disposition by states*
Traditional Dances	All states
Social and Occasional	All states
Local Festival	Ondo, Ekiti, Anambra and Imo
New Yam Festivals	Ondo, Ekiti, Anambra and Imo
Local Masquerades	All states
Festival Theatres	All states
Pategi Regatta	Niger state
Mass Wedding	Kwara and some states

Tourism as a Tool in Promoting Human Security in Nigeria

There is no doubt that Nigeria tourism resources are enormous. It is interwoven into aspects of the people's lives and therefore can aid human security on all of its seven dimensions. This is however subject to tourism development in the country.

Tourism and Economic Security: tourism can aid access to employment and income. It can also improve the GDP of the country. Nigeria has remarkable records of gross domestic product growth indices since the return to democracy in the late twentieth century (World Bank, 2016). It was also reported that Nigeria witness about seven per cent increment in gross domestic product for 17 consecutive democratic. However, this progression was not associated with matching improvement in people's lives. Majority of Nigerians are still economically unsecured, the economic environment lacks certainties, evidently seen in the poverty line of 62.6% (UNDP, 2016). Also, tourism contribution to GDP is less than 1% (World Bank, 2013). Tourism has the capacity to generate jobs in millions as well as other financially viable benefits. This is because the industry is linked to other sectors. Tourism development in Nigeria thus translates to the development of the associated sectors, hence more jobs for the people and access to basic income—which means human security.

Tourism and Food Security: tourism is capable of enabling physical and economic access to food for all individuals at all times. In Nigeria, lack of food security leads to various catastrophes like lack of food and undernourishment, especially among children, and the north has the most prevalent incidences (National Human Development report [NHDR], 2015). Tourism can enable an individual's economic access to food by empowering them with employment, providing avenue for revenue generation and aiding infrastructural development like road, which can connect people to agricultural products and produce.

Tourism and Health Security: this is another important dimension of human security that tourism can aid. Health security is targeted at ensuring maximal intensity of safety from ailments and providing education about the significance of viable lifestyles and actions as well as making available excellent Medicare (WHO, 1998). The life expectancy in the country is fifty-two years. Sixty-six per cent of all mortalities were as a result of transmissible illnesses, maternal and nutrition conditions in 2012 (WHO, 2016). The development of tourism in any area especially in rural communities translates to more investments especially by the government on social infrastructural facilities, one of which is health centres and medical facilities. While this is most times constructed for the tourists, the people also benefit.

Tourism and Environmental Security: environmental security deals with the negative consequences of degraded biophysical environments. The impact can manifest at local, state or global stages. The rating of

Environmental Law and Policy Centre Yale placed Nigeria as 134 of 178 and 119/132 in 2011 and 2012, respectively, *vis a vis* environmental security. This shows the poor state of environmental performance in the country (National Human Development Report, 2015). Tourism can promote environmental security especially under the auspices of ecological tourism where environmental sustainability is key via conservation, environmental education and promotion of environmentally friendly attitudes.

Tourism and Personal Security: personal security is a human security type with express impact on persons. It relates to visible and immediate threats to lives. No nation of the world in recent times is free of unanticipated violence against individuals: ranging from kidnapping, random shoot out, rape incidences and various forms of physical assaults. The UNDP human development report outlined some seven forms of threats that constitute personal human insecurity as follows: threats from the state (physical torture), threats from other states (war), threats from other groups of people, (ethnic tension), threats from individuals or gangs against other individuals or gangs (crime, street violence), threats directed against women (rape, domestic violence), threats directed at children due to their vulnerable and dependent states (child abuse) and self-inflicted threats (suicide, drug use) (UNDP, 1994). Tourism is an instrument of peace and advocates of human rights, the development of tourism in any country facilitates this.

Tourism and Community Security: community security involves "protection against the breakdown of law and order in the communities and other family units (such as clubs, tribes or extended families) that provide members with a reassuring sense of identity and a shared value system; the central theme in community human security discourse is making sure that the community and its inhabitant are "free from fear" (UNDP, 1994). Prominent cases of community insecurity in Nigeria include the Fulani Herdsmen crisis, Boko-Haram insurgency and Niger-Delta militancy. These cases to a very large extent have bought about a breakdown of the communal settings of lots of communities. Tension is usually as a resultant effect of heightened competitiveness over limited opportunities and assets. Tourism in itself cannot survive in an atmosphere of community insecurity, as problematic regions are projected as unsafe for people to participate in any touristic activity.

Tourism and Political Security: political security is concerned with the protection of human fundamental rights as well the liberties to stay in an area devoid of state suppression. Simply put, individuals should be able to live in societies which uphold their fundamental human liberties (UNDP, 1994). Despite the advent of democratic rule in the late twentieth century in the country, the protection and freedom to exhibit basic human rights remain questionable, as there have been incidences of law enforcement officers unlawfully killing and torturing the masses, lack of free hand of operation for press agencies, socio-political segregation as well as abuse of court mandates (Olatunji, 2014; Okeshola, 2013; Fagbadebo, 2007). Tourism likewise does not thrive under this kind of economy, as it projects an unappealing destination image.

It becomes pertinent to note that the relevance of tourism in promoting human security in Nigeria is more obvious under the auspices of economic security, food security, health security, environmental security and personal security. It is more or less dependent on the other two that is community security and political security, as tourism will not thrive in an environment where the safety of humans and their belongings is threatened and also in the face of bad political country image especially for international visitors.

Way Forward

There are a lot of constraints limiting the potentials of tourism as an incredible promotional instrument of human security in Nigeria. The classification of sub-Saharan African nations in the Tourism Development Level and Income Ranking puts Nigeria in the potential/initiating group and low-middle income country. The report shows that the countries under this category have exhibited certain interest in tourism development. However, they are constrained by inadequate control over the industry and also lack extensive infrastructural and market capabilities.

More specifically, the constraints are but not limited to (Ayodele, 2017; World Bank, 2013):

(a) Low level of awareness and inadequate stakeholders' participation;
(b) Poor governance and inappropriate conflicting policies;
(c) Poor funding;
(d) Unreliable poor database;
(e) Improper valuation of tourism resources;
(f) Inadequate infrastructure;
(g) Unfriendly business environment;

(h) Manpower problem;
(i) Poor promotion strategies;
(j) Insecurity;
(k) Poverty/poor standard of living;
(l) Rapid population growth, inadequate institutional capacity, inappropriate technologies and non-application of contemporary technologies;
(m) Lack of national tourism policy, philosophy and vision;
(n) Negative perception on tourism and hospitality services;
(o) Commercial hospitality and Africa Philosophy;
(p) Lack of tourism investments;
(q) Low levels of tourism skills.

In order to overcome this, the following is highly needed;

Stakeholders Involvement: the primary stakeholders in tourism are the visitor, government, host community, destination managers and tourism partners such as investors, industries and NGOs. The visitors are those which make conscious decision to travel, and as such without them, the industry cannot be functional. It is essential that there first be a strong political will, especially at topmost levels of governance. The role of government includes but not limited to policy formulation, coordination of other stakeholders, creation of conducive environment for investment, enhancement of market viability, infrastructural development, tourism destination promotion and marketing (World Bank, 2013). The involvement of the private sector is equally very crucial, especially in the provision of travel and tourism-related services as well creation of awareness and promotion of tourism (UNWTO, 2014). Destination mangers have the role of managing tourism activities within the destinations, taking inventory of tourism resources as well as engaging in research and monitoring. They are also involved in tourism promotion and ultimately provide unforgettable experiences to visitors. Donors are responsible for providing the much-needed financial and technological know-how in the industry which can no doubt aid tourism development (UNWTO, 2014). The participation of all the stakeholders is as such very crucial.

Tourism development: Ayodele (2017) also documented the following as a gateway for Nigerian tourism development;

(a) Setting up of a high powered commission with the following terms of reference: identify all tourism potentials/attractions; write feasibility studies of each promising tourism potential/attraction; select the most feasible potential/attractions; government should take the lead to develop the preferred options and adoption of bills and sells strategy.
(b) Encouragement of public–private partnership in tourism development to encourage diligent entrepreneurs who lack the capital and political capacity to strive.
(c) Government should create access to attractions that are inaccessible, to encourage and enhance the value of investment and patronage.
(d) Direct collaboration of government with technological and industrial countries like China, United States and UK to develop tourist attractions in Nigeria.
(e) Declaration of emergency in tourism funding.
(f) Encouragement of tourism investment.
(g) Improvement on security and infrastructure to ensure visitors confidence.
(h) Need for research to inform planning and policy
(i) Government should sponsor Tourism/Hospitality studies abroad as it was with oil/gas industry.
(j) The local people should be allowed to take vital decisions on the management of tourism and they should be well compensated. This will encourage active participation of rural communities in planning, organization and execution of projects.
(k) Benefits of management efforts and resource utilization should be accrued to the rural communities directly, either in terms of cash, bonus or provision of social amenities such as portable water, electricity, good roads, rural healthcare delivery facilities and improved educational development.
(l) National resources conservation awareness committees should be established at National, State and Local Government levels to educate policymakers, towns, cities, youths and rural people about the need for conservation and national use of our resources, using the media, organized clubs and societies in primary, secondary and tertiary institutions.

(m) Tourism Research Institute of Nigeria (TRIN) should be created to promote the development of Tourism Management in developing countries.
(n) In order to heal the suffocating economy of Nigeria, Government should create the Ministry of Tourism and Hospitality with a clear philosophy and vision to pilot tourism development.

Conclusion

Nigeria is endowed with enormous tourism attractions in her entire six geopolitical regions, most of which are located in rural areas where issues of poverty, hunger and inequality are most raging. There is no more other time than now to pursue tourism as an incredible promotional instrument of human security in Nigeria. The benefit goes beyond increase in the gross domestic product but also bring about human security which includes job security, development of health facilities and access to basic amenities and human needs which is needed for the sustenance of life. Tourism as a sector can be used to promote human security in Nigeria considering all the dimensions of human security especially economic security, food security, health security, environmental security and personal security.

References

Abiodun. (2013) in Eneji, M. A., Odey, F. A., & Bullus, M. L. (2016). Diversification of Nigerian's economy; Impact of tourism on sustainable development in Nigeria. *International Journal of Research in Humanities and Social Studies, 3*(5): 36–44.

Abomeh, O. S. (2012). Hospitality and Tourism Manpower Training and Education in Nigeria. *Afro Asian Journal of Social Science, 3*(3), 1–18.

Adebakin, M. A. (2012). National Security Challenges and Sustainable Economic Development. *EVIDENCE from Nigeria, 1*, 10–20.

Adejumo, A. A. (2011, December 16). Problems and Challenges of Insecurity of Nigeria. *News Diary Online*, pp. 4–9.

Aduloju, A. A., & Pratt, O. O. (2014). Human Security and Developmental Crisis in the Contemporary West Africa. *Journal of Human Security, 1*(1), 46–58. https://doi.org/10.12924/johs2014.10010046.

Akinyele, I. O. (2009). *Ensuring Food and Nutrition Security in Rural Nigeria: An Assessment of the Challenges, Information Needs, and Analytical Capacity.* Abuja: International Food Policy Research Institute (IFPRI).

Alfa, N. I., Adeofun, C. O., & Ologunorisa, E. T. (2008). Assessment of Changes in Aerial Extent of Lake Chad Using Satellite Remote Sensing Data. *Journal of Applied Science Environmental Management, 12*(1), 101–107.

Arowolo, O., & Fabarebo, S. (2005). *Nigeria: Contemporary Issues* (1st ed.). Educational Limited.

Ayodele, I. A. (2002). *Essentials of Tourism Management*. ISBN 978–36724–2–8. Elshaddai Global Ventures LTD, pp. 1–90.

Ayodele, I. A. (2017). *Tourism: Gateway to Good Health and Good Life*. Inaugural lecture delivered at the University of Ibadan on Thursday 12 October, 2017, p. 110.

Basu, P. K. (2003). Is sustainable tourism development possible? Broad issues concerning Australia and Papua Guinea. In R. N. Ghosh, M. A. B. Saddique and B. Gabbay (Eds.), *Tourism and economic development: Case study from Indian region*. Hampshire, England: 18–20.

Centre for Strategic & International Studies. (2018). Agriculture and Food Security in Nigeria. Downloaded from https://www.csis.orh/programs/africa-program/human-development/agriculture-and-food-security-nigeria on 6 December 2018.

Commission on Human Security (CHS). (2003). *Human Security Now: Protecting and Empowering People*. New York, NY: United Nations Publications.

Da'Silva, M. (2001). *Tourism Voice*. Lagos, Nigeria: GSL Publishing Ltd.

Eneji, M. A., Odey, F. A., & Bullus, M. L. (2016, May). Diversification of Nigeria's Economy; Impact of Tourism on Sustainable Development in Nigeria. *International Journal of Research in Humanities and Social Studies, 3*(5), 36–44. ISSN 2394–6296 (Online).

Esu, B. B. (2015). Transforming the Nigeria Tourism Industry Through Tourism Entrepreneurial Development. *African Journal of Business Management, 9*(15), 569–580.

Fagbadebo, O. (2007). Corruption, governance and political instability in Nigeria. *African Journal of Political Science and International Relations,1*(2), 028–037.

Food Security Portal (2014). Food Security Portal-Nigeria. http://www.foodsecurityportal.org/nigeria.

Gao, H., Bohn, T. J., Podest, E., & McDonald, K. C. (2011). On the Causes of the Shrinking of Lake Chad. *Environmental Research Letters, 6*, 1–11.

George, T. A. (2015). Lethal Violence Against Women in Nigeria (2006–2014): IFRA-Nigeria Working Papers Series, n 43. Downloaded from http://www.bing.com/ on 5 September 2017.

Haller, A. (2012). Growth and development through tourism in conditions of liberalisation: Theme and concepts. Paper presented at the *14th International conference 'Romanian rural tourism in context of sustainable development; present and prospect'*, 25–26 May, 2012. Vatra Dornei, Romania.

Haq, M. (1995). *Reflections on Human Development.* The book by the late Pakistani development economist, who played a pioneering role in the Human Development Report, outlines his thinking on human development and human security. Oxford: Oxford University Press.

Hobbes, T. (1996). *Leviathan* (J. C. A. Gaskin, Ed., p. 104). Oxford: Oxford University Press.

Holcomb, J. (2004). The Effect of Tourist Personal Theft on Future Travel Decisions. 1st ed. Downloaded from http://etd.fcla.edu/CF/CFE0000132/Holcomb_Judith_L_200407_MS.pdfon 18 May 2014.

Holloway, J. C. (2001). *The Business of Tourism.* Edinburgh Gate: England. Pearson Hospitality Report Nigeria by Jumia Travel. Downloaded from https://travel.jumia.com/hospitalityreportnigeria/ on September 14, 2017.

Hussein, K. D., & Gnisci, J. W. (2004). *Security and Human Security: An Overview of Concepts and Initiatives. What Implications for West Africa?* Paris, France: Organisation for Economic Co-operation and Development (OCED) Issues Paper.

International Fund for Agricultural Development (IFAD). (2012). Annual Report. IFAD, Monte Forte.

Isife, C. T. (2012). Environmental Problems in Nigeria. *Sustainable Human Development Review, 4*(1 and 2), 21–34.

Kaba, A. J. (2007). The Two West Africas: The Two Historical Phases of the West African Brain Drain. *The Journal of Pan African Studies, 1*(8), 77–92.

Matemilola, S., & Elegbede, I. O. (2017). Challenges of Food Security in Nigeria. *Open Access Library Journal, 4,* e4185. https://doi.org/10.4236/oalib.1104185.

Mathieson, A., & Wall, G. (1982). *Tourism: Economic, Physical and Social Impacts.* New York: Longman House.

McIntosh, R. W., & Goeldner, C. R. (1986). *Tourism: Principles, Practices and Philosophies* (5th ed.). New York: Wiley.

Naisbitt, J., & Naisbitt, D. (2016). *Global Game Change: How the Global Southern Belt Will Reshape Our World.* New Delhi: Sage.

National Human Development Report. (2015). Human security and human development in Nigeria (p. 126). http://hdr.undp.org/sites/default/files/2016_national_human_development_report_for_nigeria.pdf.

Northern Arizona University, Parks & Recreation Mgmt. Introduction—Online Lesson. http://www.prm.nau.edu/prm300.

Northern Arizona University. (2011). Parks & Recreation Mgmt. Introduction—Online Lesson. http://www.prm.nau.edu/prm300.

Nwagboso, C. (2012). Security Challenges and Economy of the Nigerian State (2007–2011). *American International Journal of Contemporary Research, 2*(6), 244–258.

Obasi, N. K. (2006). The Importance of Human Security in West Africa. Workshop Human Security in West Africa: Challenges, Synergies and Action for a Regional Agenda. Sahel and West Africa Club/OECD; Lome, Togo, 26–28 March 2006.

Ojo, E. O., & Adebayo, P. F. (2012). Food Security in Nigeria: An Overview. *European Journal of Sustainable Development, 1,* 199–222.

Okeshola, F. B., 2013. Human Rights Abuse by Nigerian Police in Four Selected States and the Federal Capital Territory, Abuja. *British Journal of Arts and Social Science, 13*(II), 242–250.

Olatunji, F. O. (2014). Democracy and the Challenge of the Rule of Law in Developing Democratic Society. *Journal of Integrative Humanism,* ISSN: 2026-6286.

Omonona, A. O., & Kayode, I. B. (2011). *Ecotourism: Implications on human and wildlife health* (pp. 25–36). Ibadan: Ibadan University Press.

Omorogiuwa, O., Zivkovic, J., & Ademoh, F. (2014). The Role of Agriculture in the Economic Development of Nigeria. *European Scientific Journal, 10,* 113–147.

Pettman, R. (2005). Human Security as Global Security: Reconceptualising Strategic Studies. *Cambridge Review of International Affairs, 18*(1), 137–150.

Prezelj, I. (2008). Challenges in Conceptualizing and Providing Human Security. *HUMSEC Journal Issue, 2,* 1–21.

Ramesh, T. (1997). *"From National to Human Security." Asia-Pacific Security: The Economics-Politics Nexus* (S. Harris & A. Mack, Eds., pp. 53–54). Sydney: Allen &Unwin.

Richard, J., & Deepayan, B. R. (2006). The Human Security Framework and National Human Development Reports: A Review of Experiences and Current Debates. NHDR Occasional Paper 5. 2006. Downloaded from http://hdr.undp.org/en/media/NHDR_Human_Security_GN.pdf.

Singh, A., Diop, S., & M'mayi, P. L. (2006). *Africa's Lakes: Atlas of Our Changing Environment.* Nairobi: UNEP.

Sustainable Measures. (2010). Downloaded from www.sustainablemeasures.com/Sustainability/index.html on 13 September 2017.

Trading Economics. (2018). Nigeria Youth Unemployment Rate. Downloaded from https://www.tradingeconomics.com/nigeria/youth-unemployment-rate on December 6, 2018.

TTC. (2013). Reducing Barriers to Economic Growth and Job Creation. The Travel and Tourism Competitiveness Report.

UNESCO. (2002). Mainstreaming the culture of peace. UNESCO, France, p. 26.

UNESCO. (2005). Promoting Human Security: Ethicak, Normative and Educational Frameworks in Latin America and the Caribbean. Downloaded from http://www.unesco.org/securipax.

United Nations Development Programme. (1995). *Human Development Report 1994 The Original Source of the Idea of Human Security*. Oxford: Oxford University Press.

United Nations Development Programme. (2016). About Nigeria. Downloaded from http://www.ng.undp.org/content/nigeria/en/home/countryinfo.html.

United Nations Development Programme. (1994 [2001]). *Human Development Report—New Dimensions of Human Security*. New York, NY: Oxford University Press.

United Nations Educational, Scientific and Cultural Organisation (UNESCO). (2000). Agenda for Action of the International SecuriPax Network for the Promotion of Human Security and Peace. Dowloaded from http://www.unesco.org/securipax/.

UNWTO. (2014). Nigeria—International Tourism. Downloaded from https://www.indexmundi.com/facts/nigeria/international-tourism on 26 July 2017.

World Bank. (2013). Tourism in Africa: Harnessing Tourism for Growth and Improved Livelihoods. Downloaded from www.worldbank.org/africa-tourism-report-2013-overview/ on 28 October 2018.

World Bank. (2016). GDP Growth (Annual %). Downloaded from http://data.worldbank.org/indicator/NY.GDP.MKTP.KD.ZG?contextual=aggregate&end=2015&locations=NG&start=1999&view=chart&year=2013&year_high_desc=false.

World Bank, Africa House, and ATA (Africa Travel Association). (2010). *The State of Tourism in Africa*. Joint publication of Africa House at New York University (NYU), the Africa Travel Association (ATA), and the World Bank 1 (1): p. 2.

World Health Organization. (1998). Health Promotion Glossary (No. WHO/HPR/HEP/98.1). Downloaded from http://www.who.int/healthpromotion/about/HPR%20Glossary%201998.pdf.

WHO. (2016). Nigeria. https://www.who.int/nmh/countries/nga_en.pdf.

WTTC. (2014, 2015). World Travel and Tourism Council, 2014 and 2015. The Authority on World Travel and Tourism: Travel and Tourism Economic Impact on Nigeria.

WTTC. (2017). Travel and Tourism Economic impart World 2017. Downloaded from https://www.wttc.org/-/media/files/reports/economic-impact-research/regions-2017/world2017.pdf on 26 July 2017.

Zelenika, R. (2005). *Logistički Sustavi*. Ekonomski fakultet u Rijeci, Rijeka.

CHAPTER 10

Dangerous Vision: The Insecurity of Nigerian Leadership

Kabiru Babatunde Amusa

Introduction

Governance according to Decker belongs to the powers that be.[1] He argues that in Nigeria, gangsters are those who hijack governance through fraudulent electioneering campaign, military adventurism or conspiracy. Hence, the difference between the rulers and the insurgents is that the rulers operate under law.[2] The insurgents are literarily non-elite while the leaders are.[3] The people who submit their electoral power and authority to a constituted government expect such authority to exercise power for the purpose of ensuring their security and welfare.[4] Nigeria, being one of the most populous black nations and sometimes referred to as the Giant of Africa inherited an imbalanced social and political welfare mechanism from the colonial masters. The nature and scope of the social services instituted by the colonial government varied from one region to another. This is influenced by prevailing socio-economic factors peculiar to each society. Few years after independence, Nigerians were filled with

K. B. Amusa (✉)
Department of History, University of Ibadan, Ibadan, Nigeria

K. J. Ani et al. (eds.), *Political Economy of Resource, Human Security and Environmental Conflicts in Africa*,
https://doi.org/10.1007/978-981-16-2036-2_10

admiration of fear as the leaders who occupied the previous European positions oozed nothing but an ethno-political attitude towards power.[5] The significance of such attitude became obvious in less than a decade of independence. As a result, discontent struck the land and the cry for new social identification was regenerated.

The fact that Nigeria is multilingual cannot be overemphasised. The cultural and language heterogeneity of the country which ought to be an asset became its liability when it degenerated into lack of statesmanship and visionary leadership on the part of leadership. This made it impractical for the country to have men of valour with great conscience and less ambition who could strive for emancipation. Visionary leadership is the power and ability to rule above benchmark of mediocrity on contemporary issues or challenges facing a particular geographical area or region. That is the special sense by which the qualities of a leader are perceived through the lens of transformation of the society. According to A. S. Jegede, leaders are those committed, energised people with high level of credibility, inspiration, charisma and honesty admitted by both the internally and externally bodies as well as other agencies. They enjoy an excellence social and networking abilities, which enable them, transfer the lines, ambiguities, pressures and meadow that exist between and inside of the agencies.[6] The absence of visionary leadership in Nigeria leads to the creation of a state that in turn craft some form of neo-self-identification and new social enemies.[7] Nigerians free from the shackles of colonial rule assumed that the crucial commitment of a state and its civil society is to use its powers to apportion the resources towards eradicating poverty and hunger while it assures security of livelihood and safety against the major threats and fluctuations of life, and security of decent households.[8] This hope became a mere daydream as those who led the independence movement felt that since they spearheaded national liberty activities, ruling the country had become their heritage as they viewed criticisms and oppositions to their government as an act of ungratefulness.[9] Subsequently, Nigeria and Africa in general were meant to sustain their genetics individuality and thereafter political status that were to be the consequences of the congenital form of leadership beginning from the end of colonialism.[10] Hence, Nigeria can be regarded as a cloned state of the imperialists.

The Insecurity of Governance in Nigeria

The insecurity of governance can be used interchangeably as poor leadership. Poor governance is responsible for the challenges facing the assumed unified people of Nigeria that are bifurcated by the political strategy of the leadership. The political approaches entail segregation and exclusion which implies differential access to social welfare or services that has largely been responsible for the insecurity of lives and properties. Documents show that colonial rule was not really interested in promoting integration among the various ethnic groups. Rather, it emphasized differences and hierarchy.[11] The effect of the colonial partial-prominence was responsible for the current challenges facing Nigeria's national integration, unity and harmony between the various ethnic nationalities. The conflicts in Africa and Nigeria in particular are fuelled by the politicians.[12] This has recently been reiterated by the former president of Nigeria Dr. Goodluck Ebele Jonathan in his book 'My Transition Hour' that, "My leadership was besieged and marred by these contending primordial forces, with the logos of violence and intrigues. Lining the crevices of these primordial forces are formidable modern players who are weakening the bases of their stock's primordial position for extremely selfish gains".[13] This egocentric form of leadership is responsible for the rulers' little awareness concerning the people they governed. The oblivious attitude of these leaders ignites insurgences. The insecure climate has been a continuous hindrance to the socio-economic and political attainment. This is liable for Nigeria's failure to instil an ideal sense of national citizenship, that is conscious of civic responsibility. This consecutive failure is responsible for not just unequalled crime rate in Nigeria, but also unemployment and other disastrous effect on human and national development. This insecure governance is however responsible for terrorism and insurgency that sequentially create a social consciousness and communal identity.

In precolonial Africa, political traditions included varieties of leadership styles that opened the societies to intervention.[14] This is applicable to all places colonized by the Europeans. After the independence decade, African leadership believed that the only way they could unite their nations was to find some form of cooperation among the ethnic groupings[15] often referred to as unity in diversity. The formation of Nigeria as a state, its rudiments and existence cannot be detached from its history and its leaders. The sailors of the country, including the former colonial rulers, set in place processes of regionalization and marginalization towards ethnic configuration of national governance. They began a process of rearranging the instruments of governance to fit into the interests of ethnic politics.[16] Conflict is thus used to nurture allegiance, political interest, information, as well as participation. In addition to the things that expand the trend of conflict in Nigeria, several arguments focus majorly on lack of education, mass media, urbanism, exposure, age and income. However, while Jonathan states that propaganda and rumours are responsible for insurgency, Peil argues that lack of education is considered more important than the other variables.[17]

As the leaders make use of categoric politics to maintain their sit tight syndromes, in return, the citizens adopt an iconoclastic means of requesting and collecting their share of the 'national cake'. These political attitudes and behaviour affect the socio-economic condition of the Nigerian nation. However, ethnic backgrounds of the various peoples that formed the state are essential in establishing the framework, patterns and forms of political culture. The political awareness of Nigerians and their active participation in electioneering and other socio-economic activities have been responsible for the Nigeria national and human development.[18] Even when a regime is highly dictatorial and give slight or no possibility for a defined politically awareness, there will continuously be some nuances and activities that would express the true ambitions of the individuals, nonetheless subordinated they could be beneath those in possession of power and authority.[19] Hence, political conscious citizens always hold the government responsible for their socio-economic welfare.

The principle of divide and rule, and the animosity between majority and minority groups continued. The effect on the long run sets the nation ablaze in less than a decade of independence. Yet, the political leaders engaged in the prototype of the pre-war politics of partisanship. Subsequent reforms were made to avert future occurrence of such deadly civil war through the federal government reconciliation and rehabilitation strategy. But, the differences continued to vitrine. The differences have been the sources of political disparities, suspicions or tensions among the two major bipolar regions—the North and the South; the North—broken into numerous states in three geopolitical bricks, largely Muslim. It was the centre of an Islamic empire of the Sokoto Caliphate in the pre-colonial period, dominated by Muslim populations. Especially, to those whose descendants had been part of the caliphate who generally look at the Middle East for a wide Muslim network and solidarity. While the

South is known to be a culturally divided province that comprises many states with three geopolitical units that is largely believed to be dominated by Christian.[20] They are the most socio-politically influenced as a result of the presence of the missionaries who advocated Western education. Not all embraced the foreign religions (Islam and Christianity) as practitioners of traditional religion remained. Hence, post-colonial Nigeria witnessed the epic of mutual distrust, scepticism and cynicism of modernity and religion.

The pockets of ethnic and religious groups host criticisms against ethnicity and religious preponderances as perceived hegemonic-oppressors. The criticism sometimes is communicated via bitter political objections or conflicts; forceful and lawless rivalry, factional crises and vehement rebellions stoked by political leaders who use it to uphold their status quo to defend power and authority by spreading the awareness that their ethnic group is mutually in power.[21] As a result, power keeps straddling in the hand of the major ethnic groups, while the minority groups keep feeling insecure as their interests are not well defended or represented.

Having lost power to a coalition of ethnic groupings, in turn, a cry for restructuring usurp the national quest. The continuous yell for restructuring Nigeria persisted without a delineated way for its achievement. The lack of visionary political and socio-economic ideology leads to a continuous political transfer of allegiance. The political party system in Nigeria just like every other place in the world is an institution that mobilizes the electorates on behalf of a collective set of interests, anxieties or goals. It is important because it helps nations to play an essential part in the democratic process. Thus, political party remains the only legal nationwide institution for mobilization all over the world as well as Nigeria. Various political parties in Nigeria now adopt the restructuring agenda as an attempt to at first appeal to voters' emotions and, the ethnic minorities who continuously strive for power through iconoclastic means. The persistent unbalanced political manipulation, actions and access to the national juice have caused ethnic tension between Yoruba, Ibo and Hausa/Fulani the three major ethnic groups in Nigeria have all espoused ethnic and religious conflict as a legacy through which they can hijack the national government. The federal government in return introduced several measures to curb the anti-governmental mutiny as it suits the fancies or interest of the ethnic group in power.[22]

Conflict, Insecurity and the Trajectory of Interventions

Insurgences and uprising in the Nigerian political space is one of the major means to jettison political isolation. National defence mechanism is majorly controlled by peculiar ethnic group which in turn influence the socio-economic affairs of the larger citizenry. Hence some powers that be have remained the sole determinants and benefactors of the Nigerian modern politics.[23] The interventions of this powerful elites in aspect of insurgency have continued to partition and sectionalize the Nigeria national security. The interest of this peculiar hegemonic ethnic groups cannot be downplayed in the issue of conflict, insecurity and leadership conspiracy.[24] The relocation of the Nigeria's national defence headquarters from the federal capital territory in Abuja to the north-eastern region of the country at Borno state[25] by the first elected president of the opposition party, President Muhammadu Buhari during his inaugural speech on Friday May 29, 2015 perpetrated nothing but more ethnic tensions as the border-centric defence solely testified to the sentiment of ethnic superiority and obvious manipulation of the military bureaucracy.

Subsequent to the fourth republic, several issues of insurgencies have emerged and had been solved through brutal military operations. However, the military operation is in tandem to the nature or level of conflict stroked by the people who in turn received insufficient commitment in welfare by those they entrusted with their political will. The military operations were performed in different labels to curb the rebels that questioned the infamous government, whom they considered deaf to their regional or community need. The history of government intervention in the issue of insurgency is as old as the history of the country. The establishment of different tribal militias such as Oduduwa People's Congress (OPC), Agbekoya and Afenifere in the Western region, Bakasi Boy, Niger-Delta in the South-south region, Independent People of Biafra (IPOB) and Ohanaeze Ndigbo in the East region, the Arewa People's Congress (APC), Herdsmen and Boko-Haram in the Northern region of Nigeria as a uniform response to stimuli is primarily to curtail external intervention and political oppression.[26] Several forceful arrests of militias have been carried out under several military and civilian government and not limited to the Obasanjo-Atiku regime through Buhari-Osinbajo administration. These military operations were attributed for different reasons. The history of constant uprising in the East, West and Niger Delta district of the country is traceable to the colonial root.[27] The preference and importance placed on natural resources made the Nigeria government to create the Niger Delta Development Commission (NDDC) in 2000. The description of the history of conflict and insecurity in Nigeria is impractical as large number of events have occurred over the years. However, to facilitate our understanding, it is vital to at first discuss the following: the Niger Delta militancy, the herdsmen attacks and the Boko-haram insurgence.

The Niger Delta militants were the first to revolt against environmental degradation during the Obasanjo regime; the history of mass revolt against the federal government in Nigeria has been experienced since the post-colonial era. Before the Obasanjo regime, several Niger Delta indigenes have publicly demonstrated their grievances against the federal government that has continued to exploit their land for crude oil without benefits or dividend to the native people whose farms, wells and rivers are polluted by oil. The constant revolts of Ken Saro Wiwa and the Ogoni leaders against the federal government led to their trial and conviction for treason under the military administration of Late General Sani Abacha's on November 10, 1995.[28] Less than four years of Saro-Wiwa's death sentence, there was another genocide in 1999 against the Ijaw metropolis in Odi, Bayelsa state.[29] The Odi massacre occurred in the milieu of a partial skirmish in the Niger Delta region over the aboriginal rights to oil assets and environmental safety on November 20, 1999.[30] The Odi butchery was carried out by an armed operation tagged 'Operation no Living Thing'. This military operation affected all active and able-bodied people of Odi including the aged; pregnant and nursing mothers.[31] Despite this, the oil question remains the possible most emotional issue to all. The Niger-Delta people are convinced that the oil issue is of the gravest importance to their future, and the country at large, and is the key to the sustenance of peace and stability in the Niger Delta region.

Perhaps, the most significant example of the conflicts that threatened the Nigerian state was the agitation of the independent state of Biafra. The Biafran movement at first relapsed at the termination of the Nigerian Civil War. The bloody combat fought to curb the Igbo from seceding from Nigeria after Late Col. Ojukwu's proclamation of the Republic of Biafra in 1967 ended. The end of the war gave room for national reunification. In recent time, some young generation of the Igbo led by

Nnamdi Kanu emerged the leader of the Biafran movement now Indigenous People of Biafra (IPOB). The mission of the IPOB group is to reincarnate the spirit of Ojukwu's dreamed Biafran nation. The activities of the IPOB in the eastern province of the country heightened the call for national security which leads to the introduction of a military operation tagged 'Operation Python Dance'. This military operation was established to ensure national security since a society is nothing without peace. It was designed to apprehend pro-Biafran agitators whom the Nigeria federal government perceived as enemies to national progress, activities and developments through their rebellious act. However, the South-East and the South-South regions of Nigeria have always been victimized by forceful federal government's, arbitrarily actions and the enforcement of the military order. Despite several actions embarked upon by the Herdsmen and Boko-Haram sect that have continuously threatened the national peace and security has not witness any quick or further active military actions from the federal government like other regions.

As emphasized earlier, the Ijaw and the Igbo are not the only ethnic groups in Nigeria that have threatened the peace of the country. The Hausa/Fulani factor had been a major national issue and a threat to national peace and security, influencing major ethno-religious movements in the country. The recent Boko-Haram movement emanated from the north-eastern region of the country and thence, continued to launch an attack on the people of Borno, Bauchi, Jos, Adamawa states, respectively. The ethno-religious sentiment cum fanatism known as Boko-Haram continued to manage violence shortly after the declaration of the former President Goodluck Jonathan as winner of the 2011 general elections.

Historically, the Boko-haram insurgence started as a religious violence rather than the socio-cultural and political image the appellation indicates today. The Kaduna riots that occurred between February 21 and May 23, 2000 claimed the lives of many people and left several homeless. The fight began shortly after the introduction of the sharia law in Kaduna. In September 7, 2001, the Jos riot also occurred, leaving the lives of several in disarray. In November 20–23, the Miss World riots of 2002 revolved around the killing of Mohammed Yusuf, the founder of the Boko-haram sect. This generated into further crises that called for a state of emergence in the Borno state. The event was followed in 2004 by the first and second Yelwa massacres in February 4, May 2 and the November, 28–29, 2008 Jos riots, and the January 17 through March 7, 2010 Jos riots.[32] They have unleashed anarchy that have upset the actual political, economic and security foundations of Nigeria.

The timeline for the Boko-haram uprising started in July 26 through 29, 2009 when almost one thousand soldiers were killed in the battle between Boko-haram militants and the Nigerian army. The spiritual leader of the Boko-haram insurgency Mohammed Yusuf was apprehended and handed over to the Nigerian police. The execution of Mohammed Yusuf just like that of Ken Saro-Wiwa led to another unrest and Abubakar Shekau took over the movement. In September 7, and December 31, 2010 there was a Bauchi prison break and an attack in Abuja, very close to a military barracks killing few civilians. In 2011, there were several Boko-haram attacks first in May 29 which killed several people in Abuja during the swearing in of President Goodluck Jonathan. In June 16, there was another attack on the police headquarters in Abuja, at the United Nations office in Abuja on August 6. In November 4, there was a Boko Haram attack in Damaturu, and on December 22, there were clashes between Boko-haram insurgents and Nigerian soldiers in Maiduguri and Damaturu. The Islamic fundamentalist group has been affirmed to be an international radical organisation and described to have been linked to Al Queda—another terrorist group, by the international community following the event that took place in Nigeria after the general elections in 2011.[33]

The application of extensive military force on the insurgents often takes difficult political process and negotiations. Operations such as 'Lafia D'ole', for example, have attested to a devastating conflict and exacerbating the benevolent situation in the north-eastern region of Nigeria. The actions of the military operations in different regions kept Nigerians in suspense. While subsequent news announced that the federal government defeated Boko-haram insurgents, another announced the death of some soldiers. The parties in engagement have basically remained unchanged even as their attitude and composition vary. The trend of operations as well as election periods often helps to escalate the conflict with indications of political undertones—the same government which introduced a military operation tagged 'Python Dance' not being able to apprehend the group. Many had believed that the military operation of 'Lafia D'ole' would deal a final blow to the insurgency, given President Muhammadu Buhari's promises to conquer Boko-haram in 2015. His political manifesto promised the return of the Chibok and the Datchi girls. Now, the subject matter remains in the pipeline. The president's inaugural speech of 'belong to everybody and belong to nobody' appealed to many; yet evidences consistently pointed to the opposite, particularly when he declared a cattle colony in the country, which many viewed as the Fulani Agenda.[34]

The federal government's favour of herdsmen's request for cattle colonies in every state within the country further illustrated the insincerity of the president's rhetoric. Herdsmen launched several attacks on villages around in Plateau, Benue, Kaduna, Nasarawa and Kogi states. Perceptions on the inability of the federal government increased and spread widely. In place of integrity and the character of an unbiased umpire, the federal government deployed soldiers to the scene of the events. In spite of the continuous violent rhetoric of the herdsmen in Benue, Kaduna, Nasarawa and Plateau states, the government has been unable to curb the menace significantly. It is curious to note the agility with which government introduced killer squared military operations as introduced in south-eastern and south-southern part of the country. Instead, the government brought the herdsmen out of their camps to gain cattle colonies at the doorsteps of other ethnic groups.

In examining why militants' activities occur or not occur in the early stage of independence or why it continues today, it is necessary to discuss ruminate on the socio-political conditions. Today, men of the Nigerian army and politicians seize opportunities provided by insurgency to divert money meant for national security for personal use and as conduit pipe to divert funds to other functions that are not related to its mandate.

Leadership Linkages to Insecurity

At independence, Nigeria had high hopes for the future.[35] It was the belief of many that the country, freed from the shackles of colonial rule, would achieve rapid economic growth and exercise a decisive and constructive role in African affairs in particular and world affairs in general. Indeed, power was handed over to those who had virtually all been in the corridor of power be it political or administrative office since the 1950s and had worked alongside with the British colonial officials with the objective of ensuring that political freedom could be taken in the best thinkable circumstances. But unfortunately, these men led a dispensation that plagued the country with corruption, tribalism, favouritism, unhealthy rivalry, rigging of elections, arson and all forms of political and social manoeuvrings which eventually led to the event that took place in

January 15, 1966.[36] The form and style of leadership and power politics in Nigeria since 1914 attest that leadership has been driven by the silent conspiracy of the few.[37]

Since 1970, the country's national leaders have embarked on policies that tacitly promote national integration. This policy in some cases was only perpetuated to maintain the power status quo which in turn affect the existing peace. As a result, policies made were mainly separated from any form of political obligation or development. Strategy was disconnected from societal requirements and from the cultural and historical genuineness of the people.[38] The governing method of oppression by the leaders determined the lax attitude of the governed towards appreciating governance efforts. However, the distinguishing features of leadership quality being virtue in the first case and wealth in the second were completely lacking in the contestations for leadership positions[39] that now drives people into power struggle and money politics which continually puncture the principle of natural justice.

Post-colonial Africa in general and Nigeria in particular is faced with instability. As a result, the significant thing to evoke is that those who are accountable for the implementation of power and authority be it individuals or organs of government, tribes or what could be referred as great or small cause disturbance that in turn leads to revolution. They may do so directly when they become too zealous for power. Or indirectly, when they assume too loftier that they are no longer satisfied to the main terms of equity among the people they are to governed.[40] This shows a cost push factor of the demand for power. The leaders stir up the material consciousness of the citizens, and in turn, the citizens hold the leaders responsible for affecting the standard of living either positively or negatively. Instructively, ethnic groups denied of a role in power politics as well as a share from the dividends of democracy end up being a threat to the national security.

A democratic leader is believed to play a major role in driving the democratic process towards addressing the plight of the common man. The irony of this, in Nigeria, is that the government which is meant to drive peace is not accessible as corruption and political patronage along ethnic division has eaten deep in the system. Political leaders show less concern for the needs of the people the assume are they are doing favor with their service, while the people make their needs known to the government often through protest. Commoners by their history 'have no view'[41] unlike the case in traditional leadership. This proves that the decolonization process in Nigeria was not socio-political but rather a pseudo-politico economic ideology since the suppression of the traditional authority by the colonial masters through the native law and customs remains a matter that should be within the purview of the supreme court.[42] Decker notes that between 1920 and 1960, the phase of leadership was increasingly influenced by education, business, civil service, law, journalism, labour unionism, politics, governances and administration.[43] This shows that traditional leadership was subjugated by the emergence of the neo-western educated elite who had been trained in the political philosophies of the imperial powers.

Conclusion

The lack of well-defined political vision as well as disciplined, patriotic and committed leadership is responsible for continuous primordial unrests in Nigeria. The history of insurgency in Nigeria is filled with moments when communities and individuals were robbed of socio-economic dignity as a result of dictatorship, sometimes via electoral manipulation or constitutional seizure of the state. Thus, sectionalism between the leadership and followership in straddling for dignity has remained the main strategy to dehumanise or infantilise the political structure of the country. Comprehensive redress will involve more than compensation for the physical structure of the socio-economic dignity of the citizenry which is encompassing[44] and has been gravely affected by the insecurity of the leadership and the lack of comprehensive vision of the futuristic implications of present policies. However, the real test of the nature of authority in West Africa and Nigeria in particular can only be provided through a systematic examination of the aspirations of the people or followers.[45] This is sure to reveal the basis of patriotism to the motherland. The state has become an idea of regulatory order to which people have appealed, often in the face of abuses by the very agents of the state. This has eroded the significance of leadership in Nigeria and Africa, especially with evidences of agitations and direct confrontation of the state by emotions that are politicized by religion and economy.

Since insurgency has out-rightly become an institutionalized means of expressing grievances, government should shift emphasis towards empowering traditional leaders to sustain peace and tranquillity in the society.[46] Traditional, in this sense, is the ability to deal with insurgency by developing strategies for coping with national threat and demands. Tradition and custom are invoked as a perceived source of legitimacy for new institutions of government. Ikime pinpoints that, those who parade themselves as leaders of the country need to go to the ancestors to learn the way they manage their affairs so as to be wise enough to call into play such statesmanship as it can help the nation to forge a truly United Nigeria. In spite of their differences, the people are to always exist to form a component part.[47] Nigerian leader should be conciliatory and appreciative towards traditional authority through less intervention in traditional affairs. The fact that monarchs (Oba, Obi or Emirs) are much more identified within their society cannot be overemphasized in the context of the Nigeria kingship system. It is usually with the assumption of age-old origins and automatic communal identification. The claim that chiefs (traditional rulers) discern how to convert arbitrary forces of a state into a source of defence for its people's life and property is considered the basis for chiefship[48] and should be an opportunity for generic governance to advance the course of citizens' security and rights.

Notes

1. Tunde Decker, 'Gangster Elitism: An Appraisal of Leadership in Nigeria Since 1914', *Kaduna Journal of Historical Studies*, Vol. 1, No. 9, A Publication of the Department of History, Kaduna State University, Kaduna-Nigeria, 2017, p. 391.
2. Tunde Decker, 'Gangster Elitism'.
3. Tunde Decker, 'Gangster Elitism'.
4. Alanveabee Efihraim Idyorough, *History and Philosophy of Social Welfare Services in Nigeria 1900–1960*, Aboki Publishers, p. IX.
5. S. Ademola Ajayi, *Nigerian's Search for an Enduring Political Culture; Cracks in the Wall Through Changing Scenes*, Chief Samuel Ladoke Akintola Memorial Lecture at Ladoke Akintola University of Technology, Ogbomoso, Saturday, 23 January, 2016, pp. 31–32.
6. Ayodele S. Jegede, *Collaborative Research in Practice: Experiences, Challenges and Opportunities for Academics in the Humanities*, Paper Presented at 12th WARIMA International Conference and Workshops, University of Ibadan, November 29, 2018.
7. Frank Van Acker, 'Uganda and the Lord's Resistance Army: The New Order No One Ordered', in *African Affairs: The Journal of the Royal African Society*, Vol. 103 No. 412, Oxford University Press, July 2004, p. 338.
8. David Harvey, *A Brief History of Neoliberalism*, Oxford University Press, 2005, p. 183.

9. S. Ademola Ajayi, *The 1914 Amalgamation and the Challenges of National Integration in Post-Colonial Nigeria*; Lecture delivered at Jogor Center, Ring Road, Ibadan (27 April 2013) Tonda Foundation.
10. Tunde Decker, *Matrix of Inherited Identity: A Historical Exploration of the underdog Phenomenon in Nigeria Relationship Strategies 1960–2011*, University Press PLC Ibadan, p. 3.
11. Rasheed Olaniyi, 'Ordering Urban Space and Migrant's Protests in Sabon-gari Kano 1911–1960', in *Living the city in Africa: Processes of Invention and Intervention*, Published by SGAS/SSEA, 2013, p. 63.
12. Cherry Leonardi and Martina Santschi, *Dividing Communities in South Sudan and Northern Uganda: Boundary Disputes and Land Governance*, Rift Valley Institute, London, 2016, p. 61.
13. Goodluck Jonathan, *My Transition Hours*, LWCA Publishers, p. 35.
14. Derek R. Peterson, Kodzo Gavua, and Ciraj Rassool (eds.), *The Politics of Hertiage in Africa; Economies, Histories, and Infrastructures*, Cambridge University Press, 2015, p. 2.
15. Derek R. Peterson, Kodzo Gavua, and Ciraj Rassool (eds.), *The Politics of Heritage in Africa; Economies, Histories, and Infrastructures*, Cambridge University Press, 2015, p. 1.
16. Margaret Peil, *Nigerian Politics: The People's View*, Cassell London, 1976, p. 5.
17. Margaret Peil, *Nigerian Politics.*
18. Margaret Peil, *Nigerian Politics.*
19. J Denis Derbyshire and Ian Derbyshire, *World Political System: An Introduction to Comparative Government*, Chambers Edinburgh, 1991.
20. James S. Coleman, *Nigeria Background to Nationalism*, University of California Press, 1958, p. 36.
21. Mohammed Usman, 'Ethnic Minorities and the Quest for Development', in Victor Egwemi, Terhemba Wuam and Chris S. Orngu (eds.) *Federalism, Politics and Minorities in Nigeria: Essay in Honour of Professor G.N. Hembe*, Bahiti & Dalila, Ibadan, 2014, p. 289.
22. James S. Coleman, *Nigeria Background to Nationalism*, University of California Press, 1958, p. 332.
23. Richard L. Sklar, *Nigerian Political Parties: Power in an Emergent African Nation*, Nok Publishers International New York, p. 24.
24. Goodluck Jonathan, *My Transition Hours*, LWCA Publishers, p. 22.
25. President Muhammadu Buhari, *Inaugural Speech on Friday May 29, 2015.*
26. James S. Coleman, *Nigeria Background to Nationalism*, University of California Press, 1958, p. 64.
27. S. Ademola Ajayi, *The 1914 Amalgamation and the Challenges of National Integration in Post-Colonial Nigeria*; Lecture delivered at Jogor Center, Ring Road, Ibadan (27 April 2013), Tonda Foundation, p. 16.

28. Ken Wiwa, 'Finally It Seems as if Ken Saro-wiwa, My Father, May Not Have Died in Vain', *The Guardian*, theguardian.com, Tuesday 10 November, 2015.
29. Ken Wiwa, *The Guardian*, theguardian.com, Tuesday 10 November 2015.
30. Ken Wiwa, *The Guardian*, theguardian.com, Tuesday 10 November 2015.
31. Ken Wiwa, *The Guardian*, theguardian.com, Tuesday 10 November 2015.
32. CU Okoroafor and MC Ukpabi, 'Boko Haram Insurgency and National Security in Nigeria', *International Journal of Development and Management Review*, Vol. 10, No. 1, 2015.
33. CU Okoroafor and MC Ukpabi, 'Boko Haram Insurgency and National Security in Nigeria'.
34. Ihuoma Chiedozie, 'Cattle Colonies: Buhari Pursuing Fulani Supremacy Agenda' Punch, punchng.com, 24 January 2018.
35. Adebola A. Ademeso, 'The Dialectics of Unity in Diversity: Osofisan's Proposal in Another Raft' in *Humanities Review Journal, Vol. 3 No. 1 Humanities Publisher University of Ibadan, June 2003*, p. 37.
36. Adebola A. Ademeso, 'The Dialectics of Unity in Diversity'.
37. Tunde Decker, 'Gangster Elitism'.
38. David O. Ajayi, 'Issues in Nigeria's Economic Development', in *Yoruba History and Historians: A Festschrift for Professor Gabriel Olorundare Oguntomisin*, John Archers Publishers Ibadan.
39. Tunde Decker, 'Gangster Elitism: An Appraisal of Leadership in Nigeria since 1914', *Kaduna Journal of Historical Studies*, Vol. 1, No. 9, 2017, p. 388.
40. Tunde Decker, 'Gangster Elitism', p. 390.
41. Margaret Peil, *Nigerian Politics: The People's View*, Cassell London, 1976, p. 145.
42. Tunde Decker, 'Gangster Elitism', p. 393.
43. Tunde Decker, 'Gangster Elitism', p. 393.
44. Bernadette Atuahene, *We Want What's Ours: Learning from South Africa's Land Restitution Program*, Oxford University Press, 2014, p. 21.
45. Margaret Peil, *Nigerian Politics: The People's View*, Cassell London, 1976, p. 1.
46. Cherry Leonardi, *Dealing with Government in South Sudan: Histories of Chiefship Community and State*, James Currey, 2013, p. 1.
47. Obaro Ikime, *In Search of Nigerians: Changing Patterns of Inter-Group Relations in an Evolving Nation-State*. Presidential Inaugural Lecture delivered at the 30th Congress of the Historical Society of Nigeria, Nsukka, on May 1, 1985, p. 5.
48. Cherry Leonardi, *Dealing with Government in South Sudan: Histories of Chiefship Community and State*, James Currey, 2013, p. 3.

Bibliography

African Affairs, *The Journal of the Royal African Society*, Vol. 103, No. 412, July 2004.

Atuahene Bernadette, *We Want What's Ours: Learning from South Africa's Land Restitution Program*. Oxford University Press, 2014.

Coleman S. James, *Nigeria Background to Nationalism*. University of California Press, 1958.

Decker Tunde, *Matrix of Inherited identity: A Historical Exploration of the Underdog Phenomenon in Nigeria's Relationship Strategies, 1960–2011*. University Press Ibadan, 2016.

Derbyshire J. Denis and Derbyshire Ian, *World Political System: An Introduction to Comparative Government*. Chambers Edinburgh, 1991.

Feinberg M. Harvey, *Our Land, Our Life, Our Future: Black South African Challenges to Territorial Segregation, 1913–1948*. Unisa Press Pretoria, 2005.

Harvey David, *A Brief History of Neoliberalism*, Oxford University Press, 2005.

Humanities Review Journal, Vol. 3, No. 1, June 2003.

Idyorough Alanveabee Efihraim, *History and Philosophy of Social Welfare Services in Nigeria 1900–1960*. Aboki Publishers.

Kaduna Journal of Historical Studies, Vol. 1, No. 9, 2017.

Leonardi Cherry, *Dealing with Government in South Sudan: Histories of Chiefship Community and State*. James Currey, 2013.

Leonardi Cherry and Santschi Martina, *Dividing Communities in South Sudan and Northern Uganda: Boundary Disputes and Land Governance*. Rift Valley Institute, London, 2016.

Obrist Brigit, Arlt Veit and Macamo Elisio (Eds.), *Living the City in Africa: Processes of Invention and Intervention*, Published by SGAS/SSEA, 2013.

Peil Margaret, *Nigerian Politics: The People's View*. Cassell London, 1976.

Peterson R. Derek, Kodzo Gavua, and Ciraj Rassool (eds.), *The Politics of Heritage in Africa: Economies, Histories, and Infrastructures*. Cambridge University Press, 2015.

S. Ademola Ajayi, *Nigerian's Search for An Enduring Political Culture: Cracks in the Wall Through Changing Scenes*, Chief Samuel Ladoke Akintola Memorial Lecture at Ladoke Akintola University of Technology, Ogbomoso, Saturday, 23 January 2016.

Sarro Ramon, *The Politics of Religious Change on the Upper Guinea Coast: Iconoclasm Done and Undone*. Edinburgh University Press, 2009.

Sklar L. Richard, *Nigerian Political Parties: Power in an Emergent African Nation*. Nok Publishers International New York, 1963.

Vazzadini Elena, *Lost Nationalism: Revolution, Memory & Anti-Colonial Resistance in Sudan*. James Currey, 2015.

CHAPTER 11

Inter-Group Relations and Peace Building in Pre-Colonial Africa: Focus on Agba and Izhi Environmental Conflicts

Kelechi Johnmary Ani, Lawson Onyema Chukwu, and Samuel Nwite Okoro

Introduction

Warfare has remained a form of inter-group relations among people of different ages and time. It is used to pursue defined social, economic and political interest in many societies. Recently, it graduated from a means of inter-group relations to a strategy of attaining diplomatic goals. It is also a roadmap to peace, where early warning, mediation, dialogue and third-person intervention fails.

In pre-colonial African societies, warfare was the major means which many communities used to attain their goals. According to oral tradition, communities engaged in a series of wars with their neighbours in order

K. J. Ani (✉) · L. O. Chukwu · S. N. Okoro
Department of History and Strategic Studies, Alex Ekwueme Federal University Ndufu-Alike, Ikwo, Nigeria
e-mail: kelechi.ani@funai.edu.ng

K. J. Ani et al. (eds.), *Political Economy of Resource, Human Security and Environmental Conflicts in Africa*,
https://doi.org/10.1007/978-981-16-2036-2_11

to attain or protect their existential interest. The nature of the interest differs from society to society. One of the major factors that have driven wars among communities in Africa is the contest over a given portion of land. Land occupied a fundamental place in the societal interest of many communities and groups. That is unconnected to the fact that land is used for multiple purposes. Some people need it for agricultural purpose, while others need it for business and settlement goals, thus, when the interest of one community clash with another over land, conflict and warfare becomes imminent. Several other reasons for pre-colonial Igbo warfare include abduction of sons and daughters of the land, desecration of sacred places, raids, etc. The wars were often carried out by different age grades that constituted armed forces of a particular community. In order to carry out these wars successfully, different weapons were used and many strategies were applied by the communities at war to defeat their enemies. This chapter is centred on the dynamics of intergroup warfare between the Agba people as well as Izhi people of present-day Ebonyi State and their neighbours. The chapter examined the dynamics of war between Agba and their neighbours, as well as warfare in Izhi clan, the weapons of war, those who constituted the armies and the peace building strategies adopted by the people, who were then independent communities.

Methodology

This work is an original research that adopted qualitative methodology. The researchers went to the field and extensively interviewed old men and women from Agba and Izhi communities. They also engaged in focused group discussions with five to seven persons on the dynamics of pre-colonial Agba and Izhi wars. Archival materials were extensively collected in the process for the development of this chapter while minimal level of secondary literatures was used in the process of developing this article.

Origin and Migration

Archival sources reveal that "the Agba clan is an Ibo extraction and claims relationship with the powerful Ezza clan".[1] According to oral history, it was said that Agba people migrated from their ancestral home land (Okpoku Ezekoma) in Ezza South (Onu Eke-Imoha) to the present Agba land because of clash of interest between them and their Ezza brother.

Eze Paul Ogodo Igwe said that "Agba moved from Onueke Ezza to present day Agba land because of bitter war that they engaged with Ezza their brother. On reaching Ugbodo Agba with his people, he fought with people of Oduma, Agbaebor and Ezza sub-clan after some days of war they defeated them and settled".[2] Ironically, "this claim of Ezza origin is not confirmed by the Ezza and it is known that the later drove the Agba from their earlier home in what is now Ezza land".[3] Thus, Agba, the founder of the clan, could have migrated at the same time with Ezekuna, the founder of Ezza and Ezentum, the founder of Isu from a location around Afikpo clusters. When Agba settled in the large expanse of land known today as Idembia, the Ezza invaded them after some years and pushed them further to settle in their present location.

Furthermore, Agba clan is made up of four communities, namely Amegu, Agbelu, Ohoffia and Akwurakwu. Ironically, during colonial rule Amagu and Agbelu were administered under Afikpo Division while Ohoffia and Akwurakwu were classified under the Abakaliki Division. At that time, Ohoffia and Akwurakwu sub-clans were under the Nkalagu Native Court, which holds special sessions in Ohafia main market thereby forcing Agba people to travel a long distance before their case could be heard in colonial court.

The Amegu and Agbelu sub-clans attended the Isu Native Court in Afikpo Division. That was why some people argue that the Agba people were a lost race of Isu Okoma people. Unfortunately, the demand by the people of Agba that they should be united under one colonial district never saw the light of the day due to the nature of divide and rule politics practiced by the imperial lords at that time. The same form of problem manifested among the Ezza living in Isu, which was part of Afikpo Division, as they were reluctant to pay tax at Afikpo Division.[4] However, the wider Ezza people that made up the Abakaliki Division "raised no objection to the Ezza living on the Afikpo side paying tax to Afikpo".[5] They were later united into the Abakaliki colonial division. However, before the unification, the Agba fought a number of wars with their neighbours.

Agba Warfare

Agba warfare took place in different historical epochs. Although there was no written evidence or literature to know its exact periodization, Agba people engaged in different wars at different times, as they fought with Ezza people before migrating to their present homeland. According to oral tradition, the war took place from the middle of nineteenth century and lasted intermittently to the early twentieth century.[6]

Agba people engaged in bitter war with Ezza at Onueke Imoha. The war was fought because Ezza people invaded the ancestral home land of Agba at Okpoku Ezekuna. The area was said to be a portion of land, which Ekuma Enyi, the father of Ezekoma and Ezekuna gave to Ezekoma to settle before his death.[7] Thus, according to Eze Paul Ogodo Igwe, "Agba engaged in a deadly war with Ezza, when the Agba began to lose the war, they decided to flee from their ancestral home land, Okpoku Ezekuna to settled in their present day Agba land. Agba people was pushed westward by the Ezza descendants of Ezekuna and crossing the Ebonyi River they met a group of people who has settled there before them, called Agbaebor, Ezza-Eka, and Oduma people".[8] However, according to Afoke:

> Agba people formerly occupied the area now settled by Umunwagu and Ikwuate (Idembia) in Izikworo sub-villages. When the southwards expansion of the Izikworo group of villages caught up with Agba, whose main settlements were in Ebo Ndiagu, Ochuhu Agba and Orie Agba Elu area, they put up a spirited but short-lived defence. Overcome, the Agba blocked several brine ponds in these areas with huge stones, which Idembia women later removed. After settling in their new homes for several years, Izo Imoha group of villages once more met the Agba, in their southwards expansion. They were determined this time to hold on to their land and the Izo Imoha group of villages, instead of driving away the Agba, passed over them to a wide expanse of land then uninhabited, which the Ezza called Ezzagu, meaning Ezza farm land.[9]

The first group of people in which Agba came in contact with in their new settlement was the Agbaebor people of Isu. According to oral tradition, "Agbaebor people were the original inhabitant of the area where Agba and his people first settled, that was called Ugbodo. The Agba engaged in a war with the Agbaebor people, which made them to flee farther westward.[10] Chief Moses Odi Oka noted that Agba pursed the Agbaebor people to Nkpara where they have their present-day boundary, after defeating the Agbaebor, they settled in Ugbodo.[11] On the other hand, Agbaebor oral tradition had it that at the arrival of Eze Ntum Oke and the wife in the area, there was massive expansion of land controlled by the then Isu ancestors who were hunters. The border of their land mass reached Nara, Nkerefi and Amagunze in Nkanu, Uburu in Ohozara as well as Iyonu in Ishielu, thus they willingly gave the Agba descendants the portion of land they inhabit today as they were desperately in search of a land to settle, after the Ezza has displaced them. Archival evidence reveal that "the Ezzas themselves agree that the Ezzagu settlers live on land formerly belonging to Iyono (on the North) and Isu (on the South), but all agree that the settlement was made in pre-government time, the Divisional boundary to the South includes that portion of Isu land now occupied by Ezzagu".[12] It was that act of hospitality from the Isu to the Agba that strengthened their bond of relations and enhanced their 'defence pact' in order to protect them from further enemy attack, hence they were co-opted into the Isu communities.

The Agba people engaged in war with Oduma people. The Oduma were the former inhabitant of present-day Akwurakwu, Omege and Agu Achara Agba. However, the Oduma were said to be unable to withstand the military advancement and strength of the Agba and they were forced to flee southward to the present-day Ohaofia Oduma in Abia State.[13]

Nevertheless, the deadliest war between Agba and her neighbours was the war they fought with Ezza sub-clan called Ezza-Eka as a result of territorial expansionism. This war was called Egu Obuchi war according to Gabriel Alo.[14] The Ezza-Eka people, who formerly occupied the area where Ndiagu Agba people live today, were confronted by the expanding Agba people. According to oral tradition, it was the joint military action of Oshiri and Agba warriors that made the Ezza-Eka to be pushed across the Ebonyi River. Nwali Obule said that the historic years of hostility between Oshiri and Ezza-Ekka made Agba people and Oshiri to join forces and form a formidable military alliance to fight their common enemy.[15] The Oshiri and Ezza-Ekka have engaged themselves in several years of warfare. It was also stated that the Agba were not happy with Ezza-Ekka people being the descendants of the Ezza that took over their ancestral home land. Following the popular fact that the 'enemy to my enemy is my friend', the Agba and Oshiri integrated forces and went into military fraternity to fight the Ezza sub-clan. In the conflict that followed, the Ezza-Eka was defeated by the joint military forces of the Oshiri and Agba peoples, the victorious side shared their land and settled in it".[16] Ironically, when groups conspire to fight against each other, it takes grace for them not to fall into the path of confrontation and crisis. According to Johnson Alochi, "Oshiri and Agba people cannot wedge war against each other because of the covenant both made before Egu Obuchi war".[17] The act of oath taking as a peace building strategy is widely practiced in Igbo land. The oath forces those who have taken it not to engage in anything harmful to the other group that they took the oath with.[18] Till today Agba and Oshiri live together as brothers in Ndiagu Agba.

Organization of Warfare

Agba, like many other pre-colonial African societies and communities, has no standing army or any institution of military force. Soldiers or troops were raised whenever the need arose. Pre-colonial Agba society was made up of five different age grades from where the military forces were raised. They include *Ogbo Enyimereije* (20–30 years), *Ogbo Edeagu* (30–45 years), *Ogbo Enyigwe* (45–55 years), *Ogbo Ibiniukpabi* (60–75 years) and *Ogbo Ezekome* (80–100 years). The recruitment of armies during this period was basically done by leaders of *Ogbo Ibiniukpabi* age grade. These armies were recruited from those who fall under the age grades of *Ogbo Enyimereije, Ogbo Edeagu and Ogbo Enyigwe.* Leaders of each of these age grades were ordered to examine every member of his own age grade and forward the names of able body men who they find fit for warfare to the leaders of *Ogbo Ibiniukpabi* for confirmation. After the confirmations, they were brought together under the leadership of *Okanga* or *Orchiagha* (those who have fought several wars and have mastered military tactics and strategic planning).[19]

However, all wars were seen as wars of survival for the Agba sons and daughters, and qualified person who refused joining the army was seen as saboteur of a common social contract towards Agba survival and were generally punished by the entire community. Such a person is forced to pay some fine with two goats, hen and kola nut for sacrifices to the Agba war god, *Ivome.*[20] That will serve as deterrent to others who are intending to do such. Since there was no regular army, there was no regular village or community armoury. Similarly, military training was largely ad hoc; they were trained by the *Orchiagha* or *Okanga* in the act of war and accurate marksmanship. In fact, those who constituted pre-colonial Agba armies were the able body men that were highly motivated to defend their community. Those who fell under the age grades of *Ogbo Ibiniukpabi* and *Ogbo Ezekoma* played great role when there is war as the eyes and ears of the community in consulting the ancestors and spirits as well as ensuring that the best hands were selected as warriors.

Nevertheless, before the war they will assemble on popular Agba playground called Ngangbo Ukoro to discuss how materials needed for the success of the war can be provided like foods and weapons. In the time of limited arms, hunters and farmers were mandated to gather their hunting and farm tools, which the blacksmiths quickly turn into weapons of war.[21] The community also goes to neighbouring Isu and Oshiri communities, whom they share goodwill with; to raise weapons of warfare in order to confront their enemies. In many cases, the Isu and Oshiri neighbours do not give the Agba all their weapons of war but often releases the minimal number that they believe will help them to prosecute the war. The interest of those releasing the weapons of warfare is often anchored on the idea that it was better for the Agba to prosecute the war with minimal support from them than to allow the enemies to run them down and possibly invade and harm their own territories, thus they use the act of borrowing weapons to the Agba as a strategy to reduce the negative concentric cycles of the war.

Pre-Colonial Agba Warfare Strategies

Like every pre-colonial Igbo society, Agba warfare strategies were not different. Before war, the able body men, wrestlers and hunter would assemble in Agba playground, Ngangbo Ukoro where the oldest men in the clan, the *Ogbo Ezekoma* would fortify them with charms and perform some incantations calling on the Agba war gods to grant them victory. It is imperative to note that before the war, every soldier was expected to fortify himself with charm from Agba war god called Ivome, which will offer the spirit of protectionism to the warriors. The warriors after purification were expected to absent themselves from some certain things like meeting and having sex with a lady or woman for some market days. They warriors presented Ivome with varieties of items of sacrifices like yam, goat, hen, etc., and if the warrior happened to came back with a human head, the head would be presented to Ivome too and the whole village would celebrate it and such a soldier would be initiated into the *Okanga* group with a title called *Orchiagha*[22] (Brave Commander of Battalions). Although Agba warriors were not like Ohaofia warriors who displayed their military prowess by hunting human head in different part of Igbo land, Agba warriors fought only when it was necessary to fight. It is forbidden and abomination for any Agba warrior to kill children and women in war especially pregnant woman.[23]

At the earliest period of pre-colonial Agba wars, helmets were produced from dried palm leaves (*igu*). Later, the blacksmiths in the community began to develop iron helmet. They were worn to protect head, shoulders, back and chest of the warriors. The role of women in pre-colonial Agba warfare cannot be ignored; they were assigned the responsibilities of providing water to the soldiers. The brave women followed the soldiers to the battle field; they organized themselves in groups as the soldiers were fighting in their line of warfare; the women, often organized in platoons, were providing them with water and other supporting fruits and food items at save intervals.[24]

Weapons of Warfare in Pre-Colonial Agba

Oral traditions stated that there were various weapons that were used in the pre-colonial Agba wars, which range from stone, wooden materials to the non-wooden materials of different metal shapes. Stone were the first weapon used by Agba people to fight. When war erupted, different sizes of stones were gathered by the warriors to the war front, and they would stand in far distance throwing the stone to their enemies. In the use of wood, they had the *Ngbuko*, which was a large stick used mainly in a close combat, to strike the enemy down and kill or harm him. Eku Ugbor was a short pole with a flat wide part at one end, which was used in paddling small boat or canoe. It was multipurpose weapon for attacking, striking and stabbing an enemy and was also used in the war between Agba and Oduma people.[25]

The use of metal in pre-colonial Agba warfare was as the result of the introduction or discovery of iron. The earliest metals used in Agba wars were as follows: *Oge-egbe*, which was the long-edged double sword used for amputation of warriors from the enemy camp. It was followed by the *Mpama*, which was a short-edged double sword used for stabbing. Following these weapons was another important one called *Arra* (arrow) and *Opia* (spear) which was of various sizes and design. The Agba have the long and short spear. All of which were used for stabbing and throwing it to wound an oncoming warrior. There was also the *Mbu* (shield), which was used for defense.[26]

Furthermore, the introduction of blacksmith in some part of Igbo land changed Agba weapon of warfare and strategies dramatically. There was general evidence of gun and gun powder. Oral traditions stated that "Agba people used guns in the war they fought with Ezza sub-clan". The gun used *Egbe Okwa* (Dane gun). They also used charms during warfare. The guns were produced by Nkwerre people and gun powder were obtained through trans-Atlantic slave trade.[27] The guns were one barrel and short ranged in nature. Introduction of gun brought more devastative effect on both communities that engaged in warfare.

Implications of Agba Wars on Inter-Group Relations

The Agba wars with her neighbours affected the Agba economy. It would be recalled that the Agba people were mainly agriculturist. They planted yam in large quantities and engaged in palm oil production. However, during the period of the warfare, the people's farm economy tends to collapse. When they fought and lost their war with the Ezza in Onueke, they abandoned all that they have planted for the year. They also abandoned their buildings and other investments they have made in that settlement for the Ezza. It was also stated in the oral history of the Agba that a number of Agba people who could not join their kith and kin settled down in Ezza and were assimilated by the Ezza people in the years that followed.[28]

Another major impact of the inter-group conflict between Agba and their neighbours is that it reduced the level of inter-group relations between them and their neighbours. The implication was that the Agba Clan according to W. Aston-Smith became "geographically compact and they have no close affinities with any of their neighbours".[29]

The war between Agba people and the Ezza in Onueke also had a dangerous negative influence on their bond of brotherhood. Analysts of Agba-Ezza relations have remained suspicious of the bond of brotherhood between both groups. The implication of the war on human security was that it reduced the population of Agba people drastically.

Peace-Building Strategies

The peace-building process in Agba remains multi-dimensional. The members of the Age grade often continue to meet and strategize ways to resolve or win their war with their neighbours. They do that with continuous consultation of three main priests. Those priests are the priest of Ale, Ivum and Isiagu. Every kindred have its priest of Ale, who must be a descendant of a senior family, while every sub-clan would have the priest of Ivum, which is not found in every kindred. The priests consulted the ancestors and the Almighty to discern His will on the best strategy to win a war, while advising the age grades, elders and warriors properly. The findings of the priests of Ale and Ivum as well as the opinion of the elders and age grades were often presented before the priest of Isiagu for ratification. It is his position after wide consultation with men, the ancestors and the Almighty that decides the position of the clan on the road map to peace. According to Aston-Smith, "All quarrels are reported to him and so far as possible, he preserves the peace as a recent fight between Agba and an adjoining clan was stopped by the Isiagu".[30]

The different families were also involved in conflict resolution and peacebuilding. Outside the minor issues of stealing and killing which are managed by the priest of *Ali*, whose work it is to investigate into the real culprit and pass a judicial judgement; all other offences and disputes in the community were matters for settlement between the families concerned. They might call in the elders or a particular age grade to assist in the settlement and in some cases; it was necessary also to make atonement to *Ale* (*Ani*, the earth goddess).[31] Consequently, an attempt will be made to present the pre-colonial strategic and cultural aspects of Izhi warfare, which is significantly related to that of the Agba people.

Cultural Aspects of Izhi Warfare

The place known as Izhi is located in the north-eastern part of current Ebonyi State, Nigeria. They mainly inhabit the Izhi and Abakaliki Local Government Areas of the State. A number of them are found in Ado and Oju local government of Benue State, while others are part of the Yala Local Government Area of Cross River State. "The area is a flat undulating landscape, some 120–180 m above sea level, sloping gently to the East. Erosion has exposed some volcanic rocks like the Igede hills and the hill at Abakalki".[32] The link between geography and warfare cannot be neglected. The nature of one's environment determines their degree of safety or vulnerability during warfare. Military historians have shown that pre-colonial African society were characterized by both internal and external wars fought at different times and for varieties of reasons. Others noted that the pre-colonial African people engaged in warfare using their soldiers who fought for limited objectives. Wars at that time of African history were used to display heroic might of an individual and the community at large.

The Izhi people assumed that a man who has no scar on his body is only but a mere woman in a man form whom they call *umnanyi* (a demoralized female coward) in Abakaliki dialect. As time went on, bearing of a long sharpened cutlass (*ipomu*) became a symbol for readiness to repel an aggression from an enemy faction among the Izhi people. The neighbouring Igbo communities and non-Igbo speaking communities then came to know Izhi men as people that kill and prosecute wars using cutlass especially with the onslaughts of Nwiboko Obodo. Nwiboko was reputed to have acclaimed that after 'the heaven, the earth, the next authority is him' (*Owa-a eligwe owa-a ali owa-a Nwiboko*).[33] However, most of the wars fought rightly among the Izhi themselves in their communities are skirmishes conducted to display heroic might of some powerful individuals. Although cases abound where Izhi people engaged other neighbouring ethnic groups in a campaign like the Ezza in 1902–1905,[34] they also fought with the Eru, Izigo Igboke, Otobolo and Igala.[35] It should be noted that Izhi people unlike the Ezza are not warlike; neither did they see war as a means to an end. Izhi people only resort to war when negotiations have completely failed especially when they are unjustly treated. This explains the reason why an Izhi man, in those days will butcher his enemy and off he goes to report to the communal law enforcement agency that he has killed an enemy. For him, any act of injustice needs serious punishment and a brave man must not welcome unruly behaviour of an open enemy.

The Izhi, Ikwo and Ezza trace their origin to a common ancestor called Enyi. Ironically, some people of Izhi differ on the details of the historical account. While the Amegu people accepted that their father migrated from somewhere to their land and the tomb of Ekuma Enyi is still in their soil, while the other argued that their ancestor came from heaven to Izhi. "By then heaven and earth were very close and Enyi came from heaven along a rope. But when the man did something bad, the rope fell down and man could not climb up to heaven again. That is how the first Izhi people came to live at Anmegu".[36] At the earliest period of settlement, they lived in the state of peace devoid of warfare; however, as population expanded, the insatiable needs of man began to drive conflicts and the foundation for warfare was laid.

The pre-colonial Izhi people of Ebonyi State have witnessed a number of wars fought both among themselves and with their neighbouring ethnic groups. These wars were fought mainly as a result of boundary disputes or over the illegal occupation of their land by the Eru, Otobolo, Igala and Iziogo Igboke people at that time. These people were said to have crossed Ado River (the river that separate Izhi people from Benue

State) and found their ways into the interiors of Izhi in a large mass. It should be stated that the settlers started the war while the Izhi people finished it when they could not continue to stomach the settlers' incursions. The war came to be known as *ogu* (war) Teteri in Izhi land, meaning the war of slaughtering through the throat. According to Izhi oral tradition, the settlers first started slaughtering Izhi people in a bid to maintain Eru trade oligarchy and hegemony, which lasted for many years.[37]

The second pre-colonial Izhi war to be discussed here is inter-group war, *Ogbu Agbaja war*. The Ogbu war divided the Izhi people into two inimical ethnic groups even after reconciliation was completed. It was war caused by a single man called *Nwankwo Ugo* but was fought between several numbers of communities that make up the two major ethnic groups of Izhi nation; Agbaja and Iseke. The Agbaja clan according to tradition is the first son and Iseke is second born of Nnodo Ekuma Enyi Nwegu while Ekuma Enyi Nwegu was the ancestral father of Abakaliki people—Ezza, Ikwo and Izi. As a case with every other pre-colonial Igbo society, the prosecutions of wars in Izhi were conducted by mobilizing able bodied men who have distinguished themselves through heroic display of their might in their communities or by forceful conscription into the army in the event of war. The Izhi people never had a standing army for the defence of their communities. It was accounted that during the *Ogu* Teteri period, the Izhi people were much inspired by spirit of freedom to root-out their enemies by voluntarily joining the army in a large mass. However, during the *Ogbu war*, Nwiboko Obodo forcefully conscripted the Iseke warriors that engaged the Agbaja faction.

The instrument of warfare of pre-colonial Izhi as at the periods under review was very rudimentary; ranging from *ogbu*, cutlass, dane guns, spear/arrow, stone, knife, catapult, *upyi* (flute) and *okperegede* (huge wooden gong). Nwodom Anyigbo[38] described their uses as the following. The *ogbu* was and is a combination of tree branches/sticks and bamboo stems shaped at the tips to make it destructive and easily pierce the body of enemy factions. It has the advantage of been thrown from a long distance to pin down an enemy faction and can also be used to hit down an enemy within a close range. The *mkpuma* (stones) and *ogbu* served the same purposes in prosecuting wars in pre-colonial Izhi society. The *upyi* was used to give signal to fellow warriors and for the strategic/tactical encirclement of enemy factions whenever it was blown. Whenever the *okperegede* (wooden gong) sound haphazardly in village square in the pre-colonial Izhi community, the ***umnanyi*** (cowards) always seek for hideout while the *Olwa-onla* (warriors) storm the centre stage in a heroic epic dance for the campaign to take-off. The *olwa-onla* is special breed of war heroes that have had severally went to wars and returned unbeaten with human heads. And whenever they die, another more human heads roll down for their burial. The *Okperegede* was used to inform and to assemble the masses in the village square in the event of warfare and military exercise. In the similar manner, the other remaining instruments of war listed above served general purposes across the pre-colonial African society.

The Teteri Wars

Teteri is an Izhi word which means to slain a person directly from the throat. According Nwangbonshi,[39] Teteri was a terror act initiated by the Eru, Iziogo Igboke and Otobolo who traced their origin from the present-day Benue State and the Igala from Kogi State. These people according to Nwangbonshi spread from Ado River into the hinterland of Izhi, and as time went on, they founded two popular settlements, Iziogo and Ogbala. Iziogo and Ogbala were later to turn to two popular markets in Izhi land, adopting names of the geography where they settled. The Iziogo is a popular market in Izhi Local Government Area while Ogbala is in Ebonyi Local Government Area. And in Ogbala market as of today, where major commodities are sold, still adopts the name of the former Eru people called *Ozo-eru,* meaning the base of Eru people.

Ujebe Awoke[40] avers that the setters having converted their settlements into two big markets began to reign supreme as the masters of the economy and deliberately decided to stamp-out possible opposition by act of terror, using Izhi hoodlums to reach out their targets. The Izhi people then converted the names of the settlers (Eru, Iziogo Igboke and Otobolo) and their mercenaries into a stereotype of people who live *Ndu Teteri,* meaning groups of man slaughters. They went to the length and breadth of Izhi killing prominent men and their family members alike. This onslaught of the settlers became worst when the Izhi hoodlums they employed their services decided to use this opportunity to settle vendetta. These hoodlums according to oral tradition were slaves *(Ohu)* that fled from their masters to the protection of the settlers, who had exhibited great strength and brevity.

The reign of the hoodlums as stated above gave rise to further different degrees of human rights abuses. Married women and their daughters were sexually assaulted indiscriminately under the watch of their husbands. These *Teteri* people were brutalizing Izhi men and women on their ways and in their homes and engaged in extensive looting of livelihood properties. Iboza Ochishi analysed the pathetic nature of the settlers' onslaught as thus "a few weeks after my father was made village head, he was butchered in our compound by the Eru oligarchs. Everybody fled our home for hideout and I and my elder brother was fed in the bush for more than three months by our late father's best friend because our own lives was also at stake".[41]

Oral tradition also posits that in some families, the family members were gathered together by the terrorists and they asked them to choose one person among themselves, who will continue the family circle or else face possible extinction. On the choice of a single person to continue the family circle, others will be killed by the terrifying sword of the man slaughters. Cultural activities within this period went into extinction as the people fled their villages for different places of refuge and hideout.

Just as the Izhi people would say 'the day a goat would eat an angry man's yam, the earth will bear witness against her (the untamed goat)'. When the Izhi people came to understand that hiding cannot save the menace, in one night, the *Okperegede* (wooden gong) sounded haphazardly at the different village squares and its messages were understood by people. By day break, Ogbala and Iziogo have been turned into a temporary cemetery littered with corps and their houses set ablaze. After a little resistance with the help of the Eru and others who had purchased dane guns started but the massive killing of the enemy leaders as well as the extensive burning of their settlements demoralized the Eru and they were subdued. Mbam Oduma narrated the incidents that further transpired thus:

> After Ogbala and Iziogo have fallen, the following day, our people painted themselves red with *ododo,* a traditional form of body paints for adornment (signifying danger) and when the settlers saw our people painted in red body decorations, they took to their heels down to the Ado River. Along the way to the Ado River, our people's terrifying swords sentenced as many as they can overrun to the great beyond, not minding whichever age or sex.[42]

The Izhi people believe that to put an end to whatever that bites is to chop off its head. Tradition has it that to take the settlers (Eru, Iziogo Igboke and Otobolo) captive will be an extension of evil, and therefore, they decided slaying their enemies to end their further incursions. It was in an attempt to stop Izhi people's threat to cross Ado River in further possible attacks that made Ochi Idoma, Agbo Okpekpu of Ulayi to invite Ezza people to protect them and till today the Ezza expanded from Ado River continuing to Onu-Inikiri Effium to Okwo Ijigbam across Nwenyim River located at Ulayi to Udokpo market, where Ezza have a very large population in Benue State.[43] Again, the Idoma people of Ulayi and Ijigbam who lived very close to the Ado River near Izhi renamed Izhi people, Izhingodo, a derogatory name for people that once rubbed *ododo* (a traditional form of body paints for adornment) only to unleash terror on their people.

The Izhi people after conquering the Eru, Iziogo Igboke and Igala hands down altogether then immediately crossed Ogenge River to solve what they called 'Otobolo problem' once and for all. The Otobolo people were said to having been engaged in abducting and killing Izhi people in their farms along the Ogenge River banks. This ugly menace persisted for years and increases whenever they are burying their Chiefs (Ogabbah*) and* also during *Ogbodogu* cultural festivals. It should be noted that these two events were said to require stranger's head.[44] According Eji Mbara, the battle that ensued between the Izhi people and the Otobolo people was the fiercest and dreaded among the wars Izhi fought during the precolonial period.[45]

The Otobolo people having heard the defeat of Eru people and others invited warriors from their homeland across Okpopfu Odoke River to get ready for the possible Izhi invasion. The several attempts made by the Izhi people to break into the base of Otobolo people were simultaneously repelled by Otobolo warriors and mercenaries laying ambush with their dane guns along the banks of Ogenge River. The Izhi people according to oral tradition assured themselves that a man hunted by an evil spirit does not sleep until solution is met. In the meantime, the Izhi people decided to engage the Otobolo people in the dead of night, when they might have gone to bed. Little did the Otobolo warriors imagine that Izhi people will dare to cross the deep Ogenge River in midnight. And when the warriors woke up to see Izhi people burning houses in their villages, they instead chose to go into hiding in the bushes because they were not used to night battle. Nwiziogo Okoro noted the incidents of that time, as follows:

> However, it was not success all through for the Izhi warriors because the Otobolo people unlike the Eru, Iziogo Igboke and Igala lived in scattered settlements. This made it very difficult for the few Izhi warriors who managed to cross the deep Ogenge River in the dead of the night to set all the enemy's houses ablaze before the day break. By the break, the Otobolo people who had access to dane guns were almost winning the Izhi people. They used their superior fire power and were killing the Izhi warriors in their dozens but before the middle of the day, the Otobolo ran short of firearms coupled with the ill knowledge of the use of the guns, and the reverse became the case.[46]

And when the remaining Izhi warriors who could not cross the Ogenge River in the dead of night rejoined others that crossed the river in the day that followed, it became a battle of survival for the warriors of the two camps. There was massive loss of lives on both sides but the resilience of the Izhi warriors sustained the war, which they carried to the camp of their enemies, until the Otobolo people crossed Okpopfu River to their homeland. However, the deadly marks the Otobolo people inflicted on the Izhi people before their defeat became a popular idea among the Izhi people till today. This is because the Izhi people would like to invoke the terrifying guns of Otobolo people on any erring soul by saying in their language "*Otobolo gbaja ngu ishi*" meaning "let the Otobolo people shot you on the head".

Agbaja—Iseke War

The Ogbu Agbaja war was a conflict that erupted between two sister communities in Izhi; the Iseke and Agbaja in 1887. Historically, the Agbaja and Iseke almost speak the same language and practice similar culture. Also, they are part of the Izhi people. Actually, the full name of the war is Ogbu Agbaja and Iseke War but each of the groups from their base uses the name in a way it gives glory to them. The Iseke community calls it Ogbu Agbaja War, which connotes that they beat Agbaja people hands-down in strategic calculations while the Agbaja on their own calls it Ogbu Iseke to reverse the case. However, Izhi oral tradition glorifies Ogbu Agbaja and Iseke War to the favour of former and therefore popular adoption of the name, Ogbu Agbaja War among native Izhi people.

The word *Ogbu* in Izhi means collections of sizable stones and sticks that can be used to pluck down fruits and other related things. But the word *Ogbu* as connected to this war was the weapons used to target an enemy factions in the Ogbu Agbaja and Iseke War. Once the war started, the two factions multiplied their *ogbu* and shaped the tips and edges of it to make it easily pierce through the body of a targeted enemy and indeed destructive. The Ogbu Agbaja war as popularly called divided Izhi people along two inimical and segregated lines up till today as it enshrined the Agbaja and Iseke dichotomy.[47]

The use of *Ogbu* in this war was in due to the wider Igbo culture, where individuals and groups are that shared the same cultural lineage was not allowed to bring in charms for dangerous purposes by the Ani/Ala (earth goddess), the guardian of the customs and public morality of Igbo people. The genealogical affinity between the Iseke and Agbaja clans made the use of *Ogbu* which was less dangerous, the major tool of warfare.

Nwibo Nworichi attributed the cause of Ogbu Agbaja-Iseke War to Chief Nwankwo Ugo. Nwibo accounted that Nwankwo Ugo stopped attending community social functions (payment of developmental levy and participating in village assembly) of his people, the Iseke. And when he was summoned for query by the Iseke elders, he said that he has severed his social affinity with the Iseke people. As would be expected, the elders gave him three days ultimatum to pack out to Agbaja where he has chosen on the ground of marital affinity of his mother and wife to the area. At the expiration of the three days ultimatum, the elders mobilized their youths to go and plunder and loot everything that they can lay hands on, in Nwankwo Ugo's compound. Before the day break, the youths have overrun both his compound and farms rendering him useless. And by the time Agbaja people came to understood all that have had taken place, they rallied around him and mobilized to fight for him.[48]

Another version that explained what led to Ogbu Agbaja and Iseke War was in agreement with the views of Nwibo but also added that before then, Agbaja people have been illegally encroaching a large expanse of Ibina Agalegu Iseke land. Going further, Chief Ogbaga Samuel maintained that when the Agbaja people began to fraternize with the erring Nwankwo Ugo, it triggered Iseke's annoyance over the illegal occupation of their land by the former.[49] Then, the Iseke people decided also to give all the Agbaja persons occupying or settling in any portion of their land in Ibina Agalegu Iseke two days ultimatum to vacate the land. Instead of the Agbaja persons vacating as they were instructed, they collided with their home people and sounded their *okperegede* (war song) at Okpuru Akparata Ibina in Agbaja to get ready to repel Iseke people in the ensuing warfare. Their action was quickly intercepted by the Iseke people who decided to launch a surprise attack on the Agbaja group. It should be noted that Chief Nwankwo Ugo was a bonafide citizen of Agalegu Ibina Iseke where he was residing at the onset of the war and it ragged-on.

The legendary Nwiboko Obodo of pre-colonial Izhi was said to have united all Iseke communities to fight their Agbaja brothers. However, the war started and lasted for many years. As would be expected, the Iseke fought to push the Agbaja out of their land while the latter fought to stay put in and annihilate their brothers. Be that as it may, because of their genealogical affinity, the war was characterized by extensive looting of properties, serious beatings, inflicting serious injury on the enemy targets, etc., using the *Ogbu* and catapults, while recording minimal murder due to the bond of not been allowed by *Ani,* the earth goddess to spill blood. Nwibo noted pathetically that many of those who were seriously injured cum those their properties were looted and left with nothing to feed on, passed away unto glory during and after the war.[50]

As the conflict lingered, some of the powerful individuals converted it into a game of exercising their militaristic prowess to gain more advantage over the other group. According to oral tradition, the Iseke people gradually succeeded in pushing the Agbaja out of the disputed land and because some men among them have converted the war into a game of exercising their militaristic prowess, they pushed the Agbaja towards Iyetumu, which is very close to present-day Iziogo market. But that as it said wasn't success for Iseke people as the two groups continued to attack one another. Nwangbonshi accounted that the war continued until the invasion of white men into the hinterland of Izhi. The colonial authorities intervened and brought the conflict to an end. The Europeans were said to have invited the Iseke people for negotiation at Okpuru Akparata Ibina in Agbaja. Little did they know that the intention of the Europeans was to arrest as many as were in attendance in the gathering in order to end the menace of the conflict.[51] However, the Europeans/British core targets were the Iseke people who sustained the war. But low and behold, *Ndu Cotuma* (the white men local police) landed from old Abankaleke (Abakaliki) and carted away all the Iseke attendants both men and women alike. After two years stay in *Okamkporo* (jail), they returned to see Agbaja people taking over a vast portion of their land. For the fear of the assumed wicked British colonialists, they never tried to revolt against the Agbaja people openly till even today. Today, it is only a pocket of widely scattered and separated Iseke compounds/homes that live in the midst of thousands of Agbaja compounds. However, the handful of widely scattered and separated Iseke compounds found in the midst of numerous Agbaja people have their own leadership clearly separated from those of the Agbaja control.

Conclusion

Since the evolution of communities in Africa, no is no community that does not have the story of wars that they have fought with their contiguous neighbours. Some of those conflicts were handled through diplomacy, peacebuilding or inter-group relation. In Nigeria and specifically Igbo land the Agba experienced warfare during her pre-colonial era. It is worthwhile to note that in Agba, wars were fought mainly with their neighbours in the pre-colonial era to attain communal security interests. The warriors were recruited on ad hoc bases and they were mainly hunters, wrestlers and able body men's who ranged from age of twenty to sixty years. They were also under the leadership of *Okanga* (one who have mastered war tactics, strategies of war and have the spirit of marksmanship). Both stone, wood, metal objects and guns were used as a weapon of warfare. However, during the course of the war, war songs were sang which usually induced the warriors with great strength and galvanized them into actions. The pre-colonial wars have social, economic and security implications upon the clan.

Furthermore, this chapter has been able to discuss two related wars and the one that differs a little. The differences are that while Izhi unanimously fought against the Eru, Iziogo Igboke, Igala and Otobolo as hard-core enemies, using more dangerous weapons of war against them, on the other side, in Ogbu Agbaja war which was among Izhi themselves, they limited their weaponry to some meagre weapons of war. However, one must not forget that Izhi war against Eru, Iziogo Igboke, Igala and Otobolo was retaliation for the past sins of the settlers. And therefore, the settlers supposed to pay through their nose for their undoing against Izhi people. In the like manner, the Igbo people believed that blood is thicker than water. This goes to suggest the uniqueness of Igbo norms and culture which applied herein in the execution of war even among the Izhi. The Igbo culture of executing war posits that people who share identical genealogical relations should not harm themselves in the act of warfare while people outside the confine of this genealogical affinity is openly declared a hard-core enemy to be engaged with any type of heavy weaponry.

Just as Igbo people would say, 'war is evil' (*agha di njo*) which suggest the pathetic nature of wars in anywhere and in whichever time. Even though the combatants of pre-colonial wars are gone to the great beyond, its clutches still bother the present generations. Even researches about them sometimes turn sour. However, it has helped to showcase that Africans truly have a past against the European assertions. Not only that it demonstrated the artistic wizardry of pre-colonial African in manufacturing of their weapons of warfare but also glorified the uniqueness of dissemination of vital information which is very key in winning a war. For instance, the pre-colonial Izhi used tip sharpened Ogbu, strategically chopped stones, etc., to execute wars and also used flute, wooden gong, etc., to pass useful information.

Notes

1. W. Aston-Smith, "Intelligent Report on the Agba Clan in the Abakaliki Division", OG:1469/29, National Archives Enugu, 29 July 1936, p. 1.
2. Eze Paul Ogodo Igwe, Ezeogo II of Agba Ezekoma, 73 years man, who was interviewed in his palace, Akwuruakwu, Agba on 10 May 2016.
3. W. Aston-Smith, "Intelligent Report on the Agba Clan", p. 1.
4. National Archives Enugu, "Obeagu Isu versus Ezza Land Dispute", No. Af 287 AFIDIST 3/1/29, 1929.
5. National Archives Enugu, District Office, No AB. 1558/316, Abakaliki Division, 13 July, 1948. See also G. A. Ani, *The 97 Years War*, Enugu, NP; K. J. Ani, "Unravelling the Dynamics of Colonial Experiences among the Isu of Afikpo and Owerri Divisions, South-Eastern Nigeria" in Joseph Mangut and Terhemba Wuam (Eds.) *Colonialism and the Transition to Modernity in Africa*, Ibadan: Sam-Adex Printers Sanyo, 2012, pp. 221–237; K. J. Ani and U. S. Osisioma "Ezza-Ojiegbe and Mgbalukwu-Obeagu Isu Intermittent Conflicts of 1910–2007: A Review of Migration and Culture of Hospitality to Internally Displaced Persons", *International Journal of Arts, Humanities and Management Studies*, Vol. 1, No. 1, January, 2015, pp. 1–8.
6. Chief Nwali Ali-ezza, an 87-year-old elder statesman, who was interviewed in his compound, Ndiagu, Agba on 12 May 2016.
7. Chief Alifo Gabriel, a retired farmer of 92 years, who was interviewed in his compound, Ndiagu, Agba on 12 May 2016.

8. Eze Paul Ogodo Igwe, Ezeogo II of Agba Ezekoma, 73 years, who was interviewed on his palace, Akwuruakwu, Agba on 10 May 2016.
9. J. N. Afoke, "Ezza in an Age of Expansion" in Elizabeth Isichei (Ed.) *Igbo Worlds*, London: Macmillan Education Ltd, 1977, p. 123.
10. Daniel Nwali, a retired primary school teacher of 68 years, who was interviewed in his home, Ndiagu, Agba on 15 May 2016.
11. Chief Moses Odi Oka, a dethroned Agba Chief, who was interviewed in his compound, Amegu, Agba on 12 May 2016.
12. National Archives Enugu, "Political Position of Ezzas in Ishielu", No. AB. 1272/1, District Office, Abakalki Division, 10 July, 1942, pp. 1–2.
13. Raymond Onele Oka, a palm wine taper of 64 years was interviewed in his compound, Amagu, Agba on 21 May 2016.
14. Gabriel Alo, a famer and fisher man of 67 years was interviewed in his compound, Agbelu, Agba on 10 May 2016.
15. Nwali Obule, a farmer of 85 years was interviewed in his residence, Ndiagu, Agba on 12 May 2016.
16. Nwali Obule, a farmer of 85 years cited.
17. Johnson Alochi, a palm wine taper of 66 years was interviewed in his home, Omegeokwuru, Agba, on 21 May 2016.
18. The place of oath-taking in peace Building were extensively discussed by K. J. Ani and D. I. Ajaegbo, "Historical Foundations of Conflict Management and Peace Building Strategies in Nigeria", *Ubuntu: Journal of Conflict and Social Transformation*, Vol. 4, No. 1, 2015, pp. 113–133: K. J. Ani and P. A. Alegu, "Factoring Historical and Contemporary Culture of Peace-Building for Sustainable Security and Tourism Development in Nigeria" in Kenneth C. Nwoko & Omon M. Osiki (Eds.), *Dynamics of Culture & Tourism in Africa: Perspectives on Africa's Development in the 21st Century*, Illishan Remo: Babcock University Press, 2015, pp. 471–500; K. J. Ani and U. Chukwuma, "Christianity and the Inculturation of Traditional Peace building Strategies in Igboland" in T. I. Okere (Ed.) *The Church and Igbo Society: Proceedings of the International Symposium Organized by Whelan Research Academy*, Owerri, Nigeria, Vol. 2, No. 10, Owerri: Assumpta Press, 2013, pp. 212–227.
19. Gabriel Alo, a famer and fisherman of 67 years was interviewed in his compound, Agbelu, Agba on 10 May 2016.
20. Gabriel Alo, a famer and fisher cited.
21. Simon Alobu, a retired hunter of 87 years, who was interviewed in his compound, Omegeokwuru, Agba on 21 May 2016.
22. Simon Alobu, a retired hunter of 87 years cited.
23. Simon Alobu, a retired hunter of 87 years cited.
24. Raymond Onele Oka, a palm wine taper of 64 years was interviewed in his compound, Amegu, Agba on 21 May 2016.

25. Simon Alobu, a retired hunter of 87 years, who was interviewed at his compound, Omegeokwuru, Agba on 21 May 2016.
26. Samuel Ukpai, a hunter of 70 years, who interviewed on his compound, Omegeokwuru, Agba on 14 May 2016.
27. Chief Alifo Gabriel, a retired farmer of 92 years, who was interviewed in his compound, Ndiagu, Agba on 12 May 2016.
28. Chief Alifo Gabriel, a retired farmer of 92 years cited.
29. W. Aston-Smith, "Intelligent Report on the Agba Clan", p. 2.
30. W. Aston-Smith, "Intelligent Report on the Agba Clan", p. 3.
31. W. Aston-Smith, "Intelligent Report on the Agba Clan", p. 5.
32. Nico Van Steensel, *The Izhi: Their History and Customs* (2nd Ed.), Abakalki, Abakalki: Catholic Communications Link, 2009, p. 5.
33. Form a detailed information on the man, see Uche Uwaezuoke Okonkwo and M. Ndubuisi Mbam, *He was not Given Fair Hearing: Chief Nwiboko Obodo of Colonial Abakaliki, 1893–1959*. Enugu: Madonna University Press, 2016.
34. Uchenna, Anyanwu, "The Ezza: Unsung Warriors of Igboland", *Review of Arts and Social Science*, Vol. 14, No. 2, 2005, p. 20; Kelechi Johnmary Ani, "Societal Policing and Peace Building in Abakaliki Division During the Colonial Era" in D. I. Ajaegbo, Kelechi Johnmary Ani and Paul Obiani (Eds.) *Perspectives in Igbo History and Culture: Festschrift in Honour of Mazi Professor Okoro Ijoma*, Enugu: Snaap, pp. 211–227.
35. For details on Izhi-Agila conflicts, see Ikwuta Augustine Onoja, Agila-Ezza relations up to 1980: A Study of Inter Group Relations in Nigeria, PhD Thesis, Department of History and International Studies, University of Nigeria, Nsukka, 2001, p. 207; O. Otokpa, *Agila/Ngbo: Critical Evaluation of a Border Conflict in Nigeria*, Makurdi: Oracle Publications Ltd, 2013.
36. Nico Van Steensel, *The Izhi: Their History and Customs*, p. 6.
37. Nwangbonshi Nwibo Aleke: an 86-year-old farmer and bicycle repairer was interviewed at Iziophu Iseke on September, 8, 2015.
38. Nwodom Anyigbo: an 84-year-old custodian of tradition and a farmer was interviewed at Ekirigwe Iseke on October 16, 2015.
39. Nwangbonshi Nwibo Aleke as cited.
40. Chief Ujebe Awoke: an 89-year-old custodian of traditions, hunter, artisan, farmer and palm wine tapper was interviewed at Onungele Iziophu Iseke on September 10, 2015.
41. Iboza Ochishi: an 84-year-old custodian of tradition and a farmer was interviewed at Ekirigwe Iseke on October 16, 2015.
42. Mbam Oduma: A 91-year-old farmer and an orator, who was interviewed at Azungele Iziophu, on August 17, 2015.
43. Alegu Onwoshi: A 76-year-old farmer, who was interviewed at Agalegu Ibina Iseke on August 13, 2015.

44. Nwodom Anyigbo: A 79-year-old farmer and palm wine tapper, who was interviewed at Azungele Obegu Iziophu Iseke, on July 20, 2015. The same account was recounted by Nwangbonshi Nwibo Aleke: an 86-year-old farmer and bicycle repairer, who was interviewed at Iziophu Iseke on July 15, 2015; and Chief Ujebe Awoke: an 89-year-old custodian of traditions, hunter, artisan, farmer and palm wine tapper, who was interviewed at Onungele Iziophu Iseke, on July 10, 2015.
45. Eji Mbara Odeh: An 88-year-old farmer who was interviewed at Onungele Iziophu Iseke, on September 3, 2015.
46. Chief Nwiziogo Okoro: An 89 years custodian of tradition, farmer and a petty snuff seller, who was interviewed at Onungele Iziophu Iseke, on 4 October, 2015.
47. Francis Nwuguru: A 68-year-old farmer, very knowledgeable in oral traditions, who was interviewed at Onungele Iziophu Iseke, on September 7, 2015.
48. Nwibo Nworichi: An 87-year-old farmer who was interviewed in Iziophu Iseke, on 16 October, 2015.
49. Chief Ogbaga Samuel: A 72-year-old farmer and a cabinet of Igwe Iboza Nwadumu, Iseke autonomous community, Nduegu ward 1, Onungele Azuoji Iziophu Iseke, who was interviewed on 7 October, 2015.
50. Nwibo Nworichi: An 87-year-old farmer who was interviewed in Iziophu Iseke, on 16 October, 2015.
51. Nwangbonshi Nwibo Aleke: An 86-year-old farmer and bicycle repairer, who was interviewed at Iziophu Iseke on July 15, 2015.

CHAPTER 12

The Dilemma of Natural Resources and Upsurge of Conflicts in Africa: A Cursory Look at the Marikana Management Approaches in South Africa

Chijioke Francis Onyebukwa

Introduction

African countries, such as Nigeria, Angola, South Sudan, Zimbabwe and Botswana, are among the major producers of most natural resources such as oil, natural gas, gold and platinum, which are marketed and consumed globally. For instance, despite being the largest producers of platinum, gold and diamond globally, South Africa is also endowed with immense mineral resources. Therefore, it becomes possible for government finance developmental programmes and projects that are established to enhance the living and working conditions of mining workers, as well as to improved living and environmental conditions of

C. F. Onyebukwa (✉)
Department of History and International Studies, Eastern Palm University
Ogboko, Ogboko, Nigeria

K. J. Ani et al. (eds.), *Political Economy of Resource, Human Security and Environmental Conflicts in Africa*,
https://doi.org/10.1007/978-981-16-2036-2_12

the host communities. Research findings (Maystadt et al. 2014: 724; Mehlum et al. 2006: 4) have demonstrated the direct connection between the wealth from expropriated and exploited natural resources and economic sustainability of such countries. It means that funds from mineral resources are capable of sustaining the economy of country. However, controversies surround the trickling down effect of the wealth generated from these resources with respect to the workforce and communities where these mining activities take place. Indeed, neither the direct nor indirect transmission of the above services to the workers or the societies hosting international or domestic mining companies is sufficient. Almost all mining operations in South Africa have serious direct negative effects for workers, the economy and the climate in the host communities. People who live in a mining area are obviously vulnerable to the dangerous and hazardous effects of mining operations, and their vulnerability to these detrimental impacts increases as a result of this exposure. The dilemma of those who are specifically impacted by mining's detrimental effects has not been properly resolved. Reactions to these negative implications have sparked the recurrent mining conflicts that ravage mining industries around the world, especially in Africa.

Unfortunately, this appears not to be the case. There is mounting evidence that the main players in Marikana, South Africa, the Lonmin (Pty) platinum mine, the South African government and the Congress of South African Trade Unions (COSATU) have made insufficient attempts to mitigate the impact of mining operations on employees and host communities. As a result of these factors, the citizens affected have sought valid grounds for agitation, which has devolved into labour-related civil conflicts. Consider, for instance, the complexities of the Marikana crisis, which resulted in the deaths of 34 mine employees, 78 injuries and 269 arrests (Gumede 2015: 327; Nash 2015: 387; Wasserman 2015: 375; Rapatsa 2014: 119; Chinguno 2013: 160; Elbra 2013: 555; Ledwaba 2013: 13; City Press 2 September 2012; Sinwell et al. 2012: 17), are primarily focused on bad working and living conditions, as well as low pay. There also seems to be a rift between employers and the workers' union (COSATU), which has been accused of providing inadequate and insufficient leadership during pay negotiations. McKenzie (2013: 160) described Lonmin as a mine that has been unable to provide adequate housing for all of its employees, fuelling labour-related tensions and resulting in a high number of mineworker fatalities. Leon (2012: 8) backs up this claim by stating that the majority of Lonmin employees and their families live in Nkaneng, an informal settlement with mainly shacks and little access to electricity or a proper sewerage system. McKenzie also confirms that only about 10% of the approximate 28,000 employees employed by Lonmin have been provided with housing. In response to their obvious dissatisfaction with these conditions, the Lonmin rock drill operators (RDOs) began organizing employees in July 2012 to put pressure on mine management and owners to meet their demands (Chinguno 2013: 162) for higher pay and better working and living conditions. Their monthly minimum wage demand was R12,500 (McKenzie 2013: 9). The recurrence of such violence appears to defy numerous government and mining company conflict management methods.

To lessen the detrimental effects of mining on both workers and host populations, the government and mining firms have decided that the latter should invest in construction schemes such as schools and health services such as clinics and hospitals as part of their corporate social responsibility. Despite the existence of existing rules and laws governing mining rights, mining operations and their obligations to their employees and host communities, as well as the extent of government participation, interference and resolution in conflict management, the recurrence of conflict in the South African mining sector calls into question the efficacy of such laws and institutional intervention.

Resource Mobilization Theory

The main emphasis in resource mobilization philosophy is on how organizations organize and manage resources in order to achieve a common purpose (Canel 1997: 4). According to Edwards and McCarthy (2004), the existence or lack thereof of funding continues to be a key factor in the growth, progress or failure of Social Movement Organizations (SMOs). In the growth and maintenance of social movements, resource mobilization theory emphasizes the mobilization of money and the requisite social capital. Resources and social capital could be material and non-material (Canel 1997: 4) which may include moral, cultural, social-organizational, human and material. Their work defines a resource or social capital as "something that can be potentially used by a social movement to further its goals". The explicit goal of community resource mobilization is also to pursue the group's goals, which is normally done by joint activities. The Association of Mineworkers and Construction Union (AMCU) mobilized material and non-material support in Marikana to achieve their objectives. For example, in Marikana, mineworkers spent time while engaging in the dispute and it paid off. According to time [a non-material resource] is the ultimate resource for collective action. Participants [such as mineworkers] had to devote their time to partake in a group activity [such as the Marikana conflicts], according to them (ibid).

According to Canel (1997: 2), resource mobilization theory (RMT) emphasizes the "grievances and inequalities [which were conditions experienced at Marikana], could only be considered a precondition for occurrence of social movements [and] that the passage from condition to action was contingent upon the availability of resources and changes in the opportunity for collective action". This argument clarifies the theory's possible usefulness in analysing violence in Marikana, where grievances and inequality contributed to the emergence of a social movement that resulted in confrontation.

Marikana in North West Province of South Africa

The region that is now known as Marikana was first laid out in 1870 as a farming settlement named Rooikoppes (which means "red hills" in Afrikaans) and covered about 17.54 km^2 of landmass. Before the advent of mines, it remained a renowned lucrative tobacco, maize, chilies, paprika, soya and cattle farming culture. In the 1970s, it rose to become the area's primary economic enterprise (*Wikipedia*). As a result, Marikana remained a mining town in the North West province of South Africa (within the platinum belt region), prominently located 24 kms east of Rustenburg and approximately 100 kms west of Johannesburg (McKenzie 2013: 10). It is tribal land belonging to the Bapho Ba Mogale tribal tribe, as well as land leased by the Lonmin mining corporation for its mining operations (Chinguno 2013: 7). As a result, Lonmin pays a royalty to the traditional officials, who are the land's custodians. The group, which has around 40,000 members and 7000 families, owns almost all of the province's platinum-rich regions (*New Age Newspapers* 12 June 2015: 1). Out of this figure, about 1000 people live in the Lonmin-controlled mine licensed areas, which include sections of villages adjacent to the mines, hostels, informal settlements, and low-density suburbs (Chinguno 2013: 8).

Conceptualizing Conflict

Conflict is a dynamic concept that seems to be a common occurrence in daily life. As a result, conflict continues to be an unavoidable aspect of human life at all levels. When there is a difference in concerns between parties or classes, it typically expresses itself as strain, conflict, differences, feelings or polarization, particularly when bonds are broken or absent. When relationships between individuals or communities are disrupted, for example, the effect is socioeconomic deprivation, anger, dissatisfaction, suffering and sorrow (real or anticipated), and the immediate effect is inevitable confrontation (Kohlrieser 2007: 1–2). As a result, the preceding is a property of sentiment.

People do react to the events or acts of the other side, and these responses can lead to violence, which can also lead to war. To put it another way, confrontation is a hostile or offensive way of communicating resentment and anger about incompatibility between parties and circumstances (Ganson 2011: 3). It encompasses a broad variety of nuanced goal-directed behavioural dispositions that necessitate a high level of concentration in order to comprehend unfolding scenarios or developments. As a result, conflict emerges as an interactive aspect of daily life, expressing incompatibility and contradictions between parties or groups. Persons or individuals provide subjective views of reality, and their responses are influenced by impulses, which are an important part of confrontation (Jehn 1997: 532). As a result, a vast range of diverse events, causes and circumstances have a significant impact on the understanding of conflict. Developing a common internationally accepted concept of conflict, depending on the focus, remains a major challenge for academics. As a result, there is no universally agreed-upon concept of conflict. However, a two-model approach to defining conflict tends to be sufficient and scholar concepts of conflict capture the nature of this approach. The first method focuses on a specific phenomenon, factor or condition correlated with competitive intentions, such as strike action and resistance. The second approach takes a broad view of post-conflict incidents, which influence how conflict mediation techniques are chosen (Thomas 1992: 268). Both tactics are in line with the study's two main themes: dispute and conflict resolution. Conflict is defined by early conflict scholars such as Coser (1956), as cited in Anstey (2008: 5) as, "a struggle over values and claims to scarce status, power and resources in which the aims of the opponent are to neutralize, injure or eliminate their rivals". This viewpoint depicts confrontation as a battle for ideals and claims to precious status, as well as a struggle over power and wealth. Conflict, according to this indication, is a behavioural reaction or responses to protect or maintain beliefs, limited rank, strength and energy. Obtaining these goals necessitates the prior aim of dissipating competitors. According to Thomas (1992: 265), conflict is "the process which begins when one party perceives that another party has frustrated, or is about to frustrate, some concerns of the other". In a strict sense, the dispute mechanism begins when a faction notices differences and incompatibilities in its interactions with its members or with another party. It means the disagreement arises as a result of incompatibility as well as movement or response. As a result, actual or perceived incompatibility with a party's beliefs sets the stage for disagreement among interacting parties or functions/groups within the party.

Furthermore, contemporary views see dispute as a clash between two or more people that believe they have incompatible concerns (Bloisi et al. 2003: 489). They contend that for dispute to happen, there must be a perception of the other party interfering with or completely preventing one party's issues. Goals, needs and behaviour of the other person are examples of these issues. In other words, conflict occurs when people's interests are incompatible, their interpretations of reality vary, they have unpleasant emotions, they have different values and opinions, and they disagree about common resources (Bloisi et al. 2003). By extension, a conflict situation occurs when either of the partners or groups in a partnership imposes a perceived possible incompatibility on them. Unfortunately, if the dominant party or faction persists on forcing its preferences on the other party, the confrontation situation will worsen. Further, modern scholarly propositions from Wallenstein (2012: 16) present "conflict as a social situation in which a minimum of two actors (parties) strive to acquire at the same moment in time an available set of scarce resources". To Wallenstein, striving in a strict sense realistically translates into doing something (which may include a vast range of things, including warfare) to protect scarce resources, no matter how little. According to these concepts, confrontation represents a struggle for life for those in control of the conversation and a desire for improvement for those on the receiving end, which typically results in a challenge or defeat (Kestner and Ray 2002: 23). As a result, the word "struggle" or "strife" depicts confrontation in the context of one party to a conflict remaining a persistent theoretical or actual threat to the other.

Furthermore, the meanings tend to have a general resemblance. Interdependence between parties, perceptions of incompatibility among parties involved, and the presence of some kind of interaction are among them (Thomas 1992: 264). The representation implies that disagreement is predicated on the presence of these factors in their collective form and is ostensibly played out by communicating groups. While these conflict variables may theoretically behave independently, certain inherent inevitabilities, such as the presence of interacting groups, bind them together indirectly.

The role of the sides or players in a dispute is undeniable once more. As long as the system is uncertain, fear will occur and tension will eventually arise between the system's parties (Wallenstein 2012: 17). If the other party evolves defence strategies of some kind, the effects of unpredictability between interacting parties grow anxiety and raise the likelihood of escalation of confrontation. One might argue that when a party feels anxiety in some encounter, it indicates that the party has lost interest, may have experienced defeat or is completely at odds with the changing situation, which the party perceives as a possible danger to the relationship. As a result, if a party to a conflict faces some kind of disappointment or has profound needs that cannot be fulfilled, conflict intensifies, especially, when ties are broken (Kohlrieser 2007: 2). As a result, the central feature of dispute centres around the conflicting sides. The dispute is defined by one party's overt acts and responses to the other's conduct, as well as a perceived circumstance of failure or potential danger. Conflict is a result of differences in the principles, positions, views or desires of two or more participating individuals, whether actual or imagined.

Conflict Management

Conflict is a common and almost unavoidable part of all social interactions, and it can be seen between people, associations, organizations, governments and even nations on a regular basis. Every social interaction occurs within the boundaries of covert potential conflict environment with the propensity of degeneration or escalation once triggered. Overall, conflict management is concerned with reducing the risks that may potentially lead to crisis, build some morale and lower the potential misery of the aggrieved party (Wallenstein 2012: 5). It also means the future dangers of conflict should be controlled across three levels:

(a) generate some confidence in the aggrieved party,
(b) lower possible suffering and
(c) reduce definite suffering, representing the pre-conflict, on the conflict and post-conflict levels, respectively.

The first step depicts how a pre-conflict management strategy is applied against or in an effort to avoid future conflict and its implications for the aggrieved group. The second level is concerned with reducing the aggrieved party's conflict-related effects, while the third level is concerned with the aggrieved party's post-conflict consequences. As a result, conflict management implies that it is a viable mode not only for the future pre-conflict prevention, but also for the management of conflict and post-conflict situations.

When there is a disagreement, there are two distinct outcomes: negative or positive. When there are many pending grievances over a variety of subjects, conflict continues to intensify. Furthermore, if the aggravating variables that contribute to conflict escalating are addressed, the prospects of conflict minimization improve. As a result, limiting unresolved conflicts and complaints is a sure indication of dispute de-escalation. When a dispute arises, there are many ways that can be used independently or jointly to deal with it. An approach conflict is deemed appropriate depending on the scholar and the conflict situation whether it results in successful formulation and/or solution/s to a problem (Rahim 2010: 218). Conflict is better handled using physical or psychological means, capitulation, inaction, resignation, arbitration and third-party mediation. Thomas (1992: 266), on the other hand, views competing, collaborating, compromising, avoiding and accommodating as alternatives. He goes on to categorize these into two underlying dimensions: assertiveness and cooperation. This is a "Dual Concern Model", which states that conflict mediation style selection is based on two independent variables: concern for one's own outcome and concern for the outcome of the other group. In conclusion, while assertiveness can also mean being concerned about one's own interests, being concerned about the interests of others promotes solidarity, also known as empathy. Similarly, a strong regard for the consequences of both selfish and other people's needs encourages problem solving or cooperation, while a low concern for both outcomes encourages indifference and inaction.

Conflict Management Strategies at Marikana

Multinational corporations (MNCs) face a number of significant problems, including conflict avoidance, conflict mediation and post-conflict re-building, many of which have an effect on their activities across borders. According to observers, MNCs can avoid tension between their workforce and host populations by using three main market strategies: "social investment programmes, engagement in policy dialogue and civic institution building" (Bennett 2002: 397; Nelson 2000: 45). Nelson (2000: 46) goes on to say that good conflict mediation necessitates "preventive diplomacy, fact finding and mediation mission", that deals with the three root causes of conflict: socioeconomic injustice, corruption and poverty (Bennett 2002: 398). Lonmin's and the government's conflict management techniques were available in three parts: before, during and after the Marikana shooting, providing a unique conflict management illustration along this trajectory. The aim of this example is to demonstrate the consequences of some of Lonmin's and the government's conflict resolution attempts prior to, after and after the Marikana conflict.

Lonmin Conflict Prevention Efforts

Following the incidents at Marikana, the Lonmin mining corporation has been repeatedly chastised for its lack of appropriate dispute management mechanisms. The low pay and living standards of the workforce are among the numerous strike demands. The demands of mineworkers for reforms in these fields generally increase as there are deaths in the mines as a result of inadequate working conditions. Lonmin, for example, has an inconsistent record of deaths between 2008 and 2012. The record showed a fatality rate of 3 mineworkers in 2008, 2009, 2010, 6 mineworkers in 2011 and 2 in 2012. Implicitly, this record indicates that underground safety measures were either insufficient or insufficient to reflect nationally appropriate safe working conditions for miners. As a result, some mineworker concerns about these conditions point to the MNC Lonmin's failure to remedy the deficiencies found. Unfortunately, these issues have resulted in some employees going on strike, which has resulted in violence.

Conflict avoidance, as previously mentioned, aims to avoid conflict situations. Preventing conflict thus necessitates resolving all pre-conflict causative variables. In this respect, Lonmin has shown a desire to resolve the pre-conflict causative factors that are responsible for the company's recurrence of disputes. Lonmin implemented the Safety and Sustainable Development Policy (SSDP) along this route. SSDP, which has a series of mitigation policies and programmes, is how the organization handles its environmental growth obligations. For example, the (SSDP) strategy established a stakeholders' interaction platform and a risk management mechanism to resolve some of the workforce's most pressing issues. Most of these programmes was designed in accordance with the standards and as part of Lonmin's Corporate Social Responsibility (CSR). For Lonmin, CSR profoundly projects the corporate picture and the seriousness applied to fully engaging in and implementing its social responsibilities. Lonmin listed a number of high-priority sustainable development risk areas, including deaths, severe accidents and unhealthy conduct, staff accommodation, HIV/AIDS and tuberculosis, local economic development, and stakeholder participation. To do this, Lonmin outlined a series of CSR programmes aimed at mitigating the negative effects of its operations on the citizens who are directly impacted. As a result, Lonmin has set aside a significant sum of money in the millions of rand range, as well as a significant strategic investment, in order to achieve long-term success in these fields.

Lonmin, for example, stated its commitment to "improving the quality of life of present and future generations through the convergence of economic generation, social change, and environmental protection" in its 2008 Sustainable Development Report (SDR). Lonmin's financial contributions up to 41% of its annual Social Labor Plan (SLP) allocation were set aside for the advancement of local economic community projects, according to the study. In addition, by 2011, the group had upgraded 29 hostels from hostels to family and bachelor accommodations, out of a total of 114. As a result, Lonmin's CSR is a nuanced but influential term in the company's decision-making process. Given the negative impact of mining on the climate, CSR is a way of contributing back to the community (Pesmatzoglou et al. 2014: 190). As a result, foreign corporations such as Lonmin leave economic benefits to the people who are directly impacted by their mining operations. This promotes minimal disturbance to people's social stability and the safety of families living near mines (Jenkins & Yakovleva 2006: 272). Lonmin's interaction with its CSR, by implication, serves as a means of justifying its presence and assessing progress achieved in this direction.

Stakeholder interaction groups and risk management teams are channels for maintaining ongoing communication with different stakeholders, including staff, to address their concerns. These interventionist tactics are the company's central conflict mediation techniques for preventing outbreaks of conflict. It is an engagement forum which according to Lonmin's 2009 SDR seeks to ensure that:

> They engage with those who are directly affected by our operation through the nature of our business or through proximity to our location; and with those stakeholders who demonstrated an interest in our business. We engage with our stakeholders in order to improve relations; understand their perspective and expectations; and communicate our plans and vision. We respond to our stakeholders' concerns and requests for information...We also take into consideration the interests and expectations from a range of stakeholders obtained from various stakeholders' engagement initiatives.

The implication is that these platforms provide Lonmin and its stakeholders with an ability to identify, discuss and potentially resolve possible conflict issues that arise within (its workforce) or within its immediate area which are the communities in this instance. The ability for Lonmin stakeholders to report sustainable development issues to the organization, and provides them with different ways of input to resolve these concerns, is a key feature of the company's stakeholder participation forums. Once these questions have been recognized at the stage of stakeholder participation, the organization categorizes them in order of importance for future consideration across its risk management mechanism.

In this regard, Lonmin has implemented a transparent wage rise policy that allows for discussions and settlements with local parties (workers' representatives) to ensure that its workers are paid at wages that are sustainable. The tactic influenced Lonmin's pay negotiations with the National Union of Mineworkers, according to the Department of Labour's 2011 industrial survey (NUM). The pact, which went into effect in July 2011, saw a pay increase of 8.5 to 10% for underground jobs. This is also one of the strategy's biggest success stories.

On a similar vein, the organization has been able to recognize risks related to unhealthy housing environments, which have an effect on employee security and productivity. As a result, a key thrust of the programme, especially on Lonmin's SLP, is to provide appropriate and affordable housing for its employees. Following that, the Marikana Housing Development Company (MHDC), founded in 1998, was formed to construct houses in the Marikana Extension 1 district. The aim was to provide decent housing for both staff and community residents, which could be purchased outright or leased out. As a result, as of September 30, 2012, the MHDC had constructed more than 369 houses at Karee and another 280 at Wonderkop Renamile for its employees.

In addition, Lonmin's 2012 sustainable development study stated that the company had effectively delivered decent housing to 8% of its total employees or around 4000 people. This was made possible after 19 hostel blocks were converted into 407 single units and 64 family units, accounting for 71.43% of family units and 47.07% of single units. Lonmin also mentioned that the conversion of the hostel blocks cost R89 million (USD$11 million). As a direct result of the 2011 safety summit, the organization has had the lowest fatality rate in 2012, despite seeing the highest fatality rate of 11 workers the previous year.

The South African Police Service (SAPS) and the Tactical Response Team (TRT) Option in Marikana

Historically, the South African Police Force (SAP) has been equipped to provide public security. Their implicit responsibilities include maintaining public peace and order, especially in circumstances where public order is threatened or violated (Zondi & Ukpere 2014). They also have other essential services such as neighbourhood policing, crime prevention and crime detection (Van Graan & Ukpere 2012: 10449). Since strike activities or demonstrations in South Africa typically affect public safety, SAP plays a role in maintaining public safety in such situations, especially for certain employees or citizens who would have chosen not to participate. As a result, the police continue to be the law enforcement agency in charge of protecting the public's rights and, as a result, provide primary defence services to the general public (McMichael 2014: 6).

The strike in Marikana seemed to be a threat to public order. As a result, the participation of SAP was needed at that time, based on their constitutional responsibilities. The SAP was brought in by the South

African government on purpose to bring stability and order to the turbulent Marikana environment. In other words, it is a government-mandated solution to public corruption and a law-and-order bridge in Marikana at the time (Faull 2013: 19). Lonmin called in SAP for two reasons, as previously stated: to shield its facilities from disruption and to provide cover to its employees who were employed but not part of the strike.

When the SAP arrived on the scene, they took some diplomatic steps to de-escalate the situation and disperse the crowd of protesting workers. The JOC and JOCCOM were born as a result of these strategic decisions. Additional tactics included immersive interventions aimed at persuading strikers to abandon their demands and disperse peacefully (Ledwaba 2013: 5–20). It also involved the implementation of a six-stage strike-ending technique. There were serious difficulties during the execution of some of these techniques, which ultimately led to the use of water guns, stun grenades and rubber bullets. On August 16, 2012, these tactics resulted in the shooting of protesting mineworkers (Ledwaba 2013). The fundamental thought behind these SAP reactions was to restore peace and order to Marikana. Unfortunately, the diversion plan backfired, resulting in escalating crime and the deaths of 34 people.

Lonmin and Government Post-Marikana Mitigation Efforts

Following the Marikana attack, both the government and Lonmin increased their efforts to resolve the grievances of those who were directly impacted by the company's activities. The workers' strike was effectively resolved by a wage raise resulting from a settlement between Lonmin and the workers. The strike came to an end after the confrontation and fire. The business and strike leaders reached an agreement that resulted in a 22% pay raise for RDOs, as well as an R2000 return to work bonus (Astrand & Birgersson 2014: 8). This was a very strong tactic that finally brought an end to the long-running strike and enabled the workers to return to work. The group launched a five-step plan in 2013 to rebuild its industry and, with it, fix operational, social and community problems. Employee relations, empowering workers and societies, foreign and local labour, using spent resources and facilities, and housing and lodging are among the five phases.

In conclusion, the study suggests that employee relations should be used to renegotiate union arrangements and appreciation. Lonmin said that the interests of workers and neighbourhoods should be adequately met through the Employment Value Proposition (EVP) and Community Value Proposition (CVP) (CVP). The housing and lodging plan not only gives the conversion of hostels a new lease on life, but it also raises the number of hostels that are converted. It also ensures that housing schemes are built on a continuous basis to meet the needs of its workers. Lonmin listed a series of environmental development initiatives it carried out within its operating areas as part of its commitment to the GLC. According to an article in the Daily Maverick news report on 18 August 2015, Lonmin has "identified their needs accurately, prioritized these through a collaborative process" and made serious efforts to meet them. The article summarized some of Lonmin's housing accomplishments as part of the company's effort to dowse the unrest sparked by inadequate living standards within its operating atmosphere in the city and prevent violence from reoccurring. Along this direction, Lonmin has donated over 180 hectares of land for the development of over 2,890 housing and rental units for its workers in the GLC, at a cost of over R500 million. Lonmin's proposal to construct an additional 4,000 housing units at a cost of R500 million over the next five years was echoed in the survey. Lonmin also claims to have spent R17 million tarring neighbourhood roads in Wonderkop, as well as R7.2 million enhancing water supply, affordability and usability. Another R2.5 million was invested to upgrade the sewage network at both Wonderkop and Nkaneng village settlements, according to the findings. Lonmin reiterated through its spokesperson, Memory Johnson, in a report in the *New Age Newspapers* of July 18, 2015, that:

> Lonmin had worked hard over the past two and half years to build a more open, transparent and mutually trustworthy environment, and in the process make the company a safe, better place to work. Emphasis has also been placed on the living conditions of employees and indebtedness; two burning issues that the company believes will make a profound impact on the wellbeing of employees. Since the tragic events of Marikana and following the unprecedented five-month strike in the platinum industry, Lonmin has focused its energy on rebuilding relationship with employees and their representative trade unions. The company has and continues to reach out to employees through meetings and structured workshops aimed at ensuring that any issue can be dealt with swiftly and without recourse to industrial action. (Mafisa 2015: 4)

Lonmin's renewed commitment to restoring and reclaiming confidence in its workforce, as well as improving Marikana to heal the wounds of the August 16 tragedy, is exemplified by the quote above. It also demonstrates the company's keen interest in and contribution to improving the working standards of its employees, which was one of the key factors at the conflict's nexus. In addition, as consolation, Lonmin hired some members of the families of those killed in the disaster. The wife of Makhosandile, Nonkwanele Mkhonjwa and other family members are among those who have been compensated (Mafisa 2015: 4; Mhlanga 2015: 2). The 1608 Education Trust was then formed by the corporation to ensure the education of the children of those killed in the disaster (Mafisa 2015: 4). The Trust provides funds to cover the costs of schooling for any school-aged child of the Marikana tragedy victims.

Apart from these commendable accomplishments, Lonmin and the government have collaborated on a number of collaborative development ventures, not only to build Marikana but also to improve the people's living standards and repair the tragedy's wounds. Ben Bole, the spokesperson for Local Government and Human Settlements, reaffirmed the government's commitment to improving the living standards of mining communities in the country:

> Marikana housing is part of the government's initiative to revitalize old mining towns by developing integrated and sustainable human settlements to address huge housing backlogs. The project is situated on 50 hectares of land donated by Lonmin. (Torerai 2015: 10)

Lonmin donated the property to the North West provincial government for the building of hundreds of Breaking New Ground (BNG) and Community Residential Units (CRU) houses in the Marikana extension two schemes, according to Torerai in the *New Age Newspapers* (17 August 2012). The Department of Human Settlements was supposed to provide 2,600 housing units to the Marikana population, according to the survey. By the end of 2015, the project is expected to have completed 292 BNG and 252 CRU structures in the city. This was accomplished, and on January 7, 2016, 544 completed structures totalling over R700 million were handed over to the beneficiaries (SAnews.gov.za). According to a survey published in the Platinum weekly on December 4, 2015, the houses house over 550 people (http://www.platinumweekly.co.za). Collen Maine, the MEC for Human Settlements, stated that this project is in line with and is a part of "The revitalization of distressed mining communities following the Social Accord, which was signed [by President Jacob Zuma] in October 2012 to upgrade human settlements in mining towns" (Torerai 2015: 1) and to develop social services in South African mining towns (SAnews.gov.za).

In addition, Lonmin made significant strides towards fulfilling its co-ownership commitments in accordance with BEE specifications. In reality, by December 2014, HDSA had acquired a minimum of 26% ownership in Lonmin. Ben Magara, the Chief Executive Officer (CEO) of Lonmin, said in the *New Age Newspapers* (5 December 2014) that: "We are delighted that Lonmin has successfully achieved 26 per cent ownership by HDSA's and that the ownership involves the participation of so many of their local communities and employees" (Radebe 2014: 24). Explicitly, this initiative has largely paid off BEE and HDSA's intentions. Implicitly, this change has not only established a new alliance between Lonmin and its host communities, but it has also deepened and expanded their relationship. Lonmin says; "This is a milestone that has been a long time in the making and the celebration today effectively heralds the start of a new partnership between Lonmin and its host communities" (Radebe 2014: 24).

Communities became financial partners of the business as a result of this strategic change. One of the goals of this strategy was to keep the host populations out of armed clashes while still increasing their stake in the organization by cooperation agreements. Second, it brings members of the host groups into the company's corporate climate. Finally, co-ownership allows host communities to achieve a fair degree of exposure to the company's organizational problems, especially those that impede successful resolution of their issues. As a result, both sides will have a greater view of each other, which will lead to a better friendship. To bolster this claim, Magara claimed that both of these collaborations would result in stronger ties and a greater understanding for all stakeholders, as we now all have a stake in our company's future.

Farlam Commission

One of the government's initial responses after the troubling incident at Marikana was to create the Farlam Commission. The Marikana Commission of Inquiry was established by the South African government to investigate what happened in Marikana. Each of the commission's core responsibilities was to:

> Examine matters of public, national and international concern arising out of the tragic incidents at Lonmin Mine in Marikana in the North West Province from Saturday 11th August to Thursday 16 August 2001, which led to the deaths of approximately 44 people, more than 70 persons being injured, approximately 250 people being arrested and damage and destruction of property.

The reasons surrounding and contributing to the deaths of miners will be revealed through this procedure. By extension, the commission became a mirror through which the Marikana tragedy's previously hidden causal factors could be seen. Its responsibilities give the commission a large forum to work through, allowing it to do a more thorough and efficient inquiry.

It has the following terms of reference:

> The Commission shall inquire into, make findings, report on and make recommendations concerning the following, taking into consideration the Constitution and other relevant legislation, policies and guidelines: the conduct of Lonmin in particular ..., The conduct of the Association of Mineworkers and Construction Union (AMCU), their members and officials and in particular ..." [Others are] "the conduct of the National Union of Mineworkers (NUM), its members and officials and in particular ..., The role played by the Department of Mineral Resources or any other government department or agency in relation to the incidents and whether this was appropriate in the circumstances, and consistent with their duties and obligations according to law. The conduct of individuals and loose groupings in fermenting and/or otherwise promoting a situation of conflict and confrontation, which may have given rise to the tragic incident, whether directly or indirectly.

Findings and Recommendations of the Farlam Commission

According to reports, the commission made several suggestions on the events in Marikana. However, the focus of this study is on the conflict mediation methods and techniques advocated by Lonmin and the government during the Marikana conflict. As a result, the focus of the research is on the commission's recommendations in this field. As a result, the attention will be primarily on Sections 89, 90, 91 and 92, which clearly discuss Lonmin's shortcomings in relation to the Marikana incident. This study summarizes the suggestions made in these parts in order to emphasize the argument made. Section 90 went into detail about Lonmin's inability to provide proper protections for its employees. The section likewise faulted the company's decision to instruct its workers to report for duty under the volatile and capricious situation at the time. Section 91 attributed one of the principal causes of the strike to Lonmin's failure to fulfil its responsibilities under the SLP, which the workers were trying to address. Section 92 insisted that Lonmin is to blame for not raising workers' wages, as did Implats in the wake of the crisis.

Furthermore, under the supervision of the Director of Public Prosecutions, the commission recommended a thorough inquiry to determine the extent of criminal responsibility on the part of all SAP involved in the operations, especially at scenes 1 and 2. It was also suggested that an investigation be set up to determine Major General Mbombo's (retired) and General Phiyega's fitness to hold office as a result of their involvement in the Marikana incident.

Conclusion

These actions seem to be ostentatious efforts on the part of the South African government and Lonmin to eradicate, or at the very least, ameliorate, the country's insidious social disparity. However, it seems that these attempts have failed to adequately resolve these concerns or to persuade those directly impacted by the detrimental effects of mining operations at Marikana to the contrary. Although protests about bad working and leaving conditions continue to reverberate at Marikana and Lonmin, as well as throughout the country's mining industry, the government and mining firms, paradoxically, continue to take a sluggish approach to these issues. As a result, Lonmin and the government's dispute resolution strategy for the Marikana conflict remains enigmatic and deplorable.

References

Åstrand, C., and Birgersson, L. (2014). "We Should Be a Lot Angrier": A Case Study of the Hootings.

Anstey, M. (2008). *Managing Change-Negotiating Conflict*. Juta and Company Ltd.

Bennett, J. (2002). Multinational Corporations, Social Responsibility and Conflict. *Journal of International Affairs*. Vol. 55, No 2, pp. 393–410.

Bloisi, W., Cook, C. W., & Hunsunker, P. L. (2003). Management and organisational behaviour. European Edition. McGraw-Hill, pp. 169–208.

Canel, E. (1997). New social movement theory and resource mobilization theory: The need for integration. *Community Power and Grassroots Democracy*, 189–221.

Chinguno, C. (2013). Global Issues: Marikana Massacre and Strike Violence Post-Apartheid. Available at file:///C:/Documents%20and%20Settings/useer/My%20Documents/Downloads/118-1394-1-PB.pdf. Accessed 7 March 2015. City Press, 2 September 2012.

Dube, D. (2012). Locals, Lonmin Fight. *New Age Newspapers*. 12 June 2015, pp. 1.

Edwards, B., & McCarthy, J. D. (2004). Resources and social movement mobilization. *The Blackwell Companion to Social Movements*, 116–152.

Elbra, A. D. (2013). The Forgotten Resource Curse: South Africa's Poor Experience with Mineral Extraction. *Resources Policy*. Vol. *38*, Issue 4, pp. 549–557.

Faull, A. (2013). Towards a 'New Professionalism' for the South African Police Service. *South African Review of Sociology*. Vol. 44, Issue. 2, pp. 18–35.

Ganson, B. (2011). *Business and Conflict Prevention: Towards a Framework for Action*. Geneva Peace-Building Platform, Switzerland.

Gumede, W. (2015). Marikana: A Crisis of Legitimacy in the Institutions that Form the Foundations of South Africa's 1994 Post-Apartheid Political Settlement. *Social Dynamics*. Vol. 41, Issue 2, pp. 327–343.

Jehn, K. A. (1997). A qualitative analysis of conflict types and dimensions in organizational groups. *Administrative Science Quarterly*, 530–557.

Jenkins, H., and Yakovleva, N. (2006). Corporate Social Responsibility in the Mining Industry: Exploring Trends in Social and Environmental Disclosure. *Journal of Cleaner Production*. Vol. 14, Issue 3, pp. 271–284.

Kestner, P. B., and Ray, L. (2002). *The Conflict Resolution Training Program*. Jossy-Bass Publishers USA.

Kohlrieser, G. (2007). Six essential skills for managing conflict. *Perspectives for Managers, 149*, 1–3.

Ledwaba, L. (2013). Guns and Spears: Setting the Stage. In *We Are Going to Kill Each Other Today: The Marikana Story*. Tafelberg Publishers South Africa.

Leon, P. (2012). Marikana, Mangaung and the South African Mining Industries. *Address to the South African Institute of International Affairs in Cape Town*. 30 August 2012.

Mafisa, I. (2015). Changes Since Marikana. *The New Age Newspapers*. 18 July 2015.

Maystadt. J. F., De Lucay, G., Sekeris, P. D., and Ulimwengu, J. (2014) Mineral Resources and Conflicts in DRC: A Case of Ecological Fallacy? *Oxford Economic Papers*. Vol. 66, pp. 721–749.

McKenzie, A. R. (2013). *Financialization and Labor: What Does Marikana Tell Us About Inequality in South Africa?* Issue. 1305.

McMichael, C. (2014). Police Wars and State Repression in South Africa. *Journal of Asian and African Studies*. Vol. 5, Issue 1, pp. 3–16.

Mehlum, H., Moene, K., and Trovik, R. (2006). Institutions and the Resources Curse. *The Economic Journal*. Issue 116, pp. 1–20.

Mhlanga, Z. (2015). Widows Want Compensation. *New Age Newspaper*. 9 August 2015

Nash, A. (2015). Marikana's Path. *Social Dynamics*. Vol. 41, Issue. 2, pp. 387–391.

Nelson, J. (2000). The Business of Peace. In *The Private Sector as a Partner in Conflict Prevention and Resolution*. London: International Alert, Council on Economic Priorities, The Prince of Wales Business Leaders Forum. Retrieved from http://www.internationalalert.org/sites/default/files/publications/The%20Business%20of%20Peace.pdf. Accessed January 1, 2016.

Pesmatzoglou, D., Nikolaou, I. E., Evangelinos, K. I., and Allan, S. (2014). Extractive Multinationals and Corporate Social Responsibility: A Commitment Towards Achieving the Goals of Sustainable Development or Only a Management Strategy? *Journal of International Development*. Vol. 26 Issue. 2, pp. 187–206.

Radebe, S. (2014). Tension Builds Over Lonmin BEE Deal. *New Age Newspaper* . 5 December 2014.

Rahim, M. A. (2010). *Managing Conflict in Organizations*. Transaction Publishers.

Rapatsa, M. J., and Matloga, N. S. (2014). The Practice of Strikes in South Africa: Lessons from the Marikana Quagmire. *Journal of Business Management & Social Sciences Research*. Vol. 3, Issue. 5, pp. 112–126.

Sinwell, L., et al. (2012). Introduction: Encounters in Marikana. In *Marikana: A View from the Mountain and a Case to Answer.* Jacana Media (Pty) Ltd.

Thomas, K. W. (1992). Conflict and Conflict Management: Reflections and Update. *Journal of Organizational Behavior*. Vol. 13, pp. 265–274.

Torerai, E. (2015). Houses for Marikana. *New Age Newspapers.* 17 August 2015. Vanguard News Papers of 6 March 2007

Van Graan, J., and Ukpere W. I. (2012). The Role of Impact Evaluation on Service Delivery Within the Public Sector Organizations. *African Journal of Business Management*. Vol. 6, Issue. 39, pp. 10445–10457.

Wallenstein, P. (2012). *Understanding Conflict Resolution* (3rd Edition). SAGE Publishers.

Wasserman, H. (2015). Marikana and the Media: Acts of Citizenship and a Faith in Democracy-to-Come. *Social Dynamics*. Vol. 41, Issue 2, pp. 375–386.

Zondi, Z. V., and Ukpere, W. I. (2014). Police Brutality in Post-Apartheid South Africa Reviewed. *Mediterranean Journal of Social Sciences*. Vol. 5, Issue. 3, pp. 574–579.

CHAPTER 13

Political Economy of Resource, Human Security and Environmental Conflicts in Africa: A Concluding Remark

Kelechi Johnmary Ani

Introduction

Resource has become a major determinant of domestic economy. The quantity of resources that a state has in its sovereign geography determines its economic viability, which has direct implication for societal and nation-building process across many states in the globe (Ani et al., 2018; Ani & Ojakorotu, 2018). Similarly, the degree of natural resources inherent in a society is often transformed into finished products or sold directly to other consumers as well as producers in order to accumulate capital that is needed for the development of the different sectors of a states' economy. The quest for capital accumulation often increases the number of peoples, groups, countries as well as other actors that are interested in the game of resource exploration.

K. J. Ani (✉)
Department of History & Strategic Studies, Alex Ekwueme Federal University, Ndufu-Alike, Nigeria

K. J. Ani et al. (eds.), *Political Economy of Resource, Human Security and Environmental Conflicts in Africa*,
https://doi.org/10.1007/978-981-16-2036-2_13

In many countries within Africa, the state has failed woefully in the quest to provide the social needs of the masses, thereby placing the masses on the desperate quest for economic resources. Unfortunately, in many African states, mineral resources are owned, explored and marketed by the machinery of the state. The problem arises when the masses begin to challenge state access and ownership of resources that are domiciled within their ancestral land, communities and constituencies. Often the challenge and resistance to state ownership are generated by communal or group sense of exploitation, negligence and widespread poverty in the face of high resource endowment.

Paradoxically, in Niger Delta of Nigeria and the Cabinda region of Angola, as discussed in different chapters of this book, the state has unleashed unlimited might upon all social groups and agitators, thereby leading to the increased act of taking arms by such groups which have hitherto led to the militarization of many African societies. When the informal resource agitators in the mineral resource host communities succeed in arming themselves, they begin to demand for social and environmental justice, thereby leading to mass armed conflict between them and the government. Sometimes, the confrontation could be between them and other rival local resource actors in the informal sector of their country's economy, bearing in mind that resources within their jurisdiction have become the central determinant of national commonwealth.

It is at that state of desperado to control access, extraction and sale of natural resources in a state, by different armed groups that the process of natural resources extraction qualifies as the most visible cause of conflicts and crises around the African continent. This is quite understandable given the fact that mineral resource is a gift of nature, and nature is that phenomenon that every human, group and nation claim to represent or believe to represent.

Chapter 1 introduced mineral resources and international politics of its exploration. It showed clearly how the resource-rich African continent has become overtaken by the competitive interest of the resource explorers from outside the continent. The chapter maintained that the inability of the African political elite to build and maintain sustainable oil exploring company has led to imperial multinational company's exploration of mineral resources in many African states, thereby ensuring mass impoverishment and the enthronement of resource wars. Chapter 2 focused on Chinese resource policy and human security in Africa. The chapter reveals how the Chinese relations with Africa have been on ascendancy since the turn of the new millennium in 2000. It documents scholars that have identified the phenomenal growth of the Chinese economy through exploration of African resources. The chapter argues that the need for African resources is the driving force for the Asian interest in the continent. It revealed that the resource-backed loan policy of the Chinese Government has improved infrastructure in resource-rich African countries, as well as enhanced the Foreign Direct Investment (FDI) in the continent. These have positive impact on the volume of trade, investment and economic growth in the continent. Howbeit, the impact of the resource policy as implemented on human security in the continent has not received adequate attention by stakeholders, and this is the task of the chapter. It adopts exploratory research design and depended on secondary data, which were presented qualitatively and analysed with content analysis technique. The study concludes that Chinese resource policy in Africa reinforces some aspect of human security and threatens others. It recommends the insistence on universal human rights principles as well as the observation of global best practices in labour and environmental management by African countries in negotiating and implementing the resource-backed loan agreements and other engagements with the Chinese in order to preserve human security in the continent.

Chapter 3 centred on sustainable human security in Africa and the effects of diminishing natural resources and low sovereign wealth funds. This chapter reveals that decades of mining Africa's natural resources have not yielded the desired prosperity. Instead, it has produced a paradox of plenty, which is characterized by so much wealth, but only for the privileged few, while the vast majority live in extreme poverty. What is more, decades of mining of the continent's natural resources have triggered resource depletion amid expanding frontiers of conflict, rising sovereign debts and decaying developmental infrastructures. Given these realities, coupled with evolving inventions and innovations that could render some of the natural resources redundant in the future, Africa's present is bleak and its future seems bleaker. Despite billions of dollars accruing from natural resources, only a few countries in Africa have Sovereign Wealth Funds (SWFs) for the future. And even for such countries, there is a growing debate in recent years over the merit of saving for future generations when the present generation is still languishing in penury. This chapter argues in the affirmative, pointing out that both goals are not mutually exclusive but experiences "threats" (e.g. technology, shifting natural resource value and use) that could hinder their success—threats that seem underestimated and are less widely analysed yet troubling because resource governance deficit and climate change as well as the conflicts they drive are increasingly gaining more visible attention. The chapter further re-evaluates human security in Africa beyond the present concerns and also contends that resource-rich African countries owe a debt of resource justice and management to future generations; hence, they have an ethical obligation to compensate for their depletion of natural resources. As a way forward, the chapter suggests sustainable human security approach that factors in these underestimated threats and protects the living against fear and deprivations while securing the unborn with a legacy of "wealth", functional social infrastructures and habitable environment.

Chapter 4 discussed the dynamics and complexities of natural resources and conflicts in Angola. The chapter argues that the process of natural resources extraction qualifies as the most visible cause of conflicts and crises around the world. This is quite understandable given that resources are gift of nature, and nature is that phenomenon, which every human, group and nation claims to represent, or, believe to represent them. Natural resources therefore are considered as the resources of and for all. However, following the social conflicts that emerged after the period of homoeostatic equilibrium and subsequent commencement of ownership of private property, alienation has overtaken natural resources that used to belong to all, at least theoretically, and both the state and non-state actors have been culpable in alienating others from the resource of nature (Ani et al., 2019). Natural resource actors include the state, indigenes and multinational companies and so on, and conflicts often emerge when there is clash of interest among them. Thus, in Africa, for example, natural resources have generated war and conflicts in Nigeria, Democratic Republic of Congo, South Africa and Angola to mention a few. These conflicts have led to loss of lives, internal displacement of huge parts of populations, refugees and asylum seekers that have become burdens on other nations around the world, as well as creating the multiplier problems of xenophobia. The natural resources-related conflicts can be seen to be pronounced in Africa; its effects and consequences are intertwined among nations of the world. Even multinational companies that deal in them, from what their name implies, are representatives of the business interests of many nations and are often not neutral in wars and conflicts generated by natural resources due to their exploitative tendencies. Thus, that chapter focused on the dynamics and complexities associated with natural resources in Angola. It found that natural resource conflict has led to multiple forms of resource curse, which undermined nation-building in Angola.

Chapter 5 is an Eco-Marxist critique of capitalism in Africa. The chapter centres on an Eco-Marxist critique of capitalism, with a special focus on the environmental effects of mineral resource exploitation in Africa. It revealed that as oil, gas, gold, copper, timber, etc., are exploited in Africa, there is an exploitative conspiracy between the multinational oil companies and governments in many African countries against the different poor African communities that have mineral resources in their land. The study quoted multiple negative environmental impacts of resource exploitation and the recurrence of resource curse conflicts that manifested in Niger Delta oil sites of Nigeria (Ani, 2019), gold mine areas in Ghana and South Africa as well as the copper sites in Democratic Republic of Congo and Zambia as the manifestation of the people's resistance to dehumanizing culture of resource exploitation.

Chapter 6 centres on theoretical postulation of national integration and the roles of political parties: a reflection on African and Asian countries. The study evaluates the quest for national integration by countries in Asia and Africa. It also reflects on political parties as well as theories of national integration and its implications for resource competition. The chapter revealed that most African and Asian countries bought into the concept of democracy and political parties as a viable instrument for political cohesion and development. The chapter revealed that democratic ideals have been utilized at expense of these two continents' (Asian and African) cultural beliefs, which affected development in their environments. Most of these theories of democracy that were adopted in many African and Asian states were in conformity with European and Western thoughts and against the natural beliefs of the African and Asian societies. For instance, democratic governance forcefully takes communal land and hands it over to a political sovereign through constitutional provisions, by force, thereby leading to conflicts. However, the chapter recommends that the path for national integration should be defined within multidimensional theories that will appropriate the African and Asian beliefs, traditional culture and be sensitive to her environmental configurations.

Chapter 7 is on peace-making, government and communal conflicts in Africa: evidences from Ife-Modakeke environmental crisis. Inter-communal conflict as we all know is a recurrent problem in Africa. This chapter presented the contextual discourse on the communal conflict in Nigeria before using Ife-Modakeke crisis as a case study for environmental conflict analysis. It conceptualized the key terms so as to explain the dynamics of communal conflict and its peace-making processes vis-à-vis government as the institutional mediator. It reviewed the existing studies on environmental conflicts and communal resolution with theoretical underlying assumptions. It showed that competition over land resource is central in the Ife-Modakeke environmental crisis. The chapter argued that peace-making processes demand gross attention of government in non-partisan mediation perspective. It, however, X-rayed the possible roles of government in peace-making process as well as its commitments. In concretizing the government efficacy, adaptable peace-making principles were discussed for communal conflict resolution within the socio-political space of Nigeria and beyond. That chapter concluded that government mandates, amidst other potentials, have significant current and future human rights conditions that must be respected by conflicting communities in order to create sustainable environment for peace.

Chapter 8 is on indigene-settler dichotomy and citizenship in Africa: perspectives from Otuocha and Jos environment. The affirmation of citizenship in Africa is primarily based on the primordial characteristics of indigeneity, which breeds tension between natives and settlers in diverse ways that make the primary intents and purposes of citizenship blurred in favour of myths. Indigeneship is entrenched in the national life, making it the basis of engagement as the key and characteristic feature of the state. Ironically, indigeneship fragments the Nigerian people and propels, in most cases, group contestations in both urban and rural areas. This chapter examines the ways the dialectics set by indigene-settler dichotomy frustrates citizenship in general, Otuocha, and Jos in particular and leads to conflicts. Otuocha is in Anambra East Local Government Area of Anambra State, South Eastern Nigeria, while Jos in Jos North Local Government Area of Plateau State, North Central Geopolitical zones, respectively. The chapter adopts political economy analysis using qualitative approach. The tools employed in data collection are key informant interview (KII) and non-participant observation. The study relied on content analysis of materials from key informant interviews, observations, records, oral histories, reports, memoranda, gazettes, communiqués, surveys, etc., to explain indigeneship contestations and conflicts in Otuocha and Jos environments. It reveals that tensions and conflicts in contested areas are consequences of mainly vested politicized decisions of state managers and elites over resources and not necessarily of ethnic and cultural differences. The study establishes that the contestations in Jos and Otuocha are linked to the quest for ascendancy in land and political resource control for individual and group gains, through tenuous masked mobilization of ethno-religious and other related primordial identities. The study identifies that indigene-settler dichotomy diminishes the emergence of citizenship pursued through the deployment of various default public policies of inclusion/exclusion (regionalism, federal character, quota, zoning, state of origin, etc.) that favours indigenes over settlers. The study opines that citizenship conundrum in Nigeria needs to be addressed holistically by eliminating the contradictory notions in Nigerian citizenship (constricted rights, policies and practices) in the constitution, extant laws and de-facto politics by enforcement of the rule of law, citizens' rights and residency rights.

Chapter 9 is on the role of tourism in the promoting human security in Nigeria. The chapter reveals that tourism is now the fastest growing industry worldwide with an annual growth rate of about 4%. It comprises the activities of persons travelling to and staying in places outside their usual environment for leisure, business and other purposes not related to remuneration within the place visited (Tseane-Gumbi & Ani, 2019). According to the United Nations World Tourism Organization, tourism is one of the strongest drivers of global economy. It is part of the poverty reduction strategies of more than 80% of low income countries and a major source of resource promotion. In Nigeria, most touristic activities are centred around nature and culture. An interesting fact is that unlike the oil resources which the country greatly relies on and found in higher quantities in the South-South Geopolitical zone than in the other five zones of the country, tourism is gradually developing in different parts of the country. It is observed that every local government area in the country has at least one tourism resource, which translates to nothing less than 776 tourism potential sites or attractions. Tourist environments were presented in the chapter as a solution to human insecurity as well as a good structure for the promotion of peace and conflict resolution in Nigeria. The chapter shows that human security refers to a people's orientation, integration and comprehensive framework, addressing the questions of survival and the basic needs of life. It is concerned with issues related to quality of life. The chapter revealed that the human security of the Nigerian populace is threatened by poverty, hunger, unemployment, health hazards, discrimination and ecological degradation. In addressing this, it has been advised that piecemeal policy and measures will not be sufficient; rather, a full comprehensive development strategy is required. This chapter therefore documented the various tourism attractions in the six geopolitical zones of the country. It also explored the roles of tourism in promoting human security in Nigeria putting into perspectives the seven dimensions of human security: economic security, food security, health security, environmental security, personal security, community security and political security.

Chapter 10 is on the insecurity of Nigerian leadership. The author of the chapter maintained that Nigeria is blessed with abundant human and material resources. Although these are promising enough to lead the country towards sustained prominent role in the affairs of Africa and the world at large, they have always been hindered by incessant insecurity issues such as the Boko-Haram insurgence, herdsmen attacks, militancy and others which continuously abuse the popular notion of 'Unity in Diversity' (Ani & Osisioma, 2014). This chapter argues that the lack of well-defined political vision as well as undisciplined, unpatriotic and lack of committed leadership has led to primordial sectionalism among the leadership and followership (Ani, 2011, 2013). The potential of cultural identity and values to produce neo-imaginative ideas needed for national integration, nation-building and national development has constantly been destroyed by partisan leadership who use ethnicity to maintain the status quo for selfish interest. In conclusion, leadership in Nigeria has been a driving force against security of lives and properties.

Chapter 11 centres on inter-group relations and peacebuilding in pre-colonial Africa, while focusing on Agba and Izhi environmental conflicts. It maintains that in pre-colonial African societies, warfare was the major means which many communities used to attain their goals. According to oral tradition, communities engaged in a series of wars with their neighbours in order to attain or protect their existential interest. The nature of the interest differs from society to society. One of the major factors that have driven wars among communities in Africa is the contest over a given portion of land. Land occupied a fundamental place in the societal interest of many communities and groups. That is unconnected to the fact that land is used for multiple purposes. Some people need it for agricultural purpose, while others need it for business and settlement goals; thus, when the interest of one community clashes with another over land, conflict and warfare become imminent. Several other reasons for pre-colonial Igbo warfare include abduction of sons and daughters of the land, desecration of sacred places, raids, etc. The wars were often carried out by different age grades that constituted armed forces of a particular community. In order to carry out these wars successfully, different weapons were used and many strategies were applied by the communities at war to defeat their enemies. This chapter is centred on the dynamics of inter-group warfare between the Agba people as well as Izhi people of present-day Ebonyi State and their neighbours. The chapter examined the dynamics of war between Agba and their neighbours, as well as warfare in Izhi clan, the weapons of war, those who constituted the armies and the peacebuilding strategies adopted by the people, who were then independent communities.

Chapter 12 is on the dilemma of natural resources and upsurge of conflict in Africa. The study is a cursory look at the management approach at Marikana question in South Africa. It argues that the recurrence of conflict in the mining sectors of South Africa has raised serious concerns in different quarters. The inability of mining companies, governments, workers and host communities to come to compromise on lasting solutions to this carnage deepens disaffection and fans the embers of conflict in the mining sectors of both countries. The enormous economic earnings capacity of natural resources to the economies of South Africa is not in doubt. Ironically, the conflict at Marikana is a reflection of lack of sustainable development, inequality and inequitable distribution of generated wealth particularly on the people directly affected by the negative consequences of mining activities. Against this backdrop, this paper examines the Marikana conflict with a view to understanding mining companies and government involvement and conflict management intervention approaches in the conflict. It undertakes an analysis of the conflict management approaches to assess the efficacy of mining companies as well as government intervention efforts before, during and after the conflicts. The study reveals that the conflict management efforts within the conflict were not adequate to preclude recurrence of conflict in the mining sector of South Africa. Government involvement and intervention strategies towards the conflict remain desperately inconsistent. The last chapter, which is this current chapter, summarizes the book, thereby ending the presentation and analysis.

References

Ani, Kelechi Johnmary (2011), *Politics About Failed State in Nigeria: Dialectics on Value of History to Nation Building Challenges 1960–2010*. Enugu: FirstBook.

Ani, Kelechi Johnmary (2013), "Nigerian Power Elite and Obasanjo's Violent Political Communication", *Politikja Reviste Shkencore*, NR 2: 31–46.

Ani, Kelechi Johnmary (2019), "Resource Curse and Conflict Analysis Legend: A Scholarly Profile of Professor Victor Ojakorotu" in Kelechi Johnmary Ani (Ed.), *Environmental Conflicts and Peacebuilding in Africa: A Festschrift for Victor Ojakorotu*, Academica Press: Washington and London, pp. 1–12.

Ani, Kelechi Johnmary & Ugochukwu S. Osisioma (2014), "Politics of Impoverishment in Nigeria from 1967 to Present: Fuel to Terrorism and National Insecurity", *Perspectivas—Portuguese Journal of Political Science and International Relations*, 13, 31–43.

Ani, Kelechi Johnmary & Ojakorotu Victor (2018), "Aqua Conflict, Resource Conflict, Resource Curse and the Challenge of International Cooperation Among African States", *African Renaissance,* Special Issue, December, pp. 27–42.

Ani, Kelechi Johnmary, Ebere F. Nnanwube & Victor Ojakorotu (2018), "Agriculture, Oil Resource Curse and Conflict: An Assessment of Nigerian Development Quagmire", *African Renaissance*, 15(3): 49–66.

Ani Kelechi Johnmary, Victor Ojakorotu & Uwizeyimana Dominique Emmanuel (2019), Resource and Environmental Insecurity in the Lake Chad region, *Journal of Reviews on Global Economics*, 8, 1617–1621.

Tseane-Gumbi, Lisebo A. & Ani, Kelechi Johnmary (2019), "Tourism and Transformation of the South Africa's Former Homelands: Lessons and Implications for Africa", *African Renaissance*, Special Issue, 93–108.

The manufacturer's authorised representative in the EU is Springer Nature Customer Service Centre GmbH, Europaplatz 3, 69115 Heidelberg, Germany. If you have any concerns regarding our products, please contact ProductSafety@springernature.com

Printed and bound by CPI Group (UK) Ltd, Croydon, CR0 4YY
30/09/2026
02225326-0013